D1571924

SPRINGER SERIES ON COMPARATIVE TREATMENTS FOR PSYCHOLOGICAL DISORDERS

Arthur Freeman, EdD, ABPP, Series Editor

2006: *Anger-Related Disorders: A Practitioner's Guide to Comparative Treatments*
Eva L. Feindler, PhD, Editor

2006: *Conduct Disorders: A Practitioner's Guide to Comparative Treatments*
W. Michael Nelson III, PhD, ABPP; A. J. Finch, Jr., PhD, ABPP; and Kathleen J. Hart, PhD, ABPP, Editors

2005: *Antisocial Personality Disorders: A Practitioner's Guide to Comparative Treatments*
Frederick Rotgers, PsyD, ABPP, and Michael Maniacci, PsyD, Editors

2005: *Comparative Treatments for Borderline Personality Disorder*
Arthur Freeman, EdD, ABPP; Mark Stone, PsyD; and Donna Martin, PsyD, Editors

2002: *Comparative Treatments for Anxiety Disorders*
Robert A. DiTomasso, PhD, ABPP, and Elizabeth A. Gosch, PhD, Editors

2002: *Comparative Treatments of Depression*
Mark A. Reinecke, PhD, and Michael R. Davison, PsyD, Editors

2000: *Comparative Treatments for Eating Disorders*
Katherine J. Miller, PhD, and J. Scott Mizes, PhD, Editors

2000: *Comparative Treatments for Relationship Dysfunction*
Frank M. Dattilio, PhD, ABPP, and Louis J. Bevilacqua, MEd, Editors

1999: *Comparative Treatment of Substance Abuse*
E. Thomas Dowd, PhD, and Loreen Rugle, PhD, Editors

About the Author

Eva L. Feindler, PhD, is a professor of psychology at the Long Island University Doctoral program in clinical psychology. On the Specialty Track in Family Violence and as director of the Psychological Services Clinic, she is directly involved in programs to help children and families manage their anger and resolve conflict. She received her undergraduate degree in psychology from Mount Holyoke College and her masters and doctoral degrees from West Virginia University, and she completed her clinical internship training at the Children's Psychiatric Center in Eatontown, New Jersey. Prior to her position at LIU, Dr. Feindler was an associate professor of psychology at Adelphi University, where she directed the Masters Degree program in applied behavioral technology. She has authored several books *(Adolescent Anger Control: Cognitive-Behavioral Strategies, Handbook of Adolescent Behavior Therapy, Assessment of Family Violence)* and numerous articles on parent and child anger, and she has conducted professional training workshops across the United States and internationally. She is featured on a training video, *Aggression Replacement Training.*

Dr. Feindler has served on the New York State Board for Psychology; the Board of the Nassau County Psychological Association; the Association for the Advancement of Behavior Therapy Conference, where she was Program Coordinator in 1995; the APA Commission on Violence and Youth; and the APA Task Force on Violence and the Family. Most recently she has been appointed as the cochair of the Board of Directors for ICART, the International Center for Aggression Replacement Training. She will represent North America with this international group.

Anger-Related Disorders

A Practitioner's Guide to Comparative Treatments

Eva L. Feindler, PhD

Editor

Springer Series on Comparative Treatments
for Psychological Disorders

SPRINGER PUBLISHING COMPANY

NEW YORK

Springer Publishing Company, Inc.
11 West 42nd Street
New York, NY 10036

Acquisitions Editor: Sheri W. Sussman
Production Editor: Suzanne Kastner
Cover design by Joanne Honigman
Typeset by Graphic World Inc.

06 07 08 09 10 / 5 4 3 2 1

Library of Congress Cataloging-in-Publication Data

Anger-related disorders: a practitioner's guide to comparative treatments
/edited by E. L. Feindler.
    p. cm.—(Springer series on comparative treatments for psychological disorders)
    Includes bibliographical references and index.
    ISBN 0-8261-4046-7
    1. Anger—Treatment. 2. Psychotherapy. I. Feindler, Eva L. II. Series.

RC569.5.A53A54 2006
616.89'142—dc22
                                                    2005057598

Printed in the United States of America by Maple-Vail Book Manufacturing Group.

Contents

Contents

Contributors

C. Peter Bankart, PhD, is professor of psychology at Wabash College in Crawfordsville, Indiana. He is the author of *Talking Cures: A History of Western and Eastern Psychotherapies* and has edited and contributed to several volumes on the application of Buddhist psychology.

Alison Byers, PsyD, is a founder and consultant with the Russell Byers Charter School in Philadelphia. Dr. Byers received her BA from Georgetown University, her masters in Criminology from Cambridge University, and her doctorate in Clinical Psychology from LIU CW Post. Dr. Byers assisted in the management of the Adolescent Trauma Treatment Development Center in conjunction with the Terrorism and Disaster Branch of the National Child Traumatic Stress Network, and she coordinated the Police-Mental Health Treatment Project within the Department of Psychiatry at North Shore University Hospital in Manhasset, New York.

Jerry L. Deffenbacher, PhD, is a professor of psychology and former director of training of the APA-approved doctoral program in counseling psychology in the Department of Psychology at Colorado State University. He is a fellow of the American Psychological Association, a licensed psychologist, and a diplomate of the American Board of Professional Psychology; he also serves on the editorial boards of five journals. In 2000, he co-authored with M. McKay a manual on an empirically supported intervention for anger reduction, *Overcoming Situational Anger and General Anger: Therapist Protocol* and *Client Manual.*

Daniel Eckstein, PhD, is currently associate professor of counselor education at the University of Texas–Permian Basin, Odessa. He was previously a core faculty with the Adler School of Professional Psychology, Toronto. Dr. Eckstein has a diplomate in Adlerian Studies from the North American Society of Adlerian Psychology. Dr. Eckstein is author of *Psychological Fingerprints, Leadership by Encouragement,* and *The Encouragement Process in Life-Span Development.*

Henry Edwards, MD, is a board certified psychiatrist and psychoanalyst who has maintained a private practice of general psychiatry, psychopharmacology, psychotherapy, and psychoanalysis with adolescents and adults. He is the psychiatric consultant to the Adelphi Counseling Center and the Derner Postdoctoral Program in Psychoanalysis and is a Distinguished Life Fellow in The American Psychiatric Association.

Jerry Gold, PhD, is professor of psychology and chair of the undergraduate program at the Derner Institute of Advanced Psychological Studies, Adelphi University. He received his PhD in Clinical Psychology and a Postdoctoral Certificate in Psychoanalysis from Adelphi. He is the editor of the *Journal of Psychotherapy Integration* and the author of *Key Concepts in Psychotherapy Integration* (Plenum, 1996).

Josée L. Jarry, PhD, is currently an assistant professor in the Department of Psychology at the University of Windsor, where she teaches psychodynamic psychotherapy and abnormal psychology. She also has an active research lab, the Eating Disorders and Anxiety Research Group, and is currently investigating the effects of emotional neglect and self-esteem threat on body image. Collaboratively with Dr. Sandra Paivio, Dr. Jarry is also conducting research on emotion-focused trauma therapy for adult survivors of childhood trauma and neglect.

Eli Karam is currently completing a doctoral degree in Marriage and Family Therapy at Purdue University under the guidance of Doug Sprenkle, PhD. As a recent clinical fellow at The Family Institute at Northwestern University, he has worked extensively with couples, families, and groups. He is currently collaborating on The Family Institute's Psychotherapy Change Project with Jay Lebow, PhD, and Bill Pinsof, PhD. He is a co-author of the STIC, a questionnaire designed to measure how couples and families change throughout the therapy process.

Howard Kassinove, PhD, ABPP, is professor of psychology and former chairperson of the Department of Psychology at Hofstra University in New York. He is a New York State–licensed psychologist, a certified school psychologist, and a fellow of the American Psychological Association and the Albert Ellis Institute; he is also board certified in both behavioral psychology and clinical psychology (American Board of Professional Psychology). In 1995, he edited *Anger Disorders: Definition, Diagnosis, & Treatment.* In 2002, in conjunction with Dr. R. Chip Tafrate, he published *Anger Management: The Complete Treatment Guidebook for Practitioners.*

Danielle Knafo, PhD, is an associate professor in the Clinical Psychology Doctoral Program at Long Island University's CW Post Campus. She is faculty and supervisor at Derner's Postdoctoral Program in Psychoanalysis and past faculty at Israel's Psychoanalytic Institute. She is the author of *A Self in Creation, By Herself*; is the editor of *Living with Terror, Working with Trauma: A Clinician's Handbook* (Aronson); and is co-author of *Unconscious Fantasy: Theory, Therapy, and Culture* (Analytic Press).

Jay Lebow, PhD, ABPP, is senior faculty at the Family Institute at Northwestern and is associate clinical professor at Northwestern University. He is also past-president, Division of Family Psychology, APA; fellow of APA; member of the editorial boards of JMFT and Family Process; approved supervisor AAMFT; and ABPP in family psychology. He is editor of three books, including the forthcoming *Handbook of Clinical Family Therapy.* In addition, he has authored 100 articles and book chapters for the *Annual Review of Psychology, The Psychologists' Desk Reference,* and the *Comprehensive Textbook of Psychiatry.*

Al Milliren, EdD, is professor of counseling education and coordinator of the counseling education program at the University of Texas of the Permian Basin in Odessa. He is the director of education for the West Texas Institute for Adlerian Studies in Odessa, vice president of the North American Society of Adlerian Psychology, and chair of the NASAP committee on education and professional development.

Seymour Moscovitz, PhD, is the clinical director of the Bronx Family Court Mental Service, an assistant professor of clinical psychology in the Department of Psychiatry at New York Presbyterian Hospital, and a member and graduate of the Institute for Psychoanalytic Training and

Research (2004) and a graduate of the NYU Postdoctoral Program in Psychotherapy and Psychoanalysis (1985).

Sandra C. Paivio, PhD, is professor of clinical psychology and director of the Psychotherapy Research Centre at the University of Windsor in Windsor, Ontario, Canada. She has co-authored, with Leslie Greenberg, the book *Working with Emotions in Psychotherapy*, and she has published numerous articles on emotion-focused therapy (EFT), particularly as it applies to child abuse trauma.

Paul R. Rasmussen, PhD, is associate professor of Psychology at Furman University in Greenville, South Carolina. He teaches courses in psychopathology, psychopathic personality, and counseling and psychotherapy. He is a Clinical Strategies and Contributing Review Editor for the *Journal of Individual Psychology* and has numerous publications on topics related to personality and psychopathology, stress, attention deficit disorder, the adaptive nature of affective reactions, and clinical intervention and case-conceptualization strategies.

Jill H. Rathus, PhD, is associate professor of psychology in the Clinical Psychology Doctoral Program at Long Island University in Brookville, New York. Her research and clinical interests include spouse abuse, couple distress, adolescent suicide, personality disorders, and assessment. She received intensive training in dialectical behavior therapy (DBT) from Dr. Marsha Linehan and has become a national trainer of mental health professionals in this method. Most recently, she has been adapting DBT for the treatment of intimate partner violence. She is the author of three books and is presently completing a co-authored book on DBT for suicidal adolescents.

Raymond Chip Tafrate, PhD, is a licensed psychologist in Connecticut and New York and is a fellow and supervisor at the Albert Ellis Institute. An associate professor in the Criminology and Criminal Justice Department at Central Connecticut State University, Dr. Tafrate is the director of the Graduate Program in Criminal Justice and teaches courses on anger and aggression management, correctional counseling, and research methods. In 2002, Dr. Tafrate co-authored, with Dr. Howard Kassinove, *Anger Management: The Complete Treatment Guidebook for Practitioners*, and in 2004, he co-authored, with Dr. Raymond DiGiuseppe, the *Anger Disorders Scale (ADS)*.

Sandra P. Thomas, EdD, is professor and director of the PhD Program in Nursing at the University of Tennessee, Knoxville. Dr. Thomas is the editor of *Issues in Mental Health Nursing* and the author of more than 90 journal articles, books, and book chapters. In 1996 she was named a Fellow of the American Academy of Nursing and in 1999 became a Fellow of the Society of Behavioral Medicine. She is the author of *Listening to Patients* (2002) and *Transforming Nurses' Stress and Anger.*

Robert Willhite, PhD, is currently retired and on the faculty of the Adler Graduate School of Minnesota in Hopkins. For the past 35 years, he has been active in the application of Adlerian theory and practice in the form of teaching and private practice on the local and national level. He has written three books focusing on early recollection analysis, dream analysis, and the family game of anger.

Series Editor's Note

Comparisons are odious . . .

—Cervantes, *Don Quixote*

The general view of comparisons is that they represent measurements against some standard or that they entail evaluating one experience or object against another. If one has had a sibling, one has likely come up against the parental statement, "Why can't you be like . . . ?" Teachers also invariably compare students with one another when they post grades or grade papers for all to see.

This view of comparisons is that they are somehow adversarial—one person, group, or effort "wins" and one "loses." In psychology we often use the construct of comparison as synonymous with the term *versus* (e.g., "The treatment of depression: psychotherapy versus pharmacotherapy" or "A comparison of two treatments for obsessive-compulsive disorder"). This implies that whenever there are two or more systems or objects available, one will be better than another. Yet not all comparisons are clear-cut. One choice may be appropriate for a certain subgroup, while another choice may work better in a different setting or with a different population. (This adversarial view seems to be very popular among mental health professionals. After all, we are a group that over the years have been known to circle our wagons when under attack and shoot at each other!)

Our goal in this series is to examine not who is better than whom, or what model works better than other models, but rather to examine and to compare, as cleanly as we can, the similarities and differences between different psychotherapeutic approaches. To do this most efficiently, we have used a standard client. All contributors were asked to respond to the sample case prepared by the volume editors. In this way the reader can compare the thinking, conceptualization, interventions, and questions that would be asked by the contributing authors. We have invited authors who are exemplars of a particular school, understanding that other therapists of the same school might see or do things differently. By aligning apparently diverse therapies side by side, we can look at what models share specific conceptual frameworks, philosophical biases, strategic foci, or technical interventions, as well as help us make clearer distinctions between therapeutic models.

We have set as our goal the examination of those problems most frequently seen in clinical practice. We have not seen this need for cross-model comparison as an issue of professional discipline inasmuch as these clinical syndromes are seen by psychologists, psychiatrists, nurse practitioners, social workers, pastoral counselors, and counselors.

This series sprang from four roots: first, the powerful influence of the classic "Gloria" series produced by Dr. Everett Shostrum, when he arranged for Carl Rogers (client-centered therapy), Albert Ellis (rational emotive therapy), and Fritz Perls (Gestalt therapy) to demonstrate their representative models of therapy with a standard patient, Gloria. He gave viewers the opportunity to compare and contrast the three models as practiced by the founders of the particular school of therapy.

The second influence on this series was the present state of affairs in psychotherapy. Between the models that are promoted for their purported science and efficacy and those models that are promoted for their purported humanism and eschew all of science, there are many treatment models. Without attempting to judge the value, efficacy, and importance of a model, we believe that it is important to offer mental health professionals the opportunity to make their own decisions about diverse treatment models.

The third impetus for this series was the availability of so many experts in the treatment of the broad range of psychological disorders. Both as editors and as contributing authors, it is their work that is being highlighted in this series.

Finally, this series was the result of the initial encouragement of Bill Tucker, former Acquisitions Editor of Springer Publishing Company; Dr. Ursula Springer, the Past President of Springer Publishing Company; and Sheri Sussman, Senior Vice President for Editorial. Sheri has been a guiding force for this book, for the entire Comparative Treatment series, and for a multitude of other scholarly works. When I first approached Springer Publishing with the idea for the series, they were enthusiastic and eagerly agreed to not just produce one book, but committed their resources to a series of several volumes. Given the publishing history of Springer Publishing, the breadth and quality of their book list, and the many professional groups that they reach, I can think of no better place for this series on comparative psychotherapy.

Arthur Freeman, EdD, ABPP

President, The Freeman Institute

Fort Wayne, Indiana

Acknowledgments

I want to thank my colleagues who have been in the field of anger management for their continued support and enthusiasm for my work during the past 25 years. Several of them are key authors in this volume. In particular I want to honor Arnie Goldstein in this work. He was a significant mentor to me, and his death in 2002 was a great loss for all of us who continue to work in the field of aggression replacement training.

Thanks are also in order to the 15 intelligent and dedicated clinicians who agreed to author chapters. I appreciated their respect for the deadlines, responses to my edits and feedback, and timely revisions. Together, we have produced a case examination that will interest many professionals who work with rather difficult clients. I would also like to thank Sheri Sussman, from Springer Publishing, who remained a constant support.

A person who has tirelessly devoted her time, energy, and enthusiasm for my writing projects, my assistant, Ms. Cathy Kudlack, deserves very special mention. She is an unbelievable team player, has supported all of my projects, and has been an anchor through stressful times. In addition, she has provided the most efficient and expert writing, editing, and coordination efforts behind the scene. Without her, not only would the days be less fun, but most certainly this book would have never been completed. Cathy, you continue to amaze me in all that you do.

Others have provided the more personal support; I know that they, and in particular, my daughter Jessica, will always believe in me and encourage me to embark on new ventures. My mother's spirit continues to be a gentle wind that guides me through life. She edited all of my previous manuscripts, being the "grammar expert" in the family, and I will always miss her presence on this earth.

In addition to professional training and endless dialogues with colleagues, friends, and family, I know that my work would have never expanded so without the experiences I have had with both students and clients. I truly have learned so much from each one of them; they have kept me honest, on target, and always curious. It is a blessing to have had such a wonderful stream of people in my life. I only hope that I have touched their lives as significantly as they have touched mine. In particular, I must thank "Anthony" for giving me permission to use his case as the focus of this integrative work.

Lastly, but not without great respect and affection, I want to thank Carol G. who has helped with an incredible personal as well as professional transformation, providing me with her intelligent insight, her tender guidance, and the challenge to move forward during some difficult times. Through her steady presence, her intelligence, integrity, and humor, she remained a constant in my movement toward hope and possibility. In action and through quiet "knowing," she has broadened my scope and receptivity to various other therapeutic processes and has brought me an integrated perspective in my clinical work. Carol, there are simply no words of appreciation that are adequate; I will forever cherish our dialogue and our gentle "meetings at the boundaries." I thank you from the depths of my heart and my soul for sharing the journey. You are a discovered treasure and this volume would not have happened without your support.

Foreword

Classical philosophers since the time of Aristotle and Seneca have believed that anger represented a major source of human suffering. This view of anger as a central part of human disturbance extended until the beginning of the 20th century. At that time, both Emil Kraeplin and Sigmund Freud identified anger as part of mania and mania as part of depression. Thus, two of the major figures in 20th-century psychopathology rendered anger as a secondary emotional problem to depression. Since their time, most clinicians still identify anger as a secondary emotion. This view of anger has hampered our understanding of the emotion and our knowledge of how it can become dysfunctional; most important, it has hindered our development of interventions to help those suffering from anger problems.

We clearly know much less about anger as a form of emotional disturbance compared with our knowledge of anxiety and depression. Despite the view in the clinical world that anger is a secondary emotion, all major theories on the psychology of emotions have identified anger as one of the basic universal emotions. Research on infants suggests that anger is the first negative emotion to develop and thus may be our truly primitive affect. However, even in scientific psychology, the extent of our knowledge of anger appears much less expansive compared to our knowledge of other emotions. This ignorance may limit the development of successful interventions. However, research in recent years has expanded our knowledge of anger. Anger differs from other negative emotions in several important ways. Other negative emotions motivate humans to avoid or escape the stimuli that elicit them. These emotions, such as anxiety, disgust, and sadness, elicit an avoidance behavior. Anger activates approach behaviors. People want to get close to that which arouses their anger. Also, anger is the only negative emotion that people do not wish to change. It has strong reinforcing qualities. Anger, like addictions, is a problem people do not wish to relinquish. Revenge appears to be one reason that anger is so reinforcing. Even the thought of satisfying this anger-generated motivation activates the reinforcement centers of the brain.

However, psychologists and psychotherapists have paid little attention to revenge and its role in dysfunctional anger. If you want to learn of how the drive for vengeance wrecks human life, go to the Classic or English departments of your university and read the great epics in 4,000 years of literature. We can learn a lot from these fields about anger. Anger has also been viewed as an emotion that leads to impulsive aggression. More recent research suggests that rumination and resentment are crucial aspects of the anger experience. Thus, rumination, which was always considered an important aspect of depression, may be an important target in anger treatment as well.

Because anger has been viewed as a secondary emotion by most clinical theories, no anger disorders are included in the present version of DSM-IV-TR, and this is unlikely to change in DSM-V. Despite this lack of an official DSM anger disorder, Eva Feindler has included the notion of anger-related disorders in the title of this book. What are these anger-related disorders? What do they have in common, and how are they different? Our knowledge concerning the nature and type of anger-related disorders is just beginning. Diagnosis helps clinicians organize information and develop case conceptualizations that guide treatment. Many clinicians lack general knowledge about anger and the successful strategies to treat dysfunctional anger. The development of a recognized anger diagnosis may help us organize our knowledge and thereby lead to better interventions. Also, most of the current treatments for anger assume that all people with anger disorders have the same problems and receive the same treatment. In the area of anxiety disorders, we make distinctions between panic disorder, agoraphobia, obsessive-compulsive disorder, and post-traumatic stress disorder (PTSD). Treatments vary according to these diagnostic differences. As of yet we have no recognized distinctions among angry clients that lead to differential interventions.

Chip Tafrate and I reviewed the existing outcome studies on anger treatments. We concluded that while some successful interventions for anger had been developed, these interventions were generally less successful than psychotherapeutic interventions for anxiety and depression. Also, the majority of the research focused on a narrow range of cognitive-behavioral therapies. Clearly, we need to explore a wide range of treatments to develop truly effective approaches to helping those who suffer with anger problems.

Eva Feindler has organized an outstanding list of contributors who have presented rich chapters on the treatment of anger. I have been familiar with the work of these authors for many years. Taken together, they have constructed an integrated and expanded picture of anger, its disturbance, and its treatment. Their collective wisdom will leave the readers satisfied. The organization of the books in these series around a clinical case allows for the readers not only to understand the theory and technique espoused by the authors but also to see how a specific demonstration of them is carried out. This structure recognizes the art in psychotherapy and the need to see how it is done to truly learn.

As of yet we have no clear paradigm in the treatment of dysfunctional anger. My own clinical experience has relied on many different ideas and approaches since no one approach succeeds with even a majority of clients. In fact, I recently commented to a colleague that working with angry clients has made me a more integrated psychotherapist. The strength of this book lies in the diversity of approaches presented. Understanding all of these approaches will hopefully leave the readers with a multifaceted understanding of anger and a wide range of interventions to use when their favored ones inevitable fail. I hope this book will enrich you and will make you a more integrated psychotherapist.

Ray DiGiuseppe, PhD

St. John's University

Questions for Contributors

The case of Anthony M. is derived from three 1-hour sessions of an actual client presenting in outpatient treatment with possible multiple diagnoses. This case was chosen specifically to highlight an array of anger-related difficulties not captured in DSM-IV. The contributors in this text were asked to consider the case of Anthony M. and respond to the following questions based on their theoretical orientation:

   I. Treatment. Please describe your theoretical orientation and treatment model in working with such a client.
   II. Therapist's Skills and Attributes. Describe the clinical skills or personal attributes of a treating clinician that are essential to a successful therapeutic approach.
   III. The Case of Anthony M. The goal of this book is to provide the readers with a theoretically integrated case conceptualization and a comprehensive treatment plan according to your orientation. Consider each of the following topics and questions regarding the case of Anthony M.
   A. Conceptualization, assessment, and treatment planning.
      1. What additional information would you want to assist you in conceptualizing and structuring this client's treatment? Are there any specific assessment tests/tools you would want? What would be the rationale for these?
      2. Therapeutic goals, both primary and secondary. What would be your therapeutic short- and long-term goals for this client? What level of adaptation, coping, or functioning would you see this client reaching as a result of therapy, both short and long term?

3. Length of therapy. What would be your timeline or duration for therapy? What would be the frequency and duration of sessions, and who would be included (e.g., client, parents, school personnel, legal personnel)?

4. Case conceptualization. What is your conceptualization of this client's personality, behavior, affective state, cognitions, and functioning? How would you assess the level of danger to self and others? Also include the client's strengths that could be used in therapy.

B. The therapeutic relationship. How would you describe your goals in establishing a therapeutic relationship between the therapist, client, and, if included, significant others? Examples would include the establishment of confidentiality, development of trust, boundaries, limit setting, self-disclosure, transference, and countertransference.

1. Roles in a therapeutic relationship. What are the appropriate roles of a therapist/client as well as significant others (e.g., parents, school personnel, legal authorities) in your model of treatment, and what might you do to facilitate these roles? For example, who is included and when in therapy? What is the therapist's degree of directness and activity level? For example, is the therapist more active or passive in working with such a client? To what extent is the therapeutic relationship collaborative?

C. Treatment implications and outcome.

1. Therapeutic techniques and strategies. Are there specific therapeutic techniques that you would or would not use in therapy? If so, what would they be and why? What other professionals would you want to collaborate with on this case, and how you would work together? Would you want to involve significant others in the treatment (e.g., parents, school personnel, legal representatives)? Would you assign out-of-session work (e.g., homework) with this client, and, if so, what kind?

2. Mechanisms of change. What would you see as the hope for mechanisms of change for this client, in order of relative importance?

3. Medical and nutritional issues. How would you handle any medical or psychopharmacological issues involved in working with this client? Are there any nutritional issues that you would consider in working with this adolescent?

4. Potential pitfalls. What potential pitfalls would you envision in your therapy? What do you envision as the source(s) of these difficulties, and how would you handle them? Are there any special cautions to be observed in working with this client? Are there any particular resistances that you would expect, and how would you deal with them?

5. Termination and relapse prevention. When would you consider termination to be appropriate for this client, and how would that be addressed in therapy? How would you envision relapse prevention, and how would this be structured?

CHAPTER 1

Anger-Related Disorders: Basic Issues, Models, and Diagnostic Considerations

Howard Kassinove
and Raymond Chip Tafrate

Anger, it turns out, is one of our most frequent experiences. One-third of typical community adults, as well as college students, report that they experience anger almost every day. In addition, approximately 75% of survey respondents indicate that they feel annoyed (i.e., mildly angry) multiple times during any given week (Kassinove et al., 1997). Averill's assessment of frequency (1982, 1983) indicated that adult subjects reported a mean of 7.3 incidents of anger and 23.5 incidents of annoyance per week. With regard to strength and duration, anger is typically rated as a more intense experience than annoyance and it may endure for long periods. Indeed, approximately 20% of unselected adult survey participants report that their anger lasted for more than a day (Kassinove et al., 1997). Clinically, it is well known that anger is commonly encountered in the office of practitioners (Lachmund & DiGiuseppe, 1997). Professionals who work with families are often faced with screaming interactions between married and nonmarried partners or between parents and children. Practitioners often see adults who have been privately harboring anger and fantasies of revenge for days, weeks, months, and even years. Finally, we note that for practitioners who work in specialized settings such as prisons or alternatives to incarceration programs, anger may be the emotional excess of greatest concern. Clearly, anger is a problem to be considered, evaluated, and treated across a variety of professional settings.

LACK OF ATTENTION TO ANGER

Given these data, it is surprising that so little attention has been paid to anger. Certainly, some texts have addressed anger as a specific problem to be reckoned with. These texts range from the classic work of Novaco (1975) to the more recent works of Deffenbacher and McKay (2000), Kassinove (1995), and Kassinove and Tafrate (2002). Other texts have devoted chapters to the evaluation and treatment of specific issues, such as strategies to use in the beginning phase of treatment with angry clients (Tafrate & Kassinove, 2003). However, the scientific literature has been far more oriented toward the treatment of anxiety and depression than toward anger (Kassinove & Sukhodolsky, 1995). For each article on anger, approximately 10 appear on depression and 7 appear on anxiety. Most textbooks pay minimal attention to anger or ignore it completely. As Deffenbacher and Deffenbacher (2003) have shown, introductory texts in psychology referenced anxiety, depression, and aggression 6 to 8 times more often than anger. Abnormal psychology texts referenced anxiety and depression 20 to 25 times more often than anger, and aggression 10 times more often than anger. Almost shockingly, one-fourth to one-third of texts did not reference anger *at all*. This book, then, makes an important contribution by providing practitioners with an understanding of the fundamentals of anger and a series of intervention approaches to treatment in a case where anger is the primary symptom.

Nevertheless, the question regarding our avoidance of anger remains. Why has so little been done, and why is anger so unpopular? A number of explanations exist. First, consider the statement of DiGiuseppe and Tafrate (2001), "No one likes to hug a porcupine" (p. 266). We now expand that to note that no one likes to hug a porcupine, a snake, or a skunk. Angry folks are often just plain nasty. Like the porcupine, they have sharp quills and are ready to verbally stab their practitioners, especially when the purpose of a practitioner's intervention is misinterpreted. Like the cobra, when their high self-image (see, for example, Baumeister, Smart, & Boden, 1996) is threatened, angry adults can become verbally argumentative, volatile, and at times menacing. Working with angry clients is difficult because they are often unreceptive to treatment. Like the skunk, they typically avoid interactions, and when forced to confront issues, they spray foul and unpleasant ideas about others. They almost always blame others with statements such as,

"You should bring my son into the office and fix him. He's lazy, doesn't listen, and is really out of control. I simply wouldn't be so angry if *he* would just behave himself!" Thus, because angry clients do not take personal responsibility for reducing their anger, client engagement and intervention are difficult.

Anger also has a moral tone, and clients typically think that their anger is justified. This sort of societally sanctioned anger (e.g., "Of course I'm pissed! She cheated on me, and I have a perfect right to feel angry!") limits motivation for personal change. Frankly, it is much easier to work with dependent, anxious clients who enter treatment seeking solutions for their distress (e.g., "I can't drive across bridges") and those who do not externalize blame for their problems. Nevertheless, anger is so frequent that it is critical to examine it and obtain an understanding of possible treatments when it becomes problematic.

DEFINITION AND DIFFERENTIATION OF ANGER

Effective intervention programs are based on clear definitions of the clinical issues. Unfortunately, in the case of anger there has been much confusion. Many research articles and programs of intervention simply assume that anger is the focus and proceed with an assumed general definition. Anger, in fact, has often been confused with related constructs, and what has actually been treated by the practitioner is often unclear.

The common English language definition of *anger* is, "A strong passion or emotion of displeasure or antagonism, excited by a real or supposed injury or insult to one's self or others, or by the intent to do such injury" (www.webster-dictionary.net). Kennedy (1992) wrote that, "Anger is an affective state experienced as a motivation to act in ways that warn, intimidate, or attack those who are perceived as challenging or threatening. Anger is coupled to and is inseparable from sensitivity to the perception of challenges or a heightened awareness of threats (irritability). This affective motivation and sensitivity can be experienced even if no external action occurs" (p. 150). This analysis places some emphasis on anger as a passion and motivational state that promotes approach and even aggressive actions. It also notes that anger may seem to simply appear without an immediate observable provocation but does not mention the important physical arousal that often occurs as a part of anger.

Novaco (1998) defined *anger* as, "a negatively toned emotion subjectively experienced as an aroused state of antagonism towards someone or something perceived to be the source of an aversive event" (p. 13). This definition focuses on the interpersonal nature of anger and the fact that there is usually a perceived stimulus thought to be aversive. It does not mention any associated cognitions that might distort the perception of the event or behaviors that might be associated with the experience. It considers anger to be an *emotion,* a broader term than *feeling.* Feelings have traditionally referred to subjective experiences, whereas emotions have referred to the constellation of subjective experiences, motor behaviors, and changes in the physiology of the body (Izard, 1977). In the case of anger, the emotion would refer to the conscious experience (i.e., the subjective feeling), various physiological processes such as an increased heart rate, and observable muscle or gross motor expressions (e.g., furrowed brow, clenched teeth), particularly on the face. Since the term *feeling* generally refers to the language-based, self-perceived, phenomenological state, rather than the *complex* of self-perceived states, physiological reaction patterns and associated behaviors, the definition that one uses may have an impact on the number of targets selected for change.

We propose that the following comprehensive definition be used by clinicians and researchers:

Anger is a negative, phenomenological feeling state that motivates desires for actions, usually against others, that aim to warn, intimidate, control, or attack, or gain retribution. It is associated with cognitive and perceptual distortions and deficiencies, such as the following:

Misappraisals about its importance (e.g., "It's awful")

Misappraisals about the capacity to cope (e.g., "I can't deal with this")

Justice-oriented demands (e.g., "He should treat his son fairly and with more respect")

Evaluations of others ("She should have known better than to try to cheat. She's a real dope!")

Dichotomous thinking (e.g., "Either he's my friend or he's not. It's just that simple! Is he with me or against me?")

Overgeneralization (e.g., "Since he didn't call me, it clearly means he doesn't like me")

Attributions of blame coupled with beliefs about preventability and/or intentionality (e.g., "It's all her fault. If she had really thought about it, she would not have said that. She was just trying to get his goat")

Subjective labeling of the feeling (e.g., "I feel really pissed")

Fantasies of revenge and punishment (e.g., "Now I'll teach her a real lesson!")

It is also typically, but not always, associated with the following:

Physiological changes (e.g., heart rate, sweating)

Socially constructed and reinforced patterns of behavior that define how to act when angry (e.g., using a loud voice, using profanity, pointing fingers, glaring, crossing the arms, smirking)

This definition includes the motivational and interpersonal components that are almost always present. It defines anger as a felt state that is negative and, thus, generally to be avoided. We certainly acknowledge that anger can have positive outcomes, such as motivating someone to confront an ongoing problem or to make a change. However, anger is recognized to be negative because few people get up in the morning and say, "I hope I feel really furious today." The definition recognizes the interplay of the stimulus with distorting cognitions and fits with Berkowitz's neoassociational model (1990), which proposed that aversive stimuli lead only to general arousal. Interpretations are required for the general arousal to turn into anger. The definition also fits with the hypothesis that we learn how to experience and express anger. That is, we learn to scream and when to be sarcastic by modeling our parents, friends, television characters, and so on. And, when we act in these angry ways, we receive at least some degree of intermittent reinforcement.

Of course, it is also important to clearly differentiate anger from the related concepts of hostility and aggression in order to develop interventions that target the desired variables. Unfortunately, Spielberger (1999) and Spielberger, Krasner, and Soloman (1988) have long noted that these concepts have been used almost interchangeably. The ambiguity and sometimes contradictory use of the three terms has led to confusion and difficulty with diagnosis, measurement, and treatment. At the same time, because they often co-occur, Spielberger suggested that they are all components of an anger, hostility, and aggression (AHA) syndrome.

Spielberger (1999) refers to anger as a "more fundamental concept than either hostility or aggression" (p. 19). However, he provides no explanation for the conclusion that it is more fundamental. He does note that anger refers to a "psychobiological emotional state or condition that consists of feelings that vary in intensity from mild irritation or annoyance to intense fury and rage, accompanied by activation of neuroendocrine processes and arousal of the autonomic nervous system" (p. 19). Thus, his definition also begins with subjective feelings that are associated with bodily changes. However, there is no mention of possible associated motor-behavioral actions. He then notes that "hostility involves the frequent experience of angry feelings, but this concept also has the connotation of a complex set of attitudes that include meanness and viciousness, as well as aggressive and often vindictive behavior" (p. 19). In sum, Spielberger's model refers to anger as experienced subjective feelings and bodily arousal. Hostility refers to experienced feelings and bodily arousal and behavior, and aggression refers to negative attitudes and behavior. Obviously, with so much overlap, these definitions still do not connote clear differentiation among the concepts.

This analysis is not meant to reduce the importance of Spielberger's many contributions to the analysis of anger. His work has led to many advances in theory, assessment, and intervention. This analysis does, however, point out the importance of clarifying our definitions even further if we are to develop meaningful and focused treatment programs. From our perspective, in order to understand the targets of treatment in the chapters that follow, it seems best to use the following definitions:

- *Anger* refers to an experienced negative feeling state that varies in intensity (labeled from annoyance, through anger, and then to fury) and duration (fleeting states to enduring grudges). It may occur infrequently or frequently and is associated with negative images and thoughts about the trigger, cognitive misinterpretations, and desires to warn, intimidate, control, attack, or gain retribution. Angry states may or may not be associated with physiological and motor reactions.
- *Hostility* refers to a set of negative attitudes that set the stage for anger and aggression. They represent predispositions about individuals or groups (e.g., "You can't trust adolescents. They are all crazy," or "Rednecks are simple minded" or "Jacqueline hates foreigners"). Such attitudes, or cognitive sets, increase the probability that neutral actions by the person or by members of these groups will be interpreted as wrong, unjust, purposeful, and preventable or that negative triggers will be seen to represent fundamental characteristics of the individual or group. These attitudes will often lead to increases in anger.
- *Aggression* refers to gross motor behavior, with an accompanying intent to harm. Thus, behavior that inadvertently hurts others (e.g., pain caused by a dentist) is not aggression, but corporal punishment of a misbehaving child is aggression. Aggression that follows anger is typically labeled as emotional aggression, whereas aggression that occurs in the relative absence of anger is labeled as instrumental aggression. For example, aggression that occurs as a part of gang violence is often not the result of anger. The aggressor may have no hostile attitude toward the victim and may feel no anger. Rather, the aggression occurs as a result of modeling, group

pressure, and social reinforcement. Aggression in some environments (e.g., prisons) may not represent anger as much as the individual's belief in the importance of asserting dominance in an environment where those who do not aggress will be aggressed upon. In that sense, the aggression is reinforced by the lack of aggression from others. Thus, anger may appear in the absence of aggression, and aggression may appear in the absence of anger. Yet, one of the fundamental questions for practitioners relates to the association of these two patterns of behavior.

Despite various analyses that have been put forward, the demarcation of anger from aggression remains difficult to make. For some, it may seem to be a qualitative distinction as noted by the definitions just given. For others, it may be quantitative. That is, as an aversive stimulus increases in intensity, the reaction is more likely to be called aggression rather than anger. Consider the following scenarios.

In response to discovering that a 16-year-old adolescent boy has stolen $75 from his father, the father

Thinks about how surprising the theft was. Notices his internal agitation, such as increases in heart rate, muscle tension, and images of the boy taking the money. *The father thinks it is a terrible event and believes the boy should not do such things. But, he does nothing.*

Now suppose the following additions are made:

(a) The father has *thoughts of yelling* at the boy and "grounding" him. The father, in fact, calms down and talks to the boy assertively to develop a restitution plan. (Retaliatory thoughts, but no action.)

(b) The father *actually yells*, "I can't believe you did this. You should know better. What happened? Are you stupid or something? You'll pay for this." (Demeaning and retaliatory thoughts and threatened actions.)

(c) The father yells, "I can't believe you did this. You should know better. What happened? Are you stupid or something? You'll pay for this." *The father goes to the boy's room and, while going through his dresser drawer, throws his clothing all over the floor.* (Retaliatory thoughts and some action against an inanimate object.)

(d) The father yells, "I can't believe you did this. You should know better. What happened? Are you stupid or something? You'll pay for this." The father goes to the boy's room and, while going through his dresser drawer, throws his clothing all over the floor. *Then, the father throws the boy's iPod on the floor and breaks it.* (Retaliatory thoughts and some costly action against an inanimate object.)

(e) The father yells, "I can't believe you did this. You should know better. What happened? Are you stupid or something? You'll pay for this." The father goes to the boy's room and, while going through his dresser drawer, throws his clothing all over the floor. Then, the father throws the boy's iPod on the floor and breaks it. *The boy is pushed out of the way and hits the wall as the parent leaves.* (Retaliatory thoughts, action against an object, and mild action against the boy.)

(f) The father yells, "I can't believe you did this. You should know better. What happened? Are you stupid or something? You'll pay for this." The father goes to the boy's room and, while going through his dresser drawer, throws his clothing all over the floor. Then, the father throws the boy's iPod on the floor, breaks it, and *hits the boy in the face with a belt*. (Retaliatory thoughts, action against an object, and a strong action against an object and the boy.)

In which of these scenarios would we label the father's behavior as anger and in which is it aggression? One possible qualitative demarcation might be with regard to the possibility that the stimulus *must* lead to the response. That is, if the parent hits the child with a belt, the child's body will definitely respond with blood or bruises. However, if the parent only yells or engages in negative verbal behavior, there are a variety of responses for the child. He might calmly give an explanation ("I needed the money to buy a gift for my younger sister"), he might yell ("Leave me alone. You're a screwball"), or he might hit the parent.

Thus, one possibility is to define all aversive *verbal* behavior by this parent, no matter how loud or threatening, as a separate category of anger-related behavior. Then, gross motor behavior against the child would become aggression. In between would be cases where the parent throws an item against a floor, breaks an inanimate object, and so forth, but does not touch any other person. For some, this is still aggression. For others, it would be a sign of anger because the parent most likely did not intend to harm the child by throwing a clock or iPod on the floor. This labeling issue, we believe, is both important and still unresolved.

Clinically, and perhaps most important, we have found that it is useful to make a clear distinction between the verbal and physical responses that clients may engage in when angry. Different reaction patterns (verbal versus physical) call for different levels of practitioner concern and intervention, even though both may be destructive. For example, clients who insult their children when angry may be acting in a way that will lead the child to feel inadequate, to seek revenge, or to have a weak bond with family members over the long run. However, the parent who hits the child out of anger is engaging in a behavior that will cause immediate and certain harm. Practitioners, of course, are typically required to report such incidents to their state's division of protective services.

ANGER AS A SIGNAL FOR AGGRESSION

Does anger signal aggression? Are practitioners who work with angry clients likely to become the recipients of physical attacks? The answer, it turns out, may partially depend on the intervention setting. If we use self-report data taken from unselected community adults, only 10% of respondents indicate that their anger is associated with fighting or hitting another person (Kassinove et al., 1997). In addition, although community adults who rated themselves as high on trait anger were more likely to have an associated aggression problem, their rates were still lower than might be expected from reading the daily newspapers. The typical manifestations of anger consist of arguing, yelling, complaining, using sarcasm and/or profanity, withdrawing, and holding anger in and keeping quiet. Indeed, community adults often seem to try to resolve their problems, reduce their anger, and think about positive aspects of their relationships with other people. These are the kinds of clients who are likely to be seen in private practices or outpatient settings. For private practitioners, these data indicate a relatively low probability of anger as a signal for aggression, particularly against others. At the same time, we note the importance of a good clinical interview to assess the history of aggression and the use of reliable and valid measurements to understand how clients cope with frustration and their level of anger as a personality trait.

In contrast, the situation may be quite different for practitioners who work in restricted settings, such as incarceration facilities, and for those who work with clients who suffer from other serious, comorbid psychiatric, psychological, or socioeconomic problems. In these cases, anger is more likely to be a precursor to aggression. For these individuals, the environment may contain more frustrations, their histories may contain more problematic and negative conditioning events, their thresholds for dealing with frustration are likely to be lower, and there is an increased importance of neurophysiological contributions (e.g., the catecholamines of epinephrine and norepinephrine yield a short-term, energizing hypoglycemic effect) to both anger and aggression. In these cases, undifferentiated angry arousal is more likely to be associated with, or predictive of, aggression (Robins & Novaco, 1999). Examples would include clients with post-traumatic stress disorder (PTSD), partner abusers, violent offender groups, clients with developmental delays, and so forth (Chemtob et al., 1997; Novaco, 1997; Schumacher, 2001).

In summary, angry clients are often unpleasant, do not accept personal responsibility for their anger, use moral reasons to justify maintaining their anger, typically want the practitioner to change the behavior of someone else, and present the possibility of using aversive verbal and motor behaviors against the practitioner. Although careful listening, support, reflection, and understanding of such clients is important, these are difficult skills to put into practice when anger, hostility, or aggression is present. Nevertheless, practitioners in almost all settings are likely to be faced with clients who have disordered anger experiences.

MODELS OF ANGER ASSESSMENT

The treatment of anger-related disorders can be approached from many perspectives. In later chapters, the case of Anthony is presented and treatment is reviewed from the perspectives of psychoanalysis, self-psychology, cognitive-behavioral psychology, dialectical behavior therapy, family interventions, psychopharmacology, emotion-focused treatment, Eastern spiritualism, and Adlerian psychology. In each chapter, the case is reviewed from a unique perspective with regard to the presenting problem, personal history, and anger-related difficulties. Then, intervention goals, a plan for treatment, and expected outcomes are presented. In this chapter, we review three approaches to anger for the reader. The first emerges from the psychometric literature, is based on anger states and anger traits, and is helpful with regard to diagnosis and prognosis. The second is based on client self-reports and focuses on individual episodes of anger. This second approach is helpful for understanding immediate attributions about individual anger episodes and to frame the treatment plan. The third approach is broad and represents an analysis of anger within the life system of a person. It also leads to the development of treatment strategies and a prognosis about change. We do not fully review these approaches, nor do we review the important considerations that may be represented by cultural approaches, a feminist outlook, and so on. Rather, our goal is to use these three important models as points of orientation for the chapters that follow.

Anger Traits and Angry States

The most well-known anger model has probably emerged from the work of Spielberger and his associates. In the manual for the State-Trait Anger Expression Inventory (STAXI, 1988; STAXI-2, 1999), he describes and measures anger from the perspective of states and traits. Initially described by Cattell and Scheier (1961), *traits* refer to the cross-situational likelihood of reactions, that is, the likelihood that many different stimulus events, usually negative, will lead to a state of anger. Some adults seem to experience anger often, in response to stimuli that are both obvious and hidden and that vary in the objective intensity of their aversiveness. They may become angry in response to the slightest insult, the most minimal of frustrations, lack of recognition, or any level of negative feedback. Persons with personalities that have a high level of anger are characterized as quick tempered, fiery, and hotheaded. Their anger may emerge when interacting with peers, parents, children, colleagues, sales personnel, students, or strangers in anonymous environments such as subways or supermarkets. STAXI theory also notes that such persons are likely to have a typical manner of dealing with their anger. Persons who frequently argue, yell, are sarcastic, and emit nasty verbalizations rate high on the scale of outwardly expressing anger. In the consultation office, marital partners may report such behaviors to their practitioner as constant "fighting," by which they mean verbal arguments. This mode of expressing anger outwardly is what is most commonly addressed in anger management programs.

In contrast, for some adults, anger is expressed inwardly as their normative pattern. They are fully aware of their anger, but do not show it directly to others. They may pout and have fantasies of revenge, but others do not generally know how angry they are. They may ruminate and thus hold on to their anger for long periods as a result of self-reinforcement. Finally, some people try to engage in constructive actions as a mode of operation. For adults who use anger control strategies, they may typically try to breathe deeply or relax, or they may try to engage in cognitive activities that increase tolerance and understanding. Each of these typical modes of operation is reliably assessed by the STAXI-2 (Spielberger, 1999).

Trait anger, in sum, refers to frequent increases in short-term self-perceived angry states. That is, the experiences of anger that are reported, often in detail, to practitioners. As we proposed earlier, in our comprehensive definition of anger, such experiences may consist of the simple awareness of anger and/or the awareness of cognitions related to a motivation to yell and argue or to hit something or someone. Again, these are reliably measured on the STAXI-2 and will be helpful for the purposes of diagnosis and intervention.

Recently, DiGiuseppe and Tafrate (2004) developed an Anger Disorders Scale (ADS) that is based on a five-factor model, with the domains of provocation, arousal, cognitions, motives, and behaviors. *Provocation* refers to the scope of the triggers for anger; these triggers are helpful in differentiating between diagnoses that are situationally limited (e.g., anger that appears only within parent-child interactions or only in the work environment) and those that are more generalized. The items also assess disrespect and social rejection as specific, narrow scope anger triggers.

The arousal domain of the ADS assesses reported physiological arousal (i.e., somatic tension) as well as length of the episode and the duration of anger problems. Duration is important, because a *Diagnostic and Statistical Manual* (DSM-IV-TR; APA, 2000) criterion for some emotional disorders is that they have to exist for 6 months or longer. Anger episode length also relates to adults characterized as having higher trait anger. They seem to show longer episode lengths and thus are likely to suffer more negative consequences (Deffenbacher et al., 1996; Tafrate, Kassinove, & Dundin, 2002). Unfortunately, the ADS does not include a measure of anger intensity. However, as demonstrated by Tafrate, Kassinove, and Dundin (2002), differences in intensity of anger episodes can be identified through a more idiographic, clinical approach. The intensity variable is likely to be important for treatment, the prediction of aggression, and the development of future diagnostic categories.

The cognitions domain of the ADS assesses suspiciousness, resentment, impulsivity, and rumination. *Resentment* refers to an attitude about poor treatment by life, whereas *suspiciousness* refers to a belief that others have hostile intent. For a long time, impulsivity, the lack of thoughtful delay in responding, has been considered part of the anger response and has been part of classic anger control programs based on self-instructional training (Novaco, 1975). *Rumination* refers to the tendency to place excessive focus on the anger trigger. Although the cognitions domain is reported to reflect both attitudinal and appraisal aspects, items that assess stimulus appraisals according to Ellis' and Beck's theories are absent. Such items would have been helpful to the clinician to determine, for example, whether clients were more likely to be catastrophizers versus blamers, as this knowledge would guide treatment.

The motives domain assesses characteristics such as the desire for revenge, the use of anger as a tension reduction mechanism, and as a coercive force. The behaviors domain includes assessment of the tendency to brood, to engage in aversive verbal behavior, and to act aggressively. Thus, it includes both internal cognitive-verbal behavior and gross motor behavior.

The ADS makes some significant steps forward in that it includes dimensions that are absent in other measures. DiGiuseppe and Tafrate (2004) compare both omnibus personality tests, such as the Minnesota Multiphasic Personality Inventory (MMPI) that includes an anger subscale, and specific anger inventories to their ADS and note the greater breadth of their new measure. Indeed, it is linked both to an anger model and to research findings, and it may prove to be useful in the development of formal anger diagnoses. At the same time, the ADS measures traits and not states. Because it is the anger state, or the individual anger episode, that typically causes the client to first see a clinician, trait measures help the practitioner as only one limited source of information. In contrast, richer information for the practitioner may be obtained by an individualized, clinical episode analysis, as noted in the following sections.

Standardized assessment instruments are most likely to help in the development of general hypotheses about specific client triggers or motives. For example, the Novaco Anger Scale and Provocation Inventory (2003) is another well-standardized, research-based, self-report instrument. Based on theory, it assesses the cognitive (e.g., likelihood of rumination), arousal (e.g., intensity and duration of somatic tension), behavior (e.g., indirect expression such as smashing objects), and anger regulation aspects of anger (e.g., cognitive coping and calming down). With regard to provocations, respondents report on "how true" it is that various trigger classes invoke anger. The five classes are disrespectful treatment, unfairness, frustration, annoying traits of others, and irritations such as being slowed down by another person's mistakes.

Each of these measures has clear strengths and weaknesses. The Novaco scales, for example, consider a hostile attitude to be a part of the cognitive part of anger. This may fit well with the notion that hostility is an attitude that sets the stage for anger. For example, if a client endorses the statement "Every week I meet someone I dislike," it suggests a readiness for confrontation and anger. At the same time, the lack of scales on the STAXI, ADS, or Novaco scales that assess dysfunctional cognitions from the perspective of rational emotive behavior therapy or cognitive therapy means that clinicians who work within these perspectives must look elsewhere to determine a client's specific appraisals of stimuli (triggers). And, of course, as it true of all trait scales, these scales may not reflect what led to anger at a particular moment, in response to a particular trigger, in a particular client.

The Componential Anger Episode Model

Although paper-and-pencil measures provide useful information about anger traits and typical modes of responding, in the consulting office, psychotherapeutic interventions deal with specific situations in the client's life. Typically, the client reports an event that has led to feeling angry and (hopefully) asks for help in understanding the event in order to develop a better response. Trying to modify abstract traits is not effective; rather, working on the development of better solutions for a variety of specific anger experiences is likely to lead to improved response patterns to future life problems. For this reason, many researchers and practitioners, from Gates (1926) to Anastasi, Cohen, and Spatz (1948) to Averill (1982, 1983), and to Kassinove et al. (1997), have used diary or survey methods to understand individual episodes of anger. In the office setting, such methods allow the client to talk about the self-perceived, proximal causes of anger, which can then be discussed.

Kassinove and Tafrate (2002) use a *five-stage anger episode model* to provide for a shared understanding of anger between practitioners and clients. In their model, individual episodes of anger begin with a *trigger*. Triggers may be the current negative actions of another person (e.g., a rejection) or remembrances of negative actions (e.g., "She has never appreciated what I have done for her"). They may also be relatively neutral stimuli (e.g., realizing that a child forgot to turn off a light) or even repeated positive verbal stimuli that have not been followed by behavior change (e.g., "I promise that I will stop drinking"). Almost any stimulus may be reported as the trigger for anger.

Humans are cognitive creatures and think about events. Thus, they appraise and evaluate triggers, and these *appraisals* comprise the second stage of the anger episode model. Clients will typically report that the trigger is "awful" (e.g., not receiving a desired promotion at work while the job is given to a colleague with less seniority). They report that they "can't tolerate" what has happened. They demand that events "should" be fair, according to their own perceptions. They talk in dichotomous terms about their job as bad or good, their employer as unfair or fair, and their children as lazy or gifted. The reader will recognize these appraisals as fitting the theories put forth by psychotherapist such as Ellis (1994), Ellis and Tafrate (1997), and Beck (1976, 1999).

For the beginning cognitive-behavior therapist, the difficult part of this model is distinguishing "cold" cognitions that represent noninflammatory thoughts about an event (e.g., "My boss was direct with her negative feedback") from "hot cognitions" that exacerbate anger (e.g., "My boss is out to get me. He should treat me better"). This differentiation was initially developed by Abelson (1981) and is central to understanding how clients' cognitive inflammations lead to anger. Once identified, hot cognitive appraisals of triggers can be discussed and challenged in the practitioner's office.

The anger itself consists of the experience and the expression. The *experience* portion of the model is a private event (Skinner, 1945) that is known only to the client. It consists of the intensity and duration of thoughts, images, and bodily sensations. Although all kinds of verbal distortions may occur, in conversation with the practitioner, the private experience can be communicated. Of course, based on the contingencies of the client's life (i.e., reinforcement history and current contingencies), there may be pressure to magnify the internal anger reaction (i.e., to fake high) or minimize the internal anger reaction (i.e., fake low). Verbally, clients may use a set of descriptors such as *annoyed, angry,* or *furious* to describe various self-perceived experiences. These might be descriptors that would be shared by others in their sociocultural group, or these clients may be persistent maximizers who portray all experiences as rage and fury.

Verbal, as well as motor, behaviors also represent the *expression* part of the anger episode model. Evidence suggests that the language-based verbal expression of emotions differs across cultures (e.g., Russell, 1991). Clearly, practitioners would be wise to take the cultural and linguistic background of the client into consideration when analyzing episodes.

Aside from language, the private experience of anger may be associated with expressive, public, and observable changes in the facial musculature, with flushing of the skin, with sweating, and so forth. Anger may also present with concurrent threats of aggression or actual motor actions against objects (e.g., slamming a book against a table, breaking a pencil, or hitting a wall). At the same time, when there are intentional gross motor actions against other people (e.g., hitting or shoving a child or marital partner), these actions, by definition, represent aggression. We note that most anger management programs target outward expressions of anger (e.g., yelling, aversive verbalizations, threats, hitting walls). In fact, unresolved suppressed anger may represent an equally important problem for both clients and society.

In the final stage of the anger episode model, it is noted that *outcomes* occur and that these affect future anger responses. Many of the immediate responses to the expression of anger are reinforcing for the angry person. Children, for example, may comply when a parent yells and angrily demands that homework be done "right now!" A work supervisor may respond with anger to inadequate sales attempts by a worker and demand that more telephone calls be made to generate more income. The worker will likely comply. There are also self-reinforcing effects of anger as a function of the moral tone of the feeling. The client may believe, "I'm happy that I got angry. She deserved the tongue lashing that she got from me."

Of course, not all anger is reinforced in the short term. There may be lack of compliance by the recipient of the anger, shame and/or regret in the angry person, and so on. Thus, the reinforcement for anger expression is only partial or discontinuous. Such partial reinforcement leads to resistance to extinction (i.e., maintenance) and creates the long-term habitual anger response. Many long-term outcomes of anger are also quite negative, including increased health risks for hypertension, stroke, and coronary

artery disease (Siegman & Smith, 1994; Williams et al., 2000), poor interpersonal relationships and rejection by peers (Jacobson & Gottman, 1998),
occupational ineffectiveness and maladjustment (Folger & Baron,
1996), poor decision making, and so forth (also see Kassinove &
Tafrate, 2002, and Robins & Novaco, 1999). In addition, adults with
chronic anger and other comorbid problems, including medical and psychiatric disorders and environmental stressors such as those related to
lower socioeconomic conditions, are more likely to become aggressive.
Aggression, of course, has its own set of negative consequences.
Nevertheless, as part of the fight or flight response to perceived threat, and
a partial schedule of reinforcement, anger can be difficult to modify.

The Systems Approach

The anger episode model and related diary approaches focus on the proximal causes of anger. Systems approaches (Robins & Novaco, 1999) take
a somewhat broader view and recognize that reliance on the subjective
self-monitoring of clients is likely to limit our understanding of anger.
All introspection is limited, and clients will most often report what the
culture dictates. There are prescriptions for correct and incorrect ways to
behave, and when others behave incorrectly, that person is thought to
"cause" our anger. Consider the common responses emitted by parents
such as, "Why don't you listen to me? You are making me furious" or
"You are really making Mommy mad now." The anger is culturally
justified when others do not behave "properly." This is what is typically reported in diary approaches and in the psychotherapy office to
practitioners.

Unfortunately, because anger is disruptive, when people are angry,
they are less likely to be accurate in their reports. Anger degrades their
ability to recall the sequence of events. Systems theorists look to
research and evolutionary evidence to understand anger as an automa-
tized response to stressors. This was also recognized by Kassinove and
Tafrate (2002), who noted that "much of what we do in life is actually
done on 'autopilot'" (p. 111). Anger happens, and then we make attributions about the trigger, which are likely to be related to the immediate
environment. Thus, clients most often blame others with whom they live
or work for causing their anger. When asked, they may also reveal their
cognitive interpretations about the behavior of others and indicate how
what happened was "horrible" and "should not" have occurred.
Alternatively, they may simply agree with, or model, the cognitive interpretations that have been laid out by their psychotherapist. In any case,
clients are not likely to speak of the evolutionary fight or flight reaction
and the possible long-term biological adaptive value of anger (e.g., scaring

away predators). They are unlikely to consider the possibility that their anger emerged as a result of long-term exposure to stressful conditions that lowered their threshold for coping. Furthermore, they are unlikely to think of themselves as self-controlled organisms that place themselves in environments with high stress. Indeed, with the myriad of jobs that are open to adults, it is easy to wonder why people would voluntarily work as air traffic controllers, taxicab drivers, firefighters, police officers, inner-city schools teachers, prison guards, or mental health personnel who interact with psychotic, brain-injured, abusive, or mentally disabled persons. In response to stress and loss of control, people who choose to remain in such jobs are setting the stage for personal anger experiences. Psychotherapists, as outsiders, may wonder why their clients exhibit inertia to change their environments and thereby reduce their anger. However, behaviorists would believe that this lack of inertia is not a function of agenetic behavior, because all environments have some degree of reinforcement (e.g., salary, benefits, a location close to home, prestige), and this leads people to remain where they are. Nevertheless, this combination of stress and inertia increases the automaticity of anger reactions.

ANGER COMPONENTS AND FULL SPECTRUM ANGER REACTIONS

As an emotion, anger has cognitive, physiological, and behavioral components. Each component can individually set the stage for (i.e., dispose one toward) a full-blown anger reaction. In the anger episode model presented earlier, some of the cognitive processes that may trigger anger were noted. Such beliefs and appraisals are highlighted in the well-known systems of Ellis (1962, 1973, 1994) and Beck (1963, 1971, 1976). Physiological processes also set the stage for anger. High catecholamine levels (e.g., epinephrine and norepinephrine that serve as neurotransmitters) change the threshold for anger. When adults become angry, changes occur in the cardiovascular, endocrine, and limbic systems and the muscles become tense. This suggests why some of the outcomes for long-term anger include stroke and heart disease.

At the behavioral level, it was noted that anger reactions are maintained by partial reinforcement. Sometimes, anger pays off—at least in the short run. In addition, avoidance learning is also part of the picture. By holding anger in, arguments, and even aggressive episodes, may be avoided, thus reinforcing the bottling up of unresolved anger. We all learn when to express and when not to express anger.

These three components interact with one another. Our physiological state (i.e., arousal level) will lead us to be more or less reactive to potentially provocative stimuli. This readiness may affect our cognitive system and lead us to increase our tendency to catastrophize or to appraise relatively neutral events as a sign of disapproval and rejection by others. Our history of reinforcement may also affect our tendency to interpret the behavior of others in a maladaptive manner, and we may observe others react with anger, thus increasing our own modeled anger response. Work frustrations and fatigue may combine with observing a marital partner scold a child, thus increasing our own tendency to be angry, to label the child as lazy, and to strike the child. Finally, the systems approach recognizes the centrality of homeostasis to the human system, including marriages and family organization. Many angry couples are unsatisfied and try to control their partners with verbal abuse. However, when their partner becomes too distant, they wonder what is wrong and try to get closer. Conversely, marital partners (or children) who feel smothered by relationships that are too close may become angry in order to achieve some distance from their partner (or parent). It is balance in the system that is sought. In closed environments, such as prisons, it is adaptive to be angry and "tough" in order to avoid being preyed upon. On the other hand, being too tough may make one a target by another who wants revenge. The work, family, or friendship systems call for a balance between approach and avoidance, fear and anger, closeness and distance. This will lead to inertia and a difficult therapeutic task if anger reduction is sought without considering the forces that maintain it at its present level. From this perspective, as well as others, interventions have to be multifaceted.

DIAGNOSTIC CONSIDERATIONS

Another important issue for both researchers and practitioners relates to the differentiation between normal and adaptive anger from disruptive and maladaptive anger. Certainly, some annoyance or lower-level anger reactions are adaptive. In the animal kingdom, the choice of fight or flight is paramount when meeting a potential predator. Puffing up to appear larger (e.g., the puffer fish) or raising up and spreading out parts of the body (e.g., the king cobra) presents clear warning signals to other animals. In human interchanges, raising the voice during contract negotiations with a threat to go "on strike" is a warning that important issues are on the table. Raising the voice when telling a young child to do homework may warn of the consequences of noncompliance, and expressing anger when one is ignored in a department store may lead to better service.

What then defines maladaptive anger? Traditionally, the elements of frequency, intensity, and duration have been used. Given the importance of anger, it might be expected that these elements would have already led to a set of formal diagnoses in the American Psychiatric Association's DSM-IV-TR (2000) or the World Health Organization's *International Classification of Diseases* (ICD-10, 1992). Unfortunately, this has not been the case. As noted by DiGiuseppe and Tafrate (2004), the "DSM-IV-TR fails to address the presence of anger consistently or systematically. Anger is mentioned only as a symptom that occasionally appears across divergent disorders" (p. 2).

Similar conclusions were reached earlier by Eckhardt and Deffenbacher (1995) when they examined the 1994 version of the DSM-IV. They wrote:

> . . . little progress has been evidenced in the assessment of anger in what is the most common form of clinical measurement—*diagnosis*. The most obvious indication that contemporary psychology and psychiatry have neglected anger as a clinically-relevant problem is the absence of a diagnostic category with anger as the central and defining feature (p. 35).

Eckhardt and Deffenbacher (1995) noted that the DSV-IV contained 11 Axis I disorders for anxiety-related problems and 9 Axis I disorders for mood-related disorders. However, none were available for a parallel condition of chronic, moderate, and pervasive anger. Categories existed for situational anxiety reactions (i.e., phobias) but not for situational anger reactions, such as intense anger that might occur primarily in the presence of criticism at home or at work. In the DSM-IV-TR (2000), anger-related symptoms such as irritability continue to appear only as part of Axis I and II diagnoses such as generalized anxiety disorder, PTSD, borderline personality disorder, antisocial personality disorder, and manic phases of bipolar disorder. Anger is also recognized as important in Axis III problems such as high blood pressure, stroke, and cardiovascular disease. However, anger continues to be discussed only as one of the many possible symptoms of these disorders. Also, because the disorders may be diagnosed without anger, it is not a necessary component of the diagnosis. The presence of anger is not even sufficient to make these diagnoses, because elements other than anger are required. The same situation exists with regard to the ICD-10.

In sum, our diagnostic systems have not recognized the importance of specific categories that center on anger as necessary or sufficient. This has left clinicians with the need to approximate a diagnosis for their angry clients. Indeed, Lachmund and DiGiuseppe (1997) and Lachmund, DiGiuseppe, and Fuller (2005) have shown that clinicians typically diagnose such cases as intermittent explosive disorder. Unfortunately, this diagnosis is closer to the anger-out construct and does not fit for adults who hold their anger in, dwell and ruminate about past imagined injustices, and fantasize about revenge. Practitioners who treat angry individuals are left without clear diagnostic categories that directly and clearly describe the syndrome they are treating. This is especially true for clients who hold their anger in. Adequate diagnoses will likely increase the time that practitioners spend conceptualizing cases and may lead to a greater chance of reimbursement from third-party providers. It will also allow for a fuller understanding of the frequency of maladaptive anger, which is currently hidden within other categories, and will encourage practitioners to select relevant interventions.

Given this dearth of official attention to anger, some clinical researchers have attempted to generate anger diagnoses for possible inclusion in future revisions of diagnostic systems. Eckhardt and Deffenbacher (1995), for example, proposed five anger diagnoses. The categories would reflect the general or situational nature of the anger and whether or not aggression was also present. In each one, it would have to be shown that the anger disrupts social, work, or school activities; impairs interpersonal relationships; and/or causes significant personal distress. The diagnosis could not be made without social-behavioral disruption and/or perceived distress. Their anger diagnoses are as follows:

1. *Adjustment disorder with angry mood.* This disorder reflects a maladaptive anger reaction to identifiable psychosocial stressors that occurred within 3 months after onset of the stressor. The anger persists for no more than 6 months and thus parallels adjustment disorder with anxiety, depression, or mixed emotional features. This category recognizes that some adults respond to stressors primarily with irritability and anger. The anger could be held in and perceived mostly by the person, or it could be expressed by aversive verbal communications.

2. *Situational anger disorder without aggression.* This disorder reflects the presence of a persistent (6 months or more) and consistent anger reaction to a circumscribed situation (e.g., lack of recognition by a supervisor or discourteous drivers) or to situations that share a common theme (e.g., insults, lack of compliance in completion of chores or homework by children, congested traffic patterns). The anger does not represent a chronic mood state or pervasive response pattern. Rather, it is situational or thematically specific. In addition, the client presents without significant aggressive behavior. However, in addition to raising their voices and verbally demanding responses from their children or others, such clients may curse internally, have fantasies of revenge, and so forth. Thus, the anger may be held in or expressed outwardly by aversive verbal communication.

3. *Situational anger disorder with aggression.* This disorder is used for adults who present with elevated anger *and* aggressive behavior in response to specific situations. As examples, it would apply to a worker who becomes angry when unrecognized by a supervisor and who destroys the supervisor's property (e.g., destroys a printer, lets air out of the supervisor's tires in the parking lot, scratches the supervisor's car). It would apply to a parent who screams, demeans, and hits a child who has not complied with assigned chores. In congested traffic, it would also apply to a driver who feels angry and who also drives menacingly, tailgates, makes obscene gestures, or forces the offending driver off the road. There is a *consistent* pattern of responding with aggressive behavior along with perceived anger in response to a specific provocative situation.

4. *General anger disorder without aggression.* Adults who fit this diagnosis feel chronically and pervasively angry, but they are not highly aggressive. Key elements include frequently experiencing anger in response to a wide range of situations for at least 1 year. Anger is a near-daily disruptive experience that is elicited by a wide range of stimuli. There are significant aversive verbalizations (anger-out) and/or significant thoughts and fantasies or retribution (anger-in). Aggression against objects (e.g., slamming doors) or people (e.g., children, spouses) would be infrequent and mild in intensity.

5. *General anger disorder with aggression.* Adults who fit this diagnosis experience frequent periods of generalized felt anger *and* frequent aggressive behavior. In addition to felt anger experiences, they also engage in sarcasm, demean others, make verbal threats, elevate discussions to loud arguments and yelling matches, and typically engage in physical behaviors. For example, the person might withdraw into an angry sullenness marked by terse communications and a tendency to throw or slam things around or may frequently use an anger-out mode of anger expression involving pushing, grabbing, shoving, or slapping others, as well as more severe forms of physical aggression against others, such as closed-fist blows or choking. Put differently, the individual displays either a specific habitual pattern of aggressive behaviors or a significant frequency of a number of different aggressive behaviors.

Official diagnoses are based on factors such as (1) clear criteria for the syndrome so that self-report, rating scale, and structured interview assessment instruments can be constructed; (2) research that supports the syndrome and its subcategories; and (3) the ability of clinicians to make the diagnosis and to differentiate it from related syndromes. The anger disorders suggested by Eckhardt and Deffenbacher are preliminary models open for empirical evaluation, and they are currently being reviewed and modified. Nevertheless, because there are no official diagnoses as of yet, some investigators have already used Eckhardt and Deffenbacher's categories to identify adults with anger disorders. For example, Jones and Trower (2004) recently identified clients with anger disorders by using the judgment of two clinicians to determine whether they fit into one of the five proposed diagnostic categories.

One of the criteria used by Eckhardt and Deffenbacher to make an affirmative diagnosis centers on the adaptive versus the disruptive nature of the client's anger. In an attempt to examine this issue, Tafrate, Kassinove, and Dundin (2002) looked at differences in anger among 51 community adults (mean age of 34) who were in the highest 25% (HTA) versus 42 who were in the lowest 25% (LTA) on the trait of anger, according to the STAXI standardization sample. They used self-reports, based on their componential anger episode model, to examine differences in triggers, appraisals, experiences, expressive patterns, and outcomes. As expected, there were no differences between the groups with regard to anger triggers. For all subjects combined, approximately 85% of the anger was reported to occur in response to the actions of another person, who was well known and liked or loved. This underscores the interpersonal nature of the anger experience. Furthermore, 485 of the anger events took place at home, and 45% of reported events had occurred within the prior week.

Regarding cognitive appraisals, the data showed that HTA subjects were significantly more prone to dysfunctional thinking. The mean number of dysfunctional cognitions, based on the work of Beck and Ellis, was 3.2 in HTA group and 2.0 in the LTA group. "Demandingness" (e.g., "He should have done what I told him to do" or "She ought to follow my instructions") and "Global Ratings of Others" (e.g., "She is a total jerk!" or "What a moron he is") appeared frequently (90% and 53%, respectively) in both HTA and LTA subjects. However, the HTA subjects were significantly more likely to magnify (i.e., "awfulize") the importance of the triggering event and to distort it in other ways. Such magnifications typically take the form of ignoring the objective amplitude of the trigger and instead interpreting it as being maximal in intensity. Thus, in anger, a client might suggest that it is terrible or awful when a child fails a school test rather than legitimately problematic and disadvantageous. The latter term, *disadvantageous,* is legitimate because the child might be asked to retake the exam (which takes time and effort), might be placed in a slower reading group, and so forth. In contrast, if the child is told the failure is awful, it suggests that it is the worst thing that could happen.

Mental health, we believe, includes being able to reasonably differentiate among the magnitude of the consequences of various problems.

The anger experience and expression data were interesting and consistent with what might be expected when dysfunctional appraisals interact with negative or relatively neutral triggers. HTA adults had experiences that were more frequent, more intense, and of longer duration. In the HTA group, 86% reported anger episodes at least a few times per week, as compared with only 7% in the LTA group who reported such frequencies. Indeed, 45% of the LTA subjects indicated that they "rarely, if ever" experienced anger. Using a scale of 0 to 100, subjects were asked to rate the intensity of their anger during the reported episode. The mean for HTA adults was 75 (standard deviation [SD] = 17), and the mean for LTA adults was 59 (SD = 19). The significant difference was highlighted further by the finding that one-fourth of the HTA adults indicated experienced intensities greater than 90. Regarding duration, most anger lasted for less than 1 hour. However, 45% of the HTA adults indicated that it lasted more than 1 day, versus only 17% of the LTA adults. In both groups, physical sensations were reported to be associated with the anger; these sensations included muscle tension, rapid heart rates, and headaches. However, dizziness and headache were reported significantly more often in the HTA group. These, of course, can be considered as both experiences and outcomes. In any case, these data have obvious treatment implications.

Thoughts about the event, once the anger had emerged, suggested that adults in both groups often wanted to resolve the problem, engage in some kind of avoidance, or make disapproving expressions such as glaring, frowning, or rolling the eyes. However, HTA adults had significantly greater desires to engage in negative verbalizations, physical actions, and substance abuse, or to suppress their anger and not deal with it.

Regarding actual behaviors, the reported anger episodes of HTA adults were twice as likely to be associated with aversive verbal expressions and three times as likely to be associated with motor aggression and illicit substance use. In terms of outcomes, the HTA adults reported more depression, disgust, foolishness, and shame after the anger passed. More HTA adults also reported a less frequent and weaker relationship with the other persons after the event. In contrast, the anger episode appeared to have little effect on the interpersonal relationships of the LTA adults. Finally, when asked about the long-term effects of their anger episode, HTA adults were four times more likely to report negative interpersonal outcomes.

These data suggest that adults who rank in the top quartile on trait anger are more likely to experience enduring anger, with high frequency and intensity; more likely to display a pattern of outward expressiveness;

and also more likely to experience social dysfunction and personal distress. These may be the markers for specific clinical disorders.

COMORBIDITY PATTERNS

Although anger disorders seem to exist as independent phenomena, one of the more challenging aspects of working with angry adults is understanding and prioritizing the complex comorbidity patterns that frequently exist. Indeed, addressing problematic anger reactions may be just one step in an overall treatment plan. Disordered anger can exist in the absence of other psychopathologic conditions, or it may overlap with a wide range of disorders. For this reason, we recommend using a broad-based measure of general psychopathology when working with angry clients. The Millon Clinical Multiaxial Inventory (MCMI-III; Millon, Davis, & Millon, 1997) is a good choice because it provides scores that conform closely to the DSM-IV in terms of both Axis I clinical disorders and Axis II personality profiles. Other measures of general psychopathology that can be useful for screening are the Brief Symptom Inventory (BSI; Derogatis, 1993) and the Personality Assessment Inventory (PAI; Morey, 1991).

To illustrate comorbidity issues, we provide a data set of MCMI scores for the HTA and LTA subjects described previously. The percentage of HTA or LTA adults who scored in the clinical range on Axis I disorders on the MCMI-III is shown in Table 1.1. Greater levels of

Table 1.1   Number and Percentage of High Trait Anger (HTA) and Low Trait Anger (LTA) Adults Who Met Criteria for Axis I Disorders on the MCMI-III[*,†]

| | HTA ($n = 45$) | | LTA ($n = 42$) | |
Axis I Disorder	Number	%	Number	%
Drug dependence	16	36	1	2
Alcohol dependence	9	20	1	2
Anxiety	13	29	1	2
Post-traumatic stress disorder	4	9	0	0
Depression	4	9	0	0
Dysthymia	4	9	2	5
Bipolar disorder	3	7	0	0
Delusional disorder	3	7	0	0
Thought disorder	0	0	0	0
Somatoform	1	2	0	0

[*]Base rates ≥85 are considered clinically significant.
[†]An analysis of mean base rate scores indicates that HTA adults reported significantly more symptoms than LTA adults for every disorder category.

psychopathology are noted among the HTA subjects. Although the data are presented in terms of the number of subjects who met criteria in each category, an analysis of mean base rate scores indicated that HTA subjects generally reported significantly more symptoms across each disorder category. This suggests that angry clients are likely to present with a wide range of Axis I problems. Thus, even in cases in which clients indicate anger difficulties as the primary concern, an overall screening to detect other disorders may be warranted.

Based on this small community sample, adults with anger problems seem likely to present with overlapping alcohol or drug dependence disorders. Indeed, the occurrence of comorbid substance use difficulties has been described by a number of anger researchers and is the focus of Reilly and Shopshire's treatment program (2002). In addition, and somewhat surprisingly, anxiety symptoms emerged as more frequent than depression-related difficulties. Thus, anxiety may also be a relevant co-occurring condition in angry clients.

Personality disorder information, based on MCMI-III scores, is presented in Table 1.2, in which these disorders are grouped according to the clusters indicated in DSM-IV-TR (APA, 2000). However, the MCMI-III assesses several personality patterns that are not part of the DSM-IV system (i.e., negativistic, depressive, sadistic, and masochistic personalities), and these are presented in a separate category. Although conventional clinical wisdom is that angry clients generally fall into cluster B (emotional and erratic), the data suggest that HTA adults may actually present with a wide range of dysfunctional personality patterns. Those patterns that appear to be more common in HTA adults and that would pose unique challenges for practitioners in terms of conceptualization and treatment adherence include paranoid, antisocial, borderline, and dependent personalities. For example, engaging clients with a paranoid personality disorder would likely involve more focus on the therapeutic relationship than on specific anger reduction techniques. Antisocial clients may do better with strategies that emphasize long-term consequences related to decision making. Dependent clients may require more focus on angry thoughts related to others not meeting their strongly perceived desires. Borderline clients are likely to benefit from a broader approach that emphasizes stability in relationships, thinking, and behaviors. (For specific cognitive-behavioral therapy approaches that are applicable to different personality disorders, readers are referred to Beck et al., 2004.)

Personality patterns not formally part of our diagnostic system are also commonly seen in HTA adults. The negativistic pattern corresponds to the DSM-IV-TR passive-aggressive personality disorder. Such individuals are characterized by periods of explosive anger or stubbornness,

Table 1.2 Number and Percentage of High Trait Anger (HTA) and Low Trait
Anger (LTA) Subjects Meeting Clinical Criteria for Axis II
Personality Disorders on the MCMI-III*,†

Axis II Personality Disorder	HTA (*n* = 45)		LTA (*n* = 42)	
	Number	%	Number	%
Cluster A				
Paranoid	6	13	0	0
Schizoid	3	7	0	0
Schizotypal	1	2	0	0
Cluster B				
Borderline	10	22	0	0
Antisocial	8	18	1	2
Narcissistic	8	18	7	7
Histrionic	1	2	9	21
Cluster C				
Dependent	8	18	1	2
Avoidant	2	4	1	2
Obsessive-compulsive	0	0	6	14
Miscellaneous				
Negativistic (passive-aggressive)	11	24	0	0
Depressive	8	18	2	5
Sadistic	5	11	0	0
Masochistic	4	9	0	0

*Base rates ≥85 are considered clinically significant.
†An analysis of mean base rate scores indicates that HTA adults reported significantly
more personality disorder symptoms than LTA adults for every category except
narcissistic, histrionic, and obsessive-compulsive.

intermingled with periods of guilt or shame, frequent disappointment, and
passive resistance to demands for adequate performance. This passive-
aggressive personality disorder, listed in the DSM-IV-TR in Appendix B
as a criterion set provided for further study, might appear in adults with
disordered anger experiences.

SUMMARY AND CONCLUDING REMARKS

Although anger is a frequent human experience, it has not been addressed
to the extent that it warrants. Nevertheless, a body of literature has
emerged that has helped us to understand anger and to differentiate it
from related concepts such as hostility and aggression. We have also
begun to understand the relationships among these three variables and to
differentiate common, adaptive anger from that which is maladaptive

and harmful to persons and their relationships. The literature base has led to conceptual models, assessment tools, and proposed diagnoses that will hopefully be included in future versions of the DSM and ICD and has also led to the development of effective treatment programs. Indeed, even in the absence of formal diagnoses, interventions have been developed because of the number of clients who present with anger problems in the clinical setting. We have also begun to understand some of the comorbid issues that may exist in adults who present with maladaptive anger.

In the best case, treatment would be based on diagnosis, diagnosis would be based on assessment, and assessment would be based on reliable and valid tools that are related to data and theory. We would have useful information about both the immediate causes (e.g., an aversive work environment) and the more distal causes (e.g., patterns of behavior selected by evolution) of anger. Unfortunately, we have not yet reached this best-case scenario. Rather, treatments are typically based on some degree of experience, research findings, and clinical wisdom, combined with what can be unofficially diagnosed, based on assessment tools that are incompletely related to theory and data.

Even adherents of the broader systems approach (e.g., Robins & Novaco, 1999) recognize that clinicians are "pressed with the situational imperative of needing to listen to a client who wants to talk" (p. 326). Clients, after all, rarely attribute their anger to the emergence of the species wide, fight or flight reactions, or their personal history of discontinuous reinforcement, or to increased secretion of neurotransmitters. Furthermore, treatment programs are typically based on the verbal analysis of anger episodes brought into the clinician's office. For this reason, clinicians will recognize the usefulness of Kassinove and Tafrate's anger episode model (2002).

As will be seen in the chapters in this book, the outlook for anger reduction is rather positive. Even in the absence of formal diagnoses and a complete understanding of the anger phenomenon, a number of successful treatments have been developed. This is due in no small part to the dedication of modern researchers and practitioners who have devoted their careers to the study of the long neglected phenomenon of anger.

CHAPTER 2

The Case of Anthony

Eva L. Feindler

INTRODUCTION TO THE CASE STUDY

Recent research (Eells & Lombart, 2003) has focused on meaningful differences in case formulation among therapists with respect to how clients are conceptualized, how treatment predictions are made, etiology, and expectations about course and length of treatment. Practitioner differences according to theoretical orientation, level of experience, and expertise, as well as factors both common and unique to particular psychotherapies, have been studied for quite some time.

Goldfried (1995) and Eells (1997) have suggested that practitioners use psychotherapy case formulation as a tool to organize and synthesize complex and at times contradictory information about a client, independent from orientation. A case formulation is essentially a set of hypotheses about the causes, precipitants, and maintaining influences of a person's psychological, interpersonal, and behavioral problems (Eells, 1997). Furthermore, it facilitates the tailoring of treatment to custom fit an individual case as the therapist chooses intervention techniques; anticipates pacing, implementation, and obstacles; and evaluates client progress.

Tensions and controversies abound among clinicians from various orientations with regard to what constitutes effective treatment. Ideally, according to Messer (2004), clinicians should follow an evidence-based psychotherapy practice based on the following: (1) a theoretical formulation, (2) empirically supported treatments (ESTs), (3) empirically supported therapy relationships (ESRs), (4) the clinician's accumulated practical experience, and (5) clinical judgment about a specific case.

The recent development of ESTs, based on extensive clinical trials research, is focused on diagnostic categories, which were designed to be theoretical descriptions of symptoms and on specific outcome criteria as a result of treatment techniques.

However, most clients who present in a clinical practice do not fit a specific diagnostic category and have varying contingencies operating on their entrance to treatment and motivation to change. In addition, several elements of the psychotherapy process shown to correlate with therapy outcome need consideration: quality of therapeutic alliance, therapist empathy, and collaboration on goals (Messer, 2004). Finally, Wampold (2001) identified a possible category of bona fide therapies associated with positive clinical outcome. These approaches should have a firm theoretical structure, have been practiced extensively over time, and have a research foundation even if this does not include randomized clinical traits required to be established as an EST. For all of these reasons, multiple approaches to a single clinical case formulation can and should be considered.

This book represents another in a continuing series of comparative treatments of a single case study. The descriptive material that follows is from three 1-hour sessions of an actual case presenting in an outpatient treatment facility with possible multiple diagnoses. The case was chosen specifically to highlight an array of anger-related difficulties not captured in the *Diagnostic and Statistical Manual* (DSM-IV; Kassinove, 1995).

Although the intake assessment process is necessarily based on the theoretical position or "guiding conception" of the assessor (Messer, 2004), I have tried to present sufficiently detailed information such that the selected practitioners could create a specific theoretical case formulation; describe a coherent, pragmatic, and ethical treatment plan; and predict clinical course and progress if they in fact were the treating clinician.

THE CASE OF ANTHONY

Reason for Referral

Anthony M. is seeking treatment for anger management and says that his rage spills out mostly at loved ones. These episodes have become so unpredictable and intense that his wife is threatening to divorce him if he does not get help and his three daughters say that they are afraid of him. Anthony concedes that he has been labeled as emotionally abusive by his family members. Six months ago, an embarrassing incident confirmed his awareness that he had trouble controlling his anger. While coaching the all-star game for his daughter's softball team, he became increasingly angry with the girls because of what he labeled as their "lack of competitive drive." Furious, he sat them down and verbally lambasted them, ignoring their tears. Anthony then picked up the equipment and hurled one of the bats at the backstop. Parents who witnessed this explosion called for his resignation as a manager and coach of the Little League team. He was publicly humiliated, and even though he apologized to all involved, he still feels ashamed of his behavior.

Demographic Information

Anthony is a 48-year-old white male of Italian descent and a nonpracticing Roman Catholic. Tall, stocky, and slightly graying, he lives in a two-bedroom condominium in New York, with his family, which consists of his wife and three daughters, his eldest daughter's boyfriend, and their 18-month-old daughter.

When asked to describe himself, Anthony claims to be affectionate, nurturing, emotional, and passionate. He says he has a definite "feminine" side and loves to cook. In fact, since his wife works the evening shift, Anthony is usually responsible for the family after school and throughout the evening. In his leisure time, he raises tropical fish, watches sports, and plays computer games. During his adolescent and young adult years, he collected guns and knives as a hobby, but he does not own any now because of his wife's concerns. Anthony completed only a few semesters of college and has had to struggle to find satisfying steady work.

History of Presenting Problem

Anthony realizes he uses his voice as a weapon and says that he yells, throws tantrums, and curses at family members when he is angry. Lately, he has become concerned that this pattern of explosiveness will result in his losing his family. His wife and their daughters, ages 11, 17, and 20, seem afraid to confront him about this abusive pattern and stay distant. He maintains that the triggers for his rage can be as simple as not getting his own way, and he reports being unaware of the build-up of negative emotion saying that "it just takes him by surprise."

In interacting with his wife and children, who endure the brunt of his rage, Anthony is admittedly impatient and says he has no tolerance for tardiness or stupidity. Describing his 11-year-old daughter as "brilliant," Anthony states that she tries to circumvent his anger by "playing dumb," which only seems to augment his rage. He believes his wife intentionally shows up late just to "get back at him." Thus, he finds that "waiting is torture." His impatience extends to his intolerance for waiting in any kind of line, whether it is at a bank, a store, a movie, or a theater or just waiting for others when they are late. Anthony finds lateness, stupidity, and laziness to be personal affronts and signs of disrespect.

His anger problem has intensified to such a point that Anthony feels shaky about his relationship with his wife and children. He realizes that he often provokes arguments or disagreements due to his confrontational nature and will play "devil's advocate." When family members do not comply or things do not go his way, he "blows up." When he sees he has spoiled what should have been a special occasion (e.g., when he went into a rage at Christmas because wrapping paper was strewn about the living room), he apologizes, but it is too little too late.

Guilt also seems to be a trigger for Anthony's anger, and he reports that he has many reasons to feel guilty. Often he suppresses the anger, which is triggered during conflict or crisis with loved ones. However, this lasts only so long, and then something unexpected occurs and Anthony explodes. At times in the past, he has resorted to physical violence, once with a woman he was dating, whom he suspected of cheating, and once with a male peer who "disrespected" him. However, he claims that he has not been physically aggressive toward anyone in 20 years but will throw objects, kick doors and walls, and do a great deal of screaming.

Psychological History

Family History

The third of four children, Anthony has a brother who is 6 years older, a sister who is 9 years older, and a sister who is 11 months younger than him. Both parents are still alive, retired, and living in Florida; however, he maintains relatively little contact with them or any other family members. His maternal grandmother was a dominant, negative figure in his life, but he reports being extremely close to his maternal grandfather until the age of 15, when his grandfather died of a massive heart attack. Upon his grandfather's death, Anthony recalls tremendous sadness and a depression that lasted for several months because he thought that he had "lost his best friend."

Anthony's father was a chemical engineer for an engineering company. He put himself through night school over 14 years, which was a difficult process. Although Anthony found his father to be strict, he was also someone with whom he could spend time and talk. Sometimes Anthony felt his father lived vicariously through him, particularly in relation to the many athletic pursuits enjoyed by Anthony and not by his brother. His dad coached many of the sports he was involved in and was "devastated" when Anthony quit competitive swimming in high school. Anthony describes their relationship as close but says that he has always been aware of his father's disappointment in him and lately they have become more distant.

Anthony reports that he did not like his mother, describing her as "old world." She believed in corporal punishment, so he was hit often as a child and sometimes in the face. His mother was rarely supportive or affectionate but rather was often negative. Anthony tried to avoid her in order to avoid her negativity, which he concludes, "drove his father to become a workaholic." He recalls her as being highly critical while raising all of the children but believes she was particularly demeaning to him. His mother was reportedly more focused on her oldest son and youngest daughter and even seemed distant and rejecting of his father. Anthony *never* recalls seeing any love or affection between his parents to this day and did not experience much joy in the family. In later years, his mother, who was the only girl in her family after a sister died in childhood, was forced to quit her college night school in order to take care of her own mother, who by then lived with Anthony's family. Anthony recalls his mother as very bitter and completely consumed with and controlled by her own mother.

Anthony recalls being sexually abused by a maternal uncle for approximately 5 or 6 years beginning at the age of 7. This uncle had intentions of becoming a priest but had dropped out of seminary school. The abuse occurred when the family would visit his maternal grandparents in Virginia. Because there was limited space, Anthony would be sent to stay overnight at his uncle's house down the road. The uncle would come into his bed and engage in mutual fondling and oral sex. As a young child, he loved his uncle dearly and thought he was "the greatest man in the world," obeying his rule never to mention his sexual abuse to anyone else. The uncle claimed "that it was just a special relationship." Anthony reports that he does not remember many details about the abuse and questions himself as to why he "let it" happen. During the past few years, his recall was triggered several times by particular sounds and visual flashbacks and he has had some disturbing dreams.

By the time Anthony was approaching pubescence, he no longer felt comfortable around his uncle and developed a hatred toward his grandmother for "bringing his uncle into his life." Fortunately, the family did not visit frequently after his grandfather died, and Anthony no longer spent the night at his uncle's house. When Anthony was 19 and still living at home, his uncle attempted to "visit" him in his basement apartment. The visit came to an abrupt halt when Anthony commanded his dog to "attack" and his uncle left without a word. This uncle also separately abused his older brother during the years prior to Anthony's "nighttime visits," but this was not discussed between the brothers until they were adults.

The uncle later married, became a successful government attorney, and adopted three children with his wife. At some point later, he sexually abused his oldest daughter, who has had significant struggles and confided the abuse to Anthony as an adult. The uncle is dying of cancer now and, according to Anthony, "isn't suffering enough."

While visiting with his parents for his younger sister's wedding, Anthony confronted his parents about his uncle's sexual abuse; they said that they knew he "was strange" but were unaware of the sexual inappropriateness. They did not appear to be in denial about the abuse but never apologized and seemed unfazed by his disclosure. This was extremely painful for Anthony, and he signals that conversation as the beginning of his disengagement from his own family.

In summary, Anthony's early family relationships were a mixture of idealization and disappointment. He describes having looked up to his grandfather, father, and uncle only to have each of those relationships end with Anthony experiencing much emotional pain. Relationships with his mother and grandmother were characterized as cold and rejecting while his sibling connections seemed minimal at best.

Education and Vocational History

Diagnosed with attention deficit hyperactive disorder (ADHD) in junior high school, Anthony reports being a dyslexic, impulsive child, who, despite being an academic underachiever, was a popular jock in school. Self-described as hypermasculine, he was an accomplished athlete in swimming and football. At the age of 9, he was a junior Olympic champion in swimming, a state champion in junior high, and a varsity swimmer as a high school freshman. A punter and quarterback for high school football, he received an athletic scholarship to a small southern university, only to lose that scholarship. The loss was due to a physical altercation with a "town kid" at a bar; the altercation resulted in the hospitalization of the teen and Anthony's arrest. Charges were later dropped, and Anthony managed to continue college for 1 year; however, his scholarship was canceled. Anthony then attended a local college for two semesters before dropping out, which confirmed his sense of himself as a poor "student." He had always dreamed of becoming a physical education teacher and a high school coach. At the age of 23, he tried out for a position with the New England Patriots as a punter and made it through several rounds of cuts, but in the end, he was rejected. He continued to work part-time as a coach for local youth sports teams and as a lifeguard.

Full-time employment began at the age of 25, when his father told him to "get out and get a full-time job or I'll kick you out!" At the time, he was content as a lifeguard at a local beach, playing on local teams and just "kind of hanging out." Begrudgingly, Anthony began working for an aircrafts parts company, a job his father secured for him through a family friend. This mechanic job employment lasted for 21 years. Anthony recalls that he related to his boss as a "father figure" and looked up to him. However, when he was late or absent (which was frequent), he would fight with his boss with much defiance and disrespect. Eventually, his boss ran out of patience and fired him following a particularly intense argument. Since that time, he has held four or five jobs at similar companies, but he reported never fitting in and feeling ashamed at the low starting salaries.

Now Anthony works as a projects manager for another aircraft company, a job that Anthony began 6 months ago after being let go from a previous company. Over the years, although he has supplemented his income on and off with part-time jobs, Anthony has had a history of poor work performance and describes himself as lazy and ambivalent about "working and never getting ahead." Throughout his description of this work history, Anthony's affect was quite flat and he seemed resigned to accept his patterns.

Finances have long been a source of concern in his life and in his relationship with his wife, who currently earns twice his salary. Over the years, Anthony estimates that he has lost as much as $40,000 worth of pay because he would take many days off, reportedly just sitting around the house. He admits that neither he nor his wife handles money well, which is further complicated by the fact that his wife spends a "tremendous amount" of money on clothing. However, because of his guilt over his failure to provide adequately for his family, he says nothing to his wife about her spending habits. They currently have some credit card debt, do not own a home, and have no savings.

Interpersonal History

Recently, this self-described angry, controlling, impatient, inflexible husband, father, and grandfather admits that his verbal lashings leave him feeling guilty and ashamed. During the first intake session, he spoke only of emotional and verbal abuse toward family members. Gradually, he began to discuss several episodes of physical violence in his past, which he worries may stem from his own sexual abuse by his uncle. Although Anthony's wife has emphasized his traumatic childhood as key to the understanding of his temper outbursts, he actively denies any connection and indicates that he has "dealt with the abuse."

Anthony had a reputation as a womanizer and dated frequently in high school and college. He recalls one time he became violent and hit his girlfriend when he thought she was cheating on him. He met his wife, Joanna, while he was involved with the football tryouts. She was his best friend for several years; they then fell in love and married when Anthony was 27. Anthony believes that he was Joanna's "second choice," because she had been previously engaged to her childhood sweetheart. Now the thought of losing her terrifies Anthony, and he misses the old days when she was passionate, bubbly, and excited about life with him. Both love the beach, but he enjoys swimming and bodysurfing while she would rather soak in the sun and read. Other than their children, they have few other common interests. While Joanna works out quite frequently and perhaps sports could be a joint activity, he has become less physical due to chronic sciatica. Over the past several years, he has lost nearly 40 pounds by dieting, inspired by his wife's loss of 70 pounds. Formerly quite overweight, Joanna works out daily to maintain her trim physique. Anthony seems to envy her self-control and dedication to her own fit lifestyle and envies those who can continue to be athletic. He has lost weight during the past year; however, despite this, he feels physically "unfit."

Twelve years ago, Anthony had an "emotional" affair with a female co-worker at newspaper office where he had a part-time job. He insists that they just "became best friends" because she seemed to understand him and care about him. Her husband discovered letters sent between them and threatened to expose them. Although he claims that they were never physical but simply close friends, when Anthony told his wife, she immediately assumed that it was a sexual relationship. This relationship was his main source of support during a difficult family time: his third child was born and his wife was caring for her mother, who was dying of cancer. After some counseling and tense times, the couple put this episode behind them. However, Anthony wonders if his wife still holds this against him.

Currently, Anthony has a friendship with a woman he met online in a game chat room. They discuss their similar interests of skiing, sailing, and tennis and usually talk on the computer each night. After exchanging photos over the Internet, they met for the first time when she took him out to lunch for his birthday. According to Anthony, his wife knows about the relationship and "supports [his] need for a best friend." It is clear, however, that he has become emotionally attached to this online female friend.

Regarding extended family, Anthony sees his own siblings or cousins infrequently. His brother, whom Anthony describes as bisexual, is married with three children and lives in another state. His sisters and their families live more locally, but they rarely interact. Anthony's wife is the youngest of seven children and was also sexually abused by an uncle. All of her siblings are married with children; however, his wife severed ties a decade ago due to issues related to her mother's death and disbursement of her estate. For now, there is *no* contact.

On a social level, Anthony seems outwardly skilled, yet he continues to feel isolated. Not one to let his guard down and make close friends easily, the friends he does have are mostly women who are his wife's friends. He has always had mostly female friends and struggles to find male friends he can trust. For years, his "best friend" was his wife's nephew, but he no longer has contact due to his wife's estrangement from her family.

Anthony's wife of 22 years has been a railroad conductor for the past 9 years. Joanna works mostly with men and on the nightshift because the pay is better. A direct opposite of the tall, blonde, Waspy women he used to date, she is of Puerto Rican descent, short, and dark skinned. Their ability to communicate with each other has disintegrated, and she appears to be resentful of the fact that for years he did not live up to his earning potential. According to Anthony, Joanna harbors much anger over his poor management of money, his loss of wages, and the years he did "nothing but sit on the couch and watch TV." Neither Anthony nor his wife considered that he might have been depressed or needed some help. His wife often seems "pressed for time" and will ask him to "get the girls" or do certain chores. According to Anthony, Joanna appears annoyed when the chores are not done, although she finds time to shop, work out, and have her own social life with her co-workers. As a couple, they have maintained a tradition of "Saturday night dates" for 20 years; however, recently the dinner discussions have become heated and created distance between them.

When his eldest daughter, Angela, now a college student, revealed that she was pregnant, it created intense stress between Anthony and his wife. They eventually decided that they would "adopt" their grand-daughter and raise her as their child. In the end, his daughter decided to parent her own child with the help of her now live-in boyfriend.

Her boyfriend, Jerome, is a 22-year-old African American high school graduate who is quite overweight. Anthony sees a lot of himself in Jerome, does not think he will amount to much, and sometimes puts him down. Jerome is a counselor in a group home, and Anthony assumes he has low earning potential and becomes furious with Jerome's perceived lack of responsibility (e.g., he has failed to provide a plan for health insurance for his young daughter). Angela has a seizure disorder and is quite overweight. When Angela was an infant and toddler, she and her father were inseparable, and Anthony believes perhaps he "overprotected" her because of her seizures. She neither drives nor works outside of the home but manages her classes along with child care responsibilities. Both he and his wife hope that, above all else, she finishes college, as she was a marginal high school student.

Seventeen-year-old Jackie, the middle child, has been defiant and outspoken. Because Anthony stayed consumed with firstborn Angela, he does not remember Jackie's early years and now feels guilty about this lack of attention. He reports having overcompensated lately by not making demands on her and giving in to her tantrums. He also feels badly that she does not have her own room but rather shares the living room sofa with her younger sister. Jackie is an average student in high school and plans to attend a local community college upon graduation.

The youngest child in the family is 11-year-old Savannah. She is bright, does extremely well in school, is quite athletic, and is involved in many extracurricular activities. Described as somewhat manipulative, she knows how to push her father's buttons, which further complicates his anger issues. Anthony has been very involved in her athletic pursuits, previously coaching soccer and softball through her elementary years. He says that he has great hopes that she will really succeed in life and feels most proud of her.

Living in close quarters with six other people is not easy for someone with an "anger control problem." Recently Anthony says he "broke some ground" when his youngest daughter, anticipating that his rage was about to escalate, began to cry. He used that as a cue to leave the house and cool off. Now, he is more acutely aware of his need to enter therapy so that he can better cope with his anger.

The death of his wife's 26-year-old nephew in a car accident was a recent trigger for his anger and emotional outbursts, which he tried to suppress. He said he "cried like a baby" at the funeral and could not get over a "wasted life that was cut short at such an early age." His wife, trying to process her own grief over her nephew's death, blurted out, "It's not all about you, Anthony!" leaving him confused about how to express his emotions.

Medical History

Over the years, Anthony has had several medical conditions: ADHD, sciatica, hypertension, and hiatal hernia, all of which have limited his athletic pursuits. Currently, he does not exercise and experiences chronic, mild leg and back pain. He sought marriage counseling 10 years ago initially because of his "emotional affair" but then looking to ease the stress in his marriage resulting from severe financial problems, the birth of their third child, and the death of his mother-in-law. He found the limited treatment helpful. Out of admitted shame, Anthony never wanted to disclose his history or sexual abuse to anyone other than his wife, so he never considered individual psychotherapy for himself.

Drinking and recreational drug use were a part of his teens and early adulthood. However, he says he "gave up drinking when [he] had kids." When out socially, he will sometimes have "a beer or two." There is no family history of drug and alcohol abuse.

Summary

Currently, Anthony feels like a failure and worries that time is passing him by. He admits that he does not read well and is not college educated. He does not have a strong work ethic and vacillates between respecting and envying the fact that his wife has a stronger one. Ambivalent about his current job, he says he lacks a "working man's" identity. Although he exhibits a confident bravado, Anthony admits that he does not have good self-esteem. He offers that he struggles with shame over with his past sexual abuse and guilt issues related to his lack of financial success, his outside relationships, and the emotional abuse of his family members. Stating his continued love of his wife and family, Anthony wants to understand his anger and control himself so that he does not harm others.

Assessment Results

After the first intake session, Anthony was given several self-report inventories to complete and return at the next session.

1. The *State-Trait Anger Expression Inventory* (STAXI; Spielberger, 1988) was administered. Table 2.1 presents the T-scores for all subscales as well as summary scores for State Anger (SA), Trait Anger (TA), and the Anger Expression Index (T-Ang-T). T-scores greater than 65 indicate areas of clinical concern. The low scores on SA indicate that Anthony was not experiencing much anger at the time of testing or in the testing situation. Elevated scores on the TA subscale and in particular the T-Ang-T section indicates that he usually experiences angry feelings and often feels that he is being treated unfairly. Being quick-tempered and often frustrated,

Table 2.1   Scores on the State Trait Anger
Expression Inventory

STAXI Subscale	T-score
T-Ang (trait anger)	72
T-Ang-T (angry temperament)	74
T-Ang-R (angry reaction)	56
S-Ang (state anger)	44
AX-I (anger expression) index	74
AX/Con (anger control)	30
AX-O (anger-out)	76
AX-I (anger-in)	62

persons with elevated T-Ang-T scores are impulsive and lacking in anger control but are not necessarily vindictive in attacking others. In terms of the anger expression and control subscales, results indicate endorsement of items reflecting outward expression in physical or verbal acts of aggression, such as slamming doors, yelling, making threats, and so forth. The results also indicate minimal anger control, both in monitoring and preventing outward expression and in implementing methods of anger reduction. Finally, the high anger expression indicates that Anthony experiences intense angry feelings, often expressed in aggressive behavior. Furthermore, the scoring manual suggests that persons with high AX index scores as well as elevated AX-O and AX-I scores are likely to experience difficultly in interpersonal relationships and are at greater risk for developing medical disorders.

2. On the *Beck Depression Inventory* (BDI; Beck, 1979), Anthony received a summary score of 14, indicating a mild depression.

3. The *Trauma Symptom Inventory* (TSI; Briere, 1995) was also administered.

Table 2.2 lists the T-scores Anthony received on the clinical subscales. Although only the scores on the anger irritability (AI) and the intrusive experiences (IE) subscales fall within the clinical concern range, there are elevated scores on the tension reduction behavior (TRB) and the defensive avoidance (DA) subscale. According to the TSI manual (Briere, 1995), high AI scores indicate the extent of angry mood and irritable affect and reflect either the irritability associated with post-traumatic stress disorder (PTSD) or a more chronic angry state. Items on this subscale reflect an internal experience of annoyance and bad temper such

Table 2.2   Scores on the Trauma Symptom Inventory

TSI Subscales	T-Score
a. Anxious arousal	48
b. Dissociation	49
c. Depression	49
d. Sexual concerns	43
e. Anger/irritability	74
f. Dysfunctional sexual behavior	44
g. Intrusive experiences	59
h. Impaired self-reference	45
i. Defensive avoidance	55
j. Tension reduction behavior	55

that minor difficulties or frustrations provoke contextually inappropriate angry reactions. Combined with an elevated TRB (indicating tendency to externalize distress and act out negative affect as a way to modulate or soothe negative internal states), Anthony's responses underscore his trait anger and his impulse to externalize his anger.

Scores on the IE and DA subscales support Anthony's experience of some traumatic events. Items reflect intrusive post-traumatic reactions and symptoms such as repetitive thoughts or an unpleasant previous experience. Avoidance responses to a history of aversive internal experiences that one would seek to avoid include attempts to eliminate painful thoughts or memories from conscious awareness and a desire to neutralize negative feelings about past trauma.

Diagnostic Formulations

According to information obtained during several intake interviews and the scores on assessment inventories, the initial diagnostic impression was as follows:

AXIS-I: 309.81—Post-Traumatic Stress Disorder: Delayed Onset
   Anthony's history includes recurrent intrusive recollections and disturbing dreams about his sexual abuse as a child. In addition to a crisp memory of his auditory experiences as a child ("I still hear the Velcro enclosure on his bathrobe") and the fear and helplessness he experiences, Anthony seems to have some dissociative amnesia concerning the events during ages 7 and 11 years. For the majority of his adult life, Anthony has avoided conversations about the trauma, thoughts and feelings related to the sexual abuse, and many of his own family members. A final PTSD symptom that fits is the irritability and outbursts of anger.
AXIS-I: 312.34—Intermittent Explosive Disorder
   This categorization seems logical because Anthony reports several discrete episodes of failure to resist impulses that result in serious assaultive acts.
AXIS II: 62.81—Relational Problem NOS
   This diagnosis is given to emphasize the dysfunctional interactions that currently exist between Anthony and all of the family members living with him. It is clearly his participation in the self-described "emotional abuse" of his wife and daughters that stimulated his interest in therapy.
AXIS III
   Medical conditions (i.e., hypertension, hiatal hernia, sciatica) are mild.

AXIS IV

Anthony has problems with his primary support group and work environment. He also has financial problems.

AXIS V

GAF: 60 (present); GAF: 65 (highest in last year).

Although clinicians from various orientations might have collected additional intake information or done further structured assessment, the preceding case write-up was considered in each of the chapters that follow. Clinicians were asked to consider the case material, to develop a theoretically integrated case conceptualization, and to propose a comprehensive treatment plan according to their orientation. Each author also received a list of questions to consider as they developed their clinical approach (see appendix A) and was asked to provide an overview of the theoretical orientation driving the treatment described.

CHAPTER 3

Evidence for Effective Treatment of Anger-Related Disorders

Jerry L. Deffenbacher

Although anger, especially when mild to moderate in intensity, can lead to positive outcomes, anger can also become dysfunctional and lead to negative outcomes. Dysfunctional anger is an issue frequently addressed in therapy, and recommendations or referrals for anger management are increasingly popular. As Kassinove and Tafrate (see Chapter 1) note, conceptualization and treatment planning are hampered by the absence of anger-based diagnoses. Outcome research is hindered as well, because anger populations are not defined by a common set of criteria. Until such diagnostic categories are developed and proved reliable, outcome researchers should carefully describe their samples in terms of demographics, common triggers of anger, the nature of anger and anger expression, the consequences of client anger, and other correlates and risk factors. Such information provides outcome researchers with a sense of how their populations are alike or dissimilar from other anger treatment studies in the literature and helps practitioners make informed choices regarding empirically supported interventions for a client or group with specific anger characteristics.

Adequate diagnostic and conceptual systems may not exist, but some people nonetheless experience disturbing, dysfunctional anger, anger that might benefit from therapy. But, what exactly are the treatment goals for anger reduction interventions? Dysfunctional anger might be considered a syndrome (Averill, 1982; see also Chapter 1) consisting of emotional experience (e.g., feeling furious, enraged), physiological arousal (e.g., clenched jaw, elevated heart rate), and cognitive processes (e.g., thoughts or images of revenge, derogatory and inflammatory labeling, hostile attributions). Significant personal distress (e.g., guilt, sense of being out of control) and/or significant adverse consequences to the individual or others (e.g., impaired relationships, lost jobs, legal difficulties) can result. Impairment may be related primarily to the experience of anger and its direct consequences to the person (e.g., lowered self-esteem, compromised health), but impairment may also stem from the ways in which the person responds when angry (e.g., aggression toward others or the environment, alcohol or drug use). Dysfunctional anger is elicited by various internal and external triggers. Anger often leads to reactions from the environment, particularly the interpersonal environment, and may escalate into a reciprocal angry, aggressive counterattack. Different therapies conceptually address different aspects of the anger experience and associated dysfunctional behaviors such that the trigger-cognitive-emotional-physiological-behavioral-consequence connection is altered and anger is lowered or aborted.

IS PSYCHOTHERAPY EFFECTIVE WITH ANGER?

Before turning to an evaluation of the anger reduction literature, four measurement and methodological issues should be acknowledged, because they limit, to a degree, the scope of conclusions drawn.

First, the ecological validity of outcome research is somewhat compromised. Session length and content typically have been constrained by a treatment protocol. Most interventions are 4 to 10 sessions long for a total treatment duration of 6 to 12 hours. Moreover, no studies allowed additional post-treatment contact to address new anger issues or relapse. Yet, such contact would be fairly typical and advisable in outpatient therapy. Although these conditions are appropriate for controlled outcome research, they do not map perfectly onto the more flexible environment found in outpatient psychotherapy. Even with this gap in generalization, positive findings generalize reasonably well in at least two ways. For one, conditions of therapy may generalize fairly closely in terms of a time-limited, structured intervention with a particular population (e.g., a 12-session anger reduction program for angry individuals with high blood pressure). For another, positive findings suggest an empirically supported basis from which to extend and adapt the protocol to anger-involved populations.

Second, although there are notable exceptions, such as Gerzina and Drummond's use of the report of fellow police officers (2000), most outcomes are limited to self-report. Self-report is an appropriate and valuable source of information. For example, some aspects of anger are best assessed by self-report (e.g., internal emotional and cognitive experiences of anger). They are accessible only to the individual, and self-report is therefore the appropriate avenue of assessment. Even though change in other domains might be accessed in other ways (e.g., behavioral observation of aggressive responding to role-plays or in vivo), the client's sense and report of change in these areas is still important. In addition, many studies employ self-report across multiple domains (e.g., angry emotion, anger expression, assertiveness, anger consequences, and the like), strengthening the range and breadth of constructs assessed. The fact that some self-report measures show minimal or no change and other self-report measures in the same study show change strengthens confidence in self-reported findings. If effects were due entirely to positive response bias, then change should be evidenced across all measures. Nonetheless, self-report is open to the possibility of considerable response bias, and future research should attempt to elaborate self-report with other sources (e.g., collateral informant report, in vivo physiological recordings, or archival records, such as work performance reviews, incidents of assault, and traffic citations).

Third, assessment in most studies is of the pre-post variety. Change is assessed over a considerable period of time and is necessary to assess intervention outcome. If extended to various follow-up intervals, such evaluation designs can also establish the durability of treatment effects. This approach to measuring change does little to map the course and pattern of change over the course of therapy. Change, however, is likely not to be uniform within or across people, and much is being lost in understanding the nature of anger reduction. Future research should attempt to measure anger in a more continuous, ongoing manner to establish whether there are groups with different patterns or paces of change and begin to map which anger interventions do and do not work for whom and in what response-dose-time relationships.

Fourth, there is the issue of being mandated into anger management therapy. Most studies reviewed involve voluntary, self-selected groups, such as college students with high trait anger (HTA), angry volunteers from the community, or medical patients with anger-involved problems such as cardiovascular disease. Such individuals are generally motivated to participate and to report accurately and honestly. Angry individuals who are mandated to attend anger management therapy or those strongly encouraged by external sources (e.g., employers) may not be so motivated to participate or report accurately, which poses a number of intervention and assessment problems. For one, a significant number of these individuals may not see anger as a personal problem and may attend only because they are mandated to do so, feel pressure, or wish to avoid negative systemic consequences. They are neither ready for nor good candidates for change-oriented anger interventions. This issue will be addressed in a later section on readiness. Mandated or pressured groups may also be defensive and motivated to underreport anger, especially at pretreatment assessment, which underestimates actual anger levels. When therapists build positive working alliances, trust is developed, and the experience of mandated individuals is validated, positive change may take place but the report of anger may actually increase. That is, after therapy, these clients may be more in touch with and accurately reporting anger, anger that was initially underreported because of defensiveness and lack of trust. Measurement strategies are needed that address this issue where a lack of apparent change or what appears to be a deterioration effect may actually be masked by a pretreatment "mandated" effect. For example, developing forms of retrospective self-report, use of collateral informants, and archival records may document change where simple self-report may fail. Finally, there is the issue of generalization of treatment findings. Care should be taken not to generalize findings from nonmandated to mandated groups. Groups may differ significantly in readiness, resistance, externalization, motivation to participate or report accurately, and the like. Findings may not generalize, or the nature of the interventions and assessment of change may need to be different.

So, with these caveats in mind, what is the status of anger reduction interventions? Can psychotherapy reduce anger? If so, are some interventions more effective than others? In addressing these questions, three types of psychological research will be reviewed. First, a series of meta-analyses (Beck & Fernandez, 1998; Del Vecchio & O'Leary, 2004; DiGuiseppe & Tafrate, 2003; Edmondson & Conger, 1996; Tafrate, 1995), which summarize treatment effects across several studies, will be used to draw general conclusions. Some meta-analyses also calculated effect sizes by domain of functioning or type of measurement (e.g., cognitive or emotional functioning) and/or by type of intervention (e.g., cognitive therapy or relaxation intervention). Second, meta-analyses will be supplemented by specific controlled treatment trials. All of these studies include at least one active treatment, an adequate no-treatment or minimal treatment control, and multiple measures of anger or anger-related variables (e.g., aggressive behavior). Third, a few multiple case study or quasi-experimental studies will be reviewed, although the absence of adequate controls reduces their value in establishing empirical support for the intervention. Such research, however, may provide useful hypotheses for future research and an extension of anger reduction research into new areas. In turn, this may provide practitioners with useful suggestions about interventions with individuals or groups with whom they work.

Meta-analyses suggest that psychosocial interventions reduce anger. Treatment effects differ significantly from 0.0, and the average client fares better than 76% of the controls (Beck & Fernandez, 1998). Effect sizes vary from study to study, but overall effect sizes tend to be moderate to large across meta-analyses and to suggest fairly reliable, consistent treatment effects of anger reduction interventions. This general conclusion is bolstered by two additional lines of evidence. First, some studies (e.g., Dahlen & Deffenbacher, 2000; Deffenbacher et al., 2000) employed Jacobson and Truax's reliable clinical change index (1991), a relatively stringent measure of clinically meaningful change. This index requires that the client's post-treatment score be at least 1.96 standard error of measurement below his or her pretreatment score and at least 2 standard deviations below the pretreatment mean on that measure for treatment and control participants combined. Studies using this index showed that 40% to 50% of treated participants, occasionally more, met this criterion, whereas from 0% to 5% of controls did so, suggesting meaningful clinical change with intervention and little without. Second, studies with short-term (e.g., 1-month) and long-term (e.g., 12- to 15-month) follow-ups (e.g., Deffenbacher et al., 2000; Hazaleus & Deffenbacher, 1986) reveal maintenance of effects. Thus, anger reduction appears to maintain over time, an important criterion for suggesting meaningful intervention effects. In summary, research suggests that psychotherapeutic interventions are effective and lead to meaningful change that is maintained for at least some period of time.

A closer inspection, however, suggests that this conclusion is overdrawn. There are exceptions, such an anger-focused, process-oriented group therapy based on Yalom's model (Deffenbacher et al., 1990a), but the universe of studies entered into meta-analytic studies derive almost entirely from studies of cognitive-behavioral interventions. Thus, rather than concluding that findings generally support the effectiveness of psychotherapy, it is more appropriate to conclude that there is empirical support for cognitive-behavioral interventions for anger reduction.

Interventions based on other theoretical models, such as some of those outlined in this book, may prove effective. Scientist-practitioners from these perspectives must define their anger interventions in reliable, trainable ways, such as was done with interpersonal psychotherapy in the national collaborative study on depression, and then evaluate the efficacy of these interventions with anger-involved populations. For example, an Eastern meditation intervention might be adapted for use by angry hypertensive patients or interpersonal psychotherapy for use by HTA young adults. Such controlled trials are needed to establish the efficacy of such interventions, but currently there are simply not enough studies to draw meaningful conclusions about such interventions.

IS ONE INTERVENTION MORE EFFECTIVE
THAN ANOTHER?

If cognitive-behavioral interventions are generally effective, then is there a gold standard within cognitive-behavioral interventions? Is there one intervention that has sufficient evidence that it should be recommended as the treatment of choice or at least as the baseline against which to compare interventions and from which to construct treatment protocols? Three converging lines of evidence suggest that the answer to each of these questions is "no."

First, a box score count of statistical comparisons between different types of interventions does not favor differences. Certainly, some studies found between-group differences for different interventions. For example, a relaxation intervention for angry drivers led to greater anger reduction on some measures than a cognitive-relaxation condition, whereas the cognitive-relaxation condition reduced risky behavior more than the relaxation condition (Deffenbacher et al., 2000). One social skills intervention revealed greater effects on one measure compared with another type of social skills intervention and a cognitive-relaxation intervention (Deffenbacher et al., 1994). Likewise, some between-condition differences were reported by Moon and Eisler (1983) for problem solving, social skill training, and cognitive interventions; by Tafrate and Kassinove (1998) for barb exposure with rational cognitive rehearsal compared with exposure alone; and by Stern (1999) for an intervention that combined anger and conflict management skills compared with conflict management alone. Finally, Novaco's classic study (1975) found that cognitive-relaxation and cognitive conditions did not differ greatly but both were superior to a relaxation intervention on some measures. Such between-group differences may suggest meaningful intervention differences to some readers. Caution, however, should be the watchword, and findings should not be taken out of context. Even within studies showing some between-treatment differences, the majority of comparisons between active treatments did not reveal significant differences. Highlighting the few significant between-group differences ignores or minimizes the larger backdrop of many between-condition findings that do not differ significantly. Moreover, this ignores the bulk of the rest of the outcome literature. Most studies show some treatment effects but fail to show any differences between active treatments. Thus, when these studies are added to the mix, the overall box score count does not favor between-intervention effects.

Second is the issue of replication. If a between-intervention difference is truly meaningful, then it should stand the test of time and replicate across studies. This, however, has not been the case. Between-group differences found in one study tend not to be replicated in subsequent studies. For example, differences favoring either relaxation or cognitive-relaxation interventions with angry drivers (Deffenbacher et al., 2000) failed to replicate in two subsequent studies (Deffenbacher et al., 2002; Richards et al., 2001), which found equivalent results for relaxation and cognitive-relaxation conditions. Differences favoring one social skills training format (Deffenbacher et al., 1994) failed to be replicated when the two social skills interventions were compared subsequently (Deffenbacher et al., 1996). Initial differences somewhat favoring exposure with rational restructuring over exposure alone were not replicated (Mcvey, 2000; Terracciano, 2000). The relatively stronger effects for cognitive-relaxation and cognitive conditions over relaxation reported by Novaco (1975) have not replicated either. For example, stronger effects for relaxation were found in a study with angry college students (Deffenbacher, Demm, & Brandon, 1986). Moreover, several other studies have shown relaxation to be as effective as cognitive (Dua & Swinden, 1992; Hazaleus & Deffenbacher, 1986) and cognitive-relaxation interventions (Deffenbacher and Stark, 1992; Deffenbacher et al., 2002; Dua & Swinden, 1992; Richards et al., 2001). In summary, between-treatment differences found in one study have not been replicated in other studies. Although differences between studies might account for some of the lack of replication, the overall lack of replication suggests that between-treatment differences are not reliable, robust differences in intervention effects.

Third, meta-analyses generally suggest that average effect sizes for different interventions are approximately the same, generally in the moderate to large range. Because these effect sizes are aggregated across studies, populations, and measures, meta-analyses suggest that treatments are roughly equivalent in effect. In reviewing the findings from meta-analyses, it may be tempting to look at aggregated effect sizes and draw conclusions favoring one intervention over another. Several things should caution the reader of meta-analyses from drawing firm conclusions about between-treatment conclusions. First, small differences may not be that meaningful yet are open to overinterpretation. Second, the number of studies in any cell involving meta-analyses of anger reduction studies tends to be very small. Findings from one or two studies that are extreme, either in a positive or negative direction, may skew the findings for that cell because they may be overemphasized in the overall effect size. Third, types of angry clients in each cell may not be randomly distributed. Suppose that offender populations are more difficult to treat and generally show smaller treatment effects and that offender populations are more likely to receive multicomponent interventions. The aggregate effect size for multicomponent interventions would be smaller because of the larger number of offender samples in that cell. Finally, measurement characteristics may influence and potentially confound aggregate effect sizes. Measures may differ in their sensitivity to change. If measures differ on this quality across studies in various meta-analytic comparisons, then this source of measurement characteristic could artificially inflate or deflate effect sizes for that condition and thereby the conclusions drawn about the relative effectiveness of that type of intervention. Thus, until there are many more anger outcome studies where confounds like those just noted can be controlled in the analyses and/or until large studies where highly reliable estimates of effect sizes within conditions can be conducted, it is best to conclude that cognitive-behavioral interventions were roughly equivalent in effect.

A final issue limiting the finding of differential treatment effects is that of sample size. Anger reduction research is in its infancy compared with other areas of treatment research, such as those involving anxiety or mood disorders. Large-scale, multisite treatment studies have yet to be conducted. To the contrary, n's in anger reduction research typically involve 10 to 20 participants per condition. If active treatments to be compared are at least moderately effective, this dramatically limits the statistical power needed to show between-treatment differences. Larger sample sizes are needed to address this problem and demonstrate potential differences between active treatments. The issue of sample size, however, should be placed in the context of the development of clinical science. Outcome research on anger reduction is relatively young. The first issue in a new treatment area is that of establishing effectiveness of an intervention compared with a no-treatment or minimal treatment condition. If the intervention is not effective in these comparisons, then it should not be pursued further. Sample sizes of 15 to 25 are often sufficiently powerful to demonstrate treatment effects, if they exist. It is difficult to recruit, retain, assess, and treat angry individuals. With limited resources, outcome researchers to date have been doing this most important first step, namely, that of establishing absolute effectiveness of interventions. Nonetheless, the importance of greater n and statistical power must be acknowledged and addressed as the field moves toward a more adequate assessment of relative effectiveness of interventions in the future.

In summary, the outcome research literature on anger reduction suggests positive outcomes for cognitive-behavioral interventions. There are, however, little or no replicable data that suggest one intervention is superior to another. To date, there is no gold standard intervention for anger reduction. Better funded, larger-scale, collaborative efforts are needed to establish the best practices, and then, most likely, best practices will be somewhat group specific. For example, the best interventions for anger-related cardiovascular disease in populations aged 40 to 65 may be, appropriately, quite different from those for young, angry, impulsive drivers.

WHICH INTERVENTIONS ARE EFFECTIVE?

This section describes interventions with the greatest empirical support. For each, the rationale, targeted aspect of anger, and general clinical procedures will be outlined. This will be followed by examples of findings in controlled trials and quasi-experimental studies that demonstrate the degree of effects and potential range of application.

Cognitive Interventions

Anger escalates, in part, by the ways in which a person construes and makes sense out of situations. Anger-engendering cognitive processes include things such as inflexible demands and expectations; hostile appraisals and attributions; attributions of fault, blame, and punishment; anger and aggression supportive beliefs and expectancies; coding others in highly negative ways or as the "enemy"; catastrophic or inflammatory labeling; images of revenge; and the like. Cognitive approaches to anger reduction focus on identifying and changing these anger-engendering forms of information processing. The rationale is that if the person codes events in less rigid, less demanding, more realistic ways and can cognitively guide himself or herself through the situation in calmer, more task-centered, problem-oriented ways, then the individual will react with less anger and handle the situation in a more effective manner.

Cognitive therapies are not uniform in approach, but they generally share several overlapping steps. They often begin with a cognitive rationale, assisting the person to see how his or her thinking leads to anger escalation and how changing thoughts, attitudes, and beliefs will lower anger. This is often followed by procedures (e.g., self-monitoring) that help the client become more aware of his or her triggers and reactions, with a particular emphasis on identifying anger-engendering and anger-quieting cognitions (e.g., self-dialogue, images, memories, attitudes). Anger-related cognitions are not accepted as given truths. Clients are assisted in exploring the meaning, validity, and consequences of thinking in certain ways. For example, in assessing the validity of dichotomous thinking (e.g., "I am strong or weak," "They like me or have it in for me"), the therapist might ask the client for evidence for these thoughts or for alternative explanations for the situation. The therapist might have the client visualize an angering situation, but from a very different perspective or with a very different way of thinking and see how the client feels. Some exploration might be in the form of behavioral assignments outside the therapy session. For example, the client might be asked to interview 10 people on their perceptions and interpretations of a certain angering event. Whatever the exact intervention, the goals are to shift automatic cognitive processing to controlled processing, to explore and evaluate the client's thinking, and to generate alternative ways of thinking about angering situations. Anger-lowering cognitions are then strengthened through practice. They are often rehearsed within sessions to lower anger aroused by using anger-arousing imagery or simulations of angering events. As cognitive change is strengthened within sessions, cognitive change is extended through extratherapeutic assignments. With increased success, the focus often shifts to maintenance and relapse strategies (e.g., rehearsal for relapse, booster sessions, continued recording of cognitive restructuring efforts that are sent to the therapist).

Cognitive therapy had been suggested for anger reduction (e.g., Ellis' rational emotive therapy; Ellis & Tafrate, 1997), but it was Novaco's component analysis of stress inoculation training (1975) that provided the first well-controlled study of cognitive interventions and indicated that the self-instructional component (i.e., cognitive alone) led to significant anger reduction. Although the specific content of cognitive restructuring varies from client to client, self-instructional training helps clients identify anger-engendering imagery and self-dialogue and rehearse anger-lowering self-dialogue with which they can guide themselves through provocative situations. Cognitive restructuring may include things such as coding things in less dire ways, construing events in terms of personal preferences rather than demands and commands, and challenging hostile attributions and interpretations and replacing these with calm and coping self-statements, cognitive problem-solving strategies, and self-reinforcement of self-efficacy and anger reduction. Often, these changes are rehearsed in terms of preparing for a provocation, coping with typical amounts of anger, coping with overwhelming anger, and dealing with the aftermath or cleanup of an angering event.

Novaco (1975) found that self-instructional training lowered anger, was somewhat more effective than a relaxation intervention, and was generally as effective as a combination of cognitive and relaxation interventions (i.e., stress inoculation). Subsequent studies have also supported the effectiveness of self-instructional training. Effect sizes are moderate to large for anger measures and slightly lower for measures that were not directly the focus of intervention (e.g., anxiety). Relatively few studies have included long-term follow-up, but those that have (Deffenbacher et al., 1988; Hazaleus & Deffenbacher, 1986) demonstrate long-term effects for self-instructional training. Self-instructional training has also been effective in a number of populations, such as patients with elevated blood pressure (Achmon et al., 1989), angry community volunteers (Novaco, 1975), HTA college students (Deffenbacher et al., 1988; Dua & Swinden, 1992; Hazaleus & Deffenbacher, 1986), and angry offenders (Diaz, 2000).

A partial component analysis of Beck's cognitive therapy applied to HTA college students (Dahlen & Deffenbacher, 2000) also supports the effectiveness of a cognitive-focused intervention. It may seem strange to refer to the "cognitive" component of an intervention that is specifically called *cognitive therapy*. However, Beck's version of cognitive therapy has a decidedly behavioral focus (e.g., Socratic exploration of and behavioral experiments focusing on alternative ways of handling situations), as well as cognitive change strategies. The cognitive-only component was effective compared with the control and was as effective as the full cognitive and behavioral protocol. Across measures, effect sizes were moderate to large, and 47% of clients met the reliable clinical change index, compared with 0% of the control participants.

A version of rational-emotive therapy applied to anger is also effective (Mcvey, 2000; Tafrate & Kassinove, 1998; Terracciano, 2000). Angry male community volunteers and males who experienced anger in partnered relationships were exposed to a prolonged period of exposure to denigrating, disparaging comments made to and about the client. During the exposure, they rehearsed anger-lowering statements derived from rational-emotive theory. This condition was effective compared with a control and equal to or slightly more effective than exposure alone, exposure and response prevention, or exposure plus the rehearsal of irrelevant statements.

Another effective cognitive intervention is training in problem-solving strategies. Although elements of problem solving are imbedded in other interventions, such as self-instructional training, problem solving alone focuses on training clients in discrete steps, such as problem orientation, identification of resources, identification of potential solutions, decision making, and solution enactment, and applying these strategies to anger-arousing situations. Problem-solving training was effective with HTA college students (Moon & Eisler, 1983).

In summary, although there are a number of different approaches to cognitive change for anger reduction (e.g., self-instructional training, problem solving, an adaptation of rational-emotive therapy), cognitive interventions appear more effective than control conditions and yield similar effects to other active interventions. Moreover, they have been shown to be effective with a number of anger-involved populations (e.g., HTA college students and community members, angry adjudicated individuals, hypertensive individuals), suggesting a breadth of effects as well.

Relaxation Interventions

Dysfunctional anger is often marked by heightened emotional and physiological arousal. Conceptually, relaxation interventions target this state of agitated, irritable physiological and emotional arousal. The rationale is that if clients can use arousal management skills when angry, they can become calmer and address the source of provocation with ways of thinking, problem solving, assertion, and other skills that are associated with being calmer and less aroused.

Relaxation protocols vary somewhat in design, but as with cognitive interventions, they parallel each other in a series of overlapping tasks. From client descriptions of anger and other data, the therapist notes that heightened emotional and physiological arousal is an important element of the client's experience of anger. A relaxation rationale is developed from this (i.e., if the client was able to relax and calm down, then he or she would be in a much better position to lower anger and access calmer ways of thinking about and handling the situation). The client then engage in activities (e.g., self-monitoring of anger arousal, tracking areas of tension during relaxation exercises, focusing attention on internal cues of anger arousal) that increase the client's awareness of the emotional and physiological sensations and feelings of anger and the situations in which he or she experiences heightened arousal. These become cues to which the client will apply arousal management skills later. Concurrent with these activities, the client develops a basic relaxation response, usually through progressive relaxation training, which is developed further through home practice. When the relaxation response is reasonably strong, the client is coached in brief relaxation coping skills by which he or she can more readily initiate relaxation (e.g., cue-controlled relaxation, breathing-cued relaxation, relaxation imagery, relaxation without tension, unobtrusive tension-release exercises for key areas of muscle tension). The client is now trained in session to pay attention to cues of increased arousal and to initiate relaxation skills to reduce anger arousal. Situational anger triggers might be organized in a hierarchical fashion according to the individual's typical anger response. Anger is purposefully aroused so that the client pays attention to the experience and uses relaxation skills to lower arousals. For example, clients might visualize situations that arouse anger, experience anger arousal for a brief period of say 30 to 60 seconds, and then initiate relaxation skills to reduce anger. Therapists structure this training to increase success. For example, the level of anger aroused initially might be mild to moderate, and the therapist might provide considerable assistance in initiating relaxation. However, as the client becomes more efficacious, the level of anger arousal is increased and the degree of therapist assistance is decreased. Simulations might also be used in a parallel manner. For example, a couple with anger issues might be asked to discuss an emotionally laden topic. If either experienced anger, that individual would signal the therapist and relaxation would be initiated with as much therapist assistance as needed. As clients gain skill and efficacy within sessions, application of relaxation is transferred via in vivo assignments. For example, clients may monitor anger arousal and initiate relaxation any time certain emotional or physiological cues are present or any time a certain level of anger is experienced (e.g., at a 4 on a 10-point scale of anger arousal). Clients might also contract to use relaxation in specific problem areas (e.g., an angry driver may apply relaxation every 5 minutes during a commute, or a client may prepare for and deal with a roommate or spouse regarding a difficult topic). As clients show significant gains in vivo, the focus shifts to maintenance and relapse prevention.

Several studies (e.g., Achmon et al., 1989; Deffenbacher & Stark, 1992; Deffenbacher et al., 1986, 200, 2002; Diaz, 2000; Dua & Swinden, 1992; Hazaleus & Deffenbacher, 1986; Kogan, Richards, & Deffenbacher, 2001; Richards et al., 2001; Schlichter & Horan, 1981) demonstrate significant effects for relaxation interventions compared with control conditions, effects that are typical in the moderate to large range. Relaxation interventions were also as effective as other cognitive-behavioral interventions such as cognitive and cognitive-relaxation interventions. Transfer of effects to other nontargeted emotional issues or concerns (e.g., trait anxiety) was also noted in a number of studies that included such measures (e.g., Deffenbacher et al., 1986; Richards et al., 2001). Moreover, studies that included long-term follow-ups (e.g., Deffenbacher & Stark, 1992; Deffenbacher et al., 1986; Hazaleus & Deffenbacher, 1986; Richards et al., 2001) revealed that anger reduction effects were maintained over time. Relaxation approaches have also been successfully applied with a number of anger-involved populations, such as individuals suffering from hypertension (Achmon et al., 1989; Davison et al., 1991; Haaga et al., 1994) or chronic heart disease (Bhat, 1999), HTA college students (Deffenbacher & Stark, 1992; Deffenbacher et al., 1986; Dua & Swinden, 1992; Hazaleus & Deffenbacher, 1986), angry drivers (Deffenbacher et al., 2000; Kogan, Richards, and Deffenbacher, 2001; Richards et al., 2001), and incarcerated individuals (Diaz, 2000; Schlichter & Horan, 1981).

In summary, relaxation interventions effectively reduced anger in a number of different anger-involved populations, suggesting a breadth of application. Relaxation effects appear to maintain over time and generalize to other issues and are as strong as those found for other interventions.

Behavioral Skill Interventions

Skill deficits may be involved in dysfunctional anger in at least two different ways. For one, if an individual does not have requisite skills for major life roles (e.g., parent, partner, work supervisor) or tasks (e.g., handling criticism or disappointment), then he or she may experience frustration and anger in dealing with these roles or tasks. For another, the individual may not have positive skills for handling inevitable conflict, disagreement, and hassle. The client may have learned a repertoire of dysfunctional ways (e.g., verbal or physical aggression, sullen withdrawal, substance use) of dealing with such situations. For example, much problematic anger happens in an interpersonal context. Many individuals with anger problems tend toward a hostile attributional bias and a rush to hostile, defensive judgments and conclusions. They then react abrasively and antagonistically toward others. Open, empathic, explorative, assertive communication in which opinions and feelings of others are sought and respected is in short supply. Anger and conflict may escalate, as others feel misunderstood and attacked. A cycle of reciprocal anger and aggression may ensue.

Conceptually, any anger-related skill deficit could be targeted, which suggests that anger interventions may be appropriately integrated into larger intervention efforts to reduce problem behavior. For example, cognitive and relaxation interventions might be integrated into programs designed to help abusive parents or partners deal with their children and partners in better ways or in programs to help parents and teachers deal more effectively with difficult children, such as those with attention deficit hyperactivity disorder (ADHD). Nonetheless, most skill-oriented interventions for anger reduction to date have targeted negative patterns of interpersonal communication and anger expression. The rationale is that as angry individuals develop and use more effective emotional expression, assertion, listening, and conflict management skills, they will communicate in less abrasive and intimidating and more respectful, effective ways such that anger is minimized and successful interpersonal communication and problem solving are maximized.

Because of differences in population characteristics and communication skill deficits, not every social skills program focuses on exactly the same behaviors. However, communication skill programs tend to focus on skills such as (1) monitoring and changing nonverbal aspects of aversive communication (e.g., frowns, sighs, etc., that communicate anger, impatience, and disrespect); (2) monitoring and understanding the impact of the angry person's behavior on others; (3) improving listening skills, such as listening without interruption, paraphrasing, and clarifying others' thoughts and feelings without judgment; (4) improving skills in giving others positive feedback; (5) finding respectful ways to express negative feelings, disagreement, and dissent and respectful ways to give negative feedback; (6) assertively expressing one's feelings, thoughts, and preferences; (7) setting appropriate limits; (8) learning how to negotiate and compromise; and (9) learning ways of appropriately taking a time-out. Behavioral concepts and skills are related to the client's dysfunctional anger, and the client is assisted in identifying and developing alternative, effective behaviors. Then, one or two of these behaviors (e.g., listening without interruption or talking without profanity or abusive comments) are modeled and rehearsed in some kind of role-play or simulation. The client and therapist debrief the rehearsal and provide constructive feedback. Other skill deficits are explored, and appropriate behaviors are developed and rehearsed in a similar manner. This is continued until the client has a rich repertoire of skills with which to communicate and negotiate conflict. Homework assignments are developed to transfer the improved communication patterns in vivo. Success and difficulties in vivo are discussed, and behavior is revised as needed and rehearsed again until effective skills are reliable and deployable.

There is empirical support for such skill-based interventions. For example, three early studies with angry college students (Fehrenbach & Thelen, 1981; Moon & Eisler, 1983; Rimm et al., 1974) focused on increasing assertive responding to provocation (e.g., empathic understanding, making appropriate requests) and on decreasing inappropriate behavior (e.g., profanity, threats). Treatment effect sizes were moderate to large. Deffenbacher and colleagues developed a somewhat similar social skills intervention for HTA college students (Deffenbacher et al. 1994, 1987, 1996). This program emphasized increased listening skills, skills for giving positive and negative feedback, and assertion and negotiation skills. Depending on the outcome measure, effect sizes ranged from small to large for anger reduction. Small to moderate effect sizes were found for nontargeted treatment measures such as trait anxiety. In addition, anger, anger expression, social skills changes, and anxiety reduction were maintained at 12- to 15-month follow-ups (Deffenbacher, 1988; Deffenbacher et al., 1995, 1996). The social skills interventions reviewed so far tend to be fairly structured, with the protocol specifying the behaviors to be rehearsed and in what order. Deffenbacher et al. (1994, 1996) developed an alternative format based more on the Socratic, inductive style of Beck's cognitive therapy. Angry college student clients were encouraged to identify effective communication skills and conflict management strategies. Client-identified behaviors were refined through group discussions and rehearsed through visualization of angering events or role-plays. Behavioral tryouts and experiments were contracted to transfer improved communication strategies externally. This approach led to significant anger reduction, improved anger expression, and lessened trait anxiety (moderate to large effect sizes), and effects were maintained in long-term follow-ups (Deffenbacher et al., 1995, 1996). Skill enhancement approaches have also been effective in noncollege populations. For example, a program enhancing listening and conflict management skills in adolescents and their parents improved communication and problem-solving skills and lowered experienced family conflict (Stern, 1999).

In summary, skill-oriented interventions led to a number of positive outcomes, such as lowered anger and conflict, decreased inappropriate anger expression, and increased appropriate anger expression and interpersonal communication. Effects sizes are generally moderate to large, and long-term follow-ups reveal maintenance of treatment effects. Skill interventions have been effective with angry college students and conflicted, angry families, suggesting a range of possible applications as well.

Exposure-Based Interventions

Anger, like anxiety, involves a high degree of emotional and physiological arousal. Reduction of this arousal, often achieved via an angry outburst that ends the aversive provocation of another, may have strong negative reinforcement properties. Following the logic of exposure programs from the anxiety reduction literature, it is theoretically plausible that if individuals were exposed to anger-arousing situations but not allowed to engage in aggressive or other typical behavior, then the anger would extinguish and behaviors motivated by anger reduction would decrease.

Studies involving the barb technique (i.e., exposure to intensely provoking insults, criticisms, put downs, etc.) (Mcvey, 2000; Tafrate & Kassinove, 1998; Terracciano, 2000) suggest that exposure may be an effective intervention. Tafrate and Kassinove (1998), in working with a sample of very angry adult males from the community, found that exposure alone effectively reduced anger and was as effective as or nearly as effective as the barb plus rationale-emotive condition. Terracciano (2000) replicated these findings with angry married men, as did Mcvey (2000) with a sample of angry males from the community. Grodnitsky and Tafrate (2001), in a multiple case study design, successfully extended a prolonged exposure program to angry men in a community mental health setting. Exposure-based programs have not received as much empirical support as other interventions, but they appear promising and worthy of further research and evaluation.

Multicomponent Interventions

Many anger reduction programs combine the rationale and procedures of two or more interventions and conceptually address multiple elements of dysfunctional anger arousal. One of the most studied of these is the integration of cognitive and relaxation interventions, which targets cognitive, emotional, and physiological elements. Cognitive-relaxation interventions have effectively reduced anger in HTA college students (Deffenbacher & Stark, 1992; Deffenbacher et al., 1987, 1988, 1990a, 1994, 1996 Dua & Swinden, 1992; Hazaleus & Deffenbacher, 1986), angry community volunteers (Novaco, 1975), police officers experiencing anger issues (Gerina & Drummond, 2000), and angry drivers (Deffenbacher et al., 2000, 2002; Richards et al., 2001). Treatment effect sizes are generally moderate to large, and studies that used the clinically reliable change index revealed that 40% to 50% of clients using cognitive-relaxation techniques improved this much, whereas 0% to 5% of controls did. Studies using long-term follow-ups (e.g., Deffenbacher, 1988; Deffenbacher & Stark, 1992; Deffenbacher et al., 1988, 1990a, 1995, 1996; Hazaleus & Deffenbacher, 1986; Richards et al., 2001) demonstrate long-term maintenance of anger reduction. Cognitive-relaxation therapy was also as effective as relaxation and cognitive interventions alone and social skills interventions. Thus, a combination of cognitive and relaxation interventions has considerable empirical support.

Other interventions combine cognitive and skill interventions. As noted previously, Beck's cognitive therapy focuses on assisting clients not only to identify and change anger-engendering cognitions but also to develop alternative ways of handling situations. Beck's cognitive therapy has been shown to be effective in reducing anger in HTA college students (Dahlen & Deffenbacher, 2000; Deffenbacher et al., 2000), angry drivers (Kogan et al., 2001), and angry parents at risk for committing child abuse (Whiteman, Fanshel, & Grundy, 1987). As with other interventions, treatment effect sizes were generally moderate to large, and studies using the reliable clinical change index showed that 40% to 70% of cognitive therapy clients met this criterion, whereas 0% of controls did. Treatment effects were maintained through 1-month (Dahlen & Deffenbacher, 2000; Kogan et al., 2001) and 1-year follow-ups (Deffenbacher, Richards & Kogan, 2002; Deffenbacher et al., 2000) and were as strong as the cognitive element alone (Dahlen & Deffenbacher, 2000) or a relaxation intervention (Kogan et al., 2001). Thus, Beck's multicomponent approach to cognitive therapy appears to be a promising treatment for anger as well as for many other disorders.

Many other anger management programs include, in one form or another, a focus on cognitive, emotional, physiological, and skill components. Such programs have been used with an increasingly diverse set of anger-involved populations, such as HTA college students (Deffenbacher et al., 1990b), angry veterans suffering from post-traumatic stress disorder (Chemtob et al., 1997), military personnel with anger issues (Linkh & Sonnek, 2003), adults high in Type A personality characteristics (Thurman, 1985), hypertensive individuals (Larkin & Zayfert, 1996), angry parents and their teenage offspring (Stern, 1999), caregivers to individuals experiencing dementia (Coon et al., 2003; Steffen, 2000), individuals who abuse and neglect elderly dependents (Reay & Browne, 2002), expectant mothers at risk for committing child abuse (Ravello, 2000), substance-abusing adults (Briscoe, 2002), and angry inmates and offenders (Eamon, Munchua, & Reddon, 2001). In addition, a cognitive-behavioral anger management program lowered anger and improved patterns of anger expression in men court-ordered into a domestic violence program, suggesting a value-added component of anger reduction and supporting the integration of anger reduction interventions with comprehensive programs addressing problem behavior.

In summary, interventions that combine two or more active treatment elements are effective with a variety of anger-involved populations. Where follow-ups were conducted, anger reduction effects were maintained. Where treatment comparisons have been conducted, combined programs appear to be about as effective as other programs, but in general, they are no more effective than the individual components alone or other interventions.

SINCE THERE IS NO GOLD STANDARD, SHOULD ANYTHING GO?

Since there is no clear evidence of differential treatment effectiveness, is it reasonable to conclude that practitioners can use their favorite cognitive-behavioral strategy with equal success? Rather than answer this question affirmatively, it is suggested that the literature on empirically supported interventions be used in a selective or targeted way. Clinicians can conduct a careful assessment of their client or assess and map the key elements of dysfunctional anger in the groups with which they work and then intelligently match empirically supported strategies onto those characteristics. For example, if a subgroup of hypertensive individuals experience both high levels of anger and anger suppression, then an intervention might combine relaxation for emotional-physiological arousal and skill training in appropriate emotional expression and communication for dysfunctional anger suppression. Alternatively, an individual who was chronically angry and brooding about a terminated relationship might benefit from a cognitive intervention that explored and altered themes of unfairness, narcissistic demanding, catastrophization, and dichotomous thinking. Furthermore, a highly angry, verbally abusive parent might benefit from an intervention combining relaxation, cognitive restructuring, and time-out for anger control with developmentally appropriate information about children and parent skill training to replace abusive, verbally aggressive behavior with child management competencies. That is, it is not concluded that all have won and all must have prizes. To the contrary, angry individuals and groups differ in their experience and displays of anger. The literature on empirically supported interventions can assist treatment design and planning and target those elements of the anger experience that appear most problematic.

If this strategy has merit, then let us see how themes from the treatment outcome literature might be applied to the case of Anthony. Clearly, a therapist working with Anthony would have much greater knowledge of the case, but following are some suggestive matchings of findings from the literature onto the case of Anthony.

Most, if not all, cognitive-behavioral approaches involve self-monitoring; monitoring of the triggering events for problematic anger; the cognitive, emotional, physiological, and behavioral responses to the triggers; the reactions of others; and the consequences of anger arousal as they link and sequence together. Anthony would likely benefit from such self-monitoring. He appears unaware of the nature of his anger, the triggers of that anger, and conditions that may facilitate or reduce anger reactivity. Monitoring internal states and feelings are likely to be important. States such as impatience, cognitive distraction and inability to focus well (which may be linked to ADHD), guilt, very likely depression, and perhaps anxiety should be monitored. Cognitive elements may be relevant as well, as he appears to be highly demanding, likely engages in catastrophic thinking and overgeneralizations when demands are not met, and appears to have a kind of hostile attributional bias or interpretation of others' behavior. Careful self-monitoring and clarification of themes with the therapist may help Anthony begin to see patterns in his anger and give him a sense that he may not always be out of control and at the whimsy of tumbling emotional experience.

As the triggers and themes begin to emerge, three other interventions might be initiated:

1. Anthony might be asked if he is ever able to abort or foreshorten anger episodes. With exploration, some examples will likely emerge. These often involve stepping away from or letting a situation go, which could be linked to the value of taking a time-out. It is suggested that this not be a general discussion but that the therapist and Anthony discuss specific ways of taking time-outs and that these be rehearsed until Anthony is able to effectively execute time-outs in response to a variety of triggers. That is, the nature of a time-out while dealing with his children in sporting events may be quite different from taking a time-out with one of them at home or with his wife. It is further suggested that the therapist and Anthony discuss and rehearse how he will negotiate taking time-outs with this family (i.e., getting his family to understand and support his taking a time-out when he is angry). Moreover, he should rehearse how he will initiate time-in through which he will approach and deal with the issues that angered him.

2. Anthony's anger appears to be marked by considerable emotional and physiological arousal. A relaxation intervention may be appropriate, and relaxation interventions have been successful with individuals with his level of trait anger and anger expression characteristics. After reviewing feelings and physical elements of anger arousal, his therapist may make a relatively easy transition to how relaxation may help lower his anger. If a relaxation intervention is initiated, it is suggested that it be started before significant cognitive restructuring (Deffenbacher & Lynch, 1998). Relaxation interventions appear consistent with many clients' experienced anger and do not lead to initial resistance sometimes encountered in early deployment of cognitive interventions. Thus, the therapist can begin an effective intervention while building the therapeutic alliance early in therapy and reducing resistance at the same time.

3. Cognitive restructuring appears relevant as well. Demanding, hostile attributional bias; negative interpretations of the behavior of others; as well as some of the potential cognitive themes in his guilt and depression seem appropriate for cognitive change strategies. As the therapeutic relationship is strengthened during the development of self-monitoring, relaxation, and time-out interventions, the therapist can begin to reflect on the cognitive themes apparent in self-monitoring and interviews.

Cognitive themes could be explored, with new ways of thinking developed and rehearsed along with relaxation during visualizations or simulations of angering events.

It is unclear whether other skill interventions will be needed or not. As Anthony begins to manage his anger through increased self-awareness and the application of cognitive, relaxation, and time-out strategies, he may demonstrate skills for dealing appropriately with conflict situations. However, he may not, and behavioral skill building addressing his impact on others, listening, assertive expression disagreement without intimidation and disrespect, and negotiation and compromise may be relevant.

Two other therapeutic interventions might be considered. First, family therapy may be relevant to assist Anthony, his wife, and his children to address the impact of his prior anger and to assist and support his efforts to change. Second, a referral for medication might be considered. Given Anthony's history of ADHD, a trial of appropriate medication might be warranted. Such medication might provide increased cognitive and emotional control for Anthony. Alternatively, a trial of serotonergic medications might be appropriate because they are effective with some cases of anger and impulsive aggressive behavior not dissimilar to that of Anthony.

DO THE LITERATURE AND GAPS THEREIN PROVIDE ANY OTHER SUGGESTIONS FOR PRACTITIONERS AND RESEARCHERS?

Individual or Group Therapy

Little research has been directed toward answering whether individual or group anger interventions differ in effectiveness. Individual therapy offers greater knowledge of and capacity to address the specifics of a given case and allows the practitioner to tailor the components of the treatment protocol to the client. Group therapy offers normalization of experience and provides additional alternative perspectives, greater cognitive alternatives and behavioral suggestions, more flexible opportunities for role-plays, and the like. Although there is little research addressing the relative effectiveness of individual versus group therapy, what is clear is that most outcome research has been conducted in a group format and indicates treatment effectiveness. Therefore, although legal and therapeutic reasons may suggest contraindications in some cases, practitioners should consider a group intervention. If a group intervention is used, care should be taken so that the group does not deteriorate into a place for mutual complaint and inadvertently support of anger and other dysfunctional behavior.

A Cognitive-Relaxation Intervention as a Basic Intervention for Heterogeneous Anger Groups

In some settings, practitioners may be called on to provide anger management groups for individuals experiencing widely different sources of anger. For this type of situation, it is suggested that a cognitive-relaxation intervention be considered. First, there is empirical support for cognitive-relaxation interventions for generally angry individuals. Second, relaxation and cognitive interventions are general enough to affect at least portions of most individuals' anger experiences. Third, it is hard to target specific skill elements needed when the group's anger issues differ widely. Thus, some anger reduction is likely with the economy of a group for diverse individuals.

Tailor Treatment to the Characteristics of the Individual or Population

As previously suggested, empirically supported interventions can be matched to the individual's or group's anger experience (e.g., a relaxation intervention for heightened emotional and physiological arousal). However, problem anger exists within social and cultural contexts, contexts that may support or interfere with treatment. Religious, family, and cultural values as they relate to anger and/or intervention should be identified, and interventions should be made culturally sensitive. For example, some religious groups forbid typical relaxation interventions. Care should be taken to see if culturally appropriate relaxation interventions can be identified and incorporated into therapy, should a relaxation intervention seem appropriate. For example, the impact of social sanctions should also be assessed and addressed in therapy, as is often the case when individuals are referred or mandated into anger management therapy. Such clients are often most recently angry about being in therapy. If therapeutic impasses and resistance are to be reduced, intervention should attend to the anger and resentment about having to attend. Little research to date has addressed how to make interventions sensitive to the personal attributes and cultural characteristics of angry individuals. It is suggested that researchers and practitioners working with various groups and cultural contexts actively share their experiences and efforts to effectively address group and cultural characteristics. Shared experience and strategy may mean some wheels will not have to be reinvented in the crucible of failure.

Long-Term Follow-Up, Maintenance, and Relapse Prevention

Where long-term follow-up has been included in research designs, evidence supports maintenance of intervention effects. Two issues, however, should receive further attention. First, more long-term follow-up research is needed to document whether effects continue in different populations. Effects may or may not maintain long term in different groups. Supposition of maintenance should be replaced with long-term follow-up data. Second, the value of specific maintenance and relapse prevention strategies (e.g., booster sessions) should be assessed. Problematic anger is often a long-standing, easily externalized issue. Situational contexts, such as relationships, work, court mandates, and so forth, may change such that the client may drift back toward earlier experiences and expressions of anger. It is possible that greater attention to long-term maintenance and relapse prevention might prevent this kind of drift in some clients and is in need of therapeutic and research attention.

Be Careful of Thinking "More Is Better"

Given that there are several empirically supported interventions, practitioners may be tempted to integrate multiple strategies in hopes of maximizing treatment effects. Care should be taken in making this choice. First, there is little evidence supporting the synergistic or additive effects of multicomponent interventions. In general, multicomponent interventions are no more effective than their individual components. Second, there is a practical issue to consider. If clinicians provide a time-limited intervention, which is often the case, the addition of treatment components often comes at the expense of practice. That is, as more is added, it is often rehearsal of specific strategies that suffers. Rehearsal typically comes in the latter portion of sessions, and that is what is squeezed down or out when more elements are added to the treatment protocol. Yet, such rehearsal and potential for overlearning may be critical for some individuals.

Intervention May Need to Address Resistance

Many individuals with anger problems present with a defensive posture and feel that they are being told that they are the "problem"; their feelings and behaviors are "wrong"; and "they," not others, must change. They are angry about and fight these messages in much the same ways they deal with other anger issues. Moreover, their anger may be threatening and intimidating to the therapist, and they may demonstrate attitudes and characteristics that put the therapist off (e.g., misogynist or narcissistic attitudes, beliefs that anger and aggression are justified). If not handled well, such processes may lead to clients' resisting therapy and change, to therapeutic impasses, and in some cases, to premature termination of therapy. There is minimal literature upon which to draw, but therapists might consider the following types of interventions in addressing such resistance (DiGuiseppe, Tafrate, & Eckhardt, 1994). For example, the development of the therapeutic relationship and working alliance with angry clients should receive as much or more attention than with other types of clients. The therapist need not like or accept what the angry client says or does, but he or she should listen carefully, empathically, and respectfully and attempt to actively communicate an understanding of the client's sense of loss, hurt, injustice, injury, and mistreatment, as would be done for any other client. For example, the therapist may wish to think about how he or she engages in therapeutic confrontation and cognitive change. Some active, directive approaches (e.g., Deffenbacher et al., 1988; Hazaleus & Deffenbacher, 1986) appeared to engender resistance in early sessions. Angry clients often fight and argue with challenge in therapy, as they often do in real life. However, the more Socratic, inductive approach of Beck's cognitive therapy seemed to reduce this type of resistance (Deffenbacher & Lynch, 1998). For example, if a relaxation intervention is to be used, consider introducing it early in therapy. Relaxation seems to fit well with many clients and strengthens the therapeutic alliance without increasing resistance early in therapy. Other interventions, such as cognitive restructuring or behavioral skill building, may increase resistance if introduced early and therefore would be introduced much more easily a few sessions later, after relaxation has been introduced. Interventions such as these may reduce resistance and engage angry clients more productively in therapy, especially early in therapy, when premature termination is an issue.

Intervention May Need to Address Readiness for Change

Client readiness for anger management is an important, but very under-researched, area (Howells & Day, 2003). Interventions reviewed earlier in this chapter tend to be change-oriented therapies. They assume that the client is experiencing difficulties and is at least somewhat motivated to lower his or her anger and associated problems. Many individuals with anger problems, however, are not at this stage of readiness. They may not be aware of or may deny the nature and degree of anger problems. They may totally externalize their issues, blaming others and circumstances. It is others, not them, who need to change. To them, anger and perhaps aggression may seem reasonable, natural responses to unwarranted circumstances. In a word, these individuals are not motivated for change (DiGuiseppe, Tafrate, & Eckhardt, 1994). They are at a precontemplative or at best contemplative stage of change. Action-oriented interventions are not relevant to them and do not fit their frame of reference, because they do not see themselves as experiencing an anger problem. Others (e.g., spouses, courts, employers, school systems) may not agree, and the person may end up with strong external pressures to attend anger management counseling. The person is still not likely motivated for change-oriented interventions. As other literature suggests, when interventions do not match the stage of change, they tend to be unsuccessful. With anger too, intervention should engage the person at his or her level of readiness for change. Clinicians should carefully consider and assess this issue, perhaps using assessment strategies such as the Anger Readiness to Change Questionnaire (Williams et al., 2003). Interventions such as motivational interviewing, designed to enhance readiness, probably should not be highly confrontational but instead should focus on increasing the client's awareness of his or her anger and exploring the consequences of the person's anger. Assisting clients to see that their anger may not be getting them all that they want may enhance motivation for change and make action-oriented interventions more relevant to them. However, moving automatically to action-oriented interventions for individuals not at that stage of change is likely to lead to a series of misunderstandings and impasses and might result in termination of therapy without benefit. Researchers need to develop or adapt interventions from the stages of change literature (Prochaska, Norcross, & DiClemente, 1995) and evaluate those strategies, not for anger reduction, but for change of readiness for anger reduction.

CONCLUSIONS AND SUGGESTIONS FOR THE FUTURE

The body of outcome studies for anger reduction is much smaller than that for the treatment of other emotional problems, such as anxiety and depression. Nonetheless, the literature suggests that various psychological interventions can meaningfully lower anger. This conclusion, however, should be narrowed or limited to cognitive-behavioral interventions, because nearly all outcome studies reviewed were conducted on cognitive-behavioral interventions. Other intervention strategies may prove effective; however, their efficacy awaits outcome studies with adequate measurement and controls. Small clinical trials should continue to be conducted to establish effects for newer interventions and to demonstrate whether a particular strategy is effective in understudied anger-involved populations. Larger controlled treatment trials can be conducted to evaluate relative effectiveness of interventions and to explore potential mechanisms, mediators, and moderators of change. It is also suggested that researchers turn their attention to developing and evaluating strategies for assessing and dealing with important issues heretofore receiving little research attention (e.g., assessing change in a more continuous manner; making interventions culturally sensitive and sensitive to other group characteristics; assessing client readiness for change, client resistance to change, and the potential need for and value of interventions for long-term maintenance and relapse prevention).

Although these are suggestions for the future, one may also reflect on the past of anger reduction research. Novaco's landmark study (1975) appeared 30 years ago, yet as of this writing, the body of anger reduction research is much smaller and has lagged behind that of other emotional issues, such as anxiety and depression. The question is, why is this the case? One can only speculate and consider the possibilities. Perhaps, it is because anger is relatively inconsequential and trivial as a clinical focus, and thus treatment is rarely called for. There is, however, literature that suggests that chronic and intense anger contributes to significant health, relational, vocational, legal, and other problems (e.g., Deffenbacher, 2003; Kassinove, 1995). Thus, anger does appear to have significant negative consequences that interfere with the quality of the individual's life or the lives of those around him or her. Anger is often conceptualized as an interpersonal experience in that anger expression may involve another who becomes involved in the process and who may be affected adversely. Alternatively, while clinically relevant anger may have significant adverse consequences, it, like intermittent explosive disorder, may be relatively rare and therefore not require clinical intervention very often. Again, there are clinical and research reports (e.g., Coccaro, 2003; Deffenbacher, 2003) that suggest that this is not the case and that, depending on the issues, from 2% to 6% or more of the population might benefit from anger interventions. So, the explanation for the lag in anger reduction outcome research probably does not result solely from its low base rate or lack of life interference.

Another possibility may have to with the natural tendencies of people to avoid aversive conditions. Perhaps because of the characteristics of anger itself and because of its association with aggression, anger makes mental health professionals uncomfortable and they avoid it. Our major diagnostic system, the *Diagnostic and Statistical Manual* (DSM-IV), certainly reflects this, as there are no anger-based disorders (i.e., disorders in which anger must be present for a positive diagnosis to be made) (Deffenbacher, 2003). This influences scientific research on anger reduction in a least two ways. First, the absence of consistent criteria hinders the definition and selection of clinical samples. Second, whether it should be the case or not, the absence of diagnostic criteria adversely affects research funding, because federally funded treatment research strongly favors established diagnostic groups. The absence of anger-based diagnoses thus becomes a kind of catch-22; it limits or reduces funding of treatment research on the very problems that might be funded were there established criteria. A final form of avoidance is more a political or social concern. Because anger may be associated with aggression, it can be argued that if anger is accepted as a legitimate mental health problem, then the diagnosis can be used as an excuse or explanation for aggressive, potentially illegal, even lethal behavior. Although this is a reasonable concern, it does not seem that the presence of anger-based diagnoses necessarily leads to this conclusion and the exclusion as a legitimate mental health concern. Aggressive behavior of a person with a diagnosis of antisocial, borderline, or paranoid personality disorder or intermittent explosive disorder or the self- or other-destructive behavior of a suicidal individual does not eliminate the person's legal and social culpability for his or her behavior. Such individuals can have a diagnosable mental health problem *and* be held responsible for their behavior. It seems that the same could be done for anger disorders.

If some of these speculations are accurate, then it is incumbent on anger researchers and practitioners to do at least four things:

1. They must conduct the epidemiological and risk factor research that continues to establish the frequency, degree, and nature of suffering experienced by angry individuals.
2. They must continue to establish the efficacy of well-articulated anger reduction interventions.
3. They must integrate anger and anger reduction into training programs so that future generations of therapists will be both more skilled in treating and more comfortable with angry individuals so that angry individuals can have their concerns approached with the dignity and respect given other emotional problems.
4. They must work the clinical focus of anger through the slow professional, social, and political processes to develop anger-based diagnoses, to legitimize the pain and suffering of angry individuals, pain and suffering that might be reduced by biopsychosocial interventions.

CHAPTER 4

Cultural and Gender Considerations in the Assessment and Treatment of Anger-Related Disorders

Sandra P. Thomas

Anger has long been considered a universal, primary emotion, one of the six emotions with identifiable facial expressions across cultures (Ekman, 1993). Recent research, however, has illuminated cultural and gender differences that must be considered in clinical practice. Anger is an emotional response of the whole person (Averill, 1982). That person is a rather complicated amalgam of individual personality traits, lessons learned in the family of origin, memories of experiences with mentors (and tormentors), and residuals of gender role socialization. To ensure delivery of appropriate treatment, the clinician must consider all of these influences on the behavior patterns of an adult client who presents with an anger-related disorder. The client's *culture* is the focus of this chapter.

Deploring psychology's neglect of culture, Segall, Lonner, and Berry (1998) contend that culture is the "primary shaper and molder of everyone's behavior" (p. 1107). With specific reference to the emotion of anger, Mayne and Ambrose (1999) assert that people across the globe "will largely agree about the possible causes of anger, and what an angry individual would like to do (though culture is perhaps the most important determinant of what an angry individual *actually* does)" (p. 354). In support of this assertion, there is abundant literature showing vast differences

71

in anger behaviors from culture to culture, ranging from extreme subtlety in the case of a Japanese woman creating a disorderly flower arrangement to florid public displays such as "mad dances" in West New Guinea and "running amok" in Malaysia (see Averill, 1982, and Tavris, 1989, for numerous examples of angry behaviors in other cultures). Anger is the core of several culture-bound syndromes listed in the *Diagnostic and Statistical Manual of Mental Disorders* (DSM-IV), such as *bilis* (also called *colera* or *muina*), a Latino condition caused by strongly experienced rage, and *hwa-byung,* a Korean syndrome attributed to anger suppression (American Psychiatric Association, 1994).

The meaning of anger in a specific culture is embedded in cultural beliefs about the mind, the self, society, and nature (Russell, 1991). Logically, anger is construed differently in cultures that emphasize connectedness (e.g., Japanese) versus those cultures that emphasize individualism (e.g., American). Cultural differences in anger behavior also emanate from the historical trajectories, religions, languages, and customs of a group of people. In this chapter, we pay particular attention to gender and social status as determinants of anger behavior. Gender is "nested" within culture, and status is "nested" within gender. Women have lower social status than men in every culture (United Nations Human Development Report, cited in "The War against Women," 1994), but gradations of status *within* each gender also influence anger behavior. These gradations of status are largely determined by education, occupation, and race/ethnicity.

In general, low-status people are not as assertive as high-status people (Eagly & Steffen, 1986). In the words of Fiske (1993): "The powerless attend to the powerful who control their outcomes" (p. 621). Expressing anger laterally toward one's peers or downward to subordinates is more socially acceptable than expressing anger upward toward higher-status individuals. For example, while conducting our research on Turkish women in Istanbul, we learned that a middle-class married woman was permitted to freely vent anger to her female friends or her lower-status maid (considered a peasant girl), but anger at her husband was strictly forbidden (Thomas & Atakan, 1993). Imagine two American men, both products of "Western culture," residing in the same city, working in the same Boston office building overlooking the Charles River. Now imagine the constraints on anger expression felt by the poor African American man who is the janitor in that building as compared with the constraints of the higher-status Euro-American attorney in his plush office with its sweeping river view.

In keeping with current thinking about race (e.g., Smedley & Smedley, 2005; Zuckerman, 1990), I take the position that race is a social construct; however, many people think it is real (Segall et al., 1998) and accord lower status to non-Caucasians on the basis of their skin color. Smedley and Smedley (2005) said it best: "Race as biology is fiction, racism as a social problem is real" (p. 16). Phinney (1996) suggested use of the term *ethnic group* to refer to all nondominant groups in the United States, including African Americans, Asian and Pacific Islander Americans, Native Americans, and Latinos. Sue and Sue (1999) use the term *culturally different* to refer to non-European groups, whereas others use the term *minority*. Rather than devote more space to issues of semantics, suffice it to say that this chapter examines a variety of cultural and ethnic groups with emphasis on the ways in which their traditions may influence a client's anger behavior. Because of the Eurocentric bias in much of the extant literature, nondominant groups (including women as a nondominant group) will receive greater attention in this chapter.

ASPECTS OF CULTURE THAT AFFECT ANGER BEHAVIOR

Emotions are elicited and shaped by a person's subjective evaluation of an antecedent situation or event (Lazarus, 1991; Solomon, 1993). Thus, the same event can provoke different emotions in persons from different cultures (Scherer, 1997). For example, a random act by a stranger may be judged as highly insulting by one individual but dismissed with a hearty laugh (or even ignored) by an individual with a different cultural heritage. Sizable culture effects were found for judgments of immorality and unfairness in Scherer's study of 37 different countries (1997). As noted earlier, culture also profoundly affects display rules for an emotion. In many cultures, anger is viewed as a negative emotion, virtually forbidden or taboo. The Machiguenga Indians in Peru seek to avoid anger at all costs (Johnson, Johnson, & Baksh, 1986). Utku Eskimos consider angry thoughts dangerous to social cohesion and discourage the expression of anger by cultivating acceptance of situations as they are. In the case of a snowstorm that blocks their plans, they accept the fact and build an igloo (Briggs, 1970). In many Eastern cultures, emotion is subdued to preserve harmony in relationships. For example, the Japanese have an extensive emotion lexicon, including several anger words, but they avoid direct verbal expression of negative emotion, especially in public (Tanaka-Matsumi, 1995).

In contrast to these cultures, Americans are often urged to ventilate their anger ("get that pent-up anger out; it's good for you"), perpetuating the incorrect notion that "catharsis" will diminish angry emotion. In the American business world, individuals in positions of power and dominance freely express anger. Loud cursing by the impatient Type A executive is the norm in many business settings. There is a certain degree of pride in announcing, "I told her off" or "I punched him out." The focus here is on relief of tension in the individual rather than the consequences of an outburst for interpersonal relationships. The unfortunate consequences of this egocentric focus can be seen in the increasingly uncivil interactions between Americans (e.g., epidemics of "road rage," "air rage," and "desk rage"). Recent brawls at sporting events depict a serious lessening of anger control in our society. How did we arrive at the current state of "emotional anarchy" (Tavris, 1989)? It may be worthwhile to take a closer look at the philosophical underpinnings of Western and Eastern cultural perspectives on anger.

BRIEF SYNOPSIS OF WESTERN CULTURAL PERSPECTIVES ON ANGER

In reviewing Western cultural perspectives on anger, it is important to remember that "both from place to place and from era to era, words signifying anger reside in different semantic fields, and expressions of anger take place and are received in ways that differ" (Peyroux, 1998, p. 42). Zeldin (1977) pointed out that "the history of anger has yet to be written" (p. 1120). However, insights can be gleaned from works such as those of Averill (1982), Rosenwein (1998), and Stearns and Stearns (1986). Averill (1982) examined teachings about anger during the Greco-Roman, medieval, and early modern periods, including writings of Aristotle, Aquinas, Descartes, and others. Rosenwein (1998), along with other authors in her edited volume, explored the social uses of anger in the Middle Ages, and the husband and wife team of Stearns and Stearns (1986) traced American cultural ideas about anger from the 18th through the 20th centuries. Synthesizing insights from these works, it is apparent that control of anger has been an ideal throughout much of the history of Western civilization. Although some scholars point to a cultural transformation in attitudes toward anger (i.e., from externalizing anger to internalizing it) that occurred in the 16th century, in conjunction with adoption of courtly manners (Muir, 1993), review of older texts makes it clear that anger has long been regarded as a sin, a character weakness, or a madness.

Roman philosopher Seneca produced the first complete work on anger, *De Ira*, finding nothing good to say about it (1963, originally written ca. AD 40–50). According to Seneca, "certain wise men have claimed that anger [*iram*] is temporary madness [*insanium*]" (p. 107). Other early philosophers acknowledged some positive functions of anger, such as enforcing moral standards and restoring justice, but condemned "the excesses to which anger often leads" (Averill, 1982, p. 75). Generally speaking, within Western philosophy, emotion was construed as irrational, not valued like reason—and perhaps the antithesis of reason (Solomon, 1993). Only recently have philosophers acknowledged that reason is "emotionally engaged" (Lakoff & Johnson, 1999). Damasio's neuro-science research (1994), in fact, shows that those who lose the capacity to be emotionally engaged cannot reason appropriately about social and moral issues. Sartre (1948) was one of the few philosophers to produce an entire treatise on emotion. In his book *The Emotions: Outline of a Theory,* he proposed that emotion occurs when a person's back is to the wall because of difficulties in the intransigent world; emotion is an attempt to transform that world. In this scenario, emotion serves a useful function.

Turning to Western religions, particularly the Judeo-Christian tradition, the most pervasive conceptualization of anger is sin (Campbell, 1975), although there is some recognition of "zealous" or "righteous" anger. God (and Jesus) could express righteous anger, but human anger was one of the seven deadly sins (Little, 1998). God's anger was, in fact, usually provoked by the wrongdoings of sinning humans (Saussy, 1995). Biblical passages imply that human anger is unacceptable. James 1:19–20 states "Let everyone be quick to listen, slow to speak, slow to anger, for your anger does not produce God's righteousness." Ephesians 4:31 states, "Have done with spite and passion, all angry shouting and cursing, and bad feelings of every kind." Forgiveness of offenders was recommended within both Judaism and Christianity (Brown, 2001). Little (1998), who studied the rules for monastic life in the Middle Ages, concluded that monks were not only to restrain their anger but to avoid becoming angry at all (except for formulaic liturgical "cursing" as a negotiating tool). Monks and nuns were to strive for the prized virtue of patience. Beyond the monastery walls, however, once again we see different standards, based on social status. Lords could be angry, but peasants' anger was considered illegitimate, impulsive, and destructive—never righteous or constructive (Rosenwein, 1998). Rosenwein points out "an entire repertory of conflicting norms [that] persisted side-by-side throughout the Middle ages" (pp. 242–243).

Tracing psychological conceptions of anger from Freud (1946) to the social constructionists (e.g., Harre, 1986) is beyond the scope of this chapter. Readers no doubt have some familiarity with this material. In essence, psychological conceptions of anger have evolved from the early construing of an instinctual drive that demanded expression to the social constructionist perspective exemplified by Averill and Harre. Along the way, a "ventilationist" movement occurred in the United States in the 1960s and 1970s, prompted by the research of ethologists such as Lorenz (1966) and Ardrey (1970) and by misinterpretations of Freud's catharsis concept. Although Freud (1949) did claim that holding in aggressiveness is unhealthy and leads to illness, he would have been aghast at the encounter groups and therapies such as "est" and "primal scream" that came into vogue. The American public snapped up copies of books by mental health professionals such as Rubin's *The Angry Book* (1970). Psychoanalyst Rubin wrote of a dangerous "slush fund" of unexpressed anger building up in the body, and Bach and Goldberg (1974) recommended insult clubs and family aggression festivals to discharge this slush fund of pent-up angry feelings. Although research disproved the efficacy of such activities (venting anger simply makes one angrier [Baron, 1983]) and efficacious therapies such as rational-emotive therapy (Ellis, 1976) and cognitive-behavioral therapy (Beck, 1976) were developed and researched, the legacy of the ill-advised ventilationist movement is still with us.

Indeed, what is important about examining all of these earlier Western ideas about anger is their enduring influence on contemporary culture. While modern religious writers such as Saussy (1995) have sought to dispel the notion that *all* anger is sinful (even describing a "holy" anger), a member of my research team was warned from the pulpit that "anger is only a d away from danger." Early views of anger as madness remain evident in contemporary parlance (e.g., the statement "You've gone mental," which is said disapprovingly by Britishers to an angry person). Remnants of early ideas about demonic possession may be heard in the popular American rationalization, "The devil made me do it. I wasn't myself."

Presently, within Western cultures, most people would agree that anger is a problem when it is creating difficulties in the client's work and/or family relationships. However, there are notable differences in the degree of tolerance for certain kinds of anger behaviors among regions of a Western country, especially a country with multiple diverse subcultures such as the United States. For example, physical fighting is a common occurrence in some communities, but so alarming and atypical that it prompts a call to the police in others. As in the Middle Ages, conflicting norms persist. Peyroux (1998) notes, "culture informs and frames but does not simply or uniformly determine the expression of human behavior" (p. 44).

BRIEF SYNOPSIS OF EASTERN CULTURAL PERSPECTIVES ON ANGER

Religious injunctions, as in the West, have profound influence on Eastern cultures. The Hindu *Bhagavad-Gita* (the Song of God) warns that "Lust, anger and greed . . . are the soul-destroying gates of hell" (Seldes, 1985, p. 41) and anger must be forsaken before a person can become one with Brahman. From the Buddhist point of view, anger is a form of suffering, because it produces pain for the angry person as well as for his or her victims. Anger is generated by the mind, by any threat to "our cocoon" (i.e., losing what we desire, are attached to, or identify with [Leifer, 1999]). Islam advocates moderation, tolerance, and forgiveness of human weaknesses (Guessoum, 1986). In the Koran (as in the Judeo-Christian Bible), God gets angry and the Prophet gets angry, but the message to humans in the *Hadiths* (sayings of the Prophet) is to avoid individualistic actions, giving oneself "entirely to the Common Cause, that of God and his Messenger, concentrating your thoughts, actions, and passions on it" (Ghazzal, 1998, p. 220). Control of anger is advocated in the following saying from a Hadith: "The strong man is not the good wrestler; the strong man is only he who controls himself when he is angry" (Ghazzal, 1998, p. 212). In Sufism, the mystical aspect of Islam, one aims to purify the heart of anger, envy, and jealousy (Arasteh & Sheikh, 1989). Elsewhere in the East (e.g., Japan, China), anger also has been viewed with opprobrium. The cultural expectation that anger produces only pain is evident in the Chinese proverb "If you are patient in one moment of anger, you will escape a hundred days of sorrow."

As in the West, if anger cannot be expressed directly, indirect techniques develop. Behzadi (1994) has provided an interesting glimpse of *qahr* and *ashti*, which occur in situations of interpersonal conflict in Iranian culture. *Qahr*, which has both instrumental and expressive functions, indirectly conveys to significant others that one feels angry and hurt. Displaying *qahr* (somewhat like the "silent treatment" in Western culture) evokes feelings of compassion in others, motivating them to right the wrong. *Ashti* is the last stage of *qahr*, in which reconciliation takes place.

Eastern cultural rules about anger are mediated by gender. For example, Hindu women in India view their domestic realm as sacred space; closeted within this realm, they see themselves as refined, in contrast to their husbands, who work outside the home and display "crude" emotions such as anger (*raga*) ("Midlife in Bhubaneswar," 1995). In Islam, women are considered genetically inferior to men, with deficient minds, thus requiring "training" by their husbands. This training can include punishment via beatings, although the Hadith teaches that these beatings should not result in disfigurement (Caner & Caner, 2002). Some Muslim women in the Middle East and Asia escape intolerable domestic violence by self-immolation (Campbell & Guiao, 2004).

PROBLEMS WITH CROSS-CULTURAL RESEARCH ON ANGER

Clinicians who turn to cross-cultural research to derive insights about culturally different clients will find much of the research flawed. According to Russell (1991), researchers often make inappropriate assumptions and faulty interpretations of emotions: "The questions asked, the hypotheses formulated, and the conclusions drawn . . . are built with [English] words" (p. 428), although these English words may not have equivalents in the language of the study participants. Too often, cross-cultural studies of mental health topics have been conducted by researchers from the West who "collected their data rapidly, almost perfunctorily, before returning to their . . . universities to analyze and publish the findings" (Rogler, 1999, p. 424). This approach to research has been called "safari" or "hit and run" research (Brislin, Bochner, & Lonner, 1975, p. 9). Such cultural insensitivity may be particularly problematic when studying emotions. How an ethnographer interprets people's emotions may not be the way that the people themselves do (Russell, 1991). Prolonged fieldwork, in which the ethnographer is immersed in the culture and native language, may be necessary to ascertain appropriateness of instruments or interview questions and to verify interpretations of data. Even when researchers are exploring emotion in their own country, where no language barrier exists, research on minority groups may have limitations. For example, Ponterotto (1988) found a tendency to sample only easy-to-obtain participants, failure to provide demographics of the sample, and other significant deficits in studies of minorities that were published in the *Journal of Counseling Psychology.*

PROBLEMS WITH STEREOTYPING/ASSUMING HOMOGENEITY WITHIN CULTURAL GROUPS

Even presuming that cultural anthropologists and other researchers have made accurate interpretations, there is always the danger of stereotyping. Stereotyping is an automatic, unconscious process that occurs even among persons who believe that they are not "prejudiced." Another danger is to assume homogeneity within cultural groups. "Western culture" and "Eastern culture" are enormously broad descriptors, and even when we narrow our focus to characteristic emotional expression within specific countries, such as Ireland and Italy, or regions of a country, such as Southern Appalachia, there are numerous subcultures. Moreover, individual difference variables such as gender and social status must be considered. In recent years, several books have appeared that purport to aid clinicians in understanding cultural groups and appreciating diversity (e.g., Henderson & Primeaux, 1981; Kavanagh & Kennedy, 1992; Spector, 1996). Although the intent of such texts is commendable, emphasizing group characteristics while failing to acknowledge differences *within* the various groups can foster stereotypes. For example, a typical text devotes a chapter to "Asian Americans." Sandhu (1997) points out the impossibility of generalizing about Asian Americans, given that there are 40 or more different Asian groups in the United States. Another problem is that generalizations about anger behavior among members of a "culture" may not apply to disenfranchised and marginalized minorities (Hall, Stevens, & Meleis, 1994).

As noted by Illovsky (2003), "conditions of minorities are often more a function of social, economic, and political forces and are not necessarily a function of the characteristics of the minority group" (p. ix). The aforementioned forces often prevent upward mobility of the minority, producing chronic anger and resentment. For example, in a 1994 Harris poll in the United States, African, Latin, and Asian Americans viewed whites as bigoted, bossy, and insensitive; furthermore, they perceived that whites controlled American power and wealth—and believed that whites were unwilling to share their power and wealth with non-whites ("Poll: Minorities find . . . ," 1994). Volumes of research about discriminatory practices in hiring, firing, promotion, and other forms of differential treatment on the basis of ethnicity, color, or race support the accuracy of these perceptions. Research involving blacks, Asians, Native Americans, and Latinos has revealed that the day-to-day stress of racist treatment is even more stressful than the major life events prominently featured in most stress questionnaires (Williams et al., 1997).

Unless one has experienced the cultural milieu from the perspective of a minority individual, it may be difficult to imagine what discriminatory treatment is like. Conducting research can be illuminating. White members of our biracial research team (such as I) winced as we listened to narratives of African American women, for whom racist treatment was a daily experience. As one participant put it, "Racism is like rain; if it's not falling in your location, it's gathering force somewhere nearby" (Fields et al., 1998, p. 361). An ever-present mistrust of whites was evident, as exemplified by the metaphor of the long-handled spoon:

> You look at [white] people from a distance and you feed them with that long-handled spoon. And you feed them a little bit at a time, because [if] you feed them too close to you, they'll hurt you. You don't let them get close enough to hurt you. (Fields et al., 1998, p. 363)

The genesis of the metaphor is unknown, but perhaps it could be traced to the era of slavery. Given this legacy and the ongoing racist treatment that still inflicts psychic pain, it is easy to understand why many African Americans fear, or feel uncomfortable, with the Eurocentric mental health system, militating against their seeking help from white middle-class therapists for dysphoric emotions (Scheffler & Miller, 1991; U.S. Department of Health and Human Services, 2001; U.S. Surgeon General's Report on

Mental Health, 1999). The egregious historical trauma experienced by Native Americans engenders deep mistrust of white care providers in this population as well (Struthers & Lowe, 2003). Immigrants and refugees may have even more fear of the mental health system, many of them having fled tyrannical governments (unfortunately, it is beyond the scope of this chapter to address the unique needs of immigrants and refugees).

GENDER ROLE SOCIALIZATION IN WESTERN CULTURE FOR MASCULINITY/FEMININITY AND GENDERED ANGER BEHAVIOR

Under the broad umbrella of *Western culture*, there is woman's world, with its ethos of helping, agreeing, complying, and connecting (Bernard, 1981), and man's world, with its ethos of showing toughness, competitiveness, and autonomy (Pollack, 2000). From the moment an infant is swaddled in a pink or blue receiving blanket, gender role socialization begins, becoming a major factor in the development of emotional behavior habits. According to Shields (2002), "*emotion* is identified as feminine, but *anger*, a prototypical emotion, is identified as masculine" (p. 11). Studies since the 1980s have shown that parents are more accepting of anger expression by sons (Birnbaum & Croll, 1984) and that sons are actually stimulated to aggressive action by their fathers from ages as young as 1.5 to 2 years (Miller, 1983), while fear and sadness are discouraged. In fact, fathers believe it is worse to have a son behave like a "wimp" than to have him display excessive aggression (Bacon & Ashmore, 1985). Mothers also encourage their sons to respond to angry situations with anger and retaliation (Brody, 1996). By age 3, boys act out anger physically, in hitting, pushing, and shoving, more so than girls do (Fagot, Leinbach, & Hagan, 1986). Longitudinal research by Eron, Gentry, and Schlegel (1994) showed that boys' patterns of aggressive behavior are already crystallizing by the age of 8. Competitive rough-and-tumble games on the playground teach boys that life is a contest in which they need to stay one up (Martin & Fabes, 2001; Tannen, 1994). Male sports culture perpetuates the ideal of competitive, aggressive masculinity, and failure to conform results in derogatory labels such as "girl" or "faggot" (Fine, 1987). Throughout the elementary and high school years, boys score higher on measures of overt anger than do girls (Cox, Stabb, & Hulgus, 2000).

In contrast, parents permit daughters to be more "emotional"—as long as they are not aggressive. Research shows that mothers avoid talking about anger with daughters and encourage them to repair any harm brought to others through displays of overt anger (Cross & Madson, 1997; Fivush, 1991). Traditional socialization for femininity inculcates the idea that showing anger is unattractive. Women who express their anger receive pejorative labels such as "bitch" or "shrew" (Lerner, 1985). Anger is not consistent with the cultural ideal of the selfless and ever-nurturing "perfect mother" (Bernardez, 1987). While growing up, girls often observe their mothers stifling anger or engaging in indirect expression of it through sulking—or perhaps displacing it onto children or other less powerful persons. Because direct anger expression is frowned upon, girls engage in more subtle forms of relational and social aggression, including nonverbal behaviors, such as nasty looks and threatening stares (Owens, Shute, & Slee, 2000; Simmons, 2002). The term *social aggression* was introduced in the 1980s by researchers who conducted a longitudinal study of children in grades 4 through 10; the girls engaged in behaviors such as "alienation, ostracism, or character defamation" (Cairns et al., 1989, p. 323). An alternative term, *relational aggression,* referring to girls' tendency to ignore peers when angry and exclude them during play time, was proposed by Crick and Grotpeter (1995) and came into popular parlance after extensive media coverage. More than 10 popular books on relational aggression have been published since 2000 (Geiger et al., 2004). (See Underwood [2003] and Geiger et al. [2004] for summaries of the scientific literature on girls' relational and social aggression.) Because the "silent treatment" and covert tactics (e.g., destructive gossip) do not resolve girls' disputes, their friendships are often terminated. Research on girls and women documents that rumination about painful anger experiences can continue for prolonged periods (Birditt & Fingerman, 2003).

In summary, gender-stereotypic socialization influences one's beliefs about the appropriateness of "owning" an emotion such as anger and about expressing it to others. Martin and Fabes (2001) found a "social dosage effect," in that the greater the amount of time children spend in play with same-sex peers, the greater the display of stereotypical gender-typed behavior. Perhaps neither boys nor girls learn healthy anger management. When boys learn mainly to express anger with their fists, they fail to acquire verbal facility. (In fact, Levant [1995] contended that many men have a subclinical version of alexithymia.) In later life, when men cannot settle conflicts with a few punches on the playground, they may be bereft of alternative strategies. Research shows that men who endorse the masculine gender role to a significantly greater degree are more likely to batter their partners (Schmidt, 2003). When girls learn that anger is unladylike and ugly, it may go underground, creating ongoing internal tension and distress. In our studies of both American and French women, numerous somatic symptoms of suppressed anger (e.g., stomach upset, headache, dizziness) were reported (Thomas, 2004). Women may abuse alcohol and over-the-counter drugs to medicate these uncomfortable anger-related symptoms (Grover & Thomas, 1993). In addition to somatization, Cox, Van Velsor, and Hulgus (2004) found greater depression and anxiety in women who divert anger, compared with those who express it assertively (the term *diversion* included various covert tactics, including containment and segmentation).

As mentioned previously, these generalizations about gender development and anger behavior of men and women may not apply to marginalized groups (e.g., ethnic minorities, people living in situations of poverty or abuse). For example, black women give their daughters a different message about anger than white mothers do: They prepare their daughters to mobilize anger in order to cope with the harsh realities of the world (Greene, 1990). The views of some non-European American groups are currently in flux. For example, although Muslim American women still tell themselves "Astagh-farrallah" ("God forgive me for being angry"), younger Muslim women are now doing what white U.S. women began doing in the late 1960s and 1970s—they are fighting for their rights, one of those rights being anger expression (Cox, Stabb, & Bruckner, 1999). Latinas in the study by Cox et al. expressed a similar belief. For both groups, "anger is intimately tied to the restrictions of both gender and their culture when set against the backdrop of White America" (p. 206).

The social status of an angry man or woman must always be taken into account. Maybury's (1997) study showed that the anger displays of high-status protagonists (male or female) were judged as more appropriate than the anger of low- and moderate-status protagonists. Twenge's seven-decade meta-analysis of women's assertiveness from 1931 to 1993 (2001) revealed that women's assertiveness rose and fell with their social status and the changing sociocultural environment. To wit, women's status was on the increase from 1931 to 1945, then declined from 1946 to the mid-1960s, and increased again from the late 1960s to the 1990s. (Men's scores did not demonstrate such a clear pattern of change.)

CURRENT RESEARCH ON GENDER DIFFERENCES IN ANGER

Some scholars have suggested that gender roles are changing, along with long-held taboos on various emotional behaviors. After all, some years have passed since the publication of classic papers on women's anger by Bernardez (1987), Miller (1983), and others. Girls have been exposed to tenets of the feminist movement, while boys have been exposed to the stereotypical "new male" who helps with housework and child care—and talks about his feelings. Clare (2000) contends that traditional masculinity is presently in crisis, and Levant (1995) asserts that masculinity has already collapsed, freeing men from confining gender role constraints. Some authors espouse androgyny as the new standard of mental health (Morawski, 1987). However, Plant et al. (2000) found that people are still aware of cultural and gender stereotypes of emotion and tend to believe that men experience and express anger more often than women. When asked to interpret unambiguous photos of angry faces, college students rated men's anger pose as angrier than women's (Plant et al., 2000). Spence and Buckner (2000) found that societal prescriptions for women's "niceness" remain strong. Furthermore, Jack (1999) found that women still engage in "preemptive self-condemnation" after displaying anger and aggression, conveying to others that they are cognizant of the negative connotations of their behavior and that by condemning it themselves, no further punishment is required. These findings argue against the alleged weakening of traditional anger display rules for the genders. What does other current research tell us? Findings are not entirely consistent.

Research Showing No (or Scant) Differences between Males and Females

Averill's widely cited 1982 study found no gender difference in frequency or triggers of anger (although women's anger was more intense, and women, more so than men, wanted to talk about angry incidents). In most samples, scores on measures of "trait anger" (one's general proneness to be aroused to anger) are about the same for males and females (Deffenbacher, 1992; Kopper & Epperson, 1991; Spielberger, 1991; Thomas & Williams, 1991). In a comparison of Japanese, Dutch, and Spanish college students, using vignettes about hypothetical anger-eliciting situations, gender differences in anger proneness were small or nonexistent (Ramirez, Fujihara, & van Goozen, 2001). However, it should be noted that many studies showing little difference between male and female anger involved measurement of the general proneness to become *aroused* to anger. Perhaps it is mainly in the public *display* of anger that men and women differ (see next section). Because research is so often conducted with undergraduate college students, a relatively privileged and homogeneous population, perhaps gender differences are less likely to be detected. Less social censure may result when college women express anger than when women in the culture at large do so. For example, Hatch and Forgays (2001) found that female college students were more likely to express anger overtly than were female office workers at the same college.

Research Showing Differences between Males and Females

In a questionnaire study that employed the Framingham Anger Scales, Thomas (1989) found differences between midlife males and females in two modes of anger expression. Whereas no gender differences were evident in anger suppression (anger-in) or anger vented outwardly, midlife women reported more somatic anger symptoms, such as shakiness and headache; women also scored higher on the tendency to talk about anger with a confidant. These findings were replicated in college students (Thomas & Williams, 1991), and other researchers also found that women wanted to discuss angry incidents, either with the instigator or a third party (e.g., Riley, Treiber, & Woods, 1989; Weidner, Istvan, & McKnight, 1989). A fair number of studies indicate that women experience emotions more intensely than men (e.g., Averill, 1982). New instruments, such as the Behavioral Anger Response Questionnaire (BARQ), tap additional ways of anger coping, such as diffusion and support seeking (Linden et al., 2003). On the BARQ, women reported using a wider range of anger coping styles than men, especially support seeking and anger diffusion.

Using data from Scherer's cross-cultural study involving 37 countries (1997), Fischer et al. (2004) found that men were more likely to report emotions categorized as "powerful" (e.g., anger), whereas women were more likely to report emotions categorized as "powerless" (e.g., sadness, fear, shame, guilt). However, with regard to a woman's freedom to express anger, status also enters the picture. When the 37 countries were categorized by the *status* of women, the researchers found that women reported more anger expression in countries where they have more power and status (e.g., the United States, United Kingdom) than in countries where they have lower power and status. Readers must remember, however, that even in countries like the United States, within-gender gradations of status are evident. Thomas (1993) found differences in anger expression when women were grouped according to the amount of prestige, autonomy, and control conferred by their occupation. Women in the "low prestige" category (e.g., homemakers, clerical workers) were more likely to suppress their anger. Replication of this study in men is needed.

Studies Focusing on the Meaning of Anger for Men and Women

Few previous studies have attempted to look at the antecedents of anger in men and women and their subjective experiences of angry emotionality. For more than 15 years I have led research teams conducting research about women's anger, involving more than 600 women in the United States, France, and Turkey (duMont et al., 1999; Fields et al., 1998; Thomas, 1993; Thomas & Atakan, 1993; Thomas, Smucker, & Droppleman, 1998). The focus of this program of research is anger in everyday life. The series of studies is guided by a conceptual model derived from existential and cognitive-behavioral theories of emotion (Thomas, 1991). While relying on standardized instruments in the early years (e.g., Thomas, 1989), in-depth interviews are currently used and permit study participants to ground their anger narratives in the complexities of cultural context and significant interpersonal relationships, which has been quite revealing. For example, black and white women in our 1993 study (Thomas, 1993) scored similarly on all quantitative anger measures. Only during in-depth interviews in 1998 did we discover the deep anger black women felt because of the racist treatment they encounter in daily life (Fields et al., 1998). Only in the interview studies did we discover the powerlessness that both black and white women feel when trying to get their husbands or partners to change (Fields et al., 1998; Thomas, Smucker, & Droppleman, 1998; see Thomas & Pollio [2002] for details about the philosophical underpinnings of our research methodology, derived from French philosopher Maurice Merleau-Ponty, and the specific procedure for conducting the phenomenological interviews and thematizing them).

Women's anger is most often triggered by lack of relationship reciprocity (Thomas, Smucker, & Droppleman, 1998). Study participants told us of being pressed, stretched, and almost pulled apart by multiple demands of their families. Their anger was intertwined with hurt and other painful feelings because their loved ones' actions violated an implicit relational contract. Expressing anger did not provide relief because it "breaks the circle" of relationships (Thomas et al., 1998, p. 316). Thus, anger was often muted; cooking metaphors such as "simmering," "stewing," or "slow boil" were used to describe an undercurrent of unexpressed anger within the body. Even women who were assertive at work and with friends were often reluctant to express anger to their male partners for fear of alienation or abandonment. Thus, women were presenting a false self to their partners much of the time. When anger was vented in an outburst, women expressed disbelief that they had behaved "out of character" (e.g., "I got so mad at him that I took his tea glass and shoved it in his face. He could not believe that I had done that to him. And I cried because I couldn't either" (Thomas, Smucker, & Droppleman, 1998, p. 318). Attempts to take the anger back via remorseful apology were common.

For women, chronic anger was often fueled by *vicarious stress*, that is, stressful events occurring in the lives of their significant others, over which they had no control. When asked, "What is your greatest stress?"

women did not respond in terms of the events listed on a typical stress questionnaire. They talked about their son's divorce, their grandson's illness, their husband's unemployment, an unmarried pregnant daughter, and frail elderly parents. This type of stress is particularly problematic because its consequences tend to be serious and long term, thus fueling a chronic, impotent kind of anger (Thomas, 1995). No matter how much the woman gives and cares, she cannot eradicate the stressor.

Recently, we turned our attention to men's anger, using the same in-depth interview methodology (Thomas, 2003a). Like women, the men we interviewed told their anger stories with embarrassed hesitance and nervous laughter. Like women, men often expressed guilt regarding their behavior when angry. But men differed from women in several ways, including the triggers of their anger and their choice of metaphors. Whereas women's anger was squarely grounded within their most intimate and significant relationships, men often became angered by global societal issues in which a principle was at stake or an injustice was perceived (e.g., believing the U.S. president was not doing the right thing). In essence, "a man's anger emanates from a perceived affront to his sense of control and/or his views of right and wrong" (Thomas, 2003, p. 167). Considerable anger was reported at recalcitrant mechanical objects (e.g., computers, cars, boats) or work-related problems (e.g., demanding customers, incompetent co-workers) that the men could not readily control or "fix." Metaphorically, men depicted anger as a potentially overwhelming force ("a runaway horse," "fire," "flood," or "vortex"). Unlike women, they had been forced to learn to fight in childhood to defend themselves from bullies and continued to have intense bodily arousal and impulses to hit when angry. For the most part, they no longer acted on these impulses, having eschewed physical fighting as they matured. Loss of control, as in the following example, created tremendous guilt:

> I was a Boy Scout leader. This kid and I never got along. He was not steering the canoe right. We hit the rock. And I hit him. It wasn't the right thing to do. He was startled and hurt. (Thomas, 2003a, p. 168)

Some men reported a pivotal moment when they became aware that they had the capability of killing another human with brute force (e.g., one study participant said he realized this as he had his hands around another boy's neck, choking him). As adults, to vent anger, men reported throwing hammers, hitting computers, or punching walls, although these actions provided little relief and left them feeling foolish afterward. Anger was also "shut down," "leashed," or "bridled" by withdrawing from interaction and isolating oneself. (See Thomas [2003a] for stylistic and linguistic differences between men and women while narrating anger stories and additional discussion of the findings.) In summary, these phenome-nological studies have revealed gender differences that cannot be detected in quantitative research that ignores the context of emotional experi-ences. Clearly, these gender differences have important implications for psychological intervention.

DSM GUIDELINES REGARDING CULTURAL ASSESSMENT—AND SOME CAVEATS

In the DSM-IV (APA, 1994), guidelines were provided for a "cultural formulation" to augment multiaxial diagnostic assessment. Clinicians were advised to write a narrative summary regarding (1) the cultural identity of the individual, (2) cultural explanations of the individual's ill-ness, (3) cultural factors related to psychosocial environment and levels of functioning (including role of religion and kin networks in support pro-vision), (4) cultural elements of the relationship between the individual and the clinician (especially differences in culture and social status between client and clinician), and (5) overall cultural assessment for diagnosis and care (APA, 1994). Although these guidelines were an important addition to the DSM, they are relatively brief and fail to address many issues.

Berg-Cross and Takushi-Chinen (1995) developed a 25-item inter-view that helps clinicians avoid errors of stereotyping of culturally differ-ent clients. Questions were formulated from psychodynamic, humanistic, family systems, and existential orientations. Of relevance to the clinician working with anger disorders, questions about shame and anger are included in this interview tool. Further information on this tool, and other approaches to multicultural assessment, may be found in Ponterotto, Gretchen, and Chauhan (2001). For a comprehensive assess-ment, the clinician must consider not only the client's culture but his or her gender and social status as well.

SPECIFIC ISSUES AND PROBLEMS REGARDING ASSESSMENT OF ANGER

Linguistic Considerations

Assessing a client's anger may be complicated when the client's native lan-guage was not English. Clients who learned in childhood to speak about their emotions in another language may not be able to find precise equiva-lents in English (just as some English words have no equivalents in other languages). Anger is not separate from other emotions in some languages. For example, in some African languages, the same word is used for anger and sadness (Leff, 1973). In the language of the Philippine headhunters (the Ilongot), the word *liget* covers not only anger but also grief (Rosaldo, 1984). Some languages have many words for variations of anger, whereas others have very few. The Utku Eskimos have no word for anger, whereas in the Tahitian language, there are 46 separate terms for types of *riri* (anger), indicating an elaborate cognitive structure (Levy, 1983). In Italian, distinctions are made between *rabbia* (rage), *ira* (the word you would use for God's anger), *collera* (wrath), and *furia* (a kind of blind anger in which there is a complete loss of emotional control). Although these linguistic considerations may not seem immediately relevant to the clinical practice of the average middle-class American therapist, recent studies document the multiplicity of languages now being spoken in the U.S. population. For example, 200 languages are spoken by students in the public schools in Chicago (Bracken & McCallum, 2001). Monolingual therapists may be at a distinct disadvantage in the near future.

Colloquial expressions may further complicate the task of understanding the meaning, and degree, of a client's anger. An American clinician may not understand what a British client means when he speaks of "throwing a wobbly" (which can involve alternating between despair and blaming all the others one can think of). The clinician may even need an American client to elaborate when she says she was "mad as a wet hen." Is this emotional state just as mad, or madder, than when she said "I wouldn't cross the street to piss on him if he was on fire"?

As mentioned previously, studies have shown that words in bilingual people's first language have richer meanings for them; thus, clients may tap into, and release, emotions more readily by talking about them in their first language. Altarriba (2003), who studies Latinos, recommends allowing clients to speak passionately in Spanish during a session. She asserts that even if the therapist is not bilingual, the emotional content of the story can be gleaned. Another study showed that adults who spoke Spanish as children provided more detail in Spanish than English when talking about their childhoods, providing useful insights to clinicians (Javier, Barroso, & Muqoz, 1993). These studies suggest the need, in some situations, for a therapist to collaborate with a colleague who is fluent in the client's first language.

Instrument Translation Issues

Although a fair number of anger instruments with respectable psychometric properties have been developed (e.g., Spielberger's State-Trait Anger Expression Inventory [STAXI]; see Spielberger et al. [1985] and Spielberger [1991]), clinicians should bear in mind that most were developed and normed on European American populations. It is not clear that these

instruments are appropriate to administer to culturally diverse populations, even if accurately translated, nor are there published norms to
which scores could be compared. Some cultural groups find it difficult to
respond to Likert scale items and consider English idioms confusing.
Translation of tests is expensive and difficult, and it cannot be assumed
that reliabilities will remain stable. At this writing, Spielberger's tool may
be the most often translated—known to have been translated into
Hebrew, Turkish, French, and Greek (Ayme, 2004; Ben-Zur & Zeidner,
1988; Sayar et al., 2000; Sukhodolsky, Demertzis, & Kostogiannis, 2001;
Thomas & Atakan, 1993). A final caution regarding instrumentation is
the male-oriented bias in item development, which emphasizes anger
behaviors such as hitting while excluding responses more common in
women, such as crying, consulting a confidant, and planning a problem-
solving response to the anger-producing situation (Thomas, 1993).

Instrument Social Desirability Issues

Asking people to report behaviors that are disapproved by the culture is
always a risky proposition. Do people honestly report the frequency and
intensity of their anger thoughts and behaviors, or are they tempted to
give socially desirable responses? Given the large number of studies,
including our own, that use self-report anger questionnaires, we
researchers apparently believe that study participants are reporting
behavior accurately. Harris (1996), based on her experience surveying
hundreds of university students, takes comfort in the fact that many of
the students express genuine interest in the topic of anger and wish to discuss their surveys after handing them in. However, college students are
accustomed to being tested, and clinicians should bear in mind that some
clients find it offensive or threatening to be asked to take "tests" rather
than talking about what is bothering them. When taking anger questionnaires, culturally different clients may be more concerned about pleasing
authority than about responding accurately. Paper and pencil tests should
be augmented by observing anger expression directly in the therapy session and interviewing a client's significant others about their perceptions
of the client's anger behaviors, if feasible (Mayne & Ambrose, 1999).

IMPLICATIONS FOR TREATMENT
OF ANGER-RELATED DISORDERS

There has been new interest in understanding people of other cultures
ever since the shocking events of September 11, 2001. Many Americans,
unaccustomed to enemy attacks on our own soil, have expressed the view

that "none of us will ever be the same again" (Thomas, 2003). There is no predictable endpoint of the stress engendered by 9/11, because terrorist attacks continue. Mental health professionals are struggling to understand the rage of suicide bombers and the cultural context that has produced them (Beck, 2002; Mumford, 2004). Back home, in their everyday clinical practice, clinicians are struggling to meet the needs of a clientele that is increasingly culturally diverse. Although racial and ethnic minorities comprise almost 31% of the U.S. population (U.S. Census Bureau, 2001), the clinical training of most practicing clinicians is culturally narrow and therapeutic methods are "dominated mainly by Western and anglophone paradigms" (Lunt & Poortinga, 1996, p. 504). Moreover, clinicians face an uphill battle to circumvent the sedimented cultural scripts of a lifetime. As Illovsky (2003) points out, "the counseling session lasts for only an hour, yet a person is in his or her cultural environment constantly when outside the session. That person's culture has been around and in him or her since birth. It would take an enormous act of faith, surrender, or naivete to conform to the therapist's directions—both in and out of the therapeutic session" (p. 29).

There is ample evidence that American clinicians must become more culturally competent. The U.S. Surgeon General's Report on Mental Health (1999) states that "many members of minority groups . . . experience the mental health system as the product of white, European culture . . . [finding] only clinicians who represent a white middle-class orientation, with its . . . biases, misconceptions, and stereotypes of other cultures" (p. 1). It is appalling that 50% of Hispanics (America's fastest-growing minority group) never return to a psychologist after the first session (Dingfelder, 2005). Fraga (cited in Dingfelder, 2005) attributes this dropout rate to Hispanic clients' feeling that they were not understood by the therapist and/or perceiving the therapist's values as antithetical to their own. Dropout rates of other minorities are equally dismaying. According to Ball (2001), Native Americans typically disengage after three psychological/mental health service visits. Asian Americans also tend to prematurely terminate from, and underutilize, counseling services (U.S. Department of Health and Human Services, 2001). Researchers have documented numerous barriers to mental health care access by African Americans and considerable dissatisfaction with the quality of services received (Hines-Martin et al., 2003; New Freedom Commission on Mental Health, 2003). Ivey (1995) contends, "Counseling is in the midst of a revolution, but many counselors and therapists remain unaware that it is even happening. Specifically, we are learning that our present theories and techniques are bound up with a particular and necessarily limited cultural framework" (p. 53). The Surgeon General's 2001 report on culture, race, and ethnicity even urges consideration of nontraditional modalities, such as "folk healing," that may be more culturally appropriate for some clients (U.S. Department of Health and Human Services, 2001).

What can the clinician do to provide better services to the client with an anger disorder? A cardinal mandate is inclusion of culture in the initial assessment of the client. With what aspects of the clinician's ethnic/cultural heritage does the client identify? What did the client learn about anger and its display (or inhibition) in the family of origin? To whom can anger be expressed in the client's culture (parents, teachers, friends, spouses, in-laws)? If the parents had differing cultural backgrounds—an increasingly common phenomenon in the United States—whose anger behaviors did the client tend to emulate? If a parent had anger control problems, did the client identify with the aggressor? To what extent does discrimination on the basis of ethnicity, color, gender, or race fuel the client's anger? Is the client marginalized from mainstream culture on the basis of sexual orientation, disability, or other characteristics? What violations of cultural values provoke anger? Core values worth exploration may include caring, closeness, family, justice, harmony, equality, dignity, achievement, autonomy, responsibility, brotherhood, and community (Brondolo, 2000).

To adequately serve the culturally different client, the therapist must consider his or her own values. The following white Euro-American middle-class values are well entrenched in business, politics, and health care: (1) pursuit of achievement, occupational and financial success, and status; (2) speed, activity, and efficiency; (3) youth, beauty, health, and self-reliance; (4) science and the use of technology; (5) materialism, consumerism, and use of disposable items; (6) social and geographical mobility; and (7) competitive and aggressive behavior instead of cooperation (Murray & Zentner, 1979). Given that most American therapists are white, they should reflect on the degree to which they endorse these ethnocentric values. Giordano (cited in Gottesfeld, 1981) alleges that upwardly mobile, middle-class professionals may have a personal ambivalence toward ethnicity, having left their own ethnicity and its values behind. For white therapists, self-reflection should include humble consideration of the accoutrements of the "good life" that the culture automatically confers to them by the privilege of being white. Reflecting on one's tendency to stereotype culturally different persons is essential. Although much stereotyping behavior is automatic and unconscious, a first step in reducing the tendency to stereotype minority clients is to ask oneself: What judgments am I making on the basis of this individual's skin color, accent, clothing, or demeanor? Finally, when dealing with clients who have anger-related problems, it behooves therapists to examine their own anger issues and conflict management style.

Comprehensive textbooks for multicultural counseling and therapy (MCT) are beginning to appear in the literature (e.g., Ponterotto et al., 1995; Sue & Sue, 1999), and readers are encouraged to avail themselves of these resources. However, most MCT texts do not devote extensive discussion to anger-related issues. Snippets of advice to clinicians can be found in journal articles and book chapters (e.g., Tanaki-Matsumi, 1995). For example, Gomez warns practitioners to avoid asking Hispanic clients to directly confront significant others because this tactic is incompatible with their beliefs about preservation of relationship harmony (cited in Dingfelder, 2005). Asian Americans are known to prefer clinicians who assume a consulting role when the presenting problem is of external etiology (for example, racist treatment) but take on a facilitator role (mobilizing indigenous support systems) when the problem is of internal etiology (e.g., depression) (Atkinson, Kim, & Caldwell, 1998). Clinicians who wish to enlarge their repertoire of anger control approaches could learn more about yoga, meditation, and other non-Western techniques through classes or self-study materials.

Several therapists have written edifying articles about working with clients who experience anger fueled by racial discrimination. Christensen (1995) has developed a model for therapist development of cross-cultural awareness, in which the therapist acknowledges (1) growing up in a racist society, (2) racism's effects on herself and her clients, and (3) that she may need additional training to deal with the effects of the aforementioned. Abernethy (1995) called the management of "racial anger" a critical skill in the therapist's cultural competence, pointing out that racial anger has energizing as well as destructive potential. Thompson (1996), after treating many black patients, asserted that the therapist must often perform "racial surgery" to help blacks make a distinction between those struggles that would be theirs *regardless* of race and those that might be their lot *because* of race. Illovsky (2003) warns that a white therapist's warmth and friendliness could be perceived by a minority client as superficial. Furthermore, the white therapist could be viewed as someone who obtained the job because of privileged status in the culture, or even as someone who took a job that a minority could have filled.

Some scholars have proposed that clients may fare better when matched with therapists of their own race or ethnicity. The findings of a recent meta-analysis argue against this assumption. Studies between 1991 and 2001 of outcomes for African American and Caucasian American clients and clinicians who were (or were not) racially matched were included in the analysis (Shin et al., 2005). No significant differences were found between matched and unmatched dyads with respect to overall client functioning, dropout rates, and the number of sessions attended. The researchers speculated that racial/ethnic matching may be more important for people who speak English as a second language. They also noted that similarity in attitudes, values, or personality may be more important to clients than the clinician's race or ethnicity. In a study where all the clients were Asian American and all the counselors were European American, Kim, Ng, and Ahn (2005) found that a match in client and therapist worldviews was an important factor, resulting in a stronger working alliance and client perceptions of greater empathy.

Although ethnic similarity has received little attention in the literature, at least one clinician has warned about countertransference issues that can complicate therapy when patient and therapist are ethnically similar (Gottesfeld, 1981). She describes a case of "too much psychic together-ness" when she was seeing a woman with Italian Catholic heritage like her own (p. 36). Gottesfeld (1981) had enjoyed recognizing "so many things from my own early childhood—speech inflections, words, foods, primitive ideas such as the evil eye (*malocchio*) and the horn (*cornuto*) for protection against it—that I shared with her a delicious sense of 'our thing' (*cosa nostra*)" (p. 35). The therapist's familiarity with Italian culture, however, became a detriment rather than an advantage. This case provides further food for thought about the matter of therapist-client cultural matching.

Matching of therapist and client on the basis of gender has been studied by several researchers, but none of them discovered a relationship of gender matching to treatment process, length, or outcomes (Parker-Sloat, 2003; Zlotnick, Elkin, & Shea, 1998). However, gender matching in the treatment of anger disorders has not been examined. As Jack (2001) points out, women rarely name anger as the problem for which they enter therapy (depression or anxiety may be the official presenting problem). Female clients may benefit from the self-disclosing and self-involving interventions used by a feminist therapist (Worell & Remer, 2003). These interventions, often frowned upon by traditional therapeutic approaches, may be especially important when working with female clients who have not yet discovered their anger. In a case discussed recently by Remer and Oakley (2005), the therapist's self-involving intervention was effective. "Ann," despite many positive attributes and academic success (e.g., high school valedictorian), had experienced years of being devalued by her parents. After several sessions, the therapist told Ann, "I'm very angry with your parents right now . . . If they were in the next room, I would want to express my anger to them" (p. 9). Ann found this quite revelatory. In the next session, Ann reported, "I have never considered that I had a right to be angry at them" (the parents) (p. 9). Ultimately, Ann discovered her own anger, which empowered her to confront her parents.

Some clients may benefit from participating in psychoeducational anger management (AM) group work in combination with individual counseling. Because anger is an interpersonal emotion, new modes of expression are more likely to be incorporated into one's repertoire when practiced with other people—ideally, supportive individuals who share the goal of improved anger management. Gender- or race-specific groups merit consideration. For example, AM groups designed specifically for African Americans have proved valuable because of common racist provocations faced by these individuals (Wilson, Davidson, & Reneau, 2000). Thomas (2001) has provided a model for conducting women's AM groups in the community, based on the premise that women still have some gender-specific anger issues (e.g., the old-fashioned notion that anger is unfeminine and unattractive). Women can be taught to think of their anger metaphorically as a white light, a clear, strong emotion that energizes them to combat injustice and relationship inequity (Avis, 1991). Men's AM groups may be advantageous as well. Men may need to talk with one another about the detrimental effects of socialization for aggressive masculinity. Instead of viewing cool and calm behavior as cowardly, men may need to reframe such behavior as "strong, powerful, and male" (Deffenbacher, 1992, p. 198).

Clearly, much more cross-cultural research is needed. There is insufficient research on cultural aspects of anger and effective therapeutic interventions with cross-cultural clientele, perhaps because anger itself has achieved its proper prominence as a research topic only within the past 25 years. It is unknown how cognitive-behavioral and rational-emotive therapies (i.e., those therapies with the best empirical evidence of efficacy for anger disorders) are received by clients in many cultures or what adaptations might be required. It is my hope that this chapter stimulates some readers to contribute to the clinical and/or empirical literature. A plethora of research questions and treatment issues remain to be addressed.

BRIEF REFLECTIONS ON THE CASE OF ANTHONY

Cultural issues are not prominent in the case material, as reported, although Anthony is said to be of Italian descent and his wife is of Puerto Rican descent. There may be marital issues related to cultural differences, especially vis-à-vis parenting, financial responsibility, extended family, and work ethics. It would be fruitful to explore which aspects of his cultural heritage (if any) are salient to him and which aspects of his wife's heritage may be operational in family functioning. When he described his punitive and disliked mother as "old world," one suspects that he may not have been appreciative of whatever characteristics of the Italian culture that she embodied for him. Given that his maternal grandmother and maternal uncle (his abuser) were also negative figures in his child-hood, it is improbable that Anthony developed a strong, positive identi-fication with Italian culture. Stronger in the case material are the gender issues. Perhaps initiated as a defense against the shame generated by his uncle's sexual abuse and the attention deficit hyperactivity disorder (ADHD) and dyslexia that hampered his academic achievement, Anthony developed a hypermasculine "jock" persona. Interestingly, it was during his football years when he and his wife Joanna got married. If part of his appeal for Joanna was this hypermasculine persona, her current dissatis-faction with him is understandable: He did not live up to the masculine ideal after his college years. He failed to fulfill his father's aspirations, failed to complete his education, failed to establish himself as successful as a "working man," failed to remain physically fit, and failed to be a good provider for his family. Currently, he spends more time at home parenting the children, cooking, and doing housework during the evening while his wife works. It is unclear how these typical gender stereotype reversals impact on Anthony's sense of himself. He appears to have great ambivalence toward women, exhibiting explosive anger at his wife, daughters, and the daughter's softball team, while gravitating toward female friends outside the family who "understand and care." Little information is available in Feindler's case presentation about Anthony's gender role socialization with regard to anger behavior. He appears to have identified with his disliked childhood aggressor (his mother, who hit him in the face), as evidenced by his current behavior: He has now become the aggressor with his children (although he uses his voice as the weapon to wound and control them). Anthony appears to have poor insight into his anger behavior, presenting the clinician with a substantial challenge.

CHAPTER 5

Psychoanalytic Treatment of Anger and Aggression

Danielle Knafo and Seymour Moscovitz

INTRODUCTION TO A PSYCHOANALYTIC APPROACH

We live in an age of anger, the keynote emotion for the 21st century (Knafo, 2004). We encounter rage and hatred in daily news stories of terrorist bombings, beheadings, vengeful atrocities, and ever-spiraling retaliations. On a local level, we may witness the fulminations of a rageful motorist, cut off by another driver, both seemingly absorbed in their own worlds, unaware of the existence of the other, ready to kill over a parking space.

Of all the emotions, anger is the most empowering, and next to joy, it is the most gratifying (DiGiuseppe, 2005). Fueled by a legitimate sense of injustice, anger can be the basis for reform and revolution. Distorted by self-referential ideas of persecution and betrayal, it can also motivate acts of destruction, cruelty, and revenge. How shall clinicians respond to this pandemic? Should anger be considered pathology, something to be controlled and managed? When is it adaptive for the individual and society, and when does it warrant intervention by the mental health professional?

This chapter offers a response to these questions from the perspective of contemporary psychoanalysis. We shall attempt to present an overview of analytic thought about anger and aggression and to outline a general approach to the treatment of clients who present with dysfunctional, anger-related symptoms. The case of Anthony will provide a focus to illustrate how a psychodynamic formulation of anger may be applied in the clinical setting.

Preliminary Definitions

We begin by defining the principal terms of our discussion—*aggression, anger, violence,* and *abuse*—because they have multiple meanings depending on context.

Aggression as Behavior and Instinctual Drive

In ordinary usage, *aggression* refers to behavior that aims to remove obstacles to the fulfillment of the individual's desires or aims to remove threats to the individual's well-being (Rizzuto, Meissner, & Buie, 2004). In classical psychoanalytic theory, *aggression* refers to a basic biopsychological or instinctual "drive," a motivating and propelling force within the person.

Freud (1905) originally viewed aggression as sadism, a component of the sexual instinct, and the means used to subdue the object of desire. He (1915a) later viewed aggression as a form of self-preservative instinct (an "ego" instinct), needed to protect the self against environmental threat. In this model, Freud uncoupled aggression from the sexual instinct. A third revision of instinct theory appeared in Freud's groundbreaking 1920 monograph *Beyond the Pleasure Principle,* in which he posited the existence of two major forces: eros, a life instinct that seeks to bind and unite, and thanatos, a death instinct that seeks to reduce tension to a zero point and bring the living being back to an inorganic state.

Most analysts subscribing to Freud's theory of drives have not followed this speculative and far-reaching postulation of a basic death instinct but have instead used the dual-drive theory of libido and aggression to refer to the coexistence of sexual/erotic and destructive impulses as basic to human nature. These theorists (e.g., Brenner, Arlow, Kernberg) do not view aggression as simply reactive to frustration but rather see it as a primary motive in human interactions.

In psychoanalytic theory, *aggression* is a theoretical construct referring to an unconscious motivating process or drive. What is experienced consciously or expressed in action is always a *derivative* form of the drive. As drive derivatives (or wishes for gratification) enter awareness, they are modified by the mechanisms of defense. This process is explained further in our discussion of the conflict model.

Anger as Affect Signal and Communication

Aggression also needs to be differentiated from the emotion of *anger.* In ordinary language, anger and other emotions are conscious experiences that include components of physiological arousal, thought processes, and behavior. When people are angry, they often say their "blood is boiling," reflecting their state of physical arousal; or they "see red," indicating how they perceive and cognize the world; or they "go ballistic," referring to behavior such as punching a wall or pounding their fist or shouting.

In psychiatric parlance, anger is an *affect*, like sadness, joy, pity, or fear. Psychiatric terminology (American Psychiatric Association, 2000) describes affect in terms of intensity (from mild irritation to rage), range (from narrowly constricted to broad and full ranging), stability (from fleeting and labile to consistent), and appropriateness (either to the content of one's thoughts or to the situation). When an affect is pervasive, it is often referred to as a *mood*.

Classical psychoanalysts originally viewed affects as states of tension arising from ungratified drives. Freud (1915b) viewed affect as originating at the interface of psyche and soma, mind and body, and he viewed affect expression as a way of discharging the state of tension that accumulates in the psyche. This hydraulic model of affect likened the mind to a vat that could be filled or emptied of its contents. Common expressions such as "bottled up emotion" or the view that anger can be reduced by vigorous physical activity refer to this early Freudian hydraulic model (Brenner, 1992; Freud, 1915a, 1920; Rizzuto Meissner, & Buie, 2004).

Freud (1926) later came to view affect as having a "signal" function, too, alerting the individual to the presence of danger. Some danger situations are realistic, external threats to the physical or emotional well-being of the individual and trigger *fear*. Other dangers are based on fantasized threats to the individual based on the "calamities of childhood" (Brenner, 1992), such as fear of object loss, fear of loss of love, or fear of bodily harm. Such an alarm system has an obvious adaptive value when the source of danger is real, and fear is a basic emotion necessary to survival. When the danger is more fantasized than real, however, the result is *neurotic anxiety* that can lead to symptoms and inhibitions. Freud came to view the signal function of anxiety as an intrapsychic process triggering the various unconscious defense mechanisms (e.g., denial, undoing, isolation of affect, repression, projection) to protect the psyche from internal threat.

Contemporary theorists (Fonagy et al., 2002) have also emphasized the signal function of affect and view the ability to *regulate* affect (rather than simply discharge it) as essential to healthy functioning. Anger is not a substance that needs to be eliminated or a pressure to be relieved by cathartic activity, but rather, it is a form of endopsychic communication.

Anger, like anxiety and fear, has both adaptive and maladaptive functions. It can alert the individual to injustices, frustrations, and impingements from the environment and guide instrumental behavior to correct or alleviate a situation that is inimical to the individual's well-being. It can also serve an adaptive, interpersonal, communicative function in conveying the urgency and intensity of one's needs. If based on distortion of external reality or if expressed in ways that are destructive of ties to others, anger can trigger maladaptive behavior

Violence as Instrumental or Reactive Aggression

Violence has been defined as the "intended infliction of bodily harm on another person" (Perelberg, 1999). This definition references the actual violation of another's bodily boundaries and stresses the conscious and deliberate nature of the act rather than the unconscious fantasies underlying it. *Aggression,* in contrast to violence, is a broader term that encompasses behavior ranging from self-assertion to gross destructiveness; aggression does not necessarily entail physical harm to another.

Violent acts may be further divided into those that are *predatory* versus those that are emotionally *reactive* (Meloy, 1992). Predatory acts are planned, purposeful, and carried out without emotion to obtain an instrumental gain for the predator. Reactive violent acts, by contrast, are responses to real or imagined threats to the self; they generally do not seek a clear, extrinsic goal, like monetary gain, but are necessitated by nonrational emotional needs.

A related distinction is that between *sadistic* and *nonsadistic* acts of violence or aggression. In sadistic acts, the actor perceives and obtains pleasure from the suffering of the victim. In nonsadistic acts, the actor is usually oblivious of the victim's suffering. For example, a man may push his way through a crowd to get onto a subway before the door closes, ignoring that he is stepping on other people's toes, but he does not necessarily obtain pleasure, per se, from the suffering caused by this self-centered behavior. Sadistic acts, by contrast, always involve recognition of the other's suffering, but rather than arousing compassion, this awareness brings pleasure.

Abuse as Relational Aggression

Finally, *abuse* may be defined as a form of relational aggression that attempts to exert power, domination, and control over an intimate partner by means of threats, put-downs, guilt-inducing manipulations, economic leverage, sexual coercion, and isolation from others (Dutton, 1998). Abuse may be emotional as well as physical, but it does not always entail actual violence.

Conceptualization of Anger and Aggression

A complete account of anger and aggression requires an understanding of both the individual's conscious experience and intentions as well as his or her unconscious motivations and processes. Our conceptualization will be divided into two parts: the first provides a phenomenological description of aggressive acts as experienced and justified by the actor; the second offers a psychodynamic formulation of underlying conflicts and deficits about which the actor is largely unaware.

A Phenomenological Model of Aggression

All forms of intentional aggressive behavior can be described as *means* to accomplish a variety of *ends* or *goals*.[1] Some goals have clear extrinsic value, and aggressive behavior may be an instrumental means to achieve them (e.g., a robber uses threats of violence to obtain monetary gain). Other goals have an intrinsic meaning to the individual (e.g., a batterer may use threats of violence to prevent an intimate partner from leaving home).

In its behavioral sense, then, aggression is a relational phenomenon involving an actor and a target or victim, the relationship being either *intimate* (lovers, parents, and children), *personal* (friends or co-workers), or *impersonal* (strangers, other passengers on a subway, inanimate objects). The choice of the target depends on the meaning and motivation of the act of aggression. In domestic violence, the target *must* be the intimate partner and cannot be substituted. In other forms of violence, the targets may be known to the perpetrator but not intimately (e.g., school shootings where the perpetrators seek revenge).

Although many people claim that they were "not thinking" when they committed a violent or aggressive act, even these rapidly occurring, "impulsive," and seemingly unpremeditated acts have a temporal sequence. This sequence begins with the arousal of a desire or perception of threat and culminates with the disinhibition of control. In reactive forms of aggression, anger is the usual trigger or instigator of action. Well-functioning individuals are able to stop themselves from carrying out aggressive acts, even when angered, by considering the likely negative consequences to self and others. Anxiety functions effectively as a signal causing the person to "put on the brakes." Empathy for the intended target also serves as an inhibitor, as does the anticipation of guilt, remorse, or shame if the act were executed.

People with dysfunctional anger and aggression, on the other hand, fail to consider or anticipate the likely negative consequences of their actions and lack sufficient empathy for the needs and feelings of others to deter their behavior. They may feel regret after the fact for the trouble created, but even these negative consequences do not deter future occurrences of similar behavior.

---

[1]The following discussion derives from unpublished lectures and seminars given by Robert Guglielmo, Ph.D., formerly Director of Mental Health Services, in the context of one author's (S.M.) work within the New York City Family Court.

Psychodynamic Models of Aggression and Anger

Contemporary psychoanalysis encompasses many different points of view; no single explanatory system or treatment model exists that is applicable to all clients and situations. This discussion begins with a brief review of two major psychoanalytic approaches to emotional problems: one that views symptoms as manifestations of internal *conflict* and another that regards symptoms as by-products of *deficits* in personality functioning (Livesley, 2003).

The Conflict Model. Psychoanalysis has historically viewed symptoms as products of intrapsychic conflict. In contemporary psychoanalytic conflict theory (Brenner, 1982, 1992, 2000), symptoms (and other forms of overt behavior and conscious experience) are thought to represent *compromise formations* among the competing and conflicting influences of psychic life, including our wishes and desires, inner moral prohibitions, ambitions and ideals, anxiety and other dysphoric affects, the mechanisms of defense we use to ward off these unpleasurable feelings, and the constraints of reality. The manifest behavior of the individual reflects the outcome of processes that operate outside of conscious awareness and represents a compromise among multiple determinants. Not all compromise formations are adaptive. Those that impair one's functioning and/or cause distress to the self or others often become the focus of clinical attention.

By regarding symptoms and behavior as compromise formations, psychoanalysis shifted the focus of treatment from the overt symptom to the interaction of personality factors that predispose the individual to develop symptomatic behavior. The goal of treatment is to achieve a change in the overall configuration that will then result in enduring and fundamental improvement at the overt and symptomatic level. To achieve this goal requires that the client gain increased insight and awareness of that which had previously been unconscious.

The Deficit Model. In contrast to this model of intrapsychic conflict, other theorists, such as Heinz Kohut (1971, 1972, 1977), have viewed anger, and especially *rage*, as reflecting the "disintegration" of a core self in response to empathic failures of the environment. By *environment*, these analysts refer to the other people in the individual's social world *as they exist for that individual*. For narcissistic patients, in particular, who have not developed a cohesive sense of self, other people are used as "self-objects," extensions of the person rather than separate autonomous individuals. The function of self-objects is to provide soothing and other ministrations, such as admiring, validating, and recognizing the patient as a thinking and feeling being. These functions are essential to maintain self-esteem in the face of criticism, frustration, and failure because the person with a narcissistic personality disorder is unable to provide them for himself or herself.

Developmentally, the need for self-objects is normal, indeed essential. To have a parent who "mirrors" the child's emerging self (e.g., the mother who has a gleam in her eye when her child takes a first step) or who allows the child to merge with an idealized and powerful other (e.g., the father who protects the child from harm) provides security and confidence. If environmental parents provide reasonably empathic responses to these needs and if their inevitable empathic failures are not traumatic in kind or degree, the child will develop a strong sense of self and will be able to withstand life's frustrations and setbacks with reasonable equanimity. If the parents have failed to serve these mirroring and idealizing self-object functions or have exposed the child to traumatic disruptions, the child's sense of self will be vulnerable to "narcissistic rage" (Kohut, 1972), Kohut's term for the child's response to the failure to meet these needs. Analysts following this model view anger and aggression as *reactive* to frustration, disappointment, and empathic failures of the environment rather than as primary manifestations of an aggressive "drive." The goal of treatment is to repair the deficits in personality that leave the individual vulnerable to disorganization and rage reactions.

Another deficit for individuals with anger-related problems appears in their inability to reflect on emotional experience and to comprehend its meaning. Fonagy et al. (2002) have referred to this capacity as "mentalized affectivity," a conjunction of reflective self-awareness and emotional experience. Attachment theory (Fonagy, 2001) has infused psychoanalytic theory with findings demonstrating the relationship between the security of the infant-mother bond and mentalization. Fonagy believes that in early development, the child seeks in the maternal caregiver a reflection of his or her mental states and recognition that he or she is an individual with intentions, needs, and desires. When the child is unable to find his or her self in the mind of the mother, the child is unable to develop a "theory of mind"—that is, a coherent representation of the mental states of self and others.

Lacking a capacity for mentalization creates a deficit in the ability to use verbal forms of symbolic communication of internal states of mind. Internal and external realities become confused (Perelberg, 1999), so the individual feels he or she must carry out in action what might otherwise be expressed in language, thought, play, or fantasy. Britton (1995) has remarked on the confusion between belief and fantasy in violence-prone individuals. A blurring of boundaries between fantasy and reality, thought and action, feelings and facts, body and mind, self and other characterizes the psychological functioning of these patients. As a result, it becomes necessary for such individuals to carry out actions against the body or person of the other, especially when that other represents intolerable aspects of the self that must be eliminated. As is shown in the case example, Anthony's berating his daughter's Little League team members for their lack of competitive drive reflects such a need to externalize undesirable parts of himself and to use aggressive means to coerce change in the object of the projection. Object relations theory refers to this process as *projective identification* (Klein, 1946).

The developmental goal is to cultivate the child's capacity to be aware of emotions as guides to adaptive behavior, without necessarily being compelled by emotion toward action forms of discharge. The nearly automatic link between intense anger arousal and aggressive behavior reflects a lack of self-reflective functioning and affect regulation (Krystal, 2004). When these capacities have not evolved during the normal course of development, psychoanalytic treatment may be necessary to resume a developmental process that failed to complete its full arc.

Psychoanalytic Treatment of Personality Disorder

Repetitive, self-defeating, and maladaptive expressions of anger therefore may indicate a disturbance in personality functioning rather than an isolated occurrence of poor behavioral control. As discussed in the literature (Dutton, 1998), these disorders typically fall within the spectrum of borderline personality organization. These clients exhibit personality disorders marked by pervasive disturbances in impulse control, affect regulation, self-reflective capacity, and the quality of object relations. We suggest that a modified form of psychoanalytic psychotherapy is an appropriate modality of treatment for anger-related disorders arising within severe personality disorder.

Mechanisms of Change in Psychoanalytic Psychotherapy

The therapeutic action in psychodynamic psychotherapy relies on two primary mechanisms of change: insight and internalization of the therapeutic relationship. These therapeutic factors are analogous to the distinction between conflict and deficit. In the conflict model, the therapist's clarification and interpretation of the meaning of the client's behavioral symptoms are intended to increase insight, or the awareness of previously unconscious needs, wishes, and fears. Repeatedly, and over time, this heightened awareness allows for new and more adaptive responses to situations that have evoked angry responses in the past.

Another major mechanism of change involves the therapeutic relationship itself. In psychoanalytic treatment, the habitual ways the client perceives and relates to others gradually become evident in relation to the therapist. The therapist's relatively nonjudgmental, concerned, exploratory, and empathic stance—avoiding direct methods of influence (e.g., giving advice)—allows the client's habitual relationship patterns to emerge in the foreground and become enacted in the transference. Beyond the mere repetition of old patterns, however, psychoanalytic therapy also provides an opportunity to experience a *new* relationship pattern, which then becomes internalized as a schema for current and future relationships. For example, when the therapist responds to the client's hostility not with anger or retaliation but with empathy and interest, a more benign interactional pattern is created. This new pattern of interaction is gradually internalized, altering the representational schemas that mold and influence behavior.

Empirical Evidence for the Model

Systematic, empirical research on the efficacy of psychodynamic treatment of anger-related disorders is for the most part lacking (DiGiuseppe, 2005). The dearth of studies may be attributed to two main factors. The first is the relative de-emphasis on nomothetic research in psychoanalysis in general, where the case study method has prevailed. Many analysts believe that empirical research does not do justice to the complexity and inter-relatedness of the variables at work in psychoanalytic treatment and to the unconscious processes involved. Another reason for this paucity of research is that anger-related symptoms are viewed as manifestations of more general personality functioning and disorder.

What does exist is a growing literature demonstrating the effectiveness of psychodynamic treatment for personality disorders, particularly borderline and narcissistic conditions, in which anger is frequently a prominent diagnostic feature and focus of treatment. These studies include both naturalistic and controlled designs. We briefly cite some of the major studies and meta-analyses providing empirical support for long-term psychodynamic treatment of personality disorder.

Leichsenring and Leibing (2003) conducted a meta-analysis to address the effectiveness of psychodynamic and cognitive-behavioral therapy of personality disorder in studies published between 1974 and 2001. These studies demonstrated significant effects for both treatment conditions, which were long lasting. Three studies using psychodynamic therapy showed a mean recovery rate from personality disorder of 59%.

Batemen and Fonagy (2001) also demonstrated longer-lasting benefits and more substantial gains among borderline clients treated in a psychoanalytically oriented partial hospital program, compared with those who were provided standard psychiatric treatment, over a follow-up period of 18 months after discharge. Some measures included social adjustment, self-harm, and suicide, all of which reflect better control of anger and impulsive behavior.

Perry, Banon, and Ianni (1999) performed a meta-analysis of psychodynamic, cognitive, and supportive therapy of personality disorders. All three types of treatment condition showed improvement.

Stevenson and Mears (1992) conducted an outcome study of 30 clients with borderline personality disorder who were treated with a self-psychological psychoanalytic model. Outcome measures included the number of episodes of violent and self-harming behavior, both of which symptoms showed significant improvement ($p < .001$) from assessment to conclusion of treatment (a 1-year period). These improvements were evident in a follow-up conducted 1 year after termination.

We regard these studies as a promising beginning in providing an empirically supported basis for the effectiveness of psychodynamic treatment approaches to a broad array of personality disturbances, of which anger-related disorders may be considered a subset.

THE CASE OF ANTHONY

Revised Diagnostic Impressions

In our view, Anthony's frequent episodes of dysfunctional anger may be understood as manifestations of a personality disorder. We will attempt to show that his intermittent explosions and eruptions of anger emerged in response to threats to his self-esteem and identity. Anthony's profile on the State-Trait Anger Expression Inventory (STAXI) is consistent with these long-standing and traitlike problems in impulse control. His childhood difficulties with attention, impulsivity, and low frustration tolerance suggest some neuropsychological basis to his vulnerabilities. Anthony's history of sexual abuse trauma also most likely contributed to his predisposition to rageful reactions.

Phenomenological and Psychodynamic Formulations

The sparseness of available history reflects Anthony's inability to present a coherent narrative connecting events, people, and affects in his life. What Anthony does provide by way of history is a picture of a family in which his father was strict and his mother was physically abusive. The lack of expression of affection and warmth toward Anthony may have contributed to insecure (disorganized) attachment (Fonagy, 2001), a general risk factor for later severe relationship disturbance, including violence toward intimate partners. Infants with disorganized attachment exhibit undirected and disoriented behavior upon reunion with their mothers (Fonagy, 2001).

In this context of familial relational deprivation, rejection, and maltreatment, Anthony developed a relationship with a maternal uncle, a seminary student aspiring to the priesthood, who on one hand sexually abused him but on the other hand provided attention, affection, and recognition lacking elsewhere.

A psychoanalytic understanding of the influence of trauma, such as Anthony's history of sexual abuse, emphasizes not only the actual events that occurred but also their meaning for the experiencing subject (Knafo & Feiner, 2005). During the period of sexual encounters with his uncle, Anthony does not appear to have consciously experienced this contact as abusive. It was only later, upon reaching puberty, that he became aware of its exploitative significance, giving new meaning to this part of his history. Freud referred to this delayed trauma experience as *deferred action*. Anthony's hatred and rage toward the uncle, once a loved and admired figure, and other caretakers who failed to protect him, may be viewed as a reaction to the shame he associated with the circumstances in which his affectional needs were met. Anthony's displays of anger as an adult, although inappropriate in their current context, can therefore be better understood as a repetition of the dynamic conflict triggered by association from present to past. Essentially, his outbursts represent a defensive effort, when threatened, to deny vulnerability and assert a masculine identity.

The incident that led to Anthony's referral for treatment involved his launching into a sharp rebuke to a group of 9-year-old girls whom he was coaching. Anthony berated them for their "lack of competitive drive." In Anthony's account, he was consciously attempting to motivate these children to fulfill their potential, a "principled justification" (or rationalization) for his behavior, but one that ignored the distress and harm he was causing. Phenomenologically, his actions represented a reactive, nonsadistic form of aggression. Other targets of his anger have included people (usually, although not always, female) whom he perceives in a weakened or vulnerable position.

Psychodynamically, Anthony's aggressive behavior reflects a mechanism of splitting and projective identification in which he perceives shameful, weak, and undesirable (i.e., "feminine") parts of himself in others whom he then attempts to control through coercive, angry behavior. By whipping a team of Little Leaguers into shape, he hoped to cure his own lack of masculine/phallic ambition, drive, and competitiveness.

In relation to powerful figures (usually, although not exclusively, men), another repetitive pattern emerges in which Anthony provokes anger in others and makes himself the target. For example, he remained parasitically dependent on his parents until his father threatened him when he was 25 to "Get out and get a job or I'll kick you out!" Even with this ultimatum, Anthony lacked the initiative to find a job on his own. With his father's help, he obtained employment at a company where he remained for 21 years. His boss, whom he identified as a father figure, eventually fired him for his chronic lateness and absence. Finally, his wife, a train conductor who "wears the pants in the family" and earns double his income, threatened to divorce him if he did not get help for his abusive behavior. These patterns in which Anthony either expresses anger excessively or provokes anger in others are deeply ingrained, pervasive, and long standing. They also reflect the repetitive, maladaptive, and self-defeating behavior associated with personality disorder. Although distressed by the adverse consequences of his actions, Anthony has been unable to alter his behavior.

A psychoanalytic understanding of a symptom attempts to appreciate what the client gains from his behavior, however maladaptive it might appear. Anthony's angry outbursts served multiple functions, keeping others at a distance (in accordance with his avoidant attachment style), discharging tension, disconfirming his sense of personal vulnerability, and shoring up a sense of masculine power and activity.

Strengths and Assets

Anthony exhibits several strengths that might augur favorably for a psychodynamic treatment. His shame over his failure to live up to his personal ideals and standards is a potential motivator for change, as is his distress over the suffering he has caused and continues to cause others. This distress, including some depressive symptoms, may thus be viewed as a positive prognostic sign. According to Klein (1975), the depressive position is viewed as a developmental accomplishment rather than a pathological affect state. For Kleinians, the depressive position marks the person's ability to experience concern, guilt, mourning, and desire to repair the damage one has inflicted on loved ones.

Anthony's capacity for reflective self-awareness, although not well developed, is present in nascent form and could be developed through psychotherapeutic treatment. He also has a capacity to sustain long-term relationships, as evidenced by his marital relationship and his dedication to his family. Although a principal arena for the expression of his problems, Anthony's family has nonetheless provided stability and support over the years. His "emotional affairs" may reflect both a difficulty expressing his needs within one primary relationship and a capacity to establish close connections with others. Finally, Anthony's ability to persevere in a task, as evidenced by his work history, is another positive indicator that he will be able to sustain motivation for a lengthy psychodynamic treatment that has many ups and downs.

CLINICAL ISSUES AND RECOMMENDATIONS

Psychoanalytic treatment encompasses both psychotherapy and psychoanalysis proper. Classically, psychoanalysis is conducted with three to five sessions per week in which the client lies on a couch and free-associates while the analyst remains neutral (i.e., does not favor one aspect of a conflict over another) and offers interpretations of the patient's defenses (resistance) and repetitive patterns, especially as enacted with the analyst in the treatment setting (transference). Modifications of this approach change several of these parameters, such as reducing the frequency of sessions to one to three sessions per week and using a face-to-face seating arrangement. The therapist focuses on transference as well as situations in the client's current life, with somewhat less reconstruction of early childhood precedents, although these are not excluded when relevant. The analyst may use supportive techniques, such as providing education, advice, and reassurance, all the while respecting the structure and boundaries of treatment.

This mixture of supportive and insight-oriented elements reflects the understanding that clients with anger-related personality disorders have both deficits in their functioning and intrapsychic conflicts that require exploration and interpretation. Most such clients would be unable to withstand the deprivations inherent in an unmodified analysis and might exhibit a degree of regression that would be counterproductive. To forestall such regression, it is important to anchor the client in reality, especially in the early stages of treatment, by focusing on current problems and relationships.

The treatment of Anthony would fall within this second category of modified expressive/supportive and insight-oriented psychotherapy. The recommended frequency would be at least two sessions per week, face-to-face, and sessions would be of 45 to 50 minutes in duration. These technical preferences derive from considerations of providing sufficient intensity and continuity to develop transference while forestalling untoward regression.

To achieve optimal results, an expected duration of 2 to 4 years is generally necessary. Clients such as Anthony may show some improvement in behavior or presenting symptoms within a much shorter period, yet because of the persistent and pervasive nature of his problems, we recommend a longer time frame to effect more stable and resilient change.

The need for treatment that extends beyond 1 year is supported by empirical studies (Kopta et al., 1994) that show that briefer treatments, although achieving symptom reduction within the first year, do not address traitlike features of the client's functioning.

The initial task in psychoanalytic psychotherapy is to ally us with the client's personal goals and reasons for seeking treatment. Clients with personality disorders typically do not see their habitual ways of being as the problem and often attribute their difficulties to external factors. Noting that Anthony entered treatment under an ultimatum from his wife suggests that fear of loss rather than a desire for personal change was his primary motive for seeking help. To Anthony's credit, he does perceive the negative consequences his angry outbursts are having and is distressed by a behavior pattern that he is unable to change. It should be stressed, however, that anger is like a powerful drug that immediately boosts the subject's sense of power and efficacy. As such, Anthony, like other people with anger disorders, is unlikely to easily yield behavior that has played such a crucial role in his psychic equilibrium. This *resistance* to change is expected in such a treatment and contributes to its lengthy duration.

In the initial stage of treatment, we would try to ally with that part of Anthony that realistically recognizes a need for change. We would attempt to understand his perspective, without endorsing the legitimacy of his views. We would gently challenge the means by which he expresses his needs and frustrations, asking if the approach he has used works for him. We would also empathize with the part of him that fears change and the exposure of vulnerability. The alliance would thus occur both with his nascent observing capacity and with his experience of fear and shame.

An obstacle to forming and maintaining an alliance would likely arise from Anthony's need to keep people at a distance and the gratifying aspects of his symptom. In the tight quarters of the therapeutic setting and the intimacy of a therapeutic relationship, Anthony might feel threatened by the exposure of his vulnerability. These fears could lead to a "fight or flight" response, in which Anthony might either angrily attack the therapist or take flight from treatment by prematurely terminating. We recommend preparing the client to expect such reactions as a way of decreasing the likelihood of enacting this behavior.

One issue that often arises at the outset of therapy is whether the client would do better with a male or female therapist. In Anthony's case, his history suggests difficulties in either situation. On one hand, he might provoke a punitive response from a male therapist similar to that which he received in the past from male authority figures like his father and employer. On the other hand, Anthony is likely to express ambivalent attitudes toward a female therapist, similar to his reactions to his mother, wife, and other women. Although he may initially feel more comfortable disclosing personal information to a woman (he has had several close female friends and confidants), he may be more openly angry and hostile toward a female therapist, because he would feel threatened by and envious of a competent woman (as he is with his wife), prompting disparaging or belittling remarks.

In our view, although the manifest form of Anthony's anger may differ depending on whether the therapist is male or female, the core psychodynamic issues will surface regardless of the therapist's gender. No preference, then, is indicated for either a male or female therapist. We are not suggesting, however, that Anthony's treatment will unfold in an identical, preordained manner regardless of the personal characteristics of the therapist, as each therapist/patient dyad develops its own unique and co-created interaction pattern.

Once an alliance has been provisionally established, different aspects of Anthony's needs and habitual defensive responses will become activated and repeated during the middle phase of treatment. In response, the therapist will be inevitably drawn into the client's drama and forced to play a role in these scenarios. The therapist in psychoanalytic treatment is thus not a detached onlooker but rather a "participant observer" (Sullivan, 1970).

Psychoanalysts use the phenomena of *transference* and *countertransference*, displacements from past to the present, as primary clinical data to understand the client's experiential world. The therapist conveys this understanding in the form of verbal interpretations, timed to the client's ability to hear and make use of new knowledge. The therapist also endeavors to create new patterns of experience in the here-and-now by relating to the client in a way that differs from habit and expectation. The therapeutic process therefore is not simply a repetition of old patterns but a creation of new and more adaptive interpersonal behavior guided by insight and experience.

When working with clients with anger-related characterological disorders, the therapist inevitably experiences negative feelings toward the patient (and the treatment situation) and may be drawn into actual enactments of these patterns, for example, by becoming inattentive, withdrawn, withholding, placating, preoccupied, overprotective, or openly hostile (Kernberg, 1970). These feelings and action patterns, although unpleasant, can be used to advance understanding of the conflicts being activated in the here-and-now. This goal is accomplished by recognizing the existence of these powerful feelings and attitudes and trying to "contain" and "detoxify" them so that the analyst can return the client's intolerable affects in a more palatable form (Bion, 1957). For example, if Anthony angrily rejected an interpretation, the therapist may become momentarily wounded and may wish to withdraw from the client self-protectively and angrily. Becoming aware of these action tendencies, the therapist might appreciate the client's injured self-esteem, which he induced the therapist to experience by his belittlement, and his need to get rid of an intolerable feeling in himself. The therapist could then empathically comment on the difficulty of accepting one's inadequacies and the need to disavow the experience.

If, however, the therapist enacts his or her feelings, this too can be used constructively. To continue the previous example, if the therapist started the following session late, keeping the client waiting, he or she would acknowledge the occurrence—whether mentioned by the client or not—as part of the ongoing interaction and would explore the mixture of hurt and anger at play.

Once Anthony had a better understanding and control of his anger, the next step would be to trace these patterns to an earlier period of Anthony's life. In particular, his history of early sexual abuse trauma and the strain of deprivation of emotional needs by his family would come to the fore. This component of psychoanalytic therapy is referred to as *reconstruction* and aims at giving the client a sense of continuity in life.

We believe it is necessary to postpone exploration of the past until the client is better able to tolerate feelings of vulnerability, shame, and anger in the present. Anthony would then be in a better position to view his sexual contact with his uncle as understandable in terms of his needs at the time, with less shame and rage.

Termination ideally occurs at the point when the client and therapist agree that the goals of treatment have been met. In Anthony's case, his *life goals* appear to include improving his control over his angry outbursts as well as improving his family relationships, self-esteem, and capacity to work. To help him achieve these life goals, the *treatment goals* would involve developing his capacity for self-reflection, regulation of affect, and empathy. Although there are no definitive markers that these goals have been achieved, there are indicators that would signify when change has occurred and when it is likely to endure (structural change). Because clients with anger disorders may be unreliable reporters of their behavior, it may be useful to include the client's wife or other family members to corroborate changes that have occurred.

Anthony's ability to observe his behavior, thoughts, and feelings would of course be an important marker of improvement. His ability to verbalize his emotions rather than immediately turn them into action would be an indicator of improved self-reflection and affect regulation. He would be better able to control behavior by becoming aware of anger as a signal, not as an automatic trigger for action.

We would also want Anthony to be able to mobilize aggression in his real life, empowering his ambition, sexual life, and capacity to maintain boundaries interpersonally. These changes would lessen his need to bolster his masculinity through abusive displays of anger. He would develop an ability to tolerate a range of tender or vulnerable emotions like longing, desire, and need. Finally, he would come to recognize with less self-hatred his participation in his history of sexual abuse. These gains would need to be demonstrated in a variety of situations. To acquire a new behavior pattern, frequent repetitions are needed. Psychoanalysts refer to this process as *working through*, a necessary requirement to ensure that changes are durable.

We would also expect that Anthony's capacity for play would be freed up by the time he is ready to terminate. He might learn some of this capacity for play within the treatment itself. We would predict that his inability to play would make it difficult for him to see that transference is not reality, that his feelings are not facts. To return to the referral incident, Anthony would reclaim parts of himself projected onto the 9-year-old girls he complained were lacking in competitive drive so that their failures would not be identical with his. Anthony would come to see that his involvement in his daughter's Little League was no longer play but a grim reality, an arena in which his real fears and vulnerabilities were exposed.

These changes, if achieved, would represent structural modifications in Anthony's personality. They would involve a slow and gradual process of acquiring new associational networks and patterns of interaction and more adaptive methods of coping with stress. Structural change of this order would be a product of both insight acquired through the verbal dimension of treatment (declarative knowledge) and new patterns of interaction acquired through the relationship with the therapist (procedural knowledge).

Termination would ideally occur at a point determined by the client's needs and arrived at conjointly. Often, conflicts and anxieties arise anew toward the end of a therapy, as separation is itself a new stressor and the loss of the supportive aspects of the relationship cannot be mourned until the treatment ends. Termination does not resolve all conflicts but rather allows the client to handle issues using resources developed through the treatment.

CONCLUSIONS

In this chapter, we have used the case of Anthony to illustrate, in largely hypothetical form, the basic principles and techniques used in a psychoanalytic treatment of anger-related disorders. Perhaps the most fundamental difference between analytic and other approaches is the shift of emphasis from the overt presenting symptom to the underlying personality organization. Psychoanalytic therapies aim at changing the structural configurations that predispose the individual to symptom formation under stress. The intent is to achieve more durable reduction in symptoms as well as improvements in the client's psychological capacities and resources, such as the ability to reflect on one's self, to regulate emotional experience, to maintain a cohesive and positively toned sense of self, and to achieve the capacity to relate to others as separate individuals.

The modality we suggested for clients with anger-related disorders is a modified form of psychoanalytic psychotherapy. Recognizing that such clients have both deficits in their personality development as well as intrapsychic conflicts, we proposed an approach that uses both supportive techniques (advice, direction, education) and insight-oriented interventions (clarification, confrontation, interpretation, and reconstruction). We also emphasized the importance of a new and reparative relationship with the therapist as a vehicle for change in conjunction with, and transacted through, these supportive/expressive interventions.

We consider the case of Anthony to fall within the range of indications for psychoanalytic treatment. He has sufficient internal and external resources and motivation to benefit from long-term therapy. There are formidable obstacles that a client like Anthony would present, such as a need to hold onto his anger as a way of buttressing a fragile sense of self. He is also likely to reenact his pattern of abusive relationships with the therapist. In our view, however, this potential pitfall offers the greatest promise in altering a habitual and self-defeating behavioral pattern. Psychoanalysis does not aim to eliminate anger or aggression but rather to harness these powerful emotions in the service of adaptation and survival.

CHAPTER 6

Anger Management for Adults: A Menu-Driven Cognitive-Behavioral Approach to the Treatment of Anger Disorders

Raymond Chip Tafrate and Howard Kassinove

INTRODUCTION TO
A COGNITIVE-BEHAVIORAL APPROACH

Because angry clients may present with a wide array of symptoms that might be considered dysfunctional or clinically problematic, a single cognitive-behavioral therapy (CBT) approach for anger management has not emerged as a treatment of choice. Rather, after more than three decades of treatment outcome research, an assortment of CBT techniques has begun to form the foundation of an evidence-based approach. Given our developing knowledge, the wide variability of client characteristics that practitioners encounter, and the varied settings where anger treatments are likely to be delivered, we believe that a "one-size-fits-all" program is impractical. No single intervention program is likely to be ideal for every client. For these reasons, our own anger management program (Kassinove & Tafrate, 2002), which we apply later in this chapter to the case of Anthony, is organized around four broad stages of the treatment process:

1. Preparing clients for change
2. Implementing specific change strategies
3. Helping clients accept, adapt, or adjust to difficult and unchangeable life situations
4. Maintaining change once progress has occurred

For each stage of the treatment process we present several interventions from which practitioners may choose (Table 6.1). This menu-based approach has several advantages. First, it allows for flexibility in selecting an intervention program that targets a client's specific anger symptom profile. Certainly, for example, someone who has difficulty with impulsive anger-related verbalizations to a wide range of triggers would likely benefit from a different approach than would someone who silently ruminates about a specific situation. Second, the setting where anger treatment is delivered will influence the choice of intervention. Different professional settings are likely to draw individuals with varying levels of motivation and awareness. Clients who voluntarily seek outpatient counseling may require less "preparation" than those in court-mandated

Table 6.1   Mean Effect Size (*d*), and Number of Studies for Components of Kassinove and Tafrate's Menu-Driven Program for the Treatment of Anger[*]

Treatment Process Stage	Specific Intervention	*d* (# of studies)[†]
Preparation	Motivational interviewing approach	No data
	In-session review of anger episodes	No data
	Between-session self-monitoring	No data
Change strategies	Avoidance and escape	No data
	Managing physical arousal	0.74 (*n* = 9)
	Building practical skills	0.73 (*n* = 6)
	Social problem solving	0.62 (*n* = 3)
	Exposure	0.51 (*n* = 1)
Accepting, adapting, and adjusting	Realistic interpretations	0.51 (*n* = 9)
	Fostering a more flexible philosophy	0.51 (*n* = 9)
	Forgiveness	No data
Maintaining change	Preparing for anger to re-emerge	No data

[*]Components of the menu-driven approach are adapted from *Anger management: The complete treatment guidebook for practitioners,* Copyright 2002 by Howard Kassinove and Raymond Chip Tafrate. Permission granted by Impact Publishers, Inc., PO Box 6016, Atascadero, CA 93423.
[†]Effect sizes (*d*'s) are from DiGiuseppe, R., & Tafrate, R. (2003). Anger treatment for adults: A meta-analytic review. *Clinical Psychology: Science and Practice, 10,* 70–84.

counseling. Practical concerns around implementation are also related to the setting. Incarcerated inmates may have limited access to materials such as writing tools to complete self-monitoring forms or audiotape players that would assist in developing and reviewing exposure scenes or practicing relaxation. Finally, the education, training, and skills of practitioners who routinely deliver anger treatment vary considerably. In our experience, this ranges from Ph.D.-level psychologists with extensive training in CBT interventions to case managers in alternatives to incarceration programs who have not completed an undergraduate degree program and have little knowledge of basic psychological principles. Thus, practitioner skill and experience may be factors in the choice of interventions provided.

Review of Empirical Evidence

Many of the components that make up our menu-driven approach are composed of interventions that have achieved at least a modest level of empirical support in the treatment outcome literature. At present, four meta-analytic reviews of this literature have been conducted and all have reached similar conclusions regarding *absolute efficacy*. Anger treatment is superior to doing nothing, and clients who receive treatment show moderate to strong improvement of a variety of symptoms (Beck & Fernandez, 1998; DiGiuseppe & Tafrate, 2003; Edmondson & Conger, 1996; Tafrate, 1995). The question of *component efficacy* (i.e., which specific interventions are most effective) remains largely unanswered, because many interventions have received only scant research attention while others have not been studied at all. Available effect size data for the components of our menu-driven approach and the number of studies that have examined a particular intervention are also listed in Table 6.1. Deffenbacher has already provided an in-depth discussion of effectiveness in Chapter 2.

The components that make up our menu-driven approach are overwhelmingly cognitive-behavioral in terms of concepts and origin, and many of these CBT interventions have been well investigated. Unfortunately, treatment studies examining interventions from non-CBT traditions are rare. Nonetheless, we recommend that several interventions from other orientations be considered as part of the overall treatment package, even though current data are lacking. This is especially pertinent to the *preparation* phase of treatment. Most existing studies have been conducted on volunteer research participants with little consideration given to motivational issues. Thus, in the area of anger reduction, research findings have not adequately addressed the lack of motivation for change in some clients who appear in the private offices of practitioners or in institutions such as prisons. Therefore, a preliminary preparation strategy may be necessary to achieve similar outcomes as those reported in published studies. Several preparation strategies are discussed in the following sections as part of beginning treatment with Anthony.

Basic Concepts and Assumptions

Because there are several CBT-related intervention strategies, each with histories going back a number of decades, space does not permit a detailed review of the concepts and assumptions of each intervention listed in Table 6.1. In this section, instead, we briefly review one method that is central to our treatment approach and that tends to be overlooked by both researchers and practitioners—the use of exposure methods to reduce anger symptoms. As noted in the material related to the case of Anthony, we believe that exposure is both a central component for anger reduction and a foundation for developing new skills to ward off anger reactions in the future.

Readers interested in the assumptions and concepts underlying the other interventions in the menu-driven approach will find the following references helpful. Issues related to handling client resistance and facilitating change are well reviewed by Miller and Rollnick (19991, 2002) and Hanna (2002). Relaxation interventions are covered in Benson (1975, 2000) and Suinn (1990). Skill building and assertiveness are described by Alberti and Emmons (2001), and social problem solving is discussed in detail by Chang, D'Zurilla, and Sanna (2004). Cognitive models for addressing realistic interpretations and fostering a more flexible philosophy can be found in Beck (1995), Ellis and Tafrate (1997), and Walen, DiGiuseppe, and Dryden (1992). Forgiveness interventions are described by Enright (2001), and basic concepts related to relapse prevention are discussed by Marlatt and Gordon (1985).

In terms of assumptions underlying the use of exposure procedures to reduce anger, recent theoretical work by Power and Dalgleish (1997) suggests that two separate pathways can lead to emotional arousal. One is characterized as automatic and inflexible and involves limited awareness. The second is slower, is sequential, and involves greater attention. The first pathway appears to rely on conditioning principles, whereas the second relies on higher-level cognitive processes. The first is more difficult to modify, whereas the second can be more easily brought under conscious control. This dual arousal model would explain the common report by some clients that their anger flares up quickly and they react before they can consciously alter their behavior and would also explain why cognitive interventions may be only partially effective. Exposure-based methods attempt to address the underlying conditioning and the automatic nature of some anger reactions. In theory, interventions that use a combination of exposure-based methods and cognitive restructuring will produce optimal results because both pathways to anger are addressed.

Exposure-based methods have led to the successful treatment of many human troubles, most notably those that are anxiety based. A rich theoretical literature, decades of animal research, and treatment outcome studies with clinical samples are generally supportive of the role of classical conditioning in the development of anxiety-based disorders. Unfortunately, the scientific literature on the operant or classical conditioning of anger is miniscule. We believe that anger has many self-reinforcing aspects, such as short-term compliance from others, the perception of power and control over difficult situations, tension reduction, the correction of self-righteous indignation, fulfillment of revenge fantasies, silencing of negative feedback from others, avoidance of certain topics by others, and so on. In a conditioning model, clients can learn to associate a new competing response to the triggers of their anger. Typical anger triggers could be paired with new responses, such as relaxation, cognitive coping statements, assertive verbal skills, and the ability to remain calm and not respond. Of course, these new responses require repeated rehearsal in the face of the anger triggers. Interventions that repeatedly expose clients to their anger triggers result in habituation and extinction. In addition, new responses are reinforced in the sessions and ultimately in the real world.

Several positive reports of exposure procedures with angry clients have appeared. Using the verbal barb technique, Tafrate and Kassinove (1998); Kassinove, McDermott, and Terricciano (2005); and McVey (2000) have demonstrated anger reduction in angry adult men who were repeatedly exposed to negative statements during treatment sessions. The barb procedure is described in the case application later in this chapter. Several other reports have shown anger reduction in clients who repeatedly rehearsed anger scenes in imagery (Dua & Swinden, 1992; Grodnitzky & Tafrate, 2000). Finally, Deffenbacher et al. (1988, 1995) and Deffenbacher and Stark (1992) have used anger imagery scenes within progressive muscle relaxation skill sessions. In this combined approach, relaxation plus imaginal exposure has produced better outcomes than relaxation alone (DiGiuseppe & Tafrate, 2003).

Perhaps the main reason for the relative lack of attention to exposure methods is the concern that these techniques carry more risks for angry clients (i.e., increasing their anger) and for their practitioners (i.e., becoming the target of client anger) than for anxious clients. Of course, it is important to be aware of the potential risks in using any type of procedure that has received limited research attention and that may actively evoke emotional arousal. As noted in Chapter 1, the risk may be increased for practitioners who work with patients who fit the diagnoses of post-traumatic stress disorder (PTSD), psychoses, mental retardation, and so forth. Nonetheless, we have found that in private practice–type settings, carefully planned exposure techniques promote less angry responding, decrease anger associated physical arousal, and are safe for both clients and practitioners. The key is to work collaboratively with the client, to explain what is likely to happen, and to decide jointly that exposure is a treatment of choice. A good therapeutic alliance is central to success. If the planned exercises are discussed in advance, in the context of a strong therapeutic relationship, the probability of a successful outcome is increased substantially.

THE CASE OF ANTHONY

Assessment and the Initial Approach to Treatment

Angry clients often appear in a practitioner's office because employers, family members, or the criminal justice system has coerced them into treatment. This was true in the case of Anthony, who was sent for treatment by his wife. Thus, a high percentage of adults with anger problems are ambivalent or outright resistant to the idea of making their anger experiences the target of formal treatment. Nonetheless, they are likely to be cooperative in several areas. For example, they may be comfortable complaining about perceived injustices, may be amenable to exploring ways to make others more fully understand their point of view, and are likely to become enthusiastic when discussing techniques to foster compliance in those who they view as causing their difficulties. Rather than attempting to immediately engage these folks in anger reduction techniques, it is usually better if the first few sessions are focused on increasing awareness of the costs associated with their anger experiences.

We have found the motivational interviewing framework, for understanding and engaging those with ambivalence about making a personal change, to be very effective in the beginning phase of treatment with angry clients (Miller & Rollnick, 1991, 2002). The traditional cognitive-behavioral, active-directive presentation style, which tries to convince clients that change is necessary by an examination of the evidence, rarely works. A forceful "change message" from the therapist often results in a strengthening of the client's arguments that anger is necessary, proper, and valid given the circumstances. At least initially, indirect and client-centered methods appear to be more effective. Once a commitment to change has been developed, an active-directive style, as well as a variety of CBT change strategies, will usually become more acceptable.

The initial session with Anthony would involve using *reflective statements* and *open-ended questions* to encourage him to verbalize some of the negative aspects of his anger episodes. By eliciting and differentially reinforcing verbalizations related to the problem aspects of his anger, Anthony's commitment to change would be strengthened.

Miller and Rollnick (2002) have identified four client verbalization themes believed to be predictive of behavioral change. These have been termed *self-motivational* or *change talk statements* and include *problem recognition, expression of concern, intention to change,* and *optimism.* Increasing statements about *problem recognition* is the goal of the first meeting. Evidence for the connection between client commitment language and behavioral outcomes is presented and reviewed by Amrhein et al. (2003).

In the case material, Anthony has already made statements that indicate some level of motivation. Change talk–related statements include Anthony's acknowledgment that his anger is creating distance between him and his children, his realization that his wife is threatening to leave him, and the risk of public humiliation and of losing his family. He also concedes that he feels ashamed of his outbursts while he was coaching his daughter's softball match.

To illustrate how this approach would be carried out in the first meeting, a possible dialog is presented here.

Therapist: Anthony, tell me what brings you here at this time? [open question]

Anthony: Well, it's really my wife's idea that I come here. She says that I need to get help controlling my temper.

Therapist: Sounds like things have gotten to a difficult place. [reflective statement]

Anthony: Yeah. She says if I don't change, she wants a divorce.

Therapist: That seems like a lot of pressure from her. [reflective statement]

Anthony: She's complained before. I've always had a temper, and it mostly spills out with my family.

Therapist: So it sounds like your anger has affected your family relationships. [reflective statement]

Anthony: Definitely. My daughters are afraid of me.

Therapist: What makes you think they are afraid of you? [open question]

Anthony: Well, they have gotten very distant and don't talk that much. Sometimes I see fear in their eyes when I start to get mad. Also, my wife tells me they are afraid.

Therapist: So, you can actually see it in their faces when you are angry with them. [reflective statement]

Anthony: Yeah.

Therapist: And that's not the kind of relationship you want to have with them. [reflective statement]

Anthony: No. I don't want them to be afraid of me. I just want to have a normal relationship.

Therapist: So it seems like even though it was your wife's idea that you come here, you would actually like to have better family relationships yourself. [reflective statement]

Anthony: Yeah. I don't want to lose my family. [Reflective statements and open questions can continue to be used throughout the first session to elicit from Anthony verbal statements of problem recognition. No attempt is made by the therapist to label him as having an "anger problem" or to suggest that he needs to change. Rather, it is Anthony who makes the argument for change.]

Our assessment of Anthony would involve gathering information similar to what was presented in the case description with several additional measures. First, a standardized measure of overall psychopathology would be given early in treatment to assess existing comorbidity patterns. This would immediately flag additional problems to be considered in the overall treatment plan and would reduce the likelihood of attempting interventions that have a low probability of success. Second, in addition to the State-Trait Anger Expression Inventory (STAXI), we would also include a standardized anger instrument that assesses a wider range of anger characteristics that are likely to be the focus of in-session clinical attention. This would allow the practitioner to develop an anger profile specific to Anthony. Finally, we would incorporate a strategy that allows both Anthony and the practitioner to examine specific components and consequences of individual episodes of anger. This final piece of the assessment package is considered part of the preparation phase of treatment.

Understanding Comorbidity Patterns

As noted in chapter 1, we would incorporate a broad-based measure of general psychopathology into the assessment package for clients such as Anthony. For clinical practice the Millon Clinical Multiaxial Inventory (MCMI-III; Millon, Davis, & Millon, 1997) is a good choice. Other possibilities include the Brief Symptom Inventory (BSI; Derogatis, 1993) and the Personality Assessment Inventory (PAI; Morey, 1991). Regarding Anthony's likely comorbidity patterns and potential MCMI-III scores, we would expect low scores on alcohol and substance use and an elevation on PTSD symptoms. Given Anthony's long-standing dissatisfaction with his marriage and career path, one additional diagnostic area that might emerge is dysthymic disorder. In terms of Axis II patterns, based on the descriptive information provided, potential personality disorders to consider include passive aggressive, narcissistic (due to his difficulty handling criticism and "making" everything about him), and borderline (history of instability in work, family relationships, and emotional functioning). Information related to Anthony's personality style, although not currently part of the case assessment, has the potential to influence the selection and ordering of interventions. We will proceed based on the assumption that a significant personality disorder does not exist.

Developing an Anger Profile

To more fully assess specific characteristics of anger that may lead to dysfunction and impairment we recommend the *Anger Disorders Scale* (ADS; DiGiuseppe & Tafrate, 2004). In order to demonstrate the utility of developing an anger profile, and to contrast the ADS to the STAXI, we have attempted to estimate areas of elevation based on the assessment information provided. Thus, Table 6.2 represents an expected anger profile for Anthony and highlights the organization, subscales, and factor structure of the ADS. When one is developing a profile, composite scores are examined first. Anthony's *total* ADS score would likely indicate moderate anger pathology. However, total scores may underestimate specific problem areas. His score on the higher-order *reactivity/expression* factor would likely indicate severe difficulties and would represent the area of greatest clinical concern. His higher-order *anger-in* factor score might potentially fall into the lower level of the clinical range, while his higher-order *vengeance* factor score would likely fall below the cut-off for clinical disturbance. The higher-order factor scores indicate that reactive verbal outbursts are the most salient feature of Anthony's anger episodes, although he may also experience periods of holding anger in, brooding, and thinking about perceived transgressions. A desire for revenge and retribution involving aggressive actions are not likely to show up on the ADS as a significant part of Anthony's anger profile.

An examination of individual subscale scores would likely indicate severe problems in the areas of verbal expression and the length of time anger has been a problem. Moderate difficulties would appear in the areas of impulsive behavior and the tendency to use anger coercively to control others. His scores on rumination, sensitivity to rejection, the tendency to

Table 6.2   Simulated Profile for Anthony on the Anger Disorders Scale (ADS)

ADS Scores	Not Significant	Mild	Moderate	Severe
		Level of Anger Pathology for Anthony		
Total			X	
Reactivity/expression higher-order factor				X
Scope of anger provocations	X			
Physiological arousal	X			
Duration of anger problems				X
Rumination		X		
Impulsivity			X	
Coercion			X	
Verbal expression				X
Anger-in higher-order factor		X		
Hurt/social rejection		X		
Episode length	X			
Suspiciousness	X			
Resentment	X			
Tension reduction	X			
Brooding		X		
Vengeance higher-order factor	X			
Revenge	X			
Physical aggression	X			
Relational aggression	X			
Passive aggression		X		
Indirect aggression	X			

Structure of the Anger Disorders Scale (ADS; DiGiuseppe & Tafrate, 2004).

hold anger in and brood, and the inclination to express anger by failing to comply with others' requests would also likely fall in the lower part of the clinical range.

In sum, a standardized self-report measure such as the ADS allows for profile development in a variety of anger domains and characteristics. Such a profile can be useful in designing an anger management plan that is tailored to a specific client.

Building Awareness: Assessing Individual Episodes of Anger

The focus of the next several sessions would be to understand the typical components of Anthony's anger sequence. At this stage the emphasis is still on *exploration* and not change. We prefer the use of a simple, but formal, model that provides a framework for shared understanding of the development of specific episodes of anger (Figure 6.1). In this way,

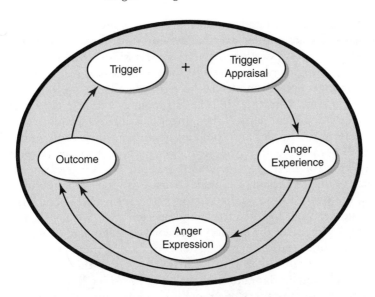

Figure 6.1 Anger Episode Model. (Adapted from Anger management: The complete treatment guidebook for practitioners, Copyright 2002 by Howard Kassinove and Raymond Chip Tafrate. Permission granted by Impact Publishers, Inc. PO Box 6016, Atascadero, CA 93423.)

practitioners and clients can jointly conceptualize anger episodes as they appear in the client's life and connect the anger episodes with both short- and long-term consequences. In treatment, we usually minimize or ignore discussions of the evolutionary value of anger and the role of hormones such as epinephrine in the initiation and maintenance of anger. The role of such factors is reviewed in Chapters 1 and 9, and our attention is on learned and cognitively mediated reactions.

The model would thus help Anthony to see that specific aversive triggers are first appraised by a set of ideas and beliefs. This combination of triggers and appraisals yields an internal anger experience that may or may not be expressed to others. In the case of Anthony, as shown on the ADS and by the case history, he would be shown that he both feels angry internally and expresses it with nasty verbalizations to others (e.g., verbally lambasting the girls of his daughter's softball team for their "lack of competitive drive"). Finally, he would be taught that these experiences and expressive patterns have both short- and longer-term outcomes. Fundamentally, Anthony would learn that his anger is caused both by his exaggerated cognitive appraisals of the trigger (e.g., poor performance by the girls on the team) and by some of the positive and reinforcing short-term consequences (e.g., temporary increased efforts by some team members, an extra hit or catch in the game that he attributes to his strong coaching approach). However, he would come to see that his appraisals lead to excessive anger and that the longer-term consequences are negative and self-defeating and far overshadow any short-term gains that might accrue. As we have described elsewhere (Kassinove & Tafrate, 2002), these include highly negative interpersonal and medical consequences.

The anger episode model has been translated into a self-monitoring tool (Kassinove & Tafrate, 2002) as a simple way to help clients understand the component parts of their anger reactions. Depending on client motivation, the model and tool can be applied in several ways. The least labor intensive, from the client's perspective, is to use the model as a structure for having a conversation about a recent and significant anger episode. Although the model is used to guide practitioner questions, the overall tone of the session is that of a casual conversation allowing the client freedom to expand on each area. We have found this strategy to be useful for developing client awareness and strengthening the therapeutic relationship while not engendering client resistance. For Anthony, we might ask him to recount step by step the components of his anger during his daughter's softball game—asking him specific questions about circumstances, his thoughts and opinions about what happened, his internal bodily reactions and fantasies, his verbal and motor expressions, and the consequences that followed the anger. When one uses this approach, it is important to stay focused on a single anger episode, to be concrete and specific, and to avoid theoretical discussions about anger in general. Reviewing one anger episode in this manner can take 20 minutes or more.

The second strategy, which can be used in subsequent sessions, is to ask the client at the beginning of the first meeting, or in the waiting room before a session, to complete a single record for the most significant anger experience that occurred since the last meeting with the therapist. This technique requires effort and begins to socialize the client into doing work on his or her patterns independently. Anthony would be asked to take 10 minutes during one of the early sessions to complete an anger episode record. The client's responses would then be discussed and, most likely, supportively corrected. This would be repeated in a series of sessions to help the client learn about his or her typical mode of reacting to aversive situations. The third strategy is to use the *anger episode record* as an ongoing self-monitoring tool, as is typical in CBT interventions. Used in this manner, the records can provide an indicator of treatment progress. The number of episodes reported early in treatment can serve as a baseline from which improvement can be measured. Other dimensions of anger can also serve as indictors of progress, depending on areas that the practitioner wishes to target. These might include average intensity of anger episodes, duration, and/or the number of episodes containing aversive or profane verbalizations or aggressive behaviors.

Developing a shared understanding of the details of the client's anger episodes is a cornerstone of the more active change strategies that follow. Without the insight that anger is having a negative impact on functioning, clients are not likely to put in the effort required to be successful with most CBT interventions. Our model connects specific anger events to consequences. Because clients often initially possess a tendency to simply blame the external world for their anger reactions, the model also highlights the *combination* of triggering events *and* client thinking patterns, along with some short-term reinforcements, as causative of anger. Thus, the role of thinking is introduced in early sessions, as is the differentiation of immediate versus delayed consequences. Finally, by examining individual episodes of anger, both the client and practitioner can specifically target key features of anger that are problematic, adding to the information obtained in the standardized assessment.

The Treatment Plan

Based on available assessment information and the probable characteristics of Anthony's anger profile, the following intervention strategies are primarily targeted at reducing his aversive verbal behaviors in interpersonal situations. We start with a basic approach, which is to shape his behavior with the deliberate use of escape maneuvers. The next group of interventions uses several types of exposure procedures in relation to common anger-eliciting triggers. Reducing his bodily arousal and automatic responding patterns is a prerequisite to building more positive skills. Thus, the exposure components of treatment form a foundation from which we would add skills such as alternative ways of thinking and communicating. Finally, through an exploration of forgiveness, we would allow him to see how his history of being sexually abused influences his thinking, emotional reactions, and behaviors in his life today and how he can "let go" of the past without forgetting about it or condoning it.

Practicing Escape: Leaving Difficult Situations Gracefully

Anthony revealed that he "broke some ground" in terms of getting a handle on his anger when he left the house to cool down after seeing that his daughter was becoming distraught when he was angry. Because he sees this as progress, getting him to leave situations when his anger begins to escalate may be a good place to start in terms of developing better control.

In general, thoughtful avoidance and escape maneuvers may be especially critical for clients whose anger puts them at risk for harming others or for suffering some type of loss, such as ending a relationship or losing a job.

Often, the immediate goal is to prevent further damage. *Avoidance* strategies can be developed collaboratively with clients in response to repetitive and predictable triggers. *Escape* strategies are also important because it is impossible to always predict situations in which conflict and anger will emerge. In Anthony's case, we would emphasize *escape* rather than avoidance when he feels anger in response to the behavior of family members.

Shaping escape behaviors can begin with simple and specific tasks that the client is likely to be successful in completing. More complex escape maneuvers can be gradually assigned. For example, in Anthony's case, we would break down the escape procedures into three steps. First, he would practice removing himself (e.g., going out for a walk to cool down) after saying one angry negative statement rather than continuing his usual verbal barrage. He would be told, "After you say something— just leave." Of course, it would take some practice for him to become aware of his reactions and to stop his verbalizations at an early stage. After he is able to complete this task, the second step would be to observe his own internal experience of anger and practice leaving before saying any type of negative statement. He would be told, "As you notice your anger build—just leave." After a number of repeated successes, the focus could then be shifted to the third step, working on more *elegant* exits. Before removing himself, Anthony would learn to tell the other person that he is becoming angry, that he is going to leave, and that he will discuss the issue at a later time. Again, a disruption of the usual pattern of aversive verbalizations associated with anger is the primary target of this strategy.

Clients who are able to implement escape in increasingly complicated steps frequently feel an initial sense of success and better self-control. Of course, these strategies have limitations in producing long-lasting changes related to effective behaviors because they do not enhance the coping skills necessary to deal more effectively with anger triggers. Avoidance and escape strategies also have the potential to exacerbate problems if they are not explained in some way to people directly involved with the client. In Anthony's case, this strategy would be explained to family members. Even if Anthony becomes proficient at removing himself gracefully, he would still have not developed better communication skills with his wife or his daughters, which would be the preferable longer-range goal. One of us recently treated a couple where the husband successfully practiced using escape to curb his verbal outbursts. Even though his spouse had agreed to the plan and was grateful that the angry verbal behavior was reduced, she quickly became dissatisfied with her husband's leaving the home. His escape strategy did not help them resolve their difficult issues around parenting and dealing effectively with household responsibilities.

In sum, we recommend that escape and avoidance be considered as short-term interventions to be used in the *early* stages of anger management to disrupt and reduce certain behaviors that have become "automatically" connected with anger experiences.

Exposure

Imagery Exposure and Relaxation Skills. Although we would like Anthony to be able to engage in more productive communication with family members, this may be difficult to accomplish if his physical activation is high. Thus, the next component of the treatment is to teach Anthony how to relax in the face of adversity. Once he can reliably achieve relaxation, the stage is set for developing additional improved cognitive and behavioral reactions to aversive triggers.

The most common relaxation technique used in mental health settings is *progressive muscle relaxation (PMR) training.* PMR involves the tensing and releasing of different muscle groups (e.g., starting with the arm muscles, then moving to the legs, stomach, chest, shoulders, neck, and face). One immediate benefit for clients with anger problems is an increased awareness of the difference between tensed and relaxed muscle groups. We recommend the creation of an audiotape recording for clients so that they can practice at home. For those unfamiliar with how to implement PMR, a more detailed description of the procedures and detailed scripts to use with clients are provided by Kassinove and Tafrate (2002), and Deffenbacher and McKay (2000). Relaxation is like many other physiological responses, and there are many ways to elicit it. Alternatives to PMR can be found in Fried (1999) and Lusk (1992), and some relaxation methods can be integrated with imagery exposure.

When working with Anthony, the therapist would review the PMR procedure in the office and give Anthony a tape to facilitate practice twice per day for 2 weeks. We suggest that the client set aside at least 30 minutes at a time when no distractions are likely. Unfortunately, experience shows that many clients will practice only once a day at best. Regular practice will help clients get to the point where they can ultimately use the procedure without the assistance of the tape.

Once relaxation skills have been practiced and clients can achieve a more relaxed state, PMR can be paired with imagery exposure to aversive triggers to further reduce angry arousal. Imagery scenes are best targeted at problematic, ongoing anger triggers. During a treatment session, Anthony and his therapist would create a scene about a typical negative interaction involving his wife. (At a later time, a separate scene might be created around an interaction with one of his daughters.) For example, Anthony would be asked to describe an argument with his wife and write it out on paper. Specific details to make the scene more realistic would be incorporated (e.g., a description of the room they were in, the temperature, what his wife was wearing, her facial expressions). The goal is to create a scene where Anthony could imagine himself participating in the events and not just observing them. When one is writing scenes, it is useful for the client and practitioner to develop an initial draft and to then add in more detail after the main ideas have been developed on paper. Scenes should generally be about 2 to 3 minutes in length. Clients sometimes report feeling some degree of anger as they are developing the scenes. This is actually desirable and indicates that the scene is on target.

In terms of integrating imagery exposure in the treatment sessions, the first step is to have Anthony use PMR to relax. Once relaxed, he would be instructed to review, in imagination, the anger scene—step by step. In initial practice experiences, it is sometimes helpful for the practitioner to verbally guide the client through the anger-provoking situation. Anthony would be asked to keep his eyes closed and to imagine the situation is *actually happening*. Anger and tension, if present, would be allowed to build as the scene unfolds. Once the scene is finished, Anthony would then be instructed to once again practice relaxation using PMR during each scene element until his physical activation is reduced. The imagery scene serves as a context in which to practice relaxation skills. The office session would begin with relaxation followed by the anger scene and a return to relaxation. Depending on the time available, this sequence may be repeated. Anthony would also be asked to repeat the sequence at home several times before the next session, using PMR to overcome activation felt while imagining the scene. Once it becomes increasingly difficult to feel anger, a second anger scene can be developed. Deffenbacher et al. (1988, 1995) and Deffenbacher and Stark (1992) have demonstrated the effectiveness of combining anger imagery with relaxation. This intervention combines two CBT procedures and consistently emerges as one of the most effective interventions for anger reduction (DiGiuseppe & Tafrate, 2003).

Verbal Barb Exposure and Response Prevention

The first step in implementing verbal barb exposure is to collaboratively develop specific exposure statements. These are known as "verbal barbs" (Kaufman & Wagner, 1972; Kimmel, 1976). *Barbs are aversive, negative words or statements designed to simulate anger triggers that occur naturally in the client's life.* It is useful to organize these statements into categories related to persons or situations that typically challenge the client (e.g., barbs from work, barbs from a spouse, barbs from à family member). With Anthony, we would first focus on having him observe interactions with his wife and write down statements that he finds the most difficult to encounter. Based on the information provided about the case, the following statements might be attributed to his wife:

1. "You only think about your own problems and nobody else's. You are so self-centered."
2. "Your inability to hold down a job means that we all have to suffer."
3. "I'm the one who has to make the money in this family."
4. "Your daughters are fed up with you and want to leave when you are around."

Again, other lists of aversive statements might be developed in other areas such as interactions with his daughters.

The next step would be a discussion about the in-session barb practice procedure. It is important not to surprise clients and to make sure that they understand what is going to happen. The therapist might say: "Anthony, I want you to practice dealing with this list of negative statements in the session with me. I am going to say a statement to you, and I would like you to listen to it and not respond. It is okay if you feel some anger. However, I do not want you to say anything at this point and I don't want you to get up out of your chair. Do you think you can do this with me?"

Most angry clients quickly understand the rationale for verbal barb exposure. Unlike anxiety-disordered clients, persons with anger problems are more readily agreeable to facing the triggers causing them difficulty. Nonetheless, a few guidelines are recommended. First, it is important to check with clients to make sure that they think they can maintain control and not react. Second, this technique should not be used with clients who do not see their anger reactions as problematic to begin with or those who do not seem to understand the rationale. In addition, any objections that emerge are best respected, although we have rarely found anyone who objects to the procedure. Third, consider comorbidity issues, such as severe mood problems, schizophrenic spectrum disorders, or current active substance use. Not everyone will be a good candidate for this procedure. Finally, check with clients at short intervals to ensure that they are maintaining good control.

Once we have a mutual understanding and agreement from Anthony, we would begin to practice the first statement. It would be delivered slowly in a flat, monotone voice. After the first delivery, Anthony would be asked to rate his internal anger arousal on a 0 to 10 scale (0 represents no anger, and 10 indicates a feeling similar to the most anger ever felt). Some clients feel some degree of physical arousal and experience a number of negative thoughts in response to the initial presentation of the first statement. Other clients do not report feeling any arousal after hearing the first statement and initially find the procedure to be silly and uncomfortable. If the reported arousal is rated greater than 2, we continue repeating the statement in the same slow, monotone voice. Clients are urged to take deep relaxing breaths to help them maintain nonreactivity. If the arousal rating is 2 or less, the intensity of the delivery can be increased. This is achieved by having the practitioner raise his or her volume, use a sharper tone, engage in a forward leaning body posture, or use a pointed finger. Following a number of successive repetitions, Anthony would likely report almost no reaction to the statement. Some clients report anger reductions very quickly, whereas others require repeated presentations. Once Anthony can hear the first statement delivered at different levels of intensity with little or no reaction, the next statement would then be presented in the same manner. This procedure would be repeated over the course of several sessions.

Through the repeated use of verbal barb exposure, it is likely that Anthony would become less reactive to verbal statements, both in session and in his home environment. With practitioner coaching, he would also learn that it was not so "terrible" to hear and absorb negative feedback from others and that he can increase his tolerance for hearing negative statements. Of course, helping Anthony not react in the usual angry manner is only the initial goal of the barb exposure. We are not recommending uniform passivity in the face of critical negative statements, nor are we advocating the continual acceptance of verbal abuse. Once clients are in greater control of their own reactions, other techniques, such as learning assertive verbal responses or problem solving to develop alternative courses of action, are added. Cognitive self-statements that promote control and lead to productive behaviors may also be programmed into verbal barb exposure practice. In Anthony's case, we want to break the conditioned automatic verbal responses and create a more stable foundation from which to develop better thinking and behavioral skills. For a more detailed description of how to implement barb exposure, readers are referred to Kassinove and Tafrate (2002).

Fostering Adaptive Thinking and Behavior

Following several weeks of imagery practice and verbal barb exposure, Anthony would likely be able to remain relaxed and calm in response to common anger triggers. Because our approach is designed to be flexible, it is difficult to prescribe a step-by-step plan from this point forward. Much would depend on Anthony's reaction to the treatment thus far, his level of progress outside of the sessions, and any potential restrictions on treatment length. Several intervention options are noted in the following sections.

Social Interaction Skills. A next possible area of focus would be to improve Anthony's social interaction behaviors. To assess his skill level, we would role-play several recent situations with his wife and have him respond in his usual pretreatment manner. The therapist would identify areas that are potentially problematic, such as eye contact, body posture, receptivity to the other person's message, and the delivery of his message. The therapist, through use of additional role-plays, would then model new and more adaptive skills. Often it is useful to engage in role-reversal wherein the practitioner plays the role of the client and the client plays the role of the "offending other." The therapist can model the new skills and combine them into a complete response. Roles are then reversed and the client practices responding with better skills. Obviously, it is important to positively reinforce any improvements, even though it may take several trials to come up with a completely improved and more effective response. The final step is to have Anthony practice the new skills in real situations and to report the results in subsequent sessions. Skills can also be evaluated and developed in other areas as well, such as work-related interactions.

At this point, we might consider having several couples sessions to further work on communication skills. Although practitioners from different orientations have varied opinions about when to involve spouses or family members, we have found that involving angry clients too early in conjoint sessions can lead to a high level of conflict in the treatment sessions themselves and can be counterproductive. Conjoint sessions tend to be beneficial only after the angry client has achieved a level of self-control and trust in the practitioner.

Cognitive Restructuring. Another potential set of interventions would focus on fostering less extreme and more flexible thinking when confronted with anger triggers. Although most treatment studies using cognitive restructuring techniques for anger reduction have examined a self-instructional training model (Meichenbaum, 1985; Novaco, 1975), the well-known theories of Beck (1964) and Ellis (1962, 1973) have also obtained an initial degree of empirical support (Deffenbacher et al., 2000; Tafrate & Kassinove, 1998). A starting point might be to have Anthony learn several *cognitive coping statements*. Again, coping statements are created collaboratively, and once developed, the client is asked to commit the statements to memory. Examples of coping statements for Anthony might include the following: (1) "It is okay to hear criticism from my wife, and I do not have to react with anger. I can tolerate hearing what she thinks, even if it is unpleasant" and (2) "Listening to what she has to say is an important part of a relationship. I do not have to agree with everything, but it is important to listen." The anger imagery scenes and verbal barbs could once again be used as context for practicing the coping statements. Anthony would rehearse the coping statements in response to both the imagery scene and barbs in the session. He would then be asked to apply the coping statements in real-life ongoing situations.

Forgiveness

Given the complexities of Anthony's case, some attention to his history of sexual abuse at the hands of his uncle seems warranted. This topic has been saved for later in the sequence of interventions because Anthony reports experiencing shame and guilt about the incidents. It does not appear as if he has ever explored how these experiences have influenced his current functioning. The hope is that after more familiarity and some success with the therapist, Anthony would be more willing to discuss his abuse history.

Anthony would be encouraged to review his abuse experiences in detail, even though it is assumed that this would be difficult for him. During this phase we would adopt a less directive attitude, emphasize a nonjudgmental stance, and highlight his strengths for having dealt with the abuse by himself for so many years. After Anthony was able to discuss the events, the next step would be to examine his interpretations and beliefs regarding the events. For example, what constructions has he developed from the experience ("Others can't be trusted. . . . You need to protect yourself because no one else will look out for you. . . . I let it happen; therefore, I deserved it. . . . I'm worthless"). Cognitive restructuring around the meaning of the experiences would be explored, and alternative interpretations would be considered (e.g., "It was not my fault, and I did not create the situation. . . . Some people cannot be trusted, but many can. . . . It is important to give people a chance before I decide that they can't be trusted. . . . It doesn't compromise my worth because I was victimized").

Depending on the presence or absence of PTSD symptoms, imaginal exposure might be considered. This would require the development of an imagery scene similar to that presented earlier, but it would be developed around the abuse experiences. The imagery scene would also be put on audiotape. Once the scene was developed and recorded, Anthony would be asked to relive the trauma for 60 minutes each day as a way of reducing arousal and negative thoughts associated with the memories. Relaxation would be incorporated, as appropriate. Greater detail regarding the use of exposure with clients who have been victims of sexual abuse can be found in Foa and Rothbaum (1998).

Finally, *forgiveness* would be presented as a way of *letting go* and moving beyond chronic feelings of anger and bitterness. The potential costs and benefits of forgiveness could be discussed. Anthony would be asked if he prefers to remain in the role of a "victim" or if he is ready to move forward. He would have to make a deliberate decision to forgive his uncle and also his parents for not protecting him. Because forgiveness involves the development of cognitive discriminations, Anthony would be asked to differentiate forgiving from forgetting, forgiving from condoning, and forgiving from excusing. He would be taught that it is possible to let go of the past and forgive and, yet, to not forget or excuse the actions of his uncle and parents. He would be helped to develop an understanding of his uncle and parents as people who behaved very badly and made serious errors. The goal would be to reduce reactivity when he thinks about the abuse, to place it in context, to develop a broader understanding of the histories and weaknesses of his uncle and parents, and to move away from the victim role. Of course, because his parents and uncle are alive, he would have the option of talking with them about the past. This can be achieved in only a moderate proportion of cases. Increased time from the original transgression and satisfying interpersonal skills and relationships increase the likelihood of success.

CLINICAL ISSUES AND RECOMMENDATIONS

Maintaining Change and Working Toward Termination

There are many positive ways to end treatment. We have found that having the client verbalize areas of progress using concrete and specific examples is a useful way to bring up the topic. In addition, we advocate many of the principles outlined by Parks and Marlatt (2000) related to a relapse prevention model.

First, the likely course of progress would be discussed. Anthony would be told that the goal of treatment has not been to eliminate all anger but rather to make anger less of a problem. Reductions in frequency, intensity, and duration of the episodes are useful goals, as well as a reduction in negative anger-related outcomes. Rumination about the past would hopefully be reduced to thinking about it on rare occasions. He would be told that ups and downs are to be expected and that even in the most successful of cases, lapses occur. Meaningful improvement is obtained over the long run, and overreacting to a lapse may undermine long-term progress. It is critical that clients resist the urge to return to old angry behavior patterns. Second, strategies for managing setbacks would be discussed, as would damage control procedures. In Anthony's case, these might include apologizing to family members, reinstating practice of earlier skills such as relaxation, using cognitive coping statements or behavioral skills, or increasing contact with the therapist. Third, Anthony and the therapist would go through a process of identifying future high-risk triggers and developing a plan to deal with each one.

Termination of treatment would begin with increased spacing of sessions. Again, depending on the client, bimonthly sessions are often a good starting point. Sessions can be further faded to monthly meetings or quarterly booster sessions. Clients are always left with the option of increasing the sessions if new and unexpected aversive events appear or old patterns reemerge.

Treatment Difficulties and Potential Obstacles

In practice, Anthony would no doubt present a variety of therapeutic challenges. His history is filled with multiple problems and negative patterns that have existed unchanged for decades. When such anger-related thinking and behavior have been practiced for more than 30 years, there will surely be some roadblocks to success. First, it is likely that there have been many short-term reinforcements that have maintained his angry outbursts. His yelling has probably led to some degree of compliance from his wife and children, at least in the early years. Because it was no doubt only intermittent compliance (reinforcement), his tendency to act with anger was actually increased in strength and it would likely take many treatment sessions to extinguish. Anthony would be considered a long-term case.

Another potential obstacle is the presence of a significant personality disorder. In this case, such disorders represent long-term, well-ingrained (maladaptive) patterns of responding to stressors. The proposed treatment model was developed based on the assumption that such a behavioral pattern does not exist to a significant degree and would not interfere with treatment. This assumption may be unwise. As noted previously, several Axis II diagnoses are possible and passive aggressive, borderline, or narcissistic seem the most likely. Maladaptive interpersonal strategies associated with any one of these patterns would interfere with the quality of the therapeutic relationship and with Anthony's ability to followthrough with cognitive and behavioral assignments. As shown in chapter 1, clients with anger problems may present with a wide range of personality disorders. Although improvements are certainly possible, the presence of such patterns often means that clients will require a longer time in treatment, exhibit less compliance, and achieve less therapeutic gain overall.

Similarly, frequent and intense anger episodes have the effect of creating chaos among work and family relationships. We have found that for some clients, it is very difficult to follow a systematic treatment approach because of the practical problems that directly emerge from the anger episodes themselves. Sometimes avoidance and escape strategies, described earlier, are necessary to create windows of relative calm.

Finally, there is always the possibility that a client such as Anthony will not see anger as a problem that needs to be changed in order to have a better quality of life. The client may, instead, use the treatment sessions simply as an opportunity to complain about unfairness that exists in current relationships. However, as noted, some of Anthony's verbalizations indicate that he is beginning to consider anger a problem, and they signal that there is at least a beginning level of a desire for change. Although ambivalence or outright resistance to making anger the target of treatment is a common obstacle, the strategies outlined in this chapter have generally worked well in creating awareness, building motivation, and preparing clients to participate in more active change interventions.

Clearly, Anthony represents a difficult case with a complex history and current clinical picture. Nevertheless, with proper assessment and a collaboratively developed, menu-driven, and flexible approach, we would be cautiously optimistic about the outcome of intervention.

CHAPTER 7

Dialectical Behavior Therapy for Anger-Related Disorders

Jill H. Rathus

INTRODUCTION TO THE DIALECTICAL BEHAVIOR THERAPY APPROACH

This chapter describes dialectical behavior therapy (DBT; Linehan, 1993a, 1993b; Linehan et al., 1991) and discusses its utility as a treatment for anger-related disorders. Following a brief review of the evidence supporting its application for anger-related problems, it describes the application of the treatment in the case of Anthony, a 48-year-old man with anger difficulties and associated problems. Finally, this chapter concludes with a section on clinical issues and recommendations.

Overview of Dialectical Behavior Therapy

Linehan (1993a) developed DBT as a treatment for chronically suicidal individuals with borderline personality disorder (BPD). DBT blends behavior therapy and crisis intervention strategies with a dialectical philosophy and Eastern spiritual practice. This blending is represented by DBT's ongoing emphasis on behavior change balanced with acceptance and validation of clients as they are, the central dialectic in the treatment. The treatment is based on Linehan's biosocial theory, which suggests that BPD arises from a transaction between a biologically based difficulty with emotion regulation and a pervasively invalidating environment.

DBT is comprehensive and flexible and is delivered over several stages of treatment designed to correspond with Linehan's notion that BPD manifests in various stages of severity and that treatment should correspond with a client's stage of disorder. Stage 1, the most severe stage, is characterized by severe behavioral dyscontrol and often life-threatening behavior; treatment goals are to establish safety, connection to treatment, and behavioral control. Stage 2 is characterized by post-traumatic stress symptoms and inhibited grieving; treatment goals are to emotionally process past traumas and loss through exposure strategies. Stage 3 is characterized by ordinary problems in living; treatment at this stage resembles standard cognitive-behavioral therapy, with a focus on problem solving and skill building. Finally, stage 4 is characterized by generally good functioning but a subjective sense of lack of fulfillment or capacity for joy; treatment is aimed at fulfillment in interpersonal, spiritual, or other realms. No specific treatment is outlined for this stage; individuals can pursue various means to achieve these aims. Because data supporting the efficacy of DBT (e.g., Linehan et al., 1991) and the DBT treatment text and skills manual (Linehan, 1993a, 1993b) address stage 1 treatment only, the remainder of this chapter focuses on the application of stage 1 DBT treatment.

Stage 1 of DBT is designed to address five particular functions: (1) to improve clients' behavioral capacities, (2) to increase clients' motivation to change, (3) to help clients generalize new behaviors to all relevant aspects of their lives, (4) to support therapists, and (5) to structure the environment to promote the success of both clients and therapists. Each of these functions is addressed through at least one mode of treatment, which typically includes individual therapy, skills training group, telephone consultation, and case consultation team for therapists. Individual therapy is framed by a hierarchy of treatment targets and the chain analysis procedure. Stage 1 targets, in order of priority, are as follows: (1) decreasing life-threatening behavior, (2) decreasing therapy-interfering behavior, (3) decreasing quality-of-life interfering behavior, and (4) increasing behavioral skills (Linehan, 1993a).

In order to identify problem behaviors, clients fill out a daily diary card to track the frequency, intensity, and times at which they occur (Linehan, 1993a). Clients bring the diary card with them to therapy, and together with the therapist, they identify the behaviors taking place during the week that are highest on the treatment hierarchy. To examine target behaviors, the DBT therapist then uses a chain analysis, which follows a standard behavior therapy "A-B-C" format (i.e., antecedents, behavior, consequences). Once the target is identified, the therapist and client exhaustively examine a critical incident in terms of precipitating events, that is, the client's feelings, bodily sensations, thoughts, images, behaviors, and ensuing events, with each representing a link on the chain (Linehan, 1993a). After exploring each precipitant, the client and therapist fully consider the function of the behavior, examining all consequences. During this stage of the chain analysis, the client and therapist also engage in problem-solving efforts, such as skill strengthening, contingency management, cognitive restructuring, or exposure, as needed.

The skills training group runs concurrently with individual therapy, although it does not need to be run by the client's own individual therapist. The skills group is divided into four distinct didactic modules: *mindfulness, distress tolerance, emotion regulation,* and *interpersonal effectiveness.* Each of these modules is taught in a manualized format and contains handouts, in vivo exercises, and homework assignments designed to help clients acquire skills (Linehan, 1993b). Phone calls with the individual therapist are available as needed, primarily to provide in vivo skills coaching for clients in challenging situations. Finally, the therapist consultation team, consisting of all individual and group DBT therapists, meets weekly to discuss cases and provide support for one another.

Regarding the efficacy of DBT, in a randomized, controlled 1-year treatment trial for women diagnosed with BPD, DBT subjects showed significant reductions in anger, suicide attempts, self-injurious behavior, and number of inpatient psychiatric days, as well as improvement in social adjustment and superior treatment retention (Linehan et al., 1991). These findings remained generally stable in a 1-year follow-up investigation (Linehan, Heard, & Armstrong, 1993; Linehan et al., 1994). In addition to the original studies supporting the efficacy of DBT for BPD, there have now been several replications (e.g., Bohus et al., 2000; Koons et al., 2001; Stanley et al., 1998; Verheul et al., 2003). Moreover, the treatment has been adapted for a variety of new populations that have problems characterized by emotional or behavioral dysregulation, which Linehan identifies as core problems of BPD. These populations include suicidal adolescents (Rathus & Miller, 2002), substance-addicted individuals (Dimeff et al., 2000; Linehan et al., 2002), individuals with eating disorders (Telch, Agras, & Linehan, 2001), depressed elderly persons (Lynch, 2000), couples with relationship distress (c.f., Fruzzetti & Iverson, 2004), forensic populations (McCann, Ball, & Ivanoff, 2000), and male perpetrators of intimate partner violence (Fruzzetti & Levensky, 2000; Rathus, Cavuoto, & Passarelli, 2006). Note that in addition to those with BPD, which features as a diagnostic criterion problems with inappropriate or excessive anger or difficulty controlling anger, distressed couples, forensic populations, and male perpetrators of intimate partner violence all have in common anger as a core clinical problem.

Conceptualization of Anger-Related Disorders

Problems with anger are conceptualized and addressed in a multitude of ways using the DBT approach. First, when anger presents as a core clinical feature, the experience and expression of anger become treatment targets that would be prioritized as behaviors interfering with quality of life, as described earlier. Thus, the therapist would routinely assess anger episodes using behavioral analysis, in which antecedents and consequences are investigated in depth. Rather than a general conceptualization of the anger problem, DBT assumes functions vary both within and across individuals and seeks to understand a given anger episode for a given person in a given context.

Having said this, it is noteworthy that Linehan and others do nevertheless identify recurrent themes that apply to the conceptualization of anger as a target behavior in treatment. First, Linehan views most impulsive and severely maladaptive behaviors (particularly suicidal behavior) as faulty problem-solving behavior, where typically, the problem to be solved is an intolerably painful affective state. In fact, she theorizes that most impulsive maladaptive behaviors stem from difficulties with *emotion regulation,* which is the frequent and intense experience of strong emotions brought on by emotional vulnerability (a tendency to be sensitive to emotional triggers and to experience strong, long-lasting emotional reactions) combined with a deficit in the capacity to modulate emotions. Thus, maladaptive behaviors represent either direct behavioral manifestations of the extreme emotion or attempts to re-regulate in the face of an extremely aversive emotional experience (Linehan, 1993a). For example, an explosion of angry behavior might impulsively accompany a buildup of intense feelings of anger, or it might represent an attempt to discharge and reduce the anger (i.e., through release of the emotion or through obtaining compliance in another).

Relatedly, Hayes (2004) and Hayes et al. (1996) discuss the notion of *experiential avoidance* as central in many disordered or maladaptive behaviors, which would include anger-related disorders. Following from the notion of anger problems stemming from difficulties with emotional regulation, such difficulties can result in experiential avoidance as a main maladaptive coping strategy. This attempt to push away unwanted internal experience represents a method of trying to manage one's emotional experience (Hayes, 2004; Hayes et al.,1996). That is, symptoms arise and are maintained as a result of avoiding painful emotions through whatever means possible (e.g., binge-eating, substance abuse, self-injurious behavior). Similarly, anger-disordered individuals might engage in aggressive behaviors toward another to relieve an aversive state of internal arousal, such as rage resulting from a partner's criticism (Babcock et al., 2004;

Fruzzetti & Levensky, 2000; Tweed & Dutton, 1998). That is, emotions produce associated action urges (e.g., anger typically occurs with the urge to verbally or physically attack or physically discharge the emotion in some other way). Failure to act on these urges tends to increase negative arousal (Bishop et al., 2004; see Carver & Scheier, 1990), whereas satisfying the action urge of an emotion tends to decrease it, at least in the short run. To the extent that satisfaction of the action urge temporarily reduces negative arousal, acting on urges becomes negatively reinforced (Adams, 1988), thereby maintaining the maladaptive pattern.

Why Dialectical Behavior Therapy for Anger-Related Disorders?

DBT is appropriate for the treatment of anger-related disorders for several reasons. First, as explicated previously, the treatment investigates the ideographic functions of anger episodes to understand the unique controlling variables of each. Second, once the functions and maintaining variables are understood, a variety of problem-solving approaches are applied as needed, including contingency management, cognitive restructuring, exposure, and skills training. Third, the particular forms of skills training taught in DBT—mindfulness, interpersonal effectiveness, distress tolerance, and emotion regulation (Linehan, 1993b)—lend themselves well to addressing problems of anger, as explicated in the following sections.

Mindfulness Training

Mindfulness training is a core treatment element in DBT, considered essential for mastery of all other capacities taught in the treatment. DBT approaches mindfulness as "psychological and behavioral versions of meditation skills usually taught in Eastern spiritual practices" (Linehan, 1993a, p. 114), particularly Buddhist traditions. Mindfulness training has particular utility for enhancing emotion regulation and for addressing problems of emotional avoidance. In fact, Bishop et al. (2004) make the case that "mindfulness approaches thus may be particularly effective for clinical syndromes in which intolerance of negative affect and subsequent behavioral avoidance play a central role" (p. 237).

Bishop et al. (2004) recently operationalized the concept of mindfulness as (1) the *self-regulation of attention,* focused and sustained on *immediate experience* while (2) relinquishing the goal of changing the experience and instead *accepting* each thought, emotion, sensation, and urge as it arises. This process, in turn, would be expected to alter the subjective meaning of these experiences. They state "mindfulness in contemporary psychology has been adapted as an approach for increasing awareness and responding skillfully to mental processes that contribute to emotional distress and maladaptive behavior" (p. 230). In particular, mindfulness-based treatment targets share qualities of emotional distress and maladaptive behavior that can be conceptualized as stemming from emotion dysregulation.

In the practice of mindfulness, one learns to cease controlling immediate emotional experience, by neither pushing it away nor clinging to it (Linehan, 1993a). One learns to notice emotions and urges without acting on them and learns to observe thoughts, bodily sensations, and surroundings without feeling a mandate to change them. Rather, one simply observes present-moment experience nonjudgmentally as it enters awareness. Implicit in the notion of observing without altering experience is the notion of accepting this experience.

Practicing mindfulness thus has clear relevance for individuals with problems of anger. Mindfulness suggests the ability to separate thought (e.g., "She's disrespected me") and emotion (anger) from action (e.g., aggression). It also enhances the ability to observe and describe emotions—a key to regulating them (Linehan, 1993a). Mindfulness training teaches the ability to pause from automatic responding, to reflect, and, with awareness, to select a response rather than react impulsively. This switching from reacting to noticing experience allows one to break the cycle of overlearned, habitual angry responding. Mindfulness also aids in inhibiting secondary elaborative processing of emotions (Bishop et al., 2004). This inhibition is useful because secondary emotions, rather than primary ones, often lead to maladaptive cognitions and behaviors (Fruzzetti & Iverson, 2004). For example, fear (primary emotion) of rejection by a partner might lead to anger (here, a secondary emotion), thoughts that the partner is behaving in a disloyal manner, and angry verbal accusations.

Interpersonal Effectiveness Skills

In the interpersonal effectiveness module of DBT, clients learn how to ask for what they want and to say no directly, while maintaining the relationship (i.e., avoiding angry escalations) and maintaining self-respect. Furthermore, clients identify and alter cognitions that interfere with interpersonal effectiveness and learn factors to consider in using their interpersonal skills most effectively, such as selecting an appropriate time and place for discussions. These skills have clear relevance for angry individuals, who often have assertiveness and conflict negotiation deficits as well as cognitions that interfere with successful interpersonal interactions.

Distress Tolerance Skills

Distress tolerance skills teach clients tools for surviving the "heat of the moment" without exploding or doing something impulsive to make a situation worse. This module includes two main sets of skills: the crisis survival skills and acceptance skills. Crisis survival skills include the abilities of distracting, self-soothing, improving the moment, and evaluating the pros and cons of acting impulsively. Acceptance skills focus on the radical acceptance of a situation exactly as it is, and they are intricately linked with mindfulness. Clearly, the distress tolerance skills have direct relevance for individuals who have difficulties with explosive anger, because they emphasize either altering or tolerating immediate, intense emotions without acting destructively on the associated action urge or doing something impulsive to numb the emotion.

Emotion Regulation Skills

The emotion regulation skills focus on the capacity to modulate emotions through several strategies. These include understanding the adaptive functions of emotions, identifying and labeling emotions (including other primary emotions that might get misinterpreted as anger), cultivating mindfulness of emotional experience (i.e., learning to observe and describe emotions without judging them or attempting to change them, and to ride out their varying intensities like a wave), learning to act opposite to the current emotional action urge and thereby reduce the intensity of emotions, and developing long-term strategies (e.g., goal setting, improved social support, mindfulness to positive experiences) to reduce emotional suffering while increasing the positive emotions. These strategies all bear directly on problems with experiencing and expressing excessive anger.

THE CASE OF ANTHONY

The case of Anthony is presented in detail in Chapter 2. Nevertheless, a summary of the case is presented here.

Anthony is a 48-year-old white man of Italian descent seeking treatment for anger management. Anthony reports that his family has labeled him as emotionally abusive. Examples of this behavior, of which he is ashamed, include blowing up at his daughter's softball team while coaching the all-star game (including furiously berating the team members and then hurling a bat at the backstop, resulting in parents calling for his resignation) and ruining special occasions (including verbally exploding at Christmas because wrapping paper was strewn about the living room).

Although he apologizes for such incidents, his family sees it as "too little too late." However, Anthony also describes himself as affectionate, nurturing, emotional, and passionate. He reports a "feminine" side, enjoying cooking and providing responsibility for the family after school and through the evening while his wife is working the evening shift.

Anthony reports yelling, throwing tantrums, and cursing at loved ones when he is angry (years ago he collected guns and knives as a hobby, but he does not have any now because of his wife's concerns). He admits that he is controlling and has lately become concerned that his pattern of explosiveness will result in losing his family. His wife and daughters seem afraid to confront him and remain distant. Triggers for his rage include feeling guilty, not getting his own way, or facing tardiness or apparent "stupidity." He believes his wife intentionally shows up late just to "get back at him," and his impatience extends to his intolerance for waiting in any kind of line whether at a bank, a store, or a theater. Anthony finds lateness, stupidity, and laziness to be personal affronts and signs of disrespect. He also reports being unaware of the buildup of negative emotion, saying "it takes him by surprise." He realizes he provokes arguments because of his confrontational nature. Often, he temporarily suppresses the anger that arises during conflict, but then something unexpected triggers it and Anthony explodes. Then he resorts to verbal abuse, and at times in the past, he has used physical violence (once with a woman he was dating, whom he suspected of cheating, and once with a male peer who disrespected him). He claims that he has not been directly physically aggressive toward anyone in 20 years; however, he has thrown objects and kicked doors and walls.

Currently, Anthony feels like a failure and worries that time is passing him by. He does not have a strong work ethic and vacillates between respecting and envying the fact that his wife has a stronger one. Ambivalent about his current job, he says he lacks a "working man's" identity. He feels a lack of confidence and admits putting on a bravado to feign confidence. He offers that he struggles with shame having to do with his past sexual abuse and guilt having to do with his lack of financial success, his outside relationships, and his emotional abuse of his family members. Stating his continued love of his wife and family, Anthony wants to understand his anger and control himself such that he does not harm others.

Case Conceptualization

Anthony is a 42-year-old man who has had chronic difficulties in relationship and vocational domains. His primary presenting problem concerns explosive anger episodes toward his family. He also exhibits marital distress and struggles with bouts of depression, symptoms of post-traumatic stress disorder (PTSD), and borderline personality features.

Developmentally, Anthony experienced pervasive invalidation in forms such as continual demeaning and corporal punishment by his mother, years of sexual abuse by an uncle, and perceived betrayal by both his parents when they reacted indifferently to his disclosure of the sexual abuse. Growing up, he repeatedly became attached to and idealized adults who ultimately disappointed him or abandoned him.

According to Linehan's biosocial theory (1993a), problems with emotion dysregulation arise from a transaction between a biologically wired emotional vulnerability (intense, long-lasting emotional reactions to even relatively minor stimuli) coupled with a pervasively invalidating environment. Such an environment often punishes displays of emotion and provides messages that one's behaviors and emotional responses are wrong, poorly reasoned, exaggerated, or manipulative. This response teaches one to mistrust one's own reactions, to look to the environment for cues of how one should think or feel, to oversimplify the ease of problem solving, and to escalate emotional displays in an attempt to be taken seriously. It also fails to teach steps necessary for emotion modulation, such as redirecting attention and behaving in a non–mood-dependent manner through steps such as focusing, distracting from distress, or self-soothing. As one's intensified expressions of emotion (e.g., anger explosions) are typically ignored or punished but on occasion attended to (i.e., intermittently reinforced), the individual learns to alternately self-invalidate (i.e., ignore, dismiss, or tune out one's own emotional signals) and express emotion with a demanding intensity.

Anthony seems by temperament to experience intense emotions, and he has a history of invalidation, seemingly leaving him without the capacities needed to modulate these emotions. He reports not recognizing his rising anger (consistent with self-invalidation) and then suddenly reacting to a trigger and exploding. He finds many situations overwhelming and defeating (e.g., work, his marital relationship) and has little idea of how to approach these problems constructively. Despite guilt over his explosive temper, he finds himself with no tools to change his destructive patterns.

The biosocial theory helps lay the foundation for DBT as it helps the therapist to view problems with emotion dysregulation compassionately and nonjudgmentally. It also helps the therapist to attend to instances of dysregulation in session, which can steer the therapy off course, and to be sensitive to avoiding repeating a pattern of invalidation of the patient (e.g., by not oversimplifying the prospect of changing behaviors). Furthermore, the major interventions in DBT share as their core goal enhancing the client's capacities for emotion modulation while providing a validating environment. As a behavioral treatment, DBT would target

Anthony's behavioral excesses (e.g., anger explosions) and deficits (e.g., ability to tolerate distress, to calm himself, to communicate assertively, to recognize internal states). The treatment would also attend to relevant contextual cues (e.g., disrespect from immediate family members) and vulnerability factors (e.g., depression, guilt, shame, intrusive traumatic memories, lack of work-derived self-esteem). The therapist would seek to identify consequences to his anger explosions that are both reinforcing (e.g., arousal reduction, sense of empowerment) and punishing (guilt, shame, and increased distance from wife and children). Behavioral analyses would target specific behavioral patterns that lead to difficulties (e.g., pursuing emotional intimacy outside of the marital relationship) as well as identify ways in which effective behaviors have been punished (e.g., getting criticized for expressing his grief over his nephew). General behavior patterns maintaining his presenting difficulties would also be examined. For example, Anthony seems to be trapped in a behavior pattern characterized by inhibited grieving and crisis-generating behavior (Linehan, 1993a). It seems clear both from the case history and assessment data that Anthony is troubled by PTSD symptoms. Suffering intrusive emotions from past trauma and loss (as indicated by his history and his assessment results on the Trauma Symptom Inventory; Briere, 1995; see Chapter 2), Anthony continually struggles to push away painful memories and images. His testing further suggests that he acts out "anger to modulate negative internal states" and seeks to avoid aversive internal experiences by "attempts to eliminate painful thoughts or memories from conscious awareness and a desire to neutralize negative feelings about past trauma" (see Chapter 2). In this behavior pattern, the continual escape behavior from such intrusive experience manifests often as impulsive behavior that results in its own negative consequences and emotional pain (i.e., "crisis-generating"); in Anthony, we see this in his emotionally abusive outbursts and his resultant distance from family members and unstable work history.

In considering the case of Anthony, it is apparent that his anger difficulties include emotional, verbal, and mild physical aggression. Although he has been directly physically aggressive only toward previous partners and not toward Joanna, he *has* repeatedly thrown objects or kicked walls and doors during his anger explosions with her. From a family violence perspective, these behaviors would be classified as mild acts of physical aggression, because they cluster with direct mild acts of physical aggression in factor analytic studies of conflict tactics used in couple relationships (Pan, Neidig, & O'Leary, 1994). The meaning of such behaviors tends to be equivalent for those witnessing them to acts of mild physical aggression, likely because they exhibit physically out-of-control behavior and suggest that the witness may be the next target of one's physically expressed rage (Pan, Neidig, & O'Leary, 1994). Moreover, the importance of Anthony's verbally and emotionally abusive behaviors toward his wife and daughters should not be minimized, particularly because many women report that a partner's psychologically aggressive behaviors have a more detrimental impact than physically aggressive behaviors. Because of reports of these behaviors, two additional assessment tools would lend important information.

First, the Psychological Maltreatment of Women Inventory (PMWI; Tolman, 1989) would assess the range and nature of psychological aggression occurring, with its two subscales: emotional-verbal abuse and dominance-isolation. Second, the Revised Conflict Tactics Scale (CTS2; Straus et al., 1996) would provide additional information on any physical aggression that may have occurred and its impact. This would be important to include because the degree of minor physical aggression is likely being under-reported (ample research evidence indicates that both male and female partners under-report incidents of physical aggression), respondents under-report aggression in face-to-face interviews relative to behaviorally specific self-report measures (see Rathus & Feindler, 2004), and any physically aggressive behavior would also be monitored and targeted in treatment. Based on the detailed case description in Chapter 2, Anthony would likely obtain high scores on the emotional-verbal abuse scale of the PMWI (Tolman, 1989), and on the CTS2 (Straus et al., 1996), he would be expected to have low scores on the negotiation scale, high scores on the psychological aggression scale, and moderate scores on the minor physical assault scale. Note that a history of trauma and also early shaming by a parent have been identified as important factors for males who grow up to be both emotionally and physically abusive (Dutton, 1995, 1999).

In terms of diagnostic categories, Anthony seems to evidence a history of major depression, characterized by his various periods of lack of motivation and anhedonia, ("sitting on the couch and doing nothing"), low self-esteem, and self-reported extended depression following his grandfather's death. This history is supported by his mild/moderate present score of 14 on the Beck Depression Inventory (see Chapter 2).

In addition to depression and PTSD, Anthony appears to meet criteria for BPD. His history of sexual abuse is a developmental factor known to be associated with deficits in emotion modulation and with a diagnosis of BPD. Anthony's features of BPD include excessive anger, emotional lability, identity confusion (seeming confusion regarding identifying with both masculine and feminine stereotypes, ambivalent work identity, ambivalent feelings about his wife's work ethic, chronic ambivalence about life choices), unstable interpersonal relationships (both within intimate and vocational contexts), and fear of abandonment. It is unclear whether he meets the additional criteria of impulsivity in at least two areas and chronic emptiness or boredom. Yet, he may meet criteria for impulsivity as he reports being a "womanizer," which may indicate a history of promiscuity; past alcohol and drug use; and explosive episodes that have caused him to lose employment. Furthermore, one gets the sense he may experience chronic emptiness, as evidenced by his lack of fulfillment from his career and his need to seek platonic "best friendships" in women. He apparently has no self-injurious behavior or suicidality and no paranoid or dissociative features, the remaining criteria for BPD. If obtaining a definitive diagnosis were important to the clinician, a standardized structured diagnostic interview would help clear up diagnostic uncertainty.

Treatment Plan

The evidence suggesting that Anthony meets criteria for BPD lends support to a DBT approach, which has been repeatedly validated as an effective treatment for BPD. Regardless of whether this diagnosis applies, however, DBT is still appropriate for Anthony's presentation given its success with other angry, emotionally dysregulated populations, as noted previously. Note that DBT is a comprehensive treatment that can address not only Anthony's anger difficulties but also his depression, PTSD, and interpersonal relationships, all factors that contribute to and maintain his anger. Moreover, DBT has been adapted for intimate partner violence (IPV), as described by Rathus, Cavuoto, and Passarelli (2006). DBT for IPV might be preferable to DBT in its original form because of the manifestation of Anthony's anger difficulties within the marriage and family and the fact that he presents with outwardly, rather than inwardly, directed aggression. DBT for IPV focuses on harm toward others within intimate relationships rather than primarily on suicidal or self-injurious behaviors.

Brief Adaptations in Dialectical Behavior Therapy for Intimate Partner Violence

In its standard form, DBT is structured to treat the problems faced by individuals with BPD, most of whom are women. While Anthony appears to meet criteria for BPD, this is not necessary for the application of DBT, which appears to be an appropriate treatment approach for anger problems and for men with abusive behavior (see Rathus, Cavuoto, & Passarelli, 2006). Such men share many characteristics with women with BPD, such as poor treatment retention, emotional dysregulation, problems with anger, confusion about self, impulsivity, and poor interpersonal skills. Thus, Rathus, Cavuoto, and Passarelli (2006) slightly modified DBT for males with abusive behavior toward an intimate partner.

The first adaptation was to expand the hierarchy of targets to include behaviors directed toward others. The category of "life-threatening behavior" was expanded to include not only self-injurious behavior but also other-directed violent behavior (particularly toward one's partner and children). In addition, the category "quality-of-life interfering behavior" was expanded to include behaviors that affect the quality of life of others (e.g., psychological abuse, verbal abuse, controlling behaviors). Authors such as O'Leary (2001) insist that a focus on forms of partner aggression other than physical aggression is imperative, because these forms of abuse have a strongly detrimental impact on recipients and might actually increase in the absence of physical aggression (Gondolf, Heckert, & Kimmel, 2002). The DBT diary card was also modified to include conflict tactics (e.g., physical, psychological, and verbal aggressive acts, along with urges to be aggressive and injury to others) and a greater number of emotions to monitor on a daily basis (anger, fear, jealousy, happiness, misery, sadness, guilt, and shame) (Figure 7.1).

Remaining minor alterations related to the skills handouts. First, Rathus et al. added a module entitled "domestic partner education," which provides psychoeducation regarding definitions of physically, verbally, and psychologically abusive behavior. For example, clients learn that throwing or slamming things is threatening to others and differs little from mild acts of physical abuse perpetrated on them directly, because the threat and perception of the perpetrator being out of control is similar. This psychoeducation module also addresses the impact of domestic violence on children, family of origin violence, common attitudes justifying abusive behavior, and the link between substance use and domestic violence. Other changes include a greater emphasis on a partner's experiences in addition to one's own (e.g., being mindful of others' experiences, or "relational mindfulness" [Fruzzetti & Levensky, 2000]), increased emphasis on empathy and partner respect in the interpersonal effectiveness module, a rewording of some of the feminine content to be more masculine, an expansion of the acceptance skills to include explicit acceptance of the partner as well as a list of difficult relationship truths that must be accepted (e.g., a partner might choose to end the relationship), and an added focus on the emotion of jealousy, which has been shown to be a significant emotional precursor to male abusive behavior (e.g., Babcock et al., 2004).

Using Dialectical Behavior Therapy with Anthony

In DBT, active treatment is preceded by a pretreatment phase, usually lasting up to several sessions. In this phase, the clinician provides a detailed orientation to the treatment and uses a variety of commitment

Dialectical Behavior Therapy Male Partner Diary Card

Initials ___ ID# ___ Filled out in session? Y/N How often did you fill out this section? _Daily 2–3x Once_ Date started _/_/_

Day & Date	Urges to be Aggressive 0–5	Conflict Tactics					Substances		Other	Emotions								Skills* 1–3
		Positive Verbal Tactics Yes/No	Negative Verbal Tactics Yes/No	Psychologically Aggressive Tactics Yes/No	Type I Physical Tactics Yes/No	Type II Physical Tactics Yes/No	Partner Injury 0–5	Alcohol/Drugs # Specify		Anger 0–5	Fear 0–5	Jealousy 0–5	Happiness 0–5	Misery/Pain 0–5	Guilt 0–5	Sadness 0–5	Shame 0–5	
Mon. /																		
Tues. /																		
Wed. /																		
Thurs. /																		
Fri. /																		
Sat. /																		
Sun. /																		

0 = Not at all; 1 = A bit; 2 = Somewhat; 3 = Rather strong; 4 = Very strong; 5 = Extremely strong

Motivation to attend group: ___ Before session (0–5) ___ After session (0–5) ___

Connection to group: ___

*USED SKILLS

1 = Did not use skills.
2 = Used them, but they did not help.
3 = Used them and they helped.

Notes:

Positive verbal tactics:
Examples:
- Discussed issues calmly
- Listened to partner's side of problem/disagreement
- Made efforts to compromise
- Respected partner's view

Negative verbal tactics:
Examples:
- Insulted or swore at partner, put partner down, belittled partner
- Would not listen to partner's point of view
- Made partner feel worthless
- Yelled and screamed

Physical tactics:

Type I examples:
- Aggressive toward property or pets (smashed, threw, kicked, hit, destroyed things)
- Pounded fist, punched wall
- Held partner down; pushed, grabbed, shoved partner; threw something at partner
- Blocked partner from leaving, restrained partner
- Slapped partner

Type II examples:
- Hit or kicked partner, choked partner
- Beat up partner
- Physically forced partner to have sex
- Threatened or used a gun or knife on partner

Psychologically aggressive tactics:

Examples:

- Threatened to hit partner, leave partner, take children away
- Monitored partner's whereabouts or friends, jealous/suspicious
- Ordered partner around, treated partner like a servant
- Prevented partner from doing something the partner wanted to do
- Humiliated partner

Partner injury scale

0 = No marks or injury.
1 = Superficial marks.
2 = Bruises or scratches **not** needing medical attention.
3 = Bruises or cuts **needing** medical attention.
4 = Broken bones or teeth; injury to eyes, nose, ears.
5 = Internal injuries; concussion or loss of consciousness.

Dialectical Behavior Therapy Male Partner Diary Card

Instructions: Circle the days you worked on each skill

	Mon.	Tues.	Wed.	Thurs.	Fri.	Sat.	Sun.
1. Wise mind	Mon.	Tues.	Wed.	Thurs.	Fri.	Sat.	Sun.
2. Observe (Just notice what's going on inside)	Mon.	Tues.	Wed.	Thurs.	Fri.	Sat.	Sun.
3. Describe (Put words on the experience)	Mon.	Tues.	Wed.	Thurs.	Fri.	Sat.	Sun.
4. Participate (Enter into the experience)	Mon.	Tues.	Wed.	Thurs.	Fri.	Sat.	Sun.
5. Do not judge (Nonjudgmental stance)	Mon.	Tues.	Wed.	Thurs.	Fri.	Sat.	Sun.
6. Stay focused (One-mindfully: in-the-moment)	Mon.	Tues.	Wed.	Thurs.	Fri.	Sat.	Sun.
7. Do what works (Effectiveness)	Mon.	Tues.	Wed.	Thurs.	Fri.	Sat.	Sun.
8. DEAR MAN (Getting what you want)	Mon.	Tues.	Wed.	Thurs.	Fri.	Sat.	Sun.
9. GIVE (Improving the relationship)	Mon.	Tues.	Wed.	Thurs.	Fri.	Sat.	Sun.
10. Cheerleading statements for worry thoughts	Mon.	Tues.	Wed.	Thurs.	Fri.	Sat.	Sun.
11. Identifying and labeling emotions	Mon.	Tues.	Wed.	Thurs.	Fri.	Sat.	Sun.

	Mon.	Tues.	Wed.	Thurs.	Fri.	Sat.	Sun.
12. PLEASE (Reduce vulnerability to emotion mind)	Mon.	Tues.	Wed.	Thurs.	Fri.	Sat.	Sun.
13. MASTER (Building mastery, feeling effective)	Mon.	Tues.	Wed.	Thurs.	Fri.	Sat.	Sun.
14. Engaging in pleasant activities	Mon.	Tues.	Wed.	Thurs.	Fri.	Sat.	Sun.
15. Working toward long-term goals	Mon.	Tues.	Wed.	Thurs.	Fri.	Sat.	Sun.
16. ACCEPTS (Distract)	Mon.	Tues.	Wed.	Thurs.	Fri.	Sat.	Sun.
17. IMPROVE the moment	Mon.	Tues.	Wed.	Thurs.	Fri.	Sat.	Sun.
18. Self-soothe (5 senses)	Mon.	Tues.	Wed.	Thurs.	Fri.	Sat.	Sun.
19. Pros and cons	Mon.	Tues.	Wed.	Thurs.	Fri.	Sat.	Sun.
20. Radical acceptance	Mon.	Tues.	Wed.	Thurs.	Fri.	Sat.	Sun.

Based on Linehan et al., 1999; Vivian & Heyman, 1996; Rathus & Cavuoto, 2000.

Figure 7.1   DBT diary card adapted for partner—violent men.

154 ANGER-RELATED DISORDERS

strategies (see Linehan, 1993a) to engage the client in the treatment process and begin building the therapeutic relationship. One of the central commitment strategies in DBT is "devil's advocate," in which the therapist points out the difficulty of therapy and attempts to let the client off the hook, allowing the client to argue why addressing the problem is imperative at this time (Linehan, 1993a). This shifts the responsibility for change from the therapist to the client and strengthens the client's motivation for therapy. A similar approach, increasingly applied to men with IPV, is known as motivational interviewing (Murphy & Baxter, 1997). Rather than confronting clients about what is harmful in their behavior, therapists using this approach asks clients to discuss how their presenting issues have been both beneficial and detrimental to them, reducing defensiveness and, again, strengthening motivation for therapy. Both of these approaches would seem important for Anthony, because discussing his guilt over his destructive anger without further shaming him would likely help cement his commitment to treatment.

Once the client is oriented to therapy and expresses commitment to participating in it, phase 1 of the treatment begins. Phase 1 treatment targets include the establishment of safety (both for oneself and, in cases in which there is outwardly directed aggressive behavior, for others), connection to treatment, and behavioral control; treatment components all contribute to attaining these goals.

At the outset of treatment, the therapist and client collaboratively identify treatment targets, according to the hierarchy. In Anthony's case, there apparently are no life-threatening behaviors—he is not suicidal and his mild acts of physical aggression at this time do not seem to pose a physical threat to others (however, should these behaviors escalate or should a thrown object pose a threat or injury, this would be treated as a top priority). Treatment-interfering behaviors, such as nonattending behavior, noncollaborative behavior, late arrival, or noncompletion of homework, would be monitored and addressed as the second priority. Quality-of-life behavior would be addressed in session as the third priority. If Anthony did not exhibit life-threatening behavior or treatment-interfering behavior, quality-of-life interfering behaviors would comprise the bulk of the treatment sessions with the primary therapist.

The therapist would work with Anthony to construct a subhierarchy of quality-of-life interfering behaviors to address, related to his presenting problems. That way, if many such behaviors occurred within a week, there would be a "road map," albeit flexible, of what to devote the session time to. Because problems with anger were the main presenting problem and these problems affect not only Anthony's but also his family's quality of life, this would surely be the top priority. This would mean that if several quality-of-life interfering behaviors took place during the week prior to therapy and an explosion of anger was among them, this would be targeted for discussion in the session. For Anthony, this category comprises intense experiences or explosions of anger, as manifested by psychological, verbal, or mild physical aggression (e.g., throwing objects) or other forms of emotional abusiveness (e.g., controlling behavior, jealous behavior, noncommunicative behavior).

Following explosive anger episodes, additional quality-of-life interfering behaviors to target might include symptoms of depression and PTSD, other behaviors that interfere with his marital relationship (e.g., his penchant for developing outside intimate relationships with women via the Internet, a behavior that hinders his intimacy with his partner and ironically makes him feel more isolated/detached, as well as guilty) and with his daughters, behaviors that might exacerbate his health problems (e.g., inadequate stress management, missed medical appointments or doses of prescribed medication), and behaviors that interfere with job success and stability. Related to this last target, if he could maintain a more stable income, not only would this contribute to improved self-esteem but it might also allow for moving to slightly larger living quarters. With seven family members living in two bedrooms, this is no doubt an ongoing stressor for Anthony (in fact, the emotion regulation skills include a section on identifying and taking steps toward short- and long-term goals, which for this client might include increased income and moving residences). Improvements in the wide range of these quality-of-life interfering behaviors would contribute to decreasing his depression and overall level of anger.

In DBT, clients fill out a diary card to monitor the target behaviors on a daily basis. The card can be customized to include targets specific to a given client. On the diary card, Anthony would monitor the aforementioned targets plus the range and intensity of the range of emotions he experiences each day. The monitoring of targeted behaviors allows the client and therapist to prioritize session content accordingly, and monitoring emotions increases awareness of emotions and, in turn, the ability to regulate them. Note that if Anthony neglected to fill out the diary card, this would be addressed with a chain analysis as a therapy-interfering behavior. After addressing this once or twice and clearing up questions or misunderstandings about the card, most clients see its central role in therapy and fill it out reliably.

After reviewing the diary card in the beginning of each session, Anthony and his therapist would develop a plan for the content of the session. One or two treatment targets, according to the DBT hierarchy, would then be addressed using the DBT chain analysis procedure, an exhaustive, moment-by-moment description of events leading to the target behavior and following it, as described earlier. After identifying central antecedents and consequences (i.e., controlling variables), the therapist and client work together to apply solutions to the problem behavior. This is done by examining the entire context and identifying links on the chain of behaviors that could have gone differently and thus resulted in a different outcome. Problem-solving strategies are applied as relevant, and new skills are practiced as needed. The following scenario exemplifies how a behavioral analysis might unfold regarding the target of Anthony's bat-hurling incident while coaching his daughter's all-star softball game.

First, the behavior (hurling the bat at the backstop) and context would be described in detail. Next, the therapist would ask Anthony to identify where the chain began, that is, to identify, to the best of his ability, what set off this particular chain of events. For the sake of this example, assume Anthony identified the precipitating event as an argument with the opposing team's coach over a play that gave the other team the lead and ultimately cost his daughter's team the game. The therapist would then ask Anthony to go back even further and identify any vulnerability factors (i.e., affective or mood states, biological factors, or environmental events that made him even more vulnerable to reacting to the precipitating event). Anthony might identify such factors as a poor night's sleep, a brief argument with his wife over her going to work on the day of the all-star game, and skipping breakfast because of rushing to make it on time, all of which led to his already feeling irritable by the start of the game. Furthermore, Anthony may have been counting on bringing his daughter's team to victory and envisioning a day of closeness with his daughter, especially important to him in light of guilt over his recent treatment of her and their growing distance. After assessing vulnerability factors, the therapist would elicit the moment-to-moment events from the event beginning the chain up to the targeted behavior. Anthony might report that engaging in, and losing, the argument with the coach might have led him to feel humiliated in front of the spectators as well as upset with himself for not controlling himself better. For this example, let's assume that in reviewing the episode, Anthony was able to identify that as his mixture of anger and humiliation grew, he became more physiologically aroused, feeling his heart pounding, his fists clenching, his brow sweating, and an urge to storm off the field. As his team started to lose, he then began pacing and having thoughts such as "I'm letting my daughter down," "I'm a lousy coach—in fact, I'm lousy at everything I do," and feeling increasingly anxious. Not focusing on his internal state but only on the game, he began getting more short-tempered with the girls on the team, criticizing them and shouting comments such as "What's wrong with you?" when they missed crucial plays. In response, the girls began looking at him angrily or outright ignoring him, which only made him angrier. When his own daughter struck out, she held up her hand toward him blocking her face and averting her eyes while walking back to the dugout, as if to say "Leave me alone," which he interpreted as hostile and disrespectful. When his team lost, he immediately felt a rush of rage, feeling his heart beating so intensely that he felt it would explode in his chest; he also felt an urge to scream at and blame his team. He immediately sat them down in the dugout and began publicly, furiously berating them for their performance and for their not listening to him during the game. As he was doing this, he saw his daughter's eyes well up with tears and spectators staring at him with disdain. He promptly felt deeply ashamed and guilty and was furious at himself for "ruining everything," showing himself to be a failure once again and further alienating his daughter. Feeling physically out of control, now with rapid breathing and a sense of being about to "jump out of his skin," he picked up the nearest bat and hurled it as hard as he could at the backstop.

Immediate negative consequences of throwing the bat included onlookers gasping in horror; his team, including his daughter, getting up and leaving the area to get away from him; and intensified shame bordering on despair. Positive consequences included relief from the unpleasant physical sensations he was experiencing, the feeling that he "got his anger out," a moment of feeling strong and in control, and a cessation of his verbal tirade. Later negative consequences that followed included his daughter giving him the silent treatment for the remainder of the weekend, his ruminations about behavior he found shameful and about his being a failure as a coach and as a father, distance from his wife for the remainder of the weekend as she sided with the daughter, and team parents calling for his resignation.

After identifying the events preceding and following the target behavior to the extent that the chain of events appears logical, the therapist would conduct a solution analysis. The solution analysis focuses on links on the chain that could have been altered to produce a different and more desirable outcome. These include focusing on both antecedents (e.g., skills training to replace problematic behavioral sequences, cognitive modification of expectancies or beliefs that support problematic behaviors, exposure to cues that elicit problem emotions/behaviors) and consequences (typically through contingency management, e.g., removing reinforcers, reinforcing other responses, adding aversive consequences). Although there are many links on this chain that could be changed to produce a different outcome, the therapist might choose to work with Anthony on a select few. For example, Anthony might work on his vulnerability factors (e.g., by working on factors that interfered with his sleep [emotion regulation skills]). Furthermore, he might have accepted his wife's work schedule and not picked an argument before the game (distress tolerance skills), or he might have discussed it with her calmly (using interpersonal effectiveness skills) several days in advance (and role-played such a conversation in session). Regarding his expectancy that this day would bring victory and enhanced closeness between him and his daughter, the therapist might work on modifying these cognitions to set a less rigid standard for a successful day. For example, he might have more realistically expected that win or lose, he is demonstrating his caring by coaching his daughter's team. As many such days accumulate, coupled with control over his anger, Anthony has a reasonable chance of building closeness with his daughter. Regarding the fight with the coach, he might have spoken assertively without escalating quickly to verbal aggression. The therapist might also use an exposure strategy to help Anthony habituate to a provocation by the opposing coach, such as by role-playing the opposing coach and having Anthony repeatedly respond to attacks without himself losing control. If Anthony had become aware of his escalating emotions, his increasing arousal, and negative cognitions following the argument with the coach, he could have practiced observing them without judgment and with a goal of effectiveness, that is, doing what would work to achieve his goals in the situation (mindfulness skills), which might have included keeping the game in perspective and refraining from criticizing the players. He could have applied distress tolerance skills, such as taking a moment to self-sooth with a cool beverage or to consider the pros and cons of acting on his anger. Furious upon losing the game, he might have again applied mindful observation of his emotions and urges and might have elected to act in opposition to his urges, for example, by calmly walking away from the team and resisting his urge to attack, or even better, by sitting down the girls and validating their feelings of disappointment and telling them they played their best. He could have noted his feeling that he would "jump out of his skin" and simply noticed its intensity wax and wane (mindfulness to current emotions, from the emotion regulation module). Because there were many punishing consequences for Anthony's explosive behavior, these might be highlighted by the therapist to enhance Anthony's attention to natural aversive consequences. In addition, the therapist would need to take care not to inadvertently reinforce maladaptive behaviors on Anthony's part. Finally, the therapist might work with Anthony on differential reinforcement of an alternative behavior, such as treating himself to something desired if he resists an explosive urge.

In addition to individual sessions, Anthony would concurrently participate in skills training sessions, which consist of a manualized didactic format with many interactive and experiential components and weekly homework assignments for practicing the skills. As delivered in standard

DBT, treatment would ideally consist of individual weekly therapy sessions plus a separate weekly skills training group. If Anthony preferred or if more feasible given the therapist's resources, Anthony could learn the skills individually through the primary therapist, although these would need to be taught in a separate session to avoid the blurring of session content and structure. However, for Anthony, the camaraderie of a group of men would probably be beneficial due to his social isolation and current lack of close male friends.

The skills modules include mindfulness, which would help with such problems as Anthony's anger building up and taking him by surprise, as well as his ability to experience anger rise in him like a wave without judging it or acting on it. Core mindfulness skills involve nonjudgmental awareness of the present moment and of aspects of the self and environment. Specifically, Anthony may have difficulty identifying what he feels, and he seems to struggle with an unstable sense of self, a sense of emptiness, and chronic ambivalence. Teaching him how to nonjudgmentally observe and describe what he is feeling and thinking in the moment would target his troubled identity development; mind-focusing and observation skills would enhance his self-knowledge while preparing him to take the needed action to skillfully reach his goals. Overall, mindfulness skills could enable Anthony to focus and make decisions with both rational and emotional input. Mindfulness helps with ambivalence and identity confusion as people access "wise mind" (an internal source of wisdom and intuitive knowing) and learn more about who they are and what their needs are.

While regular mindfulness exercises would treat the intensity and impulsive expression of anger, they serve as a form of exposure as well. That is, through mindfulness practice, Anthony would learn to experience emotions of anger, shame, anxiety/fear, guilt, and sadness, without acting in some way to avoid these experiences through some form of maladaptive behavior.

The skills modules would also include the psychoeducation module (as described previously), distress tolerance, emotion regulation, and interpersonal effectiveness. The distress tolerance skills address the impulsivity inherent in impulsive explosions of anger. Distress tolerance skills would help Anthony resist impulsive decisions and actions. These skills would address impulsivity by teaching Anthony how to effectively distract and soothe himself while considering the pros and cons of his actions. The acceptance skills in the distress tolerance module build directly on mindfulness skills and involve mastering nonjudgmental acceptance of both oneself and one's current situation. Anthony would practice experiencing and observing his thoughts, emotions, behaviors, and external environment without trying to change them. It would be important to emphasize that a nonjudgmental stance does not imply approval; Anthony can accept a situation that he cannot change (e.g., his past history of trauma, his wife's lateness, his youngest daughter's sassiness) without approving of the situation.

Emotion regulation skills address emotional sensitivity; rapid, intense mood changes; and unmodulated emotional states characterized by depression, anxiety, or problems with either overcontrolled or undercontrolled anger. Anthony would be taught how to identify and label emotions increase positive emotions, reduce vulnerability to negative emotions, and act in opposition to maladaptive emotional action urges. Building on mindfulness skills, these skills teach nonjudgmental observation and description of one's current emotion.

The interpersonal effectiveness skills focus on the clients' difficulties in maintaining consistent and rewarding relationships. Anthony has unstable, conflict-ridden relationships and experiences fear of his wife abandoning him. Also, interpersonal conflicts and frustrations are often a primary precipitating event in Anthony's anger episodes. This module can help reduce the destructive impact of Anthony's argumentative style. It seems that at times Anthony withdraws from social interactions and feels reluctant to reach out for social support. The interpersonal effectiveness module addresses these issues with both skills practice in effective communication and a cognitive therapy component aimed at thoughts interfering with successful communication of needs. Thus, the interpersonal effectiveness module would help Anthony not only in managing the inevitable conflicts with his wife, adolescent daughters, and others but also in managing his reported tendency to personalize others' behaviors (a feature common to men who engage in IPV; Holtzworth-Monroe & Hutchinson, 1993).

Stage 1 of treatment in DBT typically takes between 6 months and 1 year. Once Anthony's had reached the overall stage 1 targets of establishing safety and behavioral control, meaning, in his case, that those around him felt safe and he was no longer exploding and feeling his anger was out of control, he could begin the next stage. In stage 2 of DBT, the format typically changes to only individual weekly therapy sessions, although these might include some review of skills learned in stage 1. During this second phase, the primary focus turns toward emotionally processing the past, with a focus on unresolved trauma and grief reactions. Note that Anthony's "inhibited grieving," described in an earlier section, would begin to be addressed throughout stage 1 of DBT, primarily through mindfulness practice, which would teach noticing and accepting, rather than pushing away, aversive internal experiences. In stage 2, however, rather than conducting behavioral analyses and conducting skills training, past traumas and losses are addressed directly through exposure therapy (Linehan, 1993a). The premise is that now that the client's behaviors are under control and the client is armed with a plethora of coping resources to manage emotions without acting out destructively, a focused period of exposure to traumatic events can begin. Treating a core source of Anthony's emotion dysregulation by addressing his past traumas would be necessary for maintaining gains attained in stage 1 and continuing to build mastery over modulating his emotions. This phase would likely last an additional 6 months to 1 year, and following this, Anthony could decide whether to continue in therapy, perhaps addressing stage 3 and 4 targets, as described previously, or perhaps entering couples therapy.

CLINICAL ISSUES AND RECOMMENDATIONS

Clinical issues and recommendations for this case include identifying criteria for "graduating" to the next stage of treatment (i.e., identifying the hoped-for changes in treatment); addressing PTSD in stage 2; considering the inclusion of family members in treatment, particularly at a later stage of therapy; handling termination; and considering cautions in working with Anthony, his strengths, and the likely prognosis for this case.

DBT for Anthony's anger and related problems would likely last a minimum of 1 year, with at least 6 months devoted to stage 1 of treatment. Note that during stage 1, it is possible to schedule as-needed family sessions to work on specific problems that arise or to give the client the opportunity to rehearse new skills in an in vivo situation with the aid of therapist coaching; this might be highly useful for Anthony. Graduation from stage 1, with its focus on behavioral stability and safety, to stage 2, with its focus on emotional processing of past events, would be determined by Anthony's progress. In other words, if his family members felt safe and no longer feared him, if he felt he had gained control over his impulsive and destructive anger episodes, if at least some progress was made in his other stage 1 targets, and related to all of these gains, if he demonstrated acquisition of DBT skills, he could move on to stage 2. Normally, in stage 2, clients no longer participate in weekly skills training or fill out diary cards. However, sometimes this is decided on an individual basis, and provisions could be made for his continuing skills training if Anthony and the therapist agreed this would be worthwhile.

Similarly, Anthony's completion of stage 2 would occur when he and the therapist felt that he had sufficiently resolved his past traumas and losses through exposure work. Such a resolution would not mean that Anthony no longer experienced pain from these events but rather that his recollections of these events did not cause him to continually push away the experiences or dysregulate his emotions and behavior. The therapist would then speak with Anthony and find out if he wished to continue with therapy or to plan to terminate. One option for continuing therapy might be to begin couples or even family sessions to work on ongoing problems and stressors within the family and to teach family members the DBT skills. This could provide an environment conducive to Anthony's maintaining skill use, as well as enhance the overall family environment by teaching communication, distress tolerance, emotional regulation, and mindfulness skills to all family members. Should Anthony plan to terminate, this is done in DBT with much advance planning, and often with fading of session frequency rather than an abrupt cessation. Clients keep all skills training materials and are encouraged to refer to them for a "refresher" when needed.

Cautions in working with Anthony would include the fact that he has resisted seeking help in the past and thus might have difficulty committing to therapy or sustaining it. He is also easily frustrated and impatient and might drop out prematurely in an early stage when he experiences stressors at home and has not yet developed the capacities to handle these. Because Anthony has a history of disappointment and disillusionment in primary relationships, as well as loss and betrayal of those he cares about and looks up to, he may experience strong vulnerability and anxiety upon developing a relationship with a therapist and be a likely candidate for premature dropout. Anthony also feels lonely and seeks intimate emotional connections with others on whom he can rely and who understand him. Although an intense bond might propel therapy forward, Anthony would likely be highly sensitive to any inadvertent missteps by the therapist and might experience anger toward the therapist readily and expect to be rejected.

Precisely because patients with BPD commonly have these sensitivities, DBT emphasizes close monitoring and protection of the therapeutic relationship. First, as part of the pretreatment orientation, the clinician discusses the importance of maintaining an open and trusting therapeutic relationship. He or she normalizes rifts or fluctuations in the relationship, saying that these *will* occur and stressing the importance of open communication to resolve them (this not only protects the therapeutic alliance but also models effective behavior for outside relationships). The therapist orients the client to the use of phone calls, which in addition to in vivo coaching are used for *relationship repair.* That is, if either the therapist or client feels upset or regretful about something said in session, either is invited to phone the other to discuss it and repair the relationship promptly (rather than wait for the next session, which may result in a "no-show" if the client is upset). Second, therapy-interfering behavior is addressed as the second priority target in DBT, following only suicidal/life-threatening behaviors. Therapy-interfering behavior includes any behaviors *on the part of the client or therapist* that are interfering with the therapy. These can include noncompliance issues or lateness, as well as direct indications of changes in the therapeutic alliance, such as outbursts of rage toward the therapist or a decrease in willingness to self-disclose. Not only do therapists bring up such behaviors as they arise, but clients are invited to bring up any therapy-interfering behaviors they observe. This structure ensures that the relationship is continually monitored and aims to address problems early, before they cause irreparable damage to the therapy. Thus, Anthony might evidence a change in behavior if he felt betrayed by the therapist, and the DBT therapist would address this promptly and ideally repair the relationship while helping Anthony acquire skillful means of handling a perceived slight.

On the other hand, Anthony's strong desire for intimacy, his apparent motivation to address his anger problem, and his recent insight into his problems and their destructive impact on his family are all strengths and would likely be the motivating factors that could keep him engaged in therapy. It might even be useful to reframe his many job changes as positive in that they reflect motivation to be successful and demonstrate persistence in returning to work situations despite the difficult obstacles he has faced; the therapist could then link this stubborn persistence to working hard in therapy, even through difficult periods, and ultimately to a good prognosis. In fact, Anthony's strong motivation to improve his life and keep his family, coupled with his participation in a comprehensive treatment such as DBT, would provide him the opportunity to enhance his relationships, gain control over his behaviors and moods, and let go of his continued emotional suffering.

CHAPTER 8

Couples and Family Treatment of Anger Difficulties

Eli Karam and Jay Lebow

INTRODUCTION TO A FAMILY SYSTEMS APPROACH

What distinguishes a family systems approach from the approaches covered in most of the other chapters in this book is its primary focus on viewing individuals in the context of the systems in which they reside rather than as separate individuals. Family members are interdependent: What affects one family member subsequently affects other family members. The patterns of interaction in the family influence the behavior of each family member.

If any single idea could be said to guide family therapy, it is probably the notion of a family system, applying general systems theory to human systems (Bertalanffy, 1968). Families are social systems—simultaneous subsystems of larger systems that have their own individual subsystems (e.g., psychological, biological). Systems take on a quality of wholeness that symbolizes "the whole is greater than the sum of its parts." A system is made up of parts that are interdependent and inter-related. Families are systems that are made up of individuals (parts) who are responsive (inter-related) to each other's behaviors and a change in one part of the family system affects the other part of the system.

Human life can be organized hierarchically into systems of varying size and complexity: the individual, the family, the society, and the culture. The family is a self-maintaining system, which, like the human body, has feedback mechanisms that preserve its identity and integrity by working to restore homeostasis after a disturbance. Families have mechanisms for adapting to changed circumstances, and like individuals, they have biologically and socially determined stages of development. A family that functions poorly typically cannot adjust to change or stress because its homeostatic mechanisms are either inflexible or ineffectual.

The spouse subsystem, consisting of the husband and wife, is a refuge for the couple and a source of authority in the family. The sibling subsystem helps children learn to negotiate, compete, and cooperate with other children. Subsystems that cross generations may incorporate one parent and the children, one child and the parents, or a parent and a child. Subsystems should have boundaries that are neither too rigid nor too vague and that therefore preserve the integrity of both individuals and the family (Minuchin, 1974). In a family that functions well, the subsystems have clear boundaries, especially those between generations. The alliance between the parents is strong; they primarily support each other in front of the children and do not allow the children to arbitrate their disputes.

Another important concept relevant to working with family systems is that of differentiation. According to Bowen (1978), differentiation of self is the ability to individuate one's thought and feelings from those of the family system. People with difficulties in differentiation typically cannot separate feeling and thinking. Their intellects are flooded with feelings, they cannot think rationally, and they cannot separate their own from other people's feelings. Differentiation is manifested through understanding one's own involvement in problematic relationship systems as opposed to blaming others, yet remaining able to be emotionally related to members.

Family Systems and Violence

Client issues with anger management often involve family violence. Family violence is often under-reported (Jouriles & O'Leary, 1985), rendering it vital for the clinician working with a client with anger issues to continually assess for family violence. Because the case of Anthony features such a history of family violence, it is important to speak to the interface of systems theory and family violence.

Currently, most treatment programs for domestic violence offenders are nonsystemic approaches that focus mainly on individual characteristics that may contribute to violent behaviors (Geffner & Mantooth, 1999). The core components of these programs generally feature a pathology-centered view of the offender, and treatment consists of providing education about violence, anger management, and stress management and raising awareness of patriarchal power and control (Pence & Paymar, 1993). These psychoeducational programs usually focus on challenging participants to recognize and admit to their violent behaviors, to take full responsibility for their problems (Pence & Paymar, 1993), and to learn new ways to manage their anger. To the extent that spouses are involved, it is with an eye to raising consciousness to no longer be victims of violence, and couple and family therapy is regarded as contraindicated until the offender has been nonviolent for a full year.

Family approaches, in contrast, see the family as integral to solving the problem of violence. Early family theorists saw violence as a problem of the system, and regarded the batterer as an "identified" patient. This viewpoint was appropriately challenged by both professionals and women's groups as "blaming the victim," given the implication that batterers were only "identified" patients, carrying the symptom for the system. In particular, that aspect of early systems formulations having to do with the preeminence of circular causality (that each person's behavior led to the other's in an endless circular chain) was a very poor fit with the sequences in these cases. An implication of this view was that all participants were equally responsible for the genesis of dysfunctional behavior.

Ultimately, this led to a revision of the systemic viewpoint in these cases as well as a rethinking of the concept of circular causality. Goldner (1990), in her highly influential analysis of partner violence, pointed to the need to understand that both linear arcs of causality and circular processes are simultaneously at work in domestic violence cases. That is, the perpetrator must remain responsible for his behavior, but there also needs to be a broader understanding of how behavior in each person influences the behavior in the other. Goldner also pointed to the evidence that women in physically abusive relationships often choose to stay in those relationships even when therapists favor exiting. She argued that simple-minded positions suggesting that relationships should end when there is violence fail to account for the ambivalence felt by both wife and husband in many of these highly attached relationships in which they experience both conflict and love for one another.

Holtzworth-Munroe and Meehan (2004) added to our knowledge of domestic violence by providing an empirically based typology of different types of batterers (labeled dysphoric/borderline, generally violent/antisocial, and family only). These three types of men are influenced by different etiological factors that affect the development of violent behavior. The dysphoric/borderline men primarily confine violence to their family, carry out moderate to severe violence, and engage in sexual and psychological abuse. These batterers are emotionally volatile, are psychologically distressed, have borderline and schizoid personality disorders, have elevated levels of depression, and are more likely to have substance abuse problems. Violent/antisocial types engage in more violence outside the home than other abusive men, carry out moderate to severe violence, and engage in psychological and sexual abuse. They may have an antisocial personality disorder or psychopathology and may abuse alcohol and/or drugs. The family-only type is a group of men whose violence is less severe than that of the other two groups and who do not differ in personality or attitudes from nonviolent men.

There are cautions to heed in deciding to conduct couple therapy with batterers. In some extremely volatile couples with abusive men, couples therapy may be discouraged because it could increase the danger for the abused woman by forcing her to confront her partner directly, thus increasing the risk for future violence and potentially increasing the emotional intensity of the relationship. Not only might the woman be hesitant to disclose truth in therapy sessions, but her partner might retaliate for disclosures she makes to the therapist. In addition, conjoint treatment for some couples might be taken to suggest that the victim may be in some part responsible for the abuse because she is being asked to change her behavior in the relationship along with her partner.

Although it is not always prudent to conduct therapy with a violent couple, the majority of situations in which there is family violence can benefit from family treatment (see, for example, the research by Stith, Rosen, & McCollum, 2003). Holtzworth-Munroe (2000) advocates that the "family-only batterer" without apparent psychopathology is most likely to receive benefits from couple therapy. There are also couples in which both partners engage in physical abuse toward each other. In fact, in these types of couples, reduction in partner violence by the husband is highly dependent on whether his partner also stops her physical abuse (Gelles & Straus, 1988). Therefore, whether couple and family therapy are appropriate in situations of abuse ultimately is a matter of developing a careful assessment that describes the nature of the batterer and the couples' process. If the batterer falls into the kind of psychopathic individual that Gottman et al. (1995) have described for whom violence is calculated as a way of controlling behavior, then couple therapy is contraindicated. In contrast, in Holzworth-Munroe's typical family-only batterer, significant spouse involvement seems a key to treatment success. Certainly, the willingness of the partner who has been the recipient of violence to participate in treatment is critical.

Basic Concepts and Assumptions of an Integrative Family Systems Model

Although the approach we describe here highlights the family system, the ideal treatment is integrative in its focus rather than solely centered on the family. We believe it important to consider and work with system levels that are both larger than the family and smaller. Pinsof (1995),

Breunlin et al. (1992), and Lebow (2003a, 2004) highlight the characteristics of such a systemic integrative approach.

Problem Focused

The presenting problem is the problem for which the client system is seeking treatment and is the focus of the initial treatment phase. The client system consists of all the people who are or may be involved in the maintenance and/or resolution of the presenting problems. The therapist's conceptualization of the presenting problem might not always match what the client presents. Typically, other issues within the client system play a role in relation to the presenting problem, but sometimes, the members of the system choose not to present them for therapy. In our case study, Anthony presents himself as struggling with anger control, despite his fears that his wife is distancing herself and considering leaving him. One can imagine that when he calls for therapy, he might not even mention his marital concerns.

By virtue of engaging in treatment, families give the therapist permission to assess and explore their relational environment, but there is no clear understanding that other problems are to be the focus of treatment. In our approach to family therapy, the general guideline we follow is that in order to focus on a problem, it either must be clearly linked to the presenting problem or it must present some threat to the family that cannot be ignored. A crucial aspect of building an alliance with Anthony and the other members of the family in this case would help them see the clear connections between Anthony's problem and the family's life. So, in this case, involving Anthony's family would have a possible role in helping him to improve because his interactions with his family are relevant to his problem. The same holds true in engaging the family members, who clearly would need an explanation of why it would be helpful that they be involved. Families typically are eager to participate in trying to improve problems like Anthony's, but they may have many fears about being involved. For example, they might be afraid that the level of Anthony's anger would increase because of what they might say in therapy, that they would be blamed for the problem, or that they would be prematurely moved from a position of disengagement to closer connection before they are ready for such a connection.

In family therapy, it is essential to get a view of the presenting problem from every member of the system. In this case, in addition to relying on Anthony's subjective self-report, the therapist would initially want to meet with everyone in the system (Anthony's daughters and wife) to obtain information about the impact of anger on family functioning. During this initial family assessment session, the therapist works to form an alliance with each member of the system while simultaneously exploring his or her individual concerns and hopes for treatment. If the therapist has a good alliance with key clients, it is easier for him or her to identify and work with the problem that was not initially identified, such as Anthony's potential infidelity or depression.

Direct versus Indirect System

Following Pinsof (1995), we divide the client system into two distinct subsystems. The direct client system consists of everyone with whom the therapist works in session. The indirect client system includes all of the members of the client system who are not directly part of the therapy. The boundary between the direct and indirect systems may change often during the course of treatment. For instance, in this case, in working with the family, the therapist might choose to work with Anthony in one phase and with Anthony and his wife and/or children in another phase. Thus, Anthony's family would move from the indirect system into the direct system and back into the indirect system after a family session. Changes in the location of the indirect/direct boundary during therapy are negotiated carefully and in advance with the key clients. In this case, an early effort would be made to involve Anthony's wife in treatment given all of the relationship issues described, but substantial involvement by the children would likely wait for a time when some progress on Anthony's part was already evident.

Health Premise

The health premise (Pinsof, 1995) contends that the therapist assumes that the family system is healthy until proved dysfunctional. This premise encourages the therapist to view the family members as if they have the necessary skills to solve their presenting problem. Approaching family systems from a health perspective helps liberate both the client and the therapist to engage in healthy and adaptive problem-solving behavior without the expectation of years of therapy. However, these premises are not designed to blindly assume health at all cost. Not taking major psychopathology seriously when clearly present can be a critical error in any treatment plan.

Anthony, with his myriad of problems poses quite a challenge to the health premise. Yet, beginning with a solution-oriented focus that helps Anthony believe that he might be able to overcome his difficulties would help him both recognize his problems and build a sense of hope that these problems can be remedied.

Cost-Effectiveness

The cost-effectiveness premise encourages therapists to use the most direct and least expensive interventions before more complex, indirect, and costly ones. Behavioral intervention strategies are typically simpler and are more economical than those therapies that require the development of insight and an understanding of internal and relational dynamics. The first intervention strategies implemented with Anthony would be behavioral and cognitive ones to help him monitor his anger and develop the self-monitoring and self-soothing skills that would keep his anger under control. In a similar vein, the first interventions with the family would be to develop contracts and skills for implementing cool-down periods when explosive anger is likely to emerge.

Interpersonal Premise

Family systems approaches hold that it is better to conduct therapy within an interpersonal context whenever possible rather than in an individual session format. By involving the family members in treatment, therapists learn more about the dynamics of the client systems and family interaction processes. Also, doing therapeutic work in the presence of the other family members facilitates the opportunity for the therapist to build an alliance with all individual members of the family system. Therefore, with Anthony, treatment would be designed to bring in family members as soon as he was prepared to do so.

Adaptive Solutions

In addition to gathering information around the presenting problem, the therapist collaborates with the family system around what would be considered adaptive solutions or successful outcomes to their current problems. Typically, this entails first identifying the previously unsuccessful attempted solutions that the family has tried in their efforts to resolve the problem. This collaborative exploration by the therapist and the family of the attempted solutions is the prelude to the identification of an *adaptive solution*—a sequence of actions for the family system that has a potential of resolving the presenting problem.

The therapist must also collaborate with the clients about the suitability and appropriateness of the adaptive solution. Typically, this entails outlining the steps that need to be taken by the family in preparation for the attempted solution. For instance, Anthony needs first to decide whether he wants to try to save his relationships with his wife and daughters, and if he does, what new and reconciliatory behaviors would be needed to bring that about. Creating consensus about an adaptive solution delineates major short- and long-term goals of the therapy.

THE CASE OF ANTHONY

Clinical Assessment/Case Conceptualization

Couple and family assessment is both qualitatively and quantitatively distinct from assessment of individuals in that it offers a unique opportunity to observe problematic interpersonal communication directly and to contrast these with subjective appraisals of these events.

Because the treatment needs of the client system are in part determined through examining the clients' responses to intervention, intervention and assessment are ongoing and inseparable processes. Therefore, within our integrative approach, there are no distinct assessment and intervention phases. These two linked processes begin the moment the referring client calls for help and conclude with termination. The therapist's knowledge of the client system is always partial and continually evolving, becoming more accurate and refined as feedback from the therapist's interventions and family's reactions accumulates.

Problems are manifest on a variety of levels, and constraints on each of these levels contribute to a family's difficulty in resolving their difficulties (Breunlin et al., 1992). The focus of our integrative assessment is to understand the locus underlying a particular difficulty as well as the strengths that can be brought to bear in helping promote change. The formulation that results from this understanding leads to a treatment plan aimed at responding to the particular constraints involved.

The Biological Level

Typical biological difficulties include the physiological components of major mental disorders, learning disabilities, developmental delays, and those aspects of physical illnesses that affect behavior, cognition, and emotion. The inattentive aspect of Anthony's attention deficit hyperactivity disorder (ADHD) may impede his ability to accomplish the organizational tasks necessary for work- or parenting-related tasks. Similarly, if he struggles with an organizational learning disability, he may be unable to provide the organizational structure that his family requires. The vulnerability of his brain in managing powerful affect-laden events may also play a role in his tendency to manifest anger.

Behavioral Patterns

Family members develop habitual patterns of behavior over time after having repeated them thousands of times. Each individual member of the system has become accustomed to act in a specific manner within the family. These actions will elicit subsequent reactions from other family members over and over again. In time, sequences of interactions become habitual and repetitive and become patterns of interaction (Minuchin, 1974) that are identifiable and predictable.

Anthony displays habitual patterns of loss of control over his anger that are triggered by impatience and failure to get his own way. The interpersonal patterns and sequences in his outbursts are clear. Anthony provokes arguments or disagreements due to his confrontational nature and always plays "devil's advocate." When family members do not comply or things do not go his way, he "blows up." When Anthony recognizes that he has scared or hurt the feelings of one of his daughters or wife, he apologizes, but his family perceives it as "too little too late." As a result of his behavior, the family is afraid to confront him about this abusive pattern and stay distant.

Family Structure

The clarity and flexibility of boundaries reflect the degree of differentiation within a family system. At one extreme, boundaries can be extremely impermeable. If this is the case, the emotional and psychological distance between family members is too large, and these family members are said to be "disengaged" from one another. At the other extreme, boundaries can be far too permeable or almost nonexistent. When boundaries are very permeable, the emotional and psychological closeness between people is too great, and these family members are said to be "enmeshed." Each of these extremes is problematic and becomes a target for intervention. Interactions that are either enmeshed or disengaged can cause problems and need to be altered to establish a better balance between the closeness and distance that allows cooperation and separation. Patterns of "enmeshment" and "disengagement" can occur at the same time within subsystems in a single family.

Leadership is defined as the distribution of authority and responsibility within the family. In functional two-parent families, leadership is in the hands of the parents and they usually share authority and decision making. Therapists will examine the hierarchy (the relative power of family members) to see who is in charge of leading the family on particular tasks and who holds the family's positions of authority. Leadership should ideally reside with the parental unit; however, some supporting roles can be delegated to older children, as long as those responsibilities are not overly burdensome, are age appropriate, and are delegated by parent figures rather than usurped by the children.

Easily observable symptoms of enmeshment in our case study include Anthony's overinvolvement in his daughter's athletic endeavors and frequent participation in his children's life choices. Yet, because of

Anthony's distance from his wife and reactive behavior at home with his children, he is unable to provide the type of leadership that is appropriate for both the roles of coparent and father. In addition, instead of bringing a benevolent and supportive stance, Anthony attempts to control by intimidation and impulsivity at home. Both the marital and the sibling subsystems seem unstable and the coparenting alliance is fraught with tension.

Family Development

For family members to continue to function well as they progress through the various life stages, they must adapt in ways that fit with the particular developmental stage involved. Each time a developmental transition is reached, the family is confronted by a new set of circumstances. Perhaps one of the most stressful developmental changes occurs when children reach adolescence. This is the stage at which a large number of families are not able to adapt to developmental changes (e.g., from direct guidance to leadership and negotiation). Parents need to be involved and monitor their adolescent's life, but now they must do it from a distinctly different perspective that allows their daughter or son to gain autonomy. Clearly, Anthony has had difficulty in balancing this parental transition with his teenage daughters and more recently there is another set of generational transitions occurring with the birth of his granddaughter.

At each developmental stage, certain roles and tasks are expected of different family members. One way to determine whether the family has successfully coped with the various developmental challenges that it has confronted is to assess the appropriateness of the roles and tasks that have been assigned to each family member, considering the age and position of each person within the family. For Anthony, the multiple roles of husband, father, grandfather, and "stepfather" have not yet been articulated.

Family of Origin

Experiences in relation to family of origin often set a frame for how issues are dealt with in later life. The specter of Anthony's early experience with his family (most especially the sexual abuse and his parents' reaction to his report about it) has had a profound effect on Anthony. Thus, he has spent most of his adult life "cut off" from his family of origin. Rather than attempting to work on relationships with siblings or his mother, Anthony has instead elected to blame them for his problems and ignore their existence in favor of focusing his attentions on his own situation.

Cognitions and Emotion

Our treatment approach views cognition and emotion as the intertwined components of individual psychological process. Anthony does not confront his wife because he believes that if he does she will admit that she does not love him and will leave him. The underlying schemas in this narrative are pictures of being unattractive, worthless, weak, and fearful of abandonment and humiliation. For Anthony to confront his wife possibly would be to reaffirm his worthlessness. The belief that women are cold and domineering has also characterized Anthony's family for generations and now constrains his ability to turn toward his wife as a supportive partner and resource in helping with the structure and nurturance that he and his family need.

Psychodynamic Factors

Individuals are affected by their internalized and transformed representations of self and important others that derive from the early family experiences. Object relations become represented maladaptively through defense mechanisms such as denial, projection, transference, and projective identification.

According to the case study, Anthony's mother, much like his grandmother, was very harsh and punitive and Anthony resented her depreciating and shaming behavior. In contrast, his father was involved and supportive but seemed overly focused on his son's athletic performance. His passivity in the face of Anthony's claim of sexual abuse perpetrated by his uncle hurt and infuriated Anthony. He gradually learned that turning to his father for support or understanding was disappointing and only resulted in him feeling more lonely and abandoned.

Based on these early experiences, in his efforts to provide his children with the support they need, Anthony fears the girls will perceive him as an abusive and shaming father and that they will "hate" him as he hated his mother. In addition, Anthony may perceive his wife as being like his father—seeking her support will only exacerbate Anthony's feelings of loneliness and fear of losing her. Lastly, Anthony's propensity to view former bosses and mentors as perpetually conflictual and argumentative is a projection of his own anger at those who have hurt or let him down. He has denied, disowned, and displaced this anger much of his life, at times turning it on himself and becoming depressed.

In some family systems, the narcissistic vulnerabilities of the clients interfere with their ability to address their problems in a more adaptive manner. Typically, these vulnerabilities derive from the failures of key attachment figures, or "self-objects," to meet their narcissistic needs early in their childhoods. These include the need to be "mirrored," to "idealize," and to "twin" with key self-objects. Generally, the more vulnerable the self, the more rigid and constrained the object relations.

Anthony has these sorts of narcissistic vulnerabilities. Early in their relationship, Anthony perceived his wife as kind, sensitive, and caring. He experienced her as very different from his mother, who was aloof, critical, and unresponsive to Anthony's needs. However, as Anthony experienced his wife's growing interests and interpersonal relationships outside of the marriage, he felt alone. He lost the mirroring that he had experienced and found himself increasingly unable to communicate with her because of his childlike attachment to his wife. And in the face of this narcissistic abandonment, Anthony becomes angry. However, instead of expressing that rage directly to his wife, he lashed out at his daughters and sought the mirroring he needed from other women friends. Thus, Anthony's narcissistic vulnerability made it difficult to tolerate his wife's withdrawal and to deal with it more adaptively.

Treatment Issues and Goals

Families who have multiple problems, as in the case of Anthony, often require combining therapeutic modalities to reach treatment goals. On any one particular case, there could be multiple therapists working with different parts of the same system: an individual therapist to work with the identified client, a couple's therapist to work with husband and wife, as well as a separate family therapist to work with children and parents. In other instances, however, it is possible for one therapist trained in family systems to work in a cost-effective and integrated framework with all parts of the system. For this case, we will structure the case for simplicity and focus on the couple and family context throughout the duration of treatment and will assume there is only one therapist working with the entire system.

The therapist would begin treatment with a family session that would include all relevant members of the system—Anthony, Joanna, Angela, Jackie, and Savannah. It is also possible that Jerome, Angela's boyfriend and the father of Anthony's grandchild, would attend the initial meeting because he currently lives in the family home. Therapy begins with a definition and discussion of the presenting problem and each person's relation to it. In our case, it is likely that each family member would focus on their difficulties in dealing with Anthony's anger episodes.

An essential consideration in this case would be the frequency of individual, couple, and family sessions. There are numerous volatile issues in this family, such that the promotion of the greater degree of openness that accompanies treatment sessions might or might not be helpful depending on how family members respond to treatment. Therefore, choices about how much each therapy format would be used would depend on how family members responded to treatment. Given the establishment of a good working alliance in each therapy format, there are clearly special ways that each therapy format can contribute to the resolution of this problem. In fact, given the case description, work with the family, with the couple, and with Anthony himself is necessary to calm all the destructive forces at work in this family.

Therapeutic Alliance

The therapist's first step in working with a family is to establish a therapeutic alliance with each member of the system. The quality of the relationship between the therapist and the family is a strong predictor of whether families will come to, stay in, and improve in treatment. Research has found that the therapeutic relationship is a strong predictor of success in couple and family therapy (Pinsof, 1995). Establishing a therapeutic relationship means that the therapist must form a new system—a therapeutic system—made up of the therapist and the family. One challenge for the therapist is to establish relationships with all family members, some of whom are likely to be in conflict with one another and some of whom may not want to be in treatment.

A strong alliance is created in family therapy by being empathic, genuine, knowledgeable, and helpful in interactions with family members. Therapists further build alliance with family members by allying with various members in carefully considered ways and adapting to the family's manner of speaking and behaving. To prepare the family for change and earn a position of leadership, the therapist must show respect and support for each family member and, in turn, earn each one's trust. One of the most useful strategies that a therapist can employ in joining is to at least temporarily support the existing family leader who has the power to accept the therapist into the family, to place the therapist in a leadership role, and to keep the family in therapy. Of special note is that in building a therapeutic alliance with the family, the therapist must join with all family members, not just those with whom he or she agrees. In fact, frequently, the person with whom it is most critical to establish an alliance can be an unlikable or resistant family member.

Much of the work the therapist does to establish the therapeutic alliance involves learning family "rules" and language to better join with the family. However, the therapist cannot learn these family norms unless he or she observes family members interacting as they would "at home." Getting family members to interact in this naturalistic manner can be difficult because most families enter therapy with the assumption that their job is to tell the therapist what happened. Therefore, it is essential that therapists move themselves out of becoming central in all in-session interactions, instead encouraging family members to interact so that they can be seen behaving in their usual way.

The issues surrounding alliance and the balance in the alliance across family members are especially important in this case given Anthony's history of volatile and aggressive behavior. On one hand, the therapist must work to ensure the safety of all members in the system and, thus, must at times risk the alliance with Anthony. Furthermore, Anthony might enter family treatment anticipating rejection or feeling guilty about his anger outbursts in front of the therapist and thus adopt a resistant posture. On the other hand, Anthony must feel supported to work at his difficulties, and the family might experience that support as condoning his bad behavior. The therapist must balance a supportive stance regarding Anthony's worth as a person with a strong disapproval for all of his violent and aggressive behaviors. In order to establish an environment of safety throughout treatment, the therapist must also solicit feedback from Anthony's wife and children to understand their safety concerns about sharing information in session. Framing the core issue as helping everyone in the family with the anger (including Anthony) is likely to be a helpful intervention in building a multipartial alliance with all family members.

Creating a Treatment Plan

Once a presenting problem has been established and factors underlying the problem and family strengths have been identified, the therapist is ready to develop a treatment plan. The treatment plan lays out the strategies for intervention that will be used to help ameliorate the problem. That treatment plan is an ever-evolving blueprint that changes in response to information that accrues from observing the family respond to the treatment and to one another.

Treatments in integrative family therapy involve working with issues at the individual, couple, family, and larger system levels. For purposes of this chapter, we emphasize those strategies and interventions centered on the couple and family. Thus, although Anthony's ability to control his anger would be an integral part of our treatment of this family, we do not emphasize that work here. The reader is referred to the other treatment chapters for examples of how Anthony might learn self-control and/or explore the cognitions, affective states, and schemas that enable his lack of control or the psychodynamic processes involved.

Therapeutic Goals

The ultimate goal of integrative family therapy is resolution of the presenting problem at a level that suggests a high degree of likelihood of maintenance of change over time. To achieve that ultimate goal, integrative family therapy typically includes the accomplishment of numerous prerequisite, mediating goals.

One prominent mediating goal is to strengthen the client system by making it more competent and adaptive, at least in regard to the problems for which it is seeking help. Ultimately, it is the family who needs to take the personal initiative to do what needs to be done to resolve the presenting problem. Overall, Anthony needs to develop his skills in anger management and find ways in his daily life to receive nurturance (support/warmth) from his wife and children in order to combat his anger issues.

On a couple level, mediating goals include Anthony working conjointly with Joanna to enhance the couple's sense of spousal dependability, intimacy, confiding, and joint parenting skills. On a family level, mediating goals include collaboration so that everyone in the household can become more capable of managing expressed emotion and angry feelings in constructive ways that enhance family functioning. Other mediating family goals include Anthony sharing the insights, treatment goals, and techniques he is implementing from his individual sessions so as to enable better understanding of how the family can best be involved in the change process and improving communication and conflict negotiation skills between family members.

Tracking Change

Ongoing assessment and the tracking of change throughout the course of treatment help promote the change process. We use the Systemic Therapy Inventory of Change (STIC; Pinsof et al., 2005), a client self-report instrument that assesses six domains: individual symptoms and well-being, adult recall of childhood family of origin, current couple/marital functioning, current family functioning, child well-being and symptoms, and the therapeutic alliance. Data from this measure are collected before the beginning of each session across the course of treatment. Measures such as the STIC provide quantitative feedback for therapists and clients about individual, couple, and family progress, which can be used to inform clinical decision making during treatment.

Strategies of Intervention

Psychoeducational Strategies

Psychoeducation has a widely applicable value for helping individuals and families better cope with the problems they experience. In this case, we would include a psychoeducational component about anger presented to the entire family. The goals of this psychoeducation include (1) increasing the understanding of the biological and psychological basis of anger and (2) aiding family members (most especially Anthony) in developing realistic expectations for family functioning. As is typical in family therapy, as part of this process, Anthony would be deemed an "expert" on his own problem and would be encouraged to discuss his symptoms and current experiences related to expression of anger with his wife and daughters.

Behavioral Strategies

As stated earlier, a focus of our treatment is to shift the family from failed attempted solutions to alternative, adaptive ones. We would therefore offer Anthony and his family training in expressing anger, frustration, and disappointment in a direct, constructive manner (e.g., being brief and specific, using "I" statements), followed by instruction in compromise and negotiation. The family would be taught techniques for de-escalating conflicts and for monitoring and working with situations that might lead to angry or violent outbursts. Topics addressed here include contracting for no violence among family members, identifying early signs of intense provocation, requesting a time-out when these cues occur, and understanding the role that other contextual stressors play in heightening conflict.

Anger recognition cues allow clients to identify the physiological, behavioral, and cognitive cues of anger that precede behavioral outbursts. In addition to helping Anthony develop his own self-monitoring strategies, family members would be encouraged to give Anthony direct feedback about both verbal and nonverbal anger cues that they observe before such outbursts occur. This would allow for better identification of common elements of Anthony's anger experiences, as well as potentially high-risk situations. Once high-risk situations are identified, the family and the therapist can collaborate on appropriate ways to prevent such situations from occurring. Each element of skills training is followed by assignments to practice skill implementations at home.

Developing a workable "time-out" procedure to moderate anger would be an extremely important aspect of work with this family. We would frame the time-out as a way for Anthony or his family to stop themselves from engaging in conversations or actions that they will later regret. An appropriate length of time for the time-out would be negotiated, with the expectation that Anthony will continue his interaction with his family once the anger has subsided.

The "problem-solving" aspect of the treatment teaches the family to apply efficient problem-solving strategies and adaptive solutions to intrafamilial and extrafamilial stressors. Here we likely would use behavioral rehearsal techniques, with family members conducting structured problem solving of current difficulties during the sessions under the guidance of the therapist. In this technique, topics for problem solving are defined by the family and may include issues related to any family member, not merely those associated with the identified client.

In our work with Anthony and Joanna as a couple, behavioral inventions to improve communication, problem solving, and intimacy would be used. Given this couple's patterns, we would work with their disconnection after anger management techniques were well established, because as a couple they appear not to be able to manage the communication of painful affects. Once the anger management was well under way and the holding environment for the work established, we would help Joanna safely communicate and assert her feelings to Anthony about his periodic overinvolvement with other women, with the goal of decreasing that involvement and increasing his involvement with his wife. Anthony would be helped to express his feelings to Joanna about her increased time away from the house with "work" friends and marital disengagement, with the goal of reestablishing their traditions like "date night." This intervention is based on the hypothesis that Anthony's anger episodes derive in part from his inability to deal with his fears of rejection and rage at his mother and his wife and that if he can address those feelings and relationships, his anger should decrease.

Part of the family focus would center on eliciting feedback from everyone living in the home about the negative consequences of Anthony's rage or other objectionable behaviors observed when he is angry. The use of constructive communication skills such as "I" statements that own feelings rather than attacking and expressions of care and concern rather than expressions of blame or contempt will be critical to successful family feedback.

Family members may also have decided on limits about what they will tolerate and what they plan to do should Anthony's anger continue unchanged. Promoting communication about such limits might have an important influence on Anthony's decision making. Family members would be guided to make specific, positive requests for change from Anthony. Again, with the family, as with the couple, the promotion of direct communication would be tempered by the progress (or lack thereof) with the anger management. Safety concerns would be prioritized over other treatment goals.

Homework and Tasks

The use of tasks and homework assignments are both important components in work with families. The therapist uses tasks inside and homework outside the therapy sessions as the basic tool for facilitating new adaptive solutions and different ways of interacting. It is helpful, if possible, that a newly assigned task for the family be performed in the therapy session so that the therapist has an opportunity to observe and provide the family with suggestions and feedback to shape a successful experience. The therapist should be careful to avoid setting the family up for failure by expecting too much too soon and should try to assign tasks that are challenging yet attainable. By constantly monitoring the feedback and assessing the system's progress, the therapist can develop the appropriate task for the level of family functioning.

Although the therapist should always follow up on an assigned homework task in subsequent sessions, the families should not be expected to complete homework successfully all the time. Successful homework completion in systems requires the involvement of more than one person. Fortunately, the processing of "failed homework" in session can often lead to modifications to preexisting tasks and is a great source of information regarding the interactions that prevent a family from changing out of fixed patterns.

Cognitive Strategies

Perhaps the most widely used cognitive technique in family therapy is to offer the family a "reframe" in which the therapist creates a different perspective or "frame" of reality than the one within which the family has been operating. He or she presents this new frame to the family in a convincing manner and then uses this new frame to facilitate change. The purpose of reframing is to change perceptions and/or meaning in ways that will enable family members to change their interactions. Most of the time, in families with volatile or abusive members, anger is the target for reframing. Anger is usually exhibited as hostile, pejorative, and invalidating statements or actions. Reframing Anthony's anger might involve describing Anthony's criticism of his teenage daughter as an expression of his desire that she be successful or reframing fighting as an attempt to have some sort of connection with another family member. However, in the context of such angry destructive behavior, reframes must be offered cautiously. The other members of the family are equal clients in treatment and their physical and psychological safety must be guarded. Thus, such a reframe would be appropriate only if the family members were well into the process of changing and would not experience such a perspective as an invalidation of their own feelings in the wake of Anthony's damaging behavior.

An example will help illustrate the use of reframing negative emotions to create more positive feelings among family members. As a parent,

Anthony may feel angry that his attempts to guide his children in the "right" direction have failed and that his daughters disrespect his guidance. His daughters are likely to interpret this anger as uncaring and rejecting. Both parties may feel that the other is an adversary, which severely diminishes the possibility that they can have a genuine dialogue.

In this context, a reframe that transmutes emotions of anger, rage, and fighting into caring and compassion might be effective. We might say to Anthony, "I can see how concerned you are about your daughter. I know you care a great deal about her, and that is why you are so frustrated about trying to guide her." With this intervention, the therapist helps move both Anthony's and his daughter's perceptions from anger to concern. If the intervention is successful, Anthony might soften by saying something like, "I am very concerned. I want my child to be a success, live up to her potential and not to repeat my mistakes in life." Instead of indicating rejection, the parent is now communicating concern, care, and support for the child. Thus, this reframe would be invoked to help transform a hostile relationship between a parent and child, facilitating both positive communication and shared meaning. In addition, other family members present in the session are able to hear and observe this reframing process, which may reduce their feelings of defensiveness as well.

Emotion-Focused Strategies

Managing emotion is obviously a key to life for Anthony and his family. We already have alluded to the direct work with containing emotion that would occur in the individual treatment of Anthony. In addition, as safety needs were assured, we would work to promote more shared emotional experiencing and communication about that experiencing with all family members. The family would be encouraged to convene regular family meetings to discuss problems and goals in a frank and open manner. Toward this end, the family would learn to develop constructive expression of feelings and attitudes as well as empathic listening skills.

With Anthony and his family, the communication of affects must begin with the promotion of better understanding of feelings. Although there is a great deal of direct and indirect expression of feeling in this family, the sources of emotion appear to reside out of awareness. To cope more effectively with his own anger and rage, Anthony must identify and own his feelings. Similarly, Joanna needs to identify her feelings of anger and loss in the face of Anthony's "friendships" with other women and must learn to address the disconnect in her marriage. This work would likely entail exploring and challenging the catastrophic expectations about what will happen if they address their feelings that lay underneath their increased distance.

In the past, Joanna and Anthony have been able to address concrete stressors in their lives, including financial issues and parenting concerns, but are far less skilled in exploring the unacknowledged feelings underlying their disconnection and growing time apart. The therapist would work with Joanna and Anthony in couple sessions to promote identification with feelings, disowned needs, and aspects of the self and integrate these into relationship interactions. Other sessions might focus on the emotional issues related to their tight living quarters, their becoming grandparents, or their daughter's relationship with Jerome.

Psychodynamic Strategies

Current problems can sometimes be traced back to maladaptive involvement with families of origin and transgenerational legacies. Specific family therapy orientations address historical and transgenerational factors, including Bowen's Differentiation of Self Therapy (1978) and Boszormenyi-Nagy's Contextual Therapy (Boszormenyi-Nagy, Grunebaum, & Ulrich, 1973; Boszormenyi-Nagy & Spark, 1973). These approaches tend to use genograms (McGoldrick, Gerson, & Shellenberger, 1999) for exploring, analyzing, and modifying transgenerational sequences, as well as linking the current presenting problem to maladaptive patterns that derive from the key adult clients' families of origin.

For Anthony, transgenerational work might focus on exploring his narrative about his parents, helping him understand its impact over time and encouraging him to test its validity with his current parenting style. A central goal would be to examine whether he could break his transgenerational legacy as a parent.

On an intrapsychic level, differentiation of self involves an ability to distinguish between feeling processes and intellectual processes. Greater differentiation enables one to take I-positions in important relationships, in other words, to maintain a sense of self in an intense emotional relationship such as marriage or in the midst of shifting or uncertain circumstances. Clearly, during this time of transition, Anthony's capacity to soothe his own anxiety would be highlighted. In this situation we would coach Anthony to establish greater autonomy in his marriage without experiencing debilitating fears of abandonment and to achieve emotional intimacy in that same relationship without fear of feeling smothered.

If Anthony continues to be "stuck" in regard to attributing his angry feelings to his relationship with family or origin members, we would help him understand the ramifications of his experience in his family of origin. Anthony may look or feel independent from the family of origin, but clearly he is not. People who cut off from their original families are more likely to repeat the same patterns in their own relationships.

CLINICAL ISSUES AND RECOMMENDATIONS

Getting Caught Up in Content and Ignoring Process

The distinction between content and process is absolutely critical to family therapy. The "content" of therapy refers to what family members talk about, including their explanations for family problems, beliefs about how problems should be managed, perspectives about who or what causes the problems, and other topics. In contrast, the "process" of therapy refers to how family members interact, including the degree to which family members listen to, support, interrupt, undermine, and express emotion to one another, as well as other ways of interacting. Nonverbal behavior is usually indicative of process, as is the manner in which family members speak to one another.

The therapist's job is to help the family keep focused on (process) a single problem (content) long enough to resolve it. In turn, the experience of resolving the problem may help change the family's process so that family members can apply their newly acquired resolution skills to other problem areas. If the therapist gets lost in the family's process of shifting from one content problem to another before resolution, he or she may feel overwhelmed and thus be less likely to help the family resolve its conflicts.

Attempts by the Family to Triangulate the Therapist

Triangulation does not necessarily have to involve only family members. Sometimes a therapist can become part of a triangle as well. One of the most common strategies used by family members is to attempt to get the therapist to ally himself or herself with one family member against another. For example, one family member might say to the therapist, "Isn't it true that I am right and he is wrong?" "You know best, you tell him." "We were having this argument last night, and I told her that you had said that . . ."

Triangulation is a constraint to the process of conflicted resolution. Regardless of whether it is the therapist or a family member who is being triangulated, triangulation constrains two family members in conflict from reaching a resolution. One goal of treatment is to assist family members in resolving their conflicts on a one-to-one basis. The therapist does not want to be triangulated during conflict because the person in the middle of a triangle is rendered ineffective. If the therapist is handicapped because freedom of movement (e.g., changing alliances, choosing whom to address) has been restricted, he or she cannot work effectively.

When a family member attempts to triangulate the therapist, the therapist should direct the conflict back to the people who are involved in it. For example, the therapist might say, "Ultimately, my opinion doesn't matter. What matters is that the two of you can come to a shared understanding of the problem. I am here to help you talk, negotiate, hear each other clearly, and come to a mutual decision." In this way, the therapist places the focus of the interaction back on the family. The therapist also might respond, "I understand how difficult this is for you, but this is your family and you have to come to terms with each other, not with me."

Treatment Termination and Relapse Prevention

The case discussed in this book is a challenging one, affected by numerous difficulties on almost every system level. Yet, if alliances are successfully engaged and the treatment plan followed, it appears that there is a considerable possibility for treatment success.

It is likely that the family would initiate termination once the presenting problems were resolved. However, it would be essential at that point for the therapist to assess whether the requisite skills have been sufficiently mastered to ensure the likelihood of the maintenance of the gains that had occurred. Anger issues present a special problem in this regard in that, unless sufficient skills are developed, anger can be provoked easily again by changes in life events. It is difficult to judge how a family will handle certain life stresses until the therapist has witnessed them successfully cope with those stressors.

Assuming that the presenting problem has been resolved and the family develops a mastery of communication and anger management skills (with examples of the family managing situations that resulted in difficulty in the past), a plan for termination would be developed that would emphasize ongoing efforts to maintain the changes that have occurred (Lebow, 1995). To help family members master and retain these skills learned during treatment, the therapist reviews therapeutic gains and helps the family use effective problem-solving skills when handling stressors in the absence of the therapist. Between sessions, families are instructed to hold regular family meetings to deal with stressors that arise and to apply the problem-solving approach to attain the goals of all family members.

Even as termination approaches, Anthony and his wife and children must continue to renew their commitment to new ways to engage with one another, communicate, and problem solve. The therapist would coach Anthony to maintain his program of anger management and coach family members to support change through verbal encouragement or nonverbal gestures or by taking on family responsibilities to free up Anthony's time for treatment or self-help meetings. Given the family interaction history, as part of the termination process, Anthony and the therapist should plan for follow-up sessions after the passage of sufficient time to determine whether the changes that have occurred can be maintained and Anthony should have a clear plan to return should problems reoccur after the end of treatment (Lebow, 1994).

CHAPTER 9

Psychopharmacological Considerations in Anger Management

Henry Edwards

INTRODUCTION TO THE PSYCHOPHARMACOLOGICAL APPROACH

In response to the case of Anthony, this chapter considers the usefulness of psychopharmacological intervention in an overall treatment and anger management plan for the client. Anthony's case will be used as a vehicle to discuss some general issues involved in considering medication as part of the treatment approach to the angry client. Comments about anger and psychopharmacology are presented, followed by some details of the case that are relevant to the question of medication as an intervention strategy.

First, it must be emphasized that evaluation for, and use of, medication in the treatment of anger difficulties cannot be separated from evaluation and treatment of the whole person. Anger per se is not a mental disorder, but it can be one of the manifest symptoms of an underlying mental disorder or medical condition. Most often, however, it is not and stands alone "as the product of a complex combination of personal characteristics, environmental setting conditions, and specific antecedents" (Allen, 2000).

There is considerably less empirical support for the use of medications in the routine treatment of anger compared with its more established

189

use in the treatment of defined disorders, such as psychosis, depression, mania, and so forth. Nonetheless, the use of psychotropic drugs still tends to be a leading choice in the clinical response to anger. Perhaps this is due in part to society's strong desire and expectation of medication and other drugs to alleviate or eliminate any physical or emotional discomforts or reactions. This desire is enhanced by widespread marketing promises for medication use and clinical responsiveness based on recognition of possible effectiveness and also perhaps in part because medication as a first-line response "requires considerably less investment of career time and effort" (Allen, 2000).

However, there is a place for medications in anger management, particularly in those cases in which the anger is a prominent symptom or complicating factor in an underlying mental or medical disorder or in which the anger, in one of its more extreme forms (e.g., aggression, rage, violence) presents extreme management or safety problems. In most cases, anger is motivated by multiple psychosocial and environmental factors, which would indicate some psychosocial intervention as the first-line response. In such cases, medications may later be indicated as an adjunct if the anger is threatening or interfering with the psychotherapeutic approach.

General Psychopharmacology Issues

Psychopharmacology is the study of the actions and uses of drugs in the treatment of mental disorders and is grounded in the recognition of neurobiological bases for both normal and abnormal mental functioning. Management with medication is based on the biological activity in the brain that underlies emotional and behavioral reactions.

Prior to the 1960s and the discovery of chlorpromazine (Thorazine), the role of the brain in mental functioning was suspected, especially in the more severe forms of mental illness, such as schizophrenia, but the mechanism of action was unclear. The leading explanations of emotional, thinking, and behavioral disorders up to that time were heavily influenced by psychoanalytic and other psychological theories, with little attention given to neurobiology. However, after observing the effect of chlorpromazine on hallucinations, delusions, psychotic thinking, and aberrant behavior, more attention and research were given to the manner in which the brain itself operated in mental functioning. With increased research activity and chance findings, more chemicals were found that had a regulating effect on brain functioning. Medications (antipsychotics) having a calming and dampening effect on psychoses, such as haloperidol (Haldol), trifluoperazine hydrochloride (Stelazine), thioridazine (Mellaril), and other medications (amitriptyline [Elavil], imipramine

[Tofranil]), were observed to lift severely depressed clients out of their despair and give them hope; thus, they were added to therapists' treatment plans.

The dramatic improvements in these severe and previously poorly managed conditions stimulated research into more precise biological causes of emotional and behavioral dysfunction and led to widespread increases in the clinical use of these medications in treating mental disorders—not only the more severe psychoses and mood disorders but lesser, but still distressing, disorders and symptomology, such as anxiety, dysthymia, insomnia, hyperactivity, aggression, and so on.

It is now well established that there is a neurobiological basis for emotional, behavioral, and cognitive functioning. Normally, this biological activity is adaptive and out of conscious awareness. It prompts automatic bodily responses to environmental conditions and stimuli and thereby provides a protective function from danger and motivates the pursuit of the basic needs for food, water, reproduction, and so forth. When something goes wrong in the brain and this normal neurobiological activity malfunctions, symptoms can develop and lead to unpleasant or even dangerous emotional reactions, maladaptive behavior, or abnormal thinking disturbance.

Research evidence indicates that this malfunction is usually the result of some neurochemical or electrical imbalance in certain areas of the brain. The neurological aim of pharmacological intervention is to chemically correct or moderate this imbalance and thereby correct or at least relieve the disturbing symptomatology (e.g., depression, anxiety, psychotic behavior, agitation, anger).

The use of psychotropic medication is now a well-established component in the treatment of a variety of psychological disorders. Broadly defined, psychotropic medications are "medications that have an effect on the central nervous system to produce changes in aberrant behavior" (Meyer & Deitsch, 1996, p. 386) considering that emotional and behavioral problems are caused by a complex interaction of biological, psychological, and environmental factors, the contributions of neurobiology have greatly increased treatment options.

It is now widely accepted that any sensations, emotions, or thought must result from the activity of specific chemical and electrical activity in the brain (Hyman, 1998). This brain activity takes place in specific, identifiable neuronal circuits or pathways that are involved in the regulation of all bodily functions. From a psychopharmacological perspective, the circuits of interest are the ones that link the areas of the cortex that help us reason or plan our lives, with more deeply embedded zones in the midbrain, such as the limbic system, where emotions are processed and moods regulated. These circuits consist of linkages of neurons that are connected to one another at synapses to form specific identifiable pathways. Information that stimulates the body to respond is transmitted as electrical energy or impulses along neuronal pathways from one part of the brain to another. The flow of this energy or impulse is controlled by what happens at the synapse or junction between one neuron and the next. The impulse or information being conveyed in the so-called presynaptic neuron must cross the synaptic junction and stimulate the so-called postsynaptic neuron to continue the communication. This synaptic transmission is regulated and controlled by means of monoamines or "neurotransmitters." These neurotransmitters are produced and released at the synapse by the presynaptic neuron, cross the synaptic gap, and stimulate the postsynaptic neuron to continue the communication process. The neurotransmitters thus have a critical role to play in regulating information transmission in the brain and exert a critical influence on bodily responses.

A number of neurotransmitters are involved in overall brain activity, but the neurotransmitters primarily responsible for signaling the body to respond with feelings, behavior, or thoughts have been identified as the monoamines serotonin, norepinephrine, dopamine, and histamine. Altered levels of these monoamines at the synapse can have a marked influence on mood and behavior.

If the neurotransmitter's function is altered by an excess, deficiency, or imbalance of neurotransmitter levels, then the circuits will dysfunction and symptoms (e.g., anxiety, depression, anger) can occur. Correcting the dysfunction in the circuit (e.g., enhancing or reducing neurotransmitters to their optimal levels) can improve or even eliminate the symptoms. For example, it is known that lower-than-optimal levels of serotonin at the synapse are associated with depression and aggressive behavior. The shortage of serotonin appears to increase reactivity to stressors. Sometimes medications that increase serotonin levels can lessen the tendency toward aggression and anger (Gilligan, 1997) and symptomatically improve depression.

It seems clear that numerous mental disorders and many behavioral reactions reflect abnormal functioning or dysregulation of certain neurotransmitters at the synapse and that the psychotropic medications exert their primary influence at the synapse to regulate, stabilize, and thereby fix the neurotransmitter and electrical dysfunction or imbalance, which when successful, leads to symptom relief.

Anger and Psychopharmacology

These are certain considerations to keep in mind when an angry patient is referred for possible psychopharmacological intervention. First, anger per se is not a mental disorder but rather an emotional, behavioral reaction that involves thoughts, physiological arousal, and behavioral responses to certain internal or external stimuli (Schiraldi & Kerr, 2002). A dictionary definition of *anger* is "a strong feeling of displeasure and belligerence aroused by a real or supposed wrong . . . deep and strong feelings aroused by injury, injustice . . . the general term for sudden violent displeasure accompanied by an impulse to retaliate" (*Random House Webster's College Dictionary*, 2000, p. 47).

Anger is an understandable human emotion, easily aroused in many and experienced by everyone. What distinguishes and characterizes it from person to person is its (1) frequency of occurrence, (2) intensity (annoyance, irritation, agitation to, fury, and rage), (3) duration, (4) threshold for arousal, (5) how it is experienced, and (6) the degree of personal discomfort it causes (Schiraldi & Kerr, 2002).

Anger is often seen as one of the symptomatic manifestations of a number of defined neuropsychiatric disorders or medical conditions. For that reason, an important initial step in any psychiatric intervention is a careful evaluation to rule out any underlying mental or medical disorder. For example, anger is often seen in clients with major depressive disorders, bipolar disorder, schizophrenia, attention deficit hyperactivity disorder (ADHD), post-traumatic stress disorder (PTSD), substance abuse disorders (e.g., alcohol, phencyclidine [PCP], cocaine, and other stimulants), and serious personality disorders (e.g., borderline, antisocial, or narcissistic types). Anger is also found in numerous medical conditions, such as seizure disorder, various toxicities, hormonal imbalance, brain tumors, head injuries, and chronic pain syndromes. These superimposed or underlying psychiatric or medical problems present diagnostic challenges and treatment complications. When such a co-occurrence exists, the underlying disorder must be evaluated and appropriate treatment provided.

As a persistent symptom of some mental or medical condition, anger can complicate or delay recovery or stabilization. Anger is not only one of the possible symptoms of an underlying medical disorder but may itself be the underlying, often hidden, cause of many long-term health problems (e.g., hypertension, coronary heart disease, stroke, job injuries, headaches, backache, other chronic pain syndromes, cancer, ulcers, gastrointestinal disturbances) (Schiraldi & Kerr, 2002). Thus, anger alone or as the result or cause of another disorder or syndrome can be the source of serious discomfort, affecting the quality of life and functioning of the client and his or her significant others, and may be another indication to consider the use of medication.

As with most symptoms and emotional expressions, the biological underpinning of anger, aggression, and violent behavior all involve the neurotransmitters and the increased sensitivity of the nervous system. Severe anger-spectrum reactions seem related to either an overabundance of certain neurotransmitters, such as dopamine and norepinephrine, or a relative deficiency of other neurotransmitters, such as serotonin.

The nervous systems of many people have been so sensitized by repeated stressful experiences that they overreact to even small provocations. One biological explanation for this is that people prone to anger tend to oversecrete stress hormones such as cortisol and catecholamines. An excess of these hormones can cause shrinkage of the hippocampus, a part of the brain involved with memory. This excess of hormones enhances the effect of excessively angry memories and, coupled with the expression of anger, keeps the nervous system sensitized. Such a condition renders the person highly responsive to situations or provocations, especially those that are associated with or reminiscent of angry memories (Schiraldi & Kerr, 2002). Evidence that aggressive behavior may fluctuate over long periods in discrete cycles may be another indicator of the involvement of underlying neurobiological mechanism such as natural variations in levels of serotonin or norepinephrine (Hagerman, Bregman, & Tirosh, 1998).

The physician who is considering psychotropic intervention for anger management should be aware that anger can occur when no mental or medical disorder is present. From a practical clinical perspective, there are many intrapsychic, interpersonal, behavioral, and environmental causes for angry behavior. Ignoring this broader psychological and sociological dimension and looking at anger only as a symptom of an underlying biological dysfunction that needs correction may lead to unnecessary and noneffective medication use. Recognizing and addressing the psychosocial issues, more often than not, is the most effective approach to anger management. Kay (2002) divided anger into two broad categories: primary and secondary anger. People with *primary anger* are described as those "always on the go . . . with their motors fast all the time." They get angry when someone thwarts their desire to get something done. "Anything that gets in their way leads to anger to overcome that obstacle." *Secondary anger* is the anger used to overcome or cover up certain weak feelings, such as fear, shame, or sadness. Individuals who are afraid they are going to be deserted or who feel smothered or embarrassed get angry. Help in their cases requires "the ability to analyze the anger . . . and find that your anger quiets down when you diminish fears, shame and sad thoughts" (Hightower, 2002, p. 189).

Prescribing Psychotropic Medications for Anger Management

Because anger reactions are caused by a complex interaction of biological, psychological, and social factors, the first step before prescribing medication should be a comprehensive evaluation of the client, with attention given to indications of biological underpinnings or predispositions, signs of conscious or unconscious psychological conflicts, personality traits, sensitivities, and coping styles, and the nature of the environment or social milieu in which the anger arises. This broader evaluation will help in the selection of the most effective and efficient medication or other treatment intervention.

The use of psychotropic medications has rapidly expanded in recent years and has become an integral part of the management of mental, emotional, and behavioral disorders. However, there is a need to be realistic about what medication can accomplish in the treatment and management of anger. Medication works best and is more clearly justified in treating anger that is a part of an underlying mental disorder (e.g., schizophrenia, mania, chronic depression). This is related to the knowledge that "there is a greater biological component in the etiology of severe mental illness, in contrast to the predominant social and psychological causes of most anger and violence" (Gilligan, 1997, p. 25). When the anger is a symptom of a definitive mental or medical disorder, the underlying disorder becomes the primary focus of treatment. It would be expected that successful treatment of the underlying disorder would resolve or reduce all of its symptoms, including the anger. Medication is more effective when used to treat a diagnosable mental disorder, as listed in the *Diagnostic and Statistical Manual* (DSM-IV; APA, 1994), than when attempting to treat angry outbursts of behaviors that are reactions to, or provoked by, situational circumstances or interpersonal conflicts (i.e., where psychological and social factors play a greater role than the biological).

Nonmentally ill clients may benefit from medication if their anger escalates to an intensity that causes significant social and occupational dysfunctions, interferes with psychological treatment or management efforts, or has reached a level of rage or violence in need of immediate control. In the latter more acute and dangerous conditions, when the client seems out of control and represents a danger to self or others, medication may be needed as a form of immediate chemical restraint. Physical restraint, hospitalization, emergency room, or jail confinement may also be indicated. Except in these more severe instances, medication for anger itself is often not indicated.

Appreciating the psychosocial issues—dissatisfaction, conflicts, unhappiness, and so forth—should alert the clinician to the importance of being realistic about what can be accomplished with medications (Kaariainen, 2002). Medication does not resolve social and interpersonal problems. When medications are introduced, they should be seen as adjuncts to, and not replacements of, the ongoing psychological therapies. Anger is not "cured" with medications or even put into sustained remission. Medication can help to make the angry behavior more manageable and slow trigger-sensitive response time, giving the angry person some space, some extra time before responding to think, withdraw, negotiate, and learn and use anger management techniques being offered in therapy and counseling.

A number of psychotropic medications have been found effective in controlling or diminishing the various manifestations and degrees of anger. For convenience, they are typically divided into the following six categories based on their original and predominate behavioral effects: antipsychotic or neuroleptic, antidepressant, antimanic or mood stabilizers, antianxiety or anxiolytics, stimulants, and sedatives or hypnotics.

A brief description of these categories of medications is given in relation to their use in anger management. It is recognized that although labeled as functionally specific (e.g., antipsychotic or antidepressant), many of these drugs have been found to have broader, overlapping effectiveness in treating multiple disorders. For example, antipsychotics are also used to treat chronic depression, antidepressants are used to treat anxiety, and so on.

The Antipsychotics

The earlier, "conventional" antipsychotics, such as chlorpromazine and including haloperidol (Haldol), thioridazine (Mellaril), trifluoperazine hydrochloride (Stelazine), and fluphenazine (Prolixin), were developed and primarily used as tranquilizers in the treatment of schizophrenia and other psychoses. Although still useful, they are less frequently prescribed because of their side effects, which include tardive dyskinesia, a sometimes-permanent movement disorder (Hightower, 2002). These conventional medications have for the most part been replaced by the newer "atypical" antipsychotics such as risperidone (Risperdal), quetiapine (Seroquel), olanzapine (Zyprexa), ziprasidone (Geodon), and aripiprazole (Abilify) because of their effectiveness and lower side effect profile.

Substantial data from medication studies during the past 15 years have led to new uses of these new or atypical antipsychotics, such as in the treatment of severe depression and more severe forms of aggression when rapid control is needed. Olanzapine (Zyprexa), for example, was effective in treating temper tantrums and destructive behavior in children and adolescents with conduct disorders (Jensen, 2004). In a large retrospective study of child and adolescent psychiatric populations, it was shown that 84% of clients with a wide variety of disorders (e.g., ADHD, conduct disorder, defiant disorder, autism, Asperger's disease, depression, schizophrenia, adjustment disorder) who were treated with risperidone (Risperdal) showed improvement in aggression, psychotic symptoms, social skills, and mood disturbance (Simeon, Milin, & Walker, 2002).

The clinical use of the atypical antipsychotics has provided convincing evidence for a significant role of medication in treating aggression and intense anger in nonpsychotic disorders (e.g., borderline personality disorders, PTSD). Furthermore, when rapid control of rage or anger is indicated, treatment results with atypical antipsychotics can be seen in 1 week or in the first day, if necessary, by administering intramuscular injections. Their effectiveness makes them useful during a behavioral crisis, which might prove dangerous or violent.

The antipsychotic medications as a class seem to have their primary effect by regulating dopamine in the caudate nucleus. Dopamine is known to be involved in psychosis, but it is now thought to be significantly related to aggression, anger, irritability, and the symptoms of chronic depression as well (Meyer & Deitsch, 1996).

The Antidepressants

As the name indicates, the antidepressants were developed for the primary purpose of treating depression. The older antidepressants, monoamine oxidase inhibitors (MAOIs) such as tranylcypromine (Parnate) and phenelzine (Nardil), and the tricyclic antidepressants (TCAs) such as amitriptyline (Elavil), imipramine (Tofranil), and trazodone have for the most part been replaced by newer antidepressants, such as fluoxetine (Prozac), sertraline (Zoloft), paroxetine (Paxil), escitalopram (Lexapro), venlafaxine (Effexor), and duloxetine (Cymbalta), because they have fewer side effects and are better tolerated. Beyond their effectiveness in treating depression, the antidepressants have been found to have a calming effect on anxiety; have demonstrated usefulness in treating aggressive, angry, impulsive behavior in general; and have demonstrated effectiveness in treating the irritability or outbursts of anger often seen in clients with PTSD (Hamner & Robert, 2004). For example, fluoxetine was shown to have demonstrated efficacy on aggressive and impulsive behavior in clients with personality disorders (Coccaro & Kavoussi, 1997), and trazodone was effective in decreasing symptoms of impulsivity, hyperactivity, fighting, arguing, and losing one's temper in children (Zubieta & Alessi, 1992).

The newer antidepressants are widely considered a first option when a medication trial seems indicated for anger management because of their safety and efficacy (Hamner & Robert, 2004). However, because of their gradual onset of action (2–4 weeks), antidepressants would not be the first choice when immediate response and control are needed. The biological basis of the action of antidepressants is related to their ability to increase serotonin and norepinephrine levels in the brain.

The Antimanics/Mood Stabilizers

The antimanic or mood stabilizer drugs have been primarily useful in the treatment of manic depression or bipolar spectrum disorders characterized by recurrent mood episodes of mania and/or depression. In 1946, Cade discovered that lithium would calm mania and decrease the frequency of recurrent episodes. It was later found that lithium helped calm other hyperactive states, including rage and anger, especially of the explosive type (Campbell et al., 1984). In a study of children and adolescents ages 5 to 17 with conduct disorder and explosive aggression treated with lithium, 80% showed significant improvement (Malone et al., 2000). More recently, a group of anticonvulsant drugs has been found to have a wider use and effectiveness as mood stabilizers. divalproex sodium (Depakote), carbamazepine (Tegretol), topiramate (Topamax), and lamotrigine (Lamictal) have all shown varying degrees of effectiveness in reducing anger in explosive mood disorder.

Antianxiety or Anxiolytic Medications

Although intended for treatment of anxiety disorders and not specifically indicated for anger management, antianxiety and anxiolytic agents are often used as a quick way to calm an angry client down, or to "take the edge off." The most commonly and widely used anxiolytics are the benzodiazepines, such as alprazolam (Xanax), clonazepam (Klonopin), and lorazepam (Ativan). These medications work by increasing brain levels of gamma-aminobutyric acid (GABA), which exerts a calming effect similar to serotonin. This calming effect may indeed reduce the intensity of anger and agitation, but these medications must be used with caution. For some clients, the use of a benzodiazepine can lead to a paradoxical increase in violence similar to the disinhibiting effect of alcohol on the user's behavior (Hamner, 2004).

The potential for abuse and dependency on these medications must be kept in mind as well. Individuals with a strong need to feel better or to block out their present reality or those who have a history of substance abuse or drug-seeking behavior are likely candidates to abuse antianxiety agents(Meyer & Dietsch, 1996). Use of these medications in such cases should be clearly justified, usually for short-term use only and with the close monitoring of the client who is preferably receiving psychotherapy. Buspirone (BuSpar), a nonbenzodiazepine used in the treatment of anxiety, has certain advantages over the benzodiazepines in that it has benign side effects and low abuse potential, but it has been of limited value in treating anger.

The Stimulants

Stimulants, including amphetamine-dextroamphetamine (Adderall), methylphenidate (Concerta), and methylphenidate (Ritalin), have their primary use and effectiveness in the treatment of children and adults with ADHD. They act by increasing brain levels of norepinephrine, serotonin, and dopamine. When effective, the stimulants can reduce motor hyperactivity and impulsiveness and have shown some limited usefulness in decreasing aggressive and angry behavior in children with ADHD and conduct disorder (Jensen, 2004). Relatively little usefulness has been reported in the treatment of anger in adults.

Sedatives or Hypnotics

In addition to the abuse potential of the antianxiety agents mentioned earlier, individuals have used a number of prescription and illegal drugs inappropriately in their own attempts to control their anger and rage. Although these may offer some temporary relief, alcohol, sedatives, stimulants, and hallucinogens can actually cause an increase in their rage (Kay, 2002). There may be a longer-term calming and decrease in rage with the use of marijuana or morphine-like drugs such as heroin, but the consequences of such ongoing abuse may lead to destructive consequences, dependency, or increased tolerance and will certainly impede effective problem solving.

THE CASE OF ANTHONY

Any case referred for psychiatric opinion or intervention should begin with a broad-based assessment of the client from a biopsychosocial perspective. The case of Anthony presented in Chapter 2 will be used to illustrate some general issues involved in evaluating and treating an angry client with psychotropic medication.

Anthony, referred for "anger management," is a 48-year-old, married, white male. He is a blue collar worker and lives in cramped quarters with his employed higher-earning Puerto Rican wife, three daughters (ages 11, 17, and 20), and his oldest daughter's African American boyfriend and their 18-month-old baby. This referral immediately alerts the psychiatrist to the importance of the probable impact of multiple psychosocial factors in Anthony's presenting problem (e.g., the large number of people living in cramped quarters, different age groups, cultural and racial differences, an unmarried daughter and her boyfriend and their baby, a wife who earns more then he does).

Anthony acknowledged "trouble controlling" his anger that "spills out mostly at loved ones." However, it was noted that a primary motivation for his seeking treatment was his wife's threat to leave him if he did not get help, which raises questions about his motivation. Was he really motivated to receive help, or was he just going along to satisfy his wife and keep her from leaving? While admitting to difficulty controlling his anger, Anthony describes himself with kinder words as "affectionate, nurturing, emotional, and passionate with a feminine side . . . a man who loves to cook and is often in charge of the household."

By description, his anger seems to be intermittent, occurring in sudden, explosive outbursts, usually triggered by some specific event or situation. These episodes are typically verbal and may be temper tantrum–like in nature. Except for two reported instances, 20 years or more ago, he has not been physically assaultive. Anthony tends to justify his angry outbursts and to blame these episodes on the behavior of others. For example, he gets angry when family members or others do not comply with his wishes or do not give him his way and he is intolerant of "stupidity" and people "playing dumb." He is impatient with tardiness or being made to wait, he cannot abide laziness, and he will not allow personal affronts or disrespect. In other words, there is a pattern to his behavior in which he feels his anger is justified because of what someone did to obstruct, provoke, or disrespect him. With such an attitude, he is able to distance himself from much of the responsibility for his behavior, which allows him to see himself above others in a more powerful, righteous, or moral sense.

Anthony's long-standing anger and angry behavior is clearly a problem of significance in his life, but he has never sought personal help for it before. He does not come now on his own seeking relief from suffering as the victim of his own anger, but rather he comes at the insistence of his wife and her threat to leave him if he does not comply. This is a most important consideration when thinking of how to engage him in a treatment process in general and in thinking of the justification for medication in particular. Is the treatment for him or for others?

Because anger is not a mental disorder or diagnostic category but rather a symptomatic expression, it is important in its evaluation to look for causative factors. Is there evidence of any significant underlying mental or medical disorder that might explain the behavior or evidence that any prescription or other substance or alcohol abuse might be causing or complicating the problem?

In Anthony's case, there were no indications of any serious mental, medical, or substance abuse problems. There was no evidence of any psychosis, mania, organic brain syndrome, or identifiable anxiety disorders, and there was a denial of depression. His described behavior pattern did not suggest ADHD, even though his history reveals academic underachievement and an uneven work history. His long history of childhood sexual abuse (see following discussion) does not appear to have been processed and has been deliberately avoided or minimized by Anthony. Psychosocial factors in Anthony's developmental history and in his present life seem to predominate as explanations for his anger. The experiences of his anger seem more clearly like character traits, even though from his history these traits do not have the distinct patterns and consistency of a definable character disorder.

Anthony grew up in a family that gave him mixed experiences, and he developed mixed feelings about himself. He thought of himself on one hand as special and admired, with experiences of closeness and acceptance. On the other hand, perhaps ever more so, he suffered experiences of emotional coldness, abandonment and loss, rejection, abuse, and scorn, and he saw himself a disappointment to others. He felt close to his father, especially in relation to his father's admiration of his athletic prowess. However, Anthony also experienced his father as strict and disappointed in him. He felt disliked by his mother and described her as critical, demeaning, physically abusive to him, and rarely supportive and affectionate.

His maternal grandmother, who was a dominant family figure, treated him in a consistently negative manner. In contrast, he had a most special and extremely close relationship with his maternal grandfather. Unfortunately, Anthony was emotionally traumatized by "a great loss . . . I lost my best friend" when, at age 15, his grandfather died. Of special significance in his early history was a 4-year period, age 7 to 11, of sexual abuse by his maternal uncle. As a young child, he "loved his uncle dearly . . . thought he was the greatest man in the world." He was convinced by this uncle that what they had was just "a special relationship." It was not until pubescence that Anthony began to feel uncomfortable with his uncle, and it was not until he was an adult that he expressed hostility toward him. Although not described as traumatic at the time, it is clear that the subsequent realization of what was happening had a traumatic impact on him. Despite the inevitable post-traumatic psychological sequelae of this abuse, there was little distinct evidence of marked symptomatology or criteria to suggest a need for medications, as opposed to psychotherapy as the treatment intervention of choice.

SUMMARY, CONCLUSIONS, AND RECOMMENDATIONS

A review of Anthony's case indicates that there is not sufficient justification for medication as part of the initial treatment plan for his anger. Although his anger is clearly a significant and detrimental factor in his life, the severity of its manifestation does not indicate an immediate need for psychotropic intervention. There is little evidence to conclude that his anger is the product or symptom of any defined mental or medical disorder or that it is related to substance use or abuse.

Anthony experienced a prolonged period of sexual abuse as a child and undoubtedly has some psychological sequelae from this experience (e.g., shame, guilt, avoidance). However, it is not apparent that the level of his post-traumatic suffering warrants medical treatment. Furthermore, a diagnosis of intermittent explosive disorder was considered because of his description of explosive angry outbursts. However, although his anger can be explosive at times, the level of his aggression does not indicate a degree of severity that requires medication.

What is clear is that Anthony needs psychosocial intervention more than medication. He is clearly a candidate for psychotherapy and training in interpersonal and anger management skills, because his anger is a complicating and damaging factor in his past and present personal, marital, social, and occupational contexts. Psychotherapy would provide him the opportunity to recognize and take responsibility for his behavior. To see not only what he is doing, but why and to recognize the gain he gets from using and maintaining this angry behavior—for example, the sense of control and power it gives him, the opportunity it provides to make a lot of noise and thereby divert his attention away from examining his own insecurities, weaknesses, and other painful thoughts and memories.

Although anger was the manifest and presenting reason for Anthony's coming to therapy, a therapeutic experience, especially an insight-oriented one, could stir up and release a number of hidden or suppressed painful feelings, thoughts, or memories underlying his anger (e.g., his early history of neglect, sexual and emotional abuse, the loss of special relationships and status, failure of academic and occupational success, low self-esteem and feelings of inadequacy, his thwarted need for attachment and admiration, his guilt and fear of abandonment).

Increased arousal and awareness of these feelings and emotions could produce an exacerbation of his anger, be experienced as threatening, or reveal or lead to a significant depression. This in turn could result in more personal suffering and a resistance to or desire to take flight from therapy. Should this be the case, further consideration could then be given to the introduction of appropriate medication to his treatment regimen.

CHAPTER 10

Emotion-Focused Therapy for Anger

Josée L. Jarry and Sandra C. Paivio

INTRODUCTION TO AN EMOTION-FOCUSED THERAPY APPROACH

Theoretical Postulates of Experiential and Emotionally Focused Approaches

Emotion-focused therapy (EFT) subscribes to the general postulates of humanistic approaches concerning human functioning, such as the primacy of subjectivity and the inherent tendency toward actualization (Greenberg & Rice, 1997). EFT is also representative of current experiential theory and research (Greenberg & Paivio, 1997; Greenberg, Korman, & Paivio, 2002; Greenberg, Rice, & Elliott, 1993; Paivio & Greenberg, 1995). It integrates new findings about the importance and function of emotions (Damasio, 1999; LeDoux, 1995; Frijda, 1986; Izard, 1990b) and makes explicit the role of emotion exploration and symbolization in therapeutic change. Like other humanistic approaches, EFT adheres to the notion that what best explains human behavior is the subjective experience of reality. Attention to and symbolization of clients' subjective worlds is the raw material from which a new understanding of the self and of others can emerge.

Attention to emotions is central to the process of increased self-understanding because emotions are associated with a multimodal network of information about the self and one's experience of the world.

This network is referred to as an emotion scheme or structure whereby specific emotions are associated with specific action tendencies, thoughts, desires, and memories (Greenberg & Paivio, 1997). Thus, evoking emotions provides a direct access to associated meanings. Information associated with emotions, such as a negative view of the self, is made available through activation of the emotion structure and is now available to reprocessing and change. When traumatized individuals access the fear and helplessness experienced during abuse, they can revisit old feelings of being bad and at fault for it. The clearly identified fear is associated with cognitions and action tendencies that are incompatible with having wanted the abuse. The EFT conceptualization of emotions, classified as either primary, secondary, or instrumental, is unique within psychological theories of human functioning (Greenberg, 2002a, 2002b; Greenberg & Paivio, 1997). No single emotion, such as anger, belongs exclusively to one category, and all can travel between the following categories depending on their specific activation.

EFT Conceptualization of Emotions

Primary Emotions

Primary emotions can be adaptive or maladaptive immediate reactions to external events. They are irreducible to preceding emotions and cognition. They are direct, unmediated reactions to environmental events and are an important verbal and nonverbal (Izard, 1990a) modes of communication with others.

Emotion theory and research (e.g., Frijda, 1986) has identified a number of innate, biologically adaptive emotions, such as joy, sadness, fear, and anger, in response to objectively occurring events. Primary adaptive emotions are essential to moment-by-moment behavioral regulation because they inform the organism about the nature and valence of environmental stimuli as being either beneficial, dangerous, or simply new. Primary adaptive emotions also play an orienting role because of their association with specific action tendencies that guide behavior in the environment (Frijda, 1986). For example, fear automatically initiates a freeze or flight response and anger initiates self-protection or assertiveness.

Primary maladaptive emotions are also immediate reactions to external events that are unmediated by cognition and other affect. However, they are generated by a damaging learning history that distorts the experience of current external events and causes reactions that are incongruent with these events. Such damaging learning history can result, for example, in a core sense of self as being unworthy or vulnerable or in conditioned emotional reactions such as fear, shame, and rage in response to innocuous stimuli. Some forms of anger associated with post-traumatic stress disorder (PTSD) are typical examples of primary maladaptive emotions.

Secondary Emotions

Secondary emotions can be either reactions to primary emotions or can occur in reaction to cognitive processes. Secondary emotions in reaction to primary emotions are often defenses against primary emotions that are experienced as intolerable and/or create an intense sense of vulnerability. Common examples include feeling anger to avoid the vulnerability of fear and sadness or feeling scared of one's primary and legitimate anger. Secondary emotions also can be the result of dysfunctional thought processes. For example, secondary anxiety can result from rumination about possible threat, and anger can be activated by hostile attributions. Secondary emotions also serve to orient the organism by dictating specific behavior, but similar to primary maladaptive emotions, such behavior is incongruent with environmental events.

Instrumental Emotions

Instrumental emotions are expressed to obtain a desired reaction from others. They are used, consciously or not, to make others feel, think, or behave in a certain way and to achieve a measure of control over others. Examples include expressing anger to intimidate others and expressing sadness to elicit caring without directly asking for it. Instrumental emotions serve a manipulative function and are an indirect way of getting what one wants without having to experience the vulnerability of making direct demands or expressing authentic feelings.

Assessment of Emotions in EFT

Emotions can be classified in any of the aforementioned categories, depending on their function at any given time. To arrive at a clear understanding of the function of anger, the therapist must conduct an emotion assessment, which requires attention to the following sources and includes an evaluation of the client's capacity for emotion regulation (Greenberg & Paivio, 1997; Paivio, 1999).

Empathic Attunement

Above all, emotional assessment in EFT consists of a moment-by-moment assessment of the client's emotional experience as it unfolds in the here and now. During this process, the therapist attempts to understand the client's unique subjective experience. This is done by attending to both non-verbal cues, such as posture and vocal quality, and verbal communication about emotional states.

Knowledge of Human Emotions

Knowledge of human emotions involves the therapist's theoretical knowledge of universal human emotional responses to specific situations. Here, the therapist understands, for example, that being threatened elicits fear (LeDoux, 1995), being abandoned is likely to create sadness (Bowlby, 1980; Kendler et al., 1995; Monroe et al., 1999), and being slighted or treated disrespectfully frequently generates anger (Deffenbacher, 1999).

Knowledge of Personality Styles and Disorders

Knowledge of personality styles and disorders involves drawing on general, theoretical knowledge of personality features that influence how individuals experience and use emotions differently (Maxmen & Ward, 1995). For example, one with a more narcissistic style can be prone to experience secondary anger at perceived slight, whereas dependent individuals may be more likely to use sadness instrumentally to elicit support. Furthermore, Axis I disorders, such as PTSD and depression, also are frequently associated with irritability and anger.

Knowledge of Particular Client

Knowledge of a particular client's temperament and learning history is crucial to accurate emotion assessment. Temperament consists of biologically rooted individual differences in behavior tendencies that are present early in life and constitute the basis for personality (Bates, 1989). Emotionality is a major component of temperament (Buss & Plomin, 1975, 1984) along with sociability and activity, all three of which are relatively stable across situations but also influenced by developmental history (Rothbart & Bates, 1998). Thus, understanding a client's temperament and combining this with his or her personal history is crucial to accurate emotion assessment.

Problems with Emotion Regulation

Emotion regulation refers to the process by which individuals influence the nature, frequency, intensity, and expression of their own emotional experience (Rottenberg & Gross, 2003). According to Gross (1998), well-being is associated with the capacity to control events that elicit emotion, allowing one to experience richly diversified emotions, and the capacity to modulate the intensity of this experience and its expression.

Applying this conceptualization to anger suggests that difficulties with anger regulation can emerge from faulty control of eliciting cues, poor access to emotional experience, and insufficient upward or downward modulation of experience and expression. Anger-eliciting cues, either environmental e.g., slight) or internal (e.g., ruminative thoughts), can escape a person's awareness and thus be uncontrollable. Anger itself can be completely missing from awareness or can be over-represented to the detriment of other emotions that could be more context appropriate. Difficulties can also present themselves with the over-regulation or under-regulation of anger. Anger can be experienced as overwhelming, or it can be controlled to the point of near-complete suppression. Finally, anger expression can be thwarted by communication skill deficits or can be excessive, as in the case of gratuitous aggressive behavior. In all instances, the orienting action tendencies associated with adaptive anger are lost and anger does not fulfill its functions of assertiveness and self-protection.

Because of its emphasis on internal experiential processes, EFT is particularly well suited to the identification of emotion regulation difficulties. Specifically, as is described in Anthony's case conceptualization, difficulties with emotional awareness, together with over-regulation and under-regulation, are readily identified in the emotion assessment process of EFT.

Experiential Conceptualization of Emotions and Child Abuse, Trauma, and Neglect

Emotion-focused trauma therapy (EFTT; Paivio & Greenberg, 2000; Paivio & Nieuwenhuis, 2001; Paivio & Shimp, 1998) applies general principles of EFT to the treatment of trauma-related disorders by integrating current knowledge in the areas of trauma (van der Kolk, McFarlane, & Weisaeth, 1996), attachment (Bowlby, 1988; Sroufe, 1995), and child abuse (Briere, 1996; Herman, 1992; Myers et al., 2002). Usually, childhood abuse consists of intense experiences that excessively tax the child's capacity to process information. These experiences generate three sources of disturbance to adult functioning (Paivio & Carriere, in press).

The first source of disturbance is exposure to overwhelming affect. Recent evidence suggests that, because of the intense stress generated, traumatic events are stored in a memory system characterized by low verbal encoding and high perceptual processing (Brewin, 2001). Exposure to current stimuli akin to those involved in the original trauma evokes trauma memories (van der Kolk, 1996) as well as perceptual memories. These result, for example, in the intense sensory re-experiencing characteristic of flashbacks (Brewin, 2001). This incomplete processing of traumatic events and memories may account for the multiple areas of perceptual hypersensitivity, such as the exaggerated startle response that many PTSD sufferers experience.

Both rage and experiential avoidance are common in trauma survivors. In typical traumatic situations, the victim is powerless and the otherwise adaptive orienting value of anger is of no use. This combination of anger and helplessness can result in feelings of rage that quickly become intolerable. The victim may then rely on avoidance to cope with this rage or with other intolerable feelings generated by the abuse. Avoidance sometimes interferes with the eventual integration of trauma memories within general, autobiographical memory (Brewin, 2001) and prevents the reprocessing and integration of the trauma into an adaptive view of the self (e.g., as having been helpless in this particular situation versus in general) and the world (as being generally safe despite isolated damaging events). Avoidance of anger also compromises competence regarding this emotion and its regulation, thus the often seen alternation of indifference and explosive rage in trauma survivors.

Negative experiences with attachment figures represent a second source of disturbance. Abuse by caregivers or trusted adults damages the child's sense of self and their perceptions of relationships with others (Bowlby, 1988). Because of young children's inherent cognitive egocentrism (Piaget, 1954), abusive experiences are usually attributed to the self and generate self-blame, criticism, and a perception of the self as flawed and tainted. The betrayal inherent to abuse by caregivers also disrupts expectations of intimate relationships and shatters assumptions about their safety, creating a relationship schema where love and caring are not forthcoming. An insecure attachment style is strongly over-represented in abuse survivors (Muller, Sicoli, & Lemieux, 2000).

The third source of disturbance consists of chronic reliance on avoidance as a coping strategy. Abuse and neglect usually occur within an unsupportive context. This can be because the very individual who is in a position to provide support is also the abuser, or it may simply be because the child is too confused or disoriented to disclose the abuse and ask for support. In any case, childhood abuse usually occurs in the absence of the support or emotional coaching (Gottman, Katz, & Hooven, 1997) needed to help the child negotiate intense negative feelings. Without empathic responding, the emotions related to the trauma and their associated meaning cannot be processed and transformed into new, adaptive interpretations. Because these feelings remain painful, intense, and overwhelming, the child is likely to use experiential avoidance as a coping strategy (Paivio & Greenberg, 2000). Emotional suppression serves important protective functions at the time of the abuse. However, chronic experiential avoidance thwarts the development of emotional competence and necessarily results in problems of over-regulation or under-regulation of emotions.

Mechanisms of Change in EFT

The postulated mechanisms of change in EFT are consistent with the central role of emotion and with recent research showing that emotion facilitation and processing, combined with cognitive reflection on the meaning of emotions, are major contributors to therapeutic change (Paivio et al., 2001; Watson & Bedard, 2005; Whelton, 2004). In EFT, change is hypothesized to occur by evoking the maladaptive emotional structures currently adversely affecting the client. This requires the client to first acknowledge and recognize the presence of these emotions and then work to change them. Accessing primary adaptive emotions and the meaning attached to them makes the associated network of information and meaning about the self and the world available. This then allows the development of new adaptive behaviors aimed at fulfilling basic needs, together with a decrease in anger that is now understood as a defense.

Although the same general EFT strategies apply to EFTT, the impact of childhood trauma requires an emphasis on traumatic memories that have been incompletely processed at the time of their formation and have had a lasting damaging impact. Furthermore, childhood trauma at the hands of caregivers implies serious attachment injuries, unmet needs, and breaches of trust. Therefore, the mechanisms of change in the treatment of child abuse trauma include the development of a strong therapeutic relationship such that it can become a corrective emotional experience; the reprocessing of trauma memories; and the reprocessing of past, internalized relationships with abusive or neglectful others.

Development of a Strong Therapeutic Relationship

Empathy is defined as the capacity to understand another person's experience from his or her point of view and is both an essential context and an active intervention for addressing the emotion regulation problems associated with child abuse (Paivio & Laurent, 2001). More specifically, childhood abuse generates coping mechanisms that impair the awareness, modulation, and expression components of normal emotion regulation. In EFTT, empathy is the first condition needed for the re-establishment of this regulation.

Usually, parental empathy imparts accurate labels to the child's emotional experience. Syntonic mirroring helps the child acknowledge his or her experience and thus promotes its awareness. Seeing the experience reflected in the parents' facial expression, as well as through verbal and nonverbal behavior, provides the child with appropriate labels for the experience. By definition, abusive relationships are devoid of such empathy, and the child's emotions and interpretations of the situation are often invalidated while, at the same time, a demand is made to adhere to a counterintuitive interpretation of reality. An empathic therapeutic relationship represents a first level of corrective experience by providing this accurate mirroring of affective states, correct labeling, and appropriate expression of emotions. In addition to its inherent facilitation of affect regulation, empathy provides the context necessary to establish a strong attachment bond. The safety and trust of this relationship facilitates the exploration of painful and potentially overwhelming memories and associated feelings.

Emotional Processing of Child Abuse Memories

Childhood abuse often generates powerful, pervasive emotions and highly complex, dysfunctional meaning systems that are beyond the child's capacity for processing and integration. Highly stressful events also tend to be encoded as sensory memories that remain unavailable to verbal processing (Brewin, 2001). This prevents the higher cognitive processing of trauma-related memories and information and contributes to the maintenance of maladaptive meaning about the self and the world that results from such experiences. In addition to its desensitization effects, exposure to traumatic memories is essential to the reprocessing of the attached information and must occur to activate associated emotions and meaning system (Foa, 2000). The full exploration of these experiences in the context of advanced empathy allows the admission of new information about the self, the perpetrator, and the world and imparts a more adaptive interpretation of the original experiences. During trauma exposure exercises, EFTT actively promotes contact with previously inhibited core adaptive emotions such as sadness and anger and activates their associated adaptive action tendency.

Reprocessing of Past Relationships with Abusive or Neglectful Others

Finally, survivors of neglect and abuse are plagued by attachment difficulties with perpetrators or significant others who failed to protect them. These dysfunctional attachments are expressed in continuing emotional clinging and longing for the satisfaction of needs that were not met and contribute to an image of the self as unworthy of care and attention. In addition, these attachments contribute to disruptions of current relationships that tend to model themselves on past significant relationships. Therefore, a third mechanism of change in EFTT consists of the reprocessing of internalized relationships with abusive or neglectful others. Importantly, this reprocessing does not involve interacting with actual perpetrators in one's current life. Rather, it consists of psychologically engaging the other as experienced in the past, through evocative interventions, within the safety of the therapy setting.

The reprocessing of past relationships with perpetrators involves accessing previously inhibited needs concerning these individuals as well as the full range of emotions that were felt toward them, including sadness for the fact that needs were not and will never be satisfied. Accessing this sadness and expressing it allows the client to grieve for these losses and to eventually let go of unfulfilled hopes. Reprocessing past relationships also can help clients let go of anger at violation and at not having had their needs met or let go of defensive anger masking deeper sadness. The expression of these feelings from an assertive stance promotes a sense of entitlement to fair treatment and a view of the self as worthy of care.

Importantly, full access to emotional experience concerning the perpetrator allows the development of a more nuanced perception of this person as having been abusive because of personal shortcomings. Through this process, perpetrators are always held accountable for their actions and are sometimes forgiven if the client deems it appropriate. In either case, unresolved longing, sadness, anger, and fear toward the perpetrator can be put to rest, which fosters an increased sense of separation and autonomy.

Empirical Evidence Supporting EFT and EFTT

In a recent meta-analysis, Elliott, Greenberg, and Lietaer (2003) surveyed more than 111 outcome studies of experiential therapy, of which more than half were published since 1990. This review focused on a total of 127 adult treatment groups that ranged from inpatient psychiatric to community populations. The average treatment length was 22 sessions, and the average number of clients per study was 51.7. In this meta-analysis the average pre-post treatment effects size was 0.99 (weighted effect = 0.86) and the average mean controlled effect size was 0.89 (weighted effect = 0.78). Noticeably, in the 46 comparisons of experiential with cognitive-behavioral treatments, the pre-post effect sizes of these two approaches were equivalent. When cognitive-behavioral treatments were compared with "process directive" experiential therapies, of which EFT is a member (comprising 14 of the 46 comparisons), the process directive approach showed somewhat larger pre-post effect sizes.

In particular, EFT and EFTT both enjoy extensive empirical support. In terms of outcome, a short-term treatment (12 sessions) based on EFT principles was shown to be effective with a general population dealing with unresolved interpersonal issues from the past. This adult sample ($N = 34$) included a subset of child abuse survivors (Paivio & Greenberg, 1995). The first study of EFTT with a sample ($N = 32$) of childhood abuse survivors showed significant client improvements in multiple domains of disturbance, including PTSD symptoms, global interpersonal problems, self-affiliation, target complaints, and resolution of issues with abusive others (Paivio & Nieuwenhuis, 2001), which were maintained at 1-year follow-up. Several process outcome studies also support the posited mechanism of changes in EFT and EFTT. In a sample of childhood abuse survivors ($N = 33$), Paivio and Patterson (1999) showed that the therapeutic relationship significantly improved over the course of therapy and predicted dimensions of post-treatment change, such as general symptom distress, trauma-related symptoms, and resolution of issues with significant others from the past. Paivio et al. (2001) found that emotional engagement with trauma material independently predicted improvement in general symptom distress, trauma-related symptoms, and current relationships—over and above contributions made by the therapeutic relationship. The unique contribution of engagement with trauma material to outcome was replicated in a preliminary study of two versions of EFTT (Paivio, 2004). All of these studies were conducted with men and women who survived abuse (physical, sexual, and emotional) and neglect experiences.

The positive effect of anger exploration and expression in EFTT, per se, was recently demonstrated in two independent studies. Holowaty (2004) located, on videotapes, events that clients ($N = 27$) identified as helpful during post-treatment interviews. These events were characterized by intense expression of anger about abuse and neglect. Carriere (2003) directly studied the effects of adaptive anger experience and expression on outcome in a sample of clients ($N = 37$) receiving EFTT. Independent judges rated the quality of anger expression in videotaped therapy episodes according to five dimensions. First, anger is directed at an offending other, not at the self. Second, the anger is owned by the client through the use of "I" language and the client assertively expresses anger rather than blaming and insulting the other. Third, the expression of anger is done with a level of arousal that is appropriate to the situation and is conveyed by body posture, vocal tone, and facial expressions that are consistent with anger. Fourth, anger is differentiated from other emotions, such as sadness or fear, so that anger expression is not mixed with tears, for example. Finally, adaptive expression of anger is not simply cathartic for the purpose of venting. Adaptive anger involves meaning exploration and construction where its full expression conveys information about the self and the offending other. Results showed a significant association between adaptive anger expression and interpersonal dimensions of change, including resolution of issues with abusive or neglectful others from the past and reduced current interpersonal difficulties, and these results were maintained at follow-up. Although preliminary, these two studies support the view that the experience and expression of adaptive anger contributes to positive process and outcome in EFTT.

THE CASE OF ANTHONY

Case Conceptualization

Emotional assessment in EFT, or process diagnosis, continues throughout therapy rather than being a distinct, initial stage of therapy when the client's functioning is crystallized into a specific style or disorder (Greenberg, 2002a, 2002b). The purpose of this process diagnosis is to guide intervention that is appropriate to the client's emotional experience at any given time. To work with Anthony on his anger, the following elements would be considered.

Over-regulated Primary Adaptive Anger

As previously mentioned, primary adaptive anger is a healthy reaction to having been objectively slighted or injured by someone or something. Chronically suppressed primary adaptive anger can lead to buildups and later explosions in situations unrelated to the original insult. Anthony reports such over-regulation when he suppresses his anger during conflicts with loved ones, only to explode later. Intervention would aim at coaching Anthony to pay sufficient attention to his experience to recognize his appropriate anger and express it directly, without insulting, yelling, or being physically aggressive.

Anthony's history of abuse at the hands of his uncle clearly suggests underlying adaptive anger that has not been fully expressed and processed. This is indicated by Anthony's statement of wishing that his uncle suffered more than he currently is with cancer and his report of hatred toward his grandmother for "bringing his uncle into his life." Anthony's case also suggests unrecognized and unexpressed adaptive anger toward his parents. He may harbor resentment toward his mother for being critical and demeaning, toward his father for showing disappointment in him, and toward both of his parents for failing to support him when he disclosed the abuse. It is also possible that, as a child, he gave some indications that something was not quite right but that his parents failed to respond.

Primary Maladaptive Anger

Primary maladaptive anger is a type of stereotypical, generalized anger reaction frequently associated with PTSD. Anthony has received a diagnosis of PTSD associated with the childhood sexual abuse by his uncle. He also scored high on the "anger irritability" scale of the Trauma Symptom Inventory (TSI; Briere, 1995), which may reflect irritability associated with PTSD hypervigilance. Furthermore, his high scores on the "intrusive experience" and the "defensive avoidance" subscales of the TSI strongly support the hypothesis that some of Anthony's anger is associated with PTSD and is a generalized, maladaptive response to immediate environmental events.

Intervention with these anger states would involve exploration of Anthony's anger when there is no obvious threat in the environment. The goal would be to identify the meaning of this experience for him and how this meaning is connected to previous life events. Equally important would be the identification of primary adaptive emotions appropriate to these past and current events to arrive at the appropriate expression of these emotions.

Secondary Defensive Anger

In regard to secondary defensive anger, the goal is to assess when anger expression masks more vulnerable feelings, such as sadness, fear, and pain, which are experienced as dangerous or intolerable. These feelings can be generated by a sense of the self as being inadequate and lacking and can be defended against with secondary anger. Intervention with this type of anger aims at uncovering the masked feelings and associated information and arriving at their appropriate expression.

Several elements in Anthony's case could have promoted his development of low self-esteem. Anthony reports having felt that his mother loved him less than she loved his siblings and that his father was disappointed with him for perceived developmental failures, such as quitting the swim team. Finally, low self-esteem is likely to have resulted from the abusive experience with the uncle. Interpreting the relationship as having been purely utilitarian, with little or no genuine feelings of love from his uncle, can result in a self-perception as being unlovable.

Examples of Anthony's anger presentation supporting this hypothesis include his explosion at the girls in the "Little League" team. His rage might have stemmed from perceiving their failure as a reflection of his low level of skills. This could prompt intolerable feelings of inadequacy that are defended against with secondary anger. Another example consists of becoming furious at his wife for "purposefully" being late. It is possible that his anger not only is secondary to maladaptive beliefs but also is masking more vulnerable feelings, such as sadness about her not caring about him or feeling unimportant in her eyes, both fueled either by his own low self-image or by his perceptions of others as uncaring.

Secondary Anger Mediated by Maladaptive Beliefs

The therapist must be able to recognize when the client's anger is secondary to maladaptive core beliefs, such as being entitled to special treatment, believing certain behaviors on the part of others are completely unacceptable under any circumstances, and believing others are ill-intentioned toward the self. Anthony's maladaptive beliefs include his experience of lateness and stupidity as personal affronts, his belief that his wife is late on purpose to annoy him, and his inability to tolerate lateness from anyone or to wait in lines of any kind. Interestingly, Anthony finds that others' lateness is completely unacceptable but appears to find his own excusable, as evidenced by his lateness and absences from work and his refusal to accept his supervisor's reprimands. Although this pattern can result from low-level depression, it can also stem from a sense of entitlement to special treatment and to not having to follow the rules that apply to others.

Anthony's history of abuse may have generated maladaptive beliefs and expectations of others as being malevolent. Having suffered abuse by someone whom he admired, trusted, and loved can generate a worldview where no one can be trusted and where even those who should be most trustworthy can be exploitative, utilitarian, and oblivious of one's most basic needs and can maliciously enjoy inflicting suffering. Finally, the neglect that Anthony suffered from his parents when he told them about the abuse could further confirm his beliefs in people's lack of consideration for his needs.

Instrumental Anger

Anthony's case suggests that he uses anger instrumentally to control and manipulate others. For example, he cites using his voice as a weapon when he yells at his family, and he blows up when things do not go his way. These anger displays are at least partly aimed at intimidating others to gain compliance. Instrumental anger has likely developed from a history of reinforcement where Anthony first noticed that his anger got him what he wanted in the short term. This type of anger utilization is confronted and interpreted in EFT.

Under-regulated Anger

Anthony's history clearly indicates problems with under-regulated anger. At least three angry outbursts had significant negative consequences: the assault of a teen that cost him his scholarship and possibly his initial career plans, the verbal assault of the girls on his daughter's softball team that caused him to be fired as a coach, and the fight with his supervisor that cost him his 21-year-long position as a machinist. His report that his anger literally takes him by surprise and that he explodes in rages suggests that he is unaware of the thoughts and feelings that contribute to anger escalation and thus cannot regulate them. EFT interventions would include promoting awareness of the internal states signaling anger and the implementation of strategies to de-escalate the anger. This should be coupled with coaching on how to appropriately express anger and emotions in general.

Treatment Plan

The ultimate goal of therapy is for Anthony to gain control over his dysfunctional anger experience and expression. For this, Anthony must develop the capacity to experience and express a full range of emotions. As is typical of EFT, Anthony and the therapist will collaborate to prioritize his goals and the plan will be flexible and idiosyncratic to Anthony's particular therapeutic process.

Goals will be as follows:

1. To change the maladaptive beliefs that give rise to Anthony's cognitively mediated secondary anger. This will be achieved by accessing primary emotions (e.g., sadness) related to the negative consequences of his anger on loved ones.
2. To identify vulnerable feelings against which anger serves as a defense and to develop skills to appropriately express these emotions.
3. To decrease anger associated with PTSD by reprocessing trauma memories.
4. To access and appropriately express adaptive anger and sadness related to the sexual abuse by his uncle and his parents' failure to protect and support him.

Phase 1: Establishing the Alliance

The initial phase of EFT aims at establishing the therapeutic alliance through empathic responding, the collaborative determination of goals, and the provision of a rationale for the goals and tasks of therapy. This phase also entails arriving at a collaborative understanding of the underlying cognitive-affective determinants of the client's disturbances. Instrumental and essential to the establishment of the alliance, advanced empathy is maintained throughout the therapy process to ensure accurate understanding and labeling of the client's experience (Paivio & Laurent, 2001). Empathic responding underlies all EFT interventions and is an active change ingredient in therapy fulfilling two main functions.

Modulation of Emotional Intensity. According to Paivio and Laurent (2001), empathic responding can contribute to reducing emotional arousal by providing understanding and support. Reduced isolation and distress are inherently calming and decrease emotional arousal. Thus, intense anger can be downregulated by the feeling of finally being understood and validated. Empathy can also increase emotional arousal when reflecting emotions that were previously inhibited and over-regulated. The full experience of emotions provides access to their associated meaning, which is then available for exploration. For Anthony, empathy could lead to sufficient comfort to allow more nuanced exploration of his experience and could increase contact with previously inhibited vulnerable emotions such as fear and shame.

Increased Emotional Awareness and Understanding. Empathy increases experiential awareness by directing attention to internal experience. This is essential to the identification and expression of adaptive anger and associated meanings, as well as to the exploration of the factors contributing to maladaptive anger. Increased awareness is an essential step toward increased emotional control.

Advanced empathy and responding consists of inferring, through an empathic stance, the complex subjective experience of the client and reflecting it. Thus, rather than asking the client what he or she feels, as in psychodynamic therapy, the therapist reflects the client's emotional state. For example, when exploring with Anthony the feelings that he had when the girls on the softball team were losing, the therapist might detect fear of judgment in his depiction of the parents looking at the unfolding failure. The therapist would then tentatively reflect this fear to him and thus bring it into focus. This could be done with an intervention such as: "When you talk to me about how the parents were looking on and what you saw in their faces, it seems like you were afraid that they were thinking badly of you, that somehow, it was your fault." Thus, empathy also promotes the accurate labeling and expression of emotions, in this case, vulnerable emotions, within the context of a safe therapeutic relationship.

As this exploration unfolds, the therapist and client collaboratively formulate goals. For example, the exploration of the softball event could lead the therapist to suggest as a goal that Anthony learn to tolerate and understand the meaning behind emotions such as shame and fear rather than flying into rages. Anthony's agreement with this goal would be essential in order to give the therapist permission to direct the process.

Phase 2: Evoking and Exploring

The middle phase of therapy aims at evoking adaptive emotions and exploring secondary and instrumental emotions and the associated cognitive network. Evocation of emotionally charged material in session is important to allow for reprocessing into adaptive meaning. For example, the only way for Anthony to fully understand why he flies into rages rather than feeling the pain of being incompetent will be for him to actually feel this pain in session. This will allow him to fully experience what is intolerable for him, become desensitized to it, access associated meaning, and therefore face and resolve that specific content. During this phase, the client and therapist flexibly move between past events and present issues. For Anthony, one implication of this would be to explore the past abuse in constant connection with its consequences on his current life.

Accessing Primary Anger Associated with Child Abuse and Neglect and Addressing Secondary Defensive Anger. Because experiences of child abuse and neglect have a lasting impact on adult functioning, the sexual abuse from his uncle and the emotional neglect from his mother, combined with the eventual abandonment from his father, will constitute the core of therapy for Anthony. Much of his defensive anger likely stems from these experiences, as does his anger derived from PTSD. Essential EFT interventions will be used to understand and change defensive anger and to access and express underlying emotions as well as primary adaptive anger associated with abuse and neglect (Greenberg & Paivio, 1997). However, specialized EFTT interventions are of further use to facilitate the reprocessing of traumatic memories and resolve interpersonal issues associated with abuse and neglect and to understand the consequences of these childhood experiences.

Childhood trauma often results in the inhibition of primary adaptive emotions, such as anger and sadness, and promotes reliance on secondary defensive emotions as protection against more vulnerable feelings. Contrary to psychodynamic therapy, EFT does not primarily interpret defenses. Defensive emotions are preferably bypassed to quickly access adaptive emotions, including anger. Therefore, a major challenge is to maintain a balance between accessing and validating primary adaptive anger to help clients explore and express its meaning, while bypassing secondary anger in order to access more vulnerable underlying emotions and their associated information. The following hypothetical dialogue illustrates maintaining this balance:

Anthony: I know that he is dying from cancer right now, but that's still too good for him. He should suffer more; he's getting off easy . . .

Therapist: Yes, you are still so angry, you want to see him punished for what he did to you. Can you say more about what makes you so angry?

Anthony: He used me, took advantage of me, he handicapped me. I thought he loved me but he just used me.

Therapist: So, he hurt you very badly and the wound has not healed. It still hurts a lot, speak from that pain.

Anthony: Well, it really upsets me to think of how I was so lonely and needy.

Therapist: Yes, just a very lonely, sad child.

Anthony: I was, I was really lonely. I was ready to go to anyone who would have me. I thought he really loved me, it just broke my heart when I realized that, no, I was still alone.

Ultimately, Anthony will have to access adaptive anger and sadness toward his uncle for the sexual abuse, the betrayal of his trust, and the loss of a close relationship and toward his parents for their lack of responsiveness. EFTT will also help him appropriately express anger and indignation at poor treatment. Finally, EFTT interventions will be necessary to alleviate Anthony's symptoms of PTSD, particularly those associated with avoidance.

At this stage of therapy, making problematic material as vividly present as possible in the session is essential. Evocative empathic interventions that include metaphors and powerful images are used to bring the client's experience as alive as possible. For example:

Anthony: I still don't understand why I let it happen, what could possibly have possessed me?

Therapist: Can you see yourself as a little child? What do you see? What led that little kid to let this happen?

Anthony: Well, I was so lonely, so sick of being so lonely all the time. He seemed to want me around.

Therapist: Yes, you sound like you were just so hungry for contact, you were starved!

Anthony: I was, I really was. I think I might have done just about anything to make it stop; make the lonely feeling go away.

This dialogue illustrates how a powerful image, such as that of an emotionally starved child, helps the client access his or her sadness and the associated meaning of having been so motivated to avoid loneliness as to accept any type of contact, however exploitative. This, in turn, corrects perceptions of the self as being devious and to blame for letting the abuse happen.

Two-Chair Dialogue for Intrapsychic Conflict. Full contact with and expression of primary adaptive emotions can be hindered by different self-interruptive processes such as thoughts that one should not feel certain emotions or do certain things. To address this, clients can be invited to engage in a dialogue between the two parts of the self that are in conflict in such situations: the part that experiences the adaptive emotion (the experiencing side) and the part that interrupts it by various strategies, such as guilt, shame, fear, and anger (the critical, fearful, or blocking side). For example, in such an exercise, Anthony could be encouraged to engage in a dialogue between the vulnerable part of himself that feels unloved when his wife is late and the anxious part that feels it too risky to expose himself and judges it preferable to express anger. The goal of this kind of dialogue is to increase awareness of both sides to strengthen the experiencing side and produce a shift in the anxious or angry side. Through full emotional access, the experiencing side becomes more assertive about what it wants and the anxious or angry side accesses and expresses its values, concerns, or goals. This side can then be reassured by the experiencing side that has now gained strength and conviction about the soundness of what it wants. Such a dialogue, supported by the therapist, could proceed as follows:

Vulnerable Anthony: The other night, when Joanna was late, I felt like she did not care enough about me to be on time. That's what I would have told her from my heart.

Angry Anthony: Are you crazy?! You can't tell her that! She will take advantage of you.

Therapist: So that's what stops you, fear. The angry part of you is actually scared. How would you respond to that?

Vulnerable Anthony: Well, maybe she would not take advantage of me. I have never given her much of a chance; I always blow up at her when she is late.

Angry Anthony: Good luck, buddy. If you think she will be nice to you, be my guest! She'll take advantage of you, that's what people do.

Therapist, to vulnerable Anthony: Tell him again what you really wanted to tell her and why. Make him understand how important it is to you.

Vulnerable Anthony: I wanted to tell her how I really felt. I am sick of blowing up at her all the time. She gets hurt, clams up, won't talk to me or even look at me. I am sick of ending up alone because I blew up. I just want to be with my wife and trust her.

Angry Anthony: You are a fool! What if she uses it against you?

Therapist: Yes, the angry part of you is scared, really scared that there is no good to be had from people, even your wife. Answer to that.

Vulnerable Anthony: You know, maybe she won't hurt me. I am scared too, but I want to try it. I understand your point, but maybe you worry too much. I know what I want now, and I want to try it. I am willing to take the risk. The other way isn't working.

A dialogue like this would have the advantage of making explicit how fear gets in the way of experiencing and expressing primary vulnerable emotions and bringing into focus the reasons and importance of his defensive anger. Once aware of his fear, Anthony could further process these thoughts and emotions under more rational control. He could, for example, revisit the assumption that Joanna would take advantage of him and perhaps realize that it comes from the experience with his uncle, who did take advantage of him. His wife may not if he gave her a chance.

Imaginal Confrontation. Another technique that may be considered is imaginal confrontation (IC). IC is a powerful exposure-based procedure developed to promote the resolution of issues with significant others. It consists of making psychological contact with significant others from the past to express previously inhibited thoughts and feelings. In EFTT, the goal of IC is the exploration of trauma feelings and memories and the resolution of lingering bad feelings, needs, and longings toward abusive and neglectful others from the past. The IC procedure is based on an empirically verified model of resolution using a Gestalt-derived empty chair dialogue (Greenberg & Foerster, 1996; Greenberg & Malcolm, 2002) adapted specifically for work with adult survivors of abuse. Steps in the resolution process include accessing negative perceptions of the other, fully expressing emotions such as sadness and anger, accessing and expressing entitlement to unmet needs, and, finally, arriving at changed perceptions of self and others. Paivio et al. (2001) showed that IC predicted resolution of abuse issues, improvement in trauma-related symptoms, and improvement in interpersonal relationships.

Markers for initiating the IC procedure are the presence of unresolved feelings related to the abusive or neglectful significant other from the past and the fact that the feelings are currently experienced but are not fully differentiated or expressed. When markers of hurt, blame, and complaint are present, the therapist invites the client to vividly imagine the other sitting in an empty chair and to address the other directly. The client is directed to imagine the other as that person was at the time of the abuse or neglect and to tell that person his or her thoughts and feelings about the abuse. The therapist often gives the instruction of making the other person understand how the client feels and the impact that the abuse has had on him or her.

During this procedure, clients typically move in and out of dialogue with the imagined other, depending on how much support they need from the therapist and depending on what emotion they wish to express. While expressing anger directly to the imagined abusive or neglectful other is empowering, the expression of sadness requires safety, and one needs to trust that the other will respond with compassion. Therefore, clients often cannot express sadness to an imagined abusive, uncaring other because they appropriately do not wish to be vulnerable with this person (Paivio & Greenberg 2000); they can, however, be encouraged to express sadness to the therapist. Perceptions of the perpetrator also shift throughout therapy. If, for example, the client can imagine the perpetrator as being remorseful and somewhat capable of acknowledging the negative impact of what he or she did or if the client feels sufficiently strengthened by a previous assertive anger expression, then the client may choose to express sadness directly to the imagined perpetrator.

The full experience and expression of these feelings aids in the construction of new meaning. As exemplified previously, fully experiencing how loved he felt by his uncle and how precious it was for him to feel special could help Anthony understand why he "did not stop it." This would contribute to improving his low self-esteem associated with having gone along with the abuse. IC would also be most important for Anthony as a venue to express primary adaptive anger at having been used and betrayed. Contacting this legitimate anger would help access the conviction that he did not deserve to be treated this way and would provide a sense of entitlement to unmet needs, such as genuine love and protection. This would in turn promote the development of a self-image that is deserving of good treatment, thus further correcting self-esteem injuries. For Anthony, this could also result in a clear sense that what was done to him was wrong and that his uncle was to blame for what happened, not him.

IC is a powerful technique that can be stressful (Paivio & Jarry, 2002). Paivio et al. (2001) reported that approximately one third of their sample ($N = 37$) did not substantially participate in the IC after its initial introduction in session four. It is unclear whether this was because clients were anxious concerning the performance demands of IC or because clients were overwhelmed by the evocative nature of the procedure. In any case, for clients who cannot or will not participate in IC, evocative empathy (EE) can be used to evoke and explore trauma material. In EE, the client expresses thoughts and feelings to the therapist in a context of advanced empathic responding that simultaneously promotes maximum psychological contact with the perpetrator. The treatment principles of EE are identical to those of IC; however, clients are not invited to imagine this person sitting in the chair and do not engage in a dialogue with this person. Rather, the therapist invites clients to imagine the other in their mind's eye, attend to how they feel toward the perpetrator, and express these feelings to the therapist. In this fashion, the goals of resolution can be attained without engaging in an actual dialogue with an imagined perpetrator.

For Anthony, either IC or EE could be used with the consistent goal of widening and deepening his experiential access and symbolization and his capacity for appropriate expression. These techniques also promote the construction of new meaning about the self, the significant other, and the relationship between the self and this person. This new repertoire of emotions and communication skills could help to counteract his anger outbursts and reduce his level of "background" anger. At this stage, strategies similar to those used in cognitive-behavioral therapy (CBT) also could be taught to promote emotion regulation. These could include time-outs to de-escalate anger and allow the identification of alternative feelings and specific assertive expression skills.

Addressing Anger Secondary to Core Maladaptive Beliefs. In terms of anger generated by core maladaptive beliefs, EFT interventions typically do not directly dispute the legitimacy of such beliefs or change them through cognitive restructuring, although these interventions can be integrated within the EFT process of therapy as is outlined later in this chapter. Typical EFT interventions would aim at evoking and amplifying the individual's experience of the *consequences* of their anger. These identified consequences would then be used to heighten motivation to change the maladaptive cognitions at the source of the anger. This process would be similar to that of motivational interviewing, for example, where discrepancies between problem behavior and goals, values, and ideals are emphasized (Miller & Rollnick, 2002).

Anthony's anger has had significant negative consequences on his life in general and on his interpersonal relationships in particular. His anger appears to be a significant obstacle to closeness with his family, and he reports feeling "guilty" about exploding at them. EFT interventions could consist of identifying and amplifying his desire to be close to his family and the sadness of ruining this with his anger. Being intensely aware of these feelings could in turn increase his awareness of his desire to change and result in increased motivation to do so. Exploring and amplifying his sadness at the distance with his family and using it as a motivator for change could proceed as follows:

Therapist: So, you feel guilty about the impact of your anger on your family. This is not what you want.

Client: No, it's not. I don't like them being afraid of me.

Therapist: What does that do to you when you see the fear on their face? Can you see one of them now, in your mind's eye? What's that like?

Client: I just really don't like it. My youngest daughter, I can still see her face last time, how her eyes got all teary, she turned red. I can't stand it!

Therapist: It sounds devastating to you, your own child getting so scared. Sounds like it's making you so sad to see her like this.

Client: It does, that's not what I want with my kids.

Therapist: Tell me what you want.

Client: I want to feel close to them, I want them to be able to trust me, to come to me with problems. I want to be a dad to my kids.

Therapist: It sounds like that would mean so much to you, to be close to them, have them trust you.

EFT's conceptualization of anger secondary to core maladaptive beliefs is compatible with the CBT conceptualization; anger is more likely when individuals engage in specific primary and secondary appraisals (Deffenbacher, 1999). Primary appraisals leading to anger consist of feeling that one should not be exposed to the irritant and are intensified if one feels that others intentionally imposed hardship on the self. Secondary appraisals leading to anger include feeling that one should not have to cope with the irritant and that anger is an appropriate response. Anthony shows clear signs of engaging in dysfunctional primary and secondary appraisals. For example, his lack of tolerance for "tardiness and stupidity" suggest that he appraises these behaviors as inexcusable or intentional and that he should not have to endure these behaviors or manage the negative feelings that they evoke in him and that he is entitled to his anger in such circumstances.

Strategies used to change maladaptive cognitions are similar in EFT and in CBT approaches, such as Ellis' ABC model (1991), where *A* refers to an activating event, *B* refers to beliefs about the activating event, and *C* stands for the consequences of A as modified by B. Both heighten awareness of negative feelings and contributory thoughts, encourage access to alternative adaptive thoughts, and direct the client's attention to the different impact of the new thoughts on their emotional state. However, in CBT, these appraisals are quickly confronted and disputed. EFT, on the other hand, relies more on a shift whereby heightened awareness of implicit core maladaptive belief can initiate spontaneous questioning in the client. For example, once clearly aware of his appraisal that Joanna is being callous toward him, Anthony may start to spontaneously question this appraisal. Such a shift could be detectable in a statement such as: "Wait a minute, does she really not care about me? What if she does? After all, she has stuck by me for all these years." However, if this shift does not take place, then confrontation, very similar to that used in CBT, is appropriate to promote a change in thinking.

Therefore, integrative EFT interventions with Anthony would include exploring and making explicit his assumptions and beliefs and, if necessary, confronting him with their absurdity. Assuming a strong therapeutic alliance, the therapist could also use "irreverence" as in dialectical behavioral therapy (Linehan & Schmidt, 1995) and confront beliefs about tardiness with an intervention such as: "Oh, so it was OK for *you* to be late for all these years at your first job. You had a right, and you had reasons, but *they* don't! When they do it, it's to get to you!" An intervention like this should be done in a tone of affiliative humor and, again, only within a strong therapeutic alliance. Anthony would then be encouraged to replace his dysfunctional thoughts with more adaptive cognitions with a prompt such as: "What other reason could there be for your wife being late?" These interventions (awareness and confrontation) and EFT strategies aimed at increasing emotional contact with motivators for change are likely to potentiate each other resulting in a synergistic effect.

Addressing Instrumental Anger. As described earlier, Anthony uses anger to manipulate others into behaving according to his wishes, without having to face the vulnerability of directly expressing his needs. The EFT therapist would confront this, explore underlying needs, and coach Anthony to be assertive about what he wants. Here, EFT interventions share some features with assertiveness training, whereby the therapist makes explicit the manipulative aspect of Anthony's instrumental anger, in this case, trying to coerce and intimidate Joanna by yelling at her. The therapist also might encourage Anthony to assertively express his needs while tolerating the fear of being rejected. This then could be followed by an integration of assertiveness training.

Phase 3: Restructuring and Integration

Changes in Self-Perceptions. Full access to and expression of primary emotions is thought to produce a gradual shift whereby clients become more aware of unmet needs, desires, and the associated action tendencies (Greenberg & Paivio, 1997), which provide behavioral guidance for actual change in the present. In the case of abuse survivors, awareness of needs often is followed by a feeling of entitlement to having those needs met. Combined with validation from the therapist, the client can re-experience himself or herself as an innocent child who was undeserving of the abuse and who had a right to affectionate care. This sense of entitlement promotes adaptive perception of the self as being worthy of this attention and care.

Changes in Perception of Abusive or Neglectful Others. Another important result of emotional access and symbolization consists of changes in perceptions of the perpetrator. At the beginning of therapy, clients usually harbor feelings of hurt and deep resentment combined with longing for the needs that were never met in their relationship. One important goal of promoting psychological contact with perpetrators is to modify clients' perceptions of this person as having the power to hurt them or to satisfy their needs if only they agreed to do so. Having a chance to fully experience and express these feelings and needs, and being validated by the therapist, helps clients finally complete a grieving process that frees them from these concerns. Once this is accomplished, clients feel more powerful and manage to actually feel good about themselves. This enables them to access empathic resources toward the perpetrator that facilitates understanding of their motives. For example, clients may come to see the perpetrator as experiencing their own despair, as being mentally ill, or as being cruel because of personal shortcomings, while holding them responsible for having been abusive or for not having provided appropriate care. This is distinctly different from the minimization of abuse, such as making excuses for the perpetrator, which often imitates true resolution in the early stage of therapy. Authentic modification in the perception of the other, from powerful and evil to being limited and lacking results in differentiation of the self from the perpetrator and understanding that the perpetrator acted for their own independent reasons. This contributes to undoing clients' perceptions that they somehow are to blame for what happened and could facilitate grieving for what this ineffective perpetrator was unable to provide and for the loss of innocence.

In summary, this phase is focused on restructuring perceptions of the self and of the other through the activation of emotion memories and their associated meaning about the self and others. This includes the emergence of needs and, eventually, feelings of entitlement to having those needs met. In the case of Anthony, this new awareness would help change his feelings of inadequacy and the necessity for anger to protect him from powerful others. It would also widen his repertoire of emotional experience and expression, thus diminishing his reliance on anger as his main emotional outlet.

CLINICAL ISSUES AND RECOMMENDATIONS

Timeline and Anticipated Outcome

Both EFT and EFTT, conducted in 12 to 20 sessions, have demonstrated efficacy (Greenberg & Malcolm, 2002; Jarry & Paivio, 2004; Paivio & Greenberg, 1995; Paivio & Nieuwenhuis, 2001). The features of Anthony's case point to a positive outcome in a reasonable timeline since he appears highly motivated, has had no previous treatment, and has experienced no treatment failure. Because he is largely unaware of the origins of his anger and does not understand it, he is likely to benefit significantly from interventions aimed at increasing experiential awareness and self-understanding.

There are few signs of personality disorder in Anthony's history except for mild narcissistic features exemplified in his sense of entitlement to privileged treatment in terms of work attendance and punctuality. In narcissistic personality organizations, anger is conceptualized as a defense against fragile self-esteem (Rhodewalt & Morf, 1998). EFT's consistent use of empathy likely contributes to improve self-esteem and therefore to diminish anger. In fact, alliance in EFTT is strongly associated with improved self-esteem (Paivio, 2004; Paivio & Patterson, 1999; Paivio et al., 2001). Improved self-esteem, combined with appropriate confrontation and greater access to vulnerable feelings, should also diminish feelings of entitlement, along with the anger they generate. Finally, Anthony's motivation to change is evident in his report of having already started using management strategies to "cool off" instead of exploding.

Despite these predictors of positive outcome, Anthony has a long history of costly aggressive behavior. The chronicity and frequency of his outbursts suggest that he relies heavily on anger as a form of expression for various emotions and that it may be difficult for him to change. Anthony also needs to considerably enlarge his repertoire of emotional experience and expression, which, in itself, will be challenging. Anthony would thus benefit from at least 20 individual therapy sessions.

Treatment Difficulties

Clients' experience and expression of anger in session can be overwhelming and can dominate or derail the therapy process. This is especially so with a client like Anthony, who uses anger to defend himself precisely

from the vulnerable emotions that EFT would target. Therefore, directing and redirecting Anthony's attention to these vulnerable emotions
while avoiding the trap of defensive anger will require the therapist and
Anthony to agree that anger is all too easy to experience and that he
needs to access other emotions. For this, Anthony must give the therapist
permission to be directive, and both the therapist and Anthony need to
collaboratively endeavor to maintain the focus on vulnerable emotions.
With a clear understanding of the goal of the therapist's directness,
Anthony is more likely to agree to try to access and express other emotions without experiencing the therapist as excessively controlling and
thus prevent alliance ruptures. For example, the therapist could direct
Anthony to remain connected with sadness with interventions such as:
"Let's stay away from your anger right now. Stay in touch with your sadness and talk to me from that sadness. What makes you so sad?"

Another possible treatment difficulty could be Anthony's family.
When he starts to change and attempts to communicate vulnerable emotions instead of exploding, family members might be suspicious and
remain distant. This is liable to be hurtful to him and trigger the old
defense of becoming angry because his new openness is not immediately
recognized for what it is and supported by loved ones. These hurdles will
need to be processed with the therapist. Anthony must take responsibility and accept his role in their distrust and fear of him, that he is not entitled to his family's trust, and that he must earn it with behavior change
over time. It is also possible that the damage is irreparable, that the level
of trust that he aspires to will never be there. He would then have to tolerate his sadness about this and grieve for what he has lost.

Couples' sessions could be helpful to bring Joanna on board with
Anthony's personal progress. EFT for couples is a well-developed area
of EFT (Johnson & Greenberg, 1985, 1988) and has recently been
adapted for use with trauma survivors (Johnson, 2002). From an anger
perspective, the goal of couples' EFT would be to give Anthony a chance
to express primary vulnerable emotions to his wife within the safety of
the therapeutic relationship. These sessions would also provide Joanna
with the support needed to share feelings with her husband without
fearing an unregulated angry outburst. From a trauma perspective, the
goal of couples' EFT is to create enough safety in the marital relationship for the trauma survivor to experience it as a corrective experience
and for both partners to not be further traumatized by current relationship injuries resulting from past trauma. This is done by facilitating
each partner's access to the other's subjective experience via mutual
emotional expression.

EFT for traumatized couples also attends to the creation of a safe
relationship outside of therapy sessions such that reparative work can be

ongoing between sessions and after therapy is completed. More specifically, in these sessions, Joanna would be made privy to Anthony's traumatic experiences and their impact on him, she would get to share his
emotional reactions to such experiences, and she would have a chance to
express her feelings regarding these experiences. Both partners would
also have a chance to discuss how they wish to manage the sequelae of
the trauma in their daily lives. Both the anger and the trauma element of
the couple's work could be significant contributors to Anthony's progress
and the maintenance of his gains after the end of therapy.

Treatment Termination and Relapse Prevention

Anthony is likely to become quite attached to the therapist because of the
intensity of the therapeutic work, and this could make termination difficult for him. If he is successful, he is also likely to be extremely grateful
for his improvements, as he is motivated to change and keep his family.
Furthermore, Anthony currently is quite unaware of his experience and
he will discover much about himself through his work with the therapist.
On the other hand, he is capable of forming meaningful attachments with
others, for example, his Internet friend, which could help the termination
process. His improved family relationships will also help him feel connected and cared for.

Given his long history of angry outbursts and because of the multidetermined nature of his anger, relapses, at least in the form of temporary anger bouts, are very likely. To prevent long-term relapse,
follow-up combined with refresher sessions are indicated. Anthony is
likely to discover new, unknown triggers for his anger that will necessi-
tate ad hoc short-term therapeutic work. Other useful elements to prevent relapse could include participating in a support group for adult
survivors of abuse and/or participating in an anger management group;
Anthony should also be encouraged to regularly read about anger and
its management.

In sum, there are a number of salient clinical issues in the case of
Anthony. One consists of balancing anger management with exploring
and accessing anger and other emotions during therapy sessions. Another
involves differentiating among different types of anger with the goal of
learning appropriate expression of inhibited adaptive anger to access
adaptive information; exploring and changing secondary anger; and
finally confronting instrumental anger together with finding alternative,
healthy ways of getting his needs met. Central issues also concern the
variety of emotional experiences and cognitions associated with the
sexual abuse at the hands of his uncle and the resolution of attachment
injuries resulting from this abuse.

CHAPTER 11

Treating Anger with Wisdom and Compassion: A Buddhist Approach

C. Peter Bankart

INTRODUCTION TO A BUDDHIST APPROACH

In this chapter we explore the application of Buddhist theory and practice to the challenge of helping a Western psychotherapy client achieve greater peace of mind and control over angry thoughts and impulses. Buddhism is one of the world's oldest religions, but it is a relative newcomer to the practical world of Western psychotherapy. The history of various attempts over the past century to marry the wisdom of Buddhism with the secular aims and methods of humanistic psychology (broadly construed) has been described elsewhere (Bankart, 1997, 2000, 2003a; Bankart et al., 1992). In general, my conclusion is that the best match between East and West is found in applying Buddhist wisdom in a cognitive behavioral framework where a significant effort is made to repair and reconcile the Cartesian split between soma and psyche.

Much of the teachings of the Buddha require remarkably little modification to inform the therapeutic work of a current-day cognitive therapist. Take, for example, this passage from the *Dhammapada*, the collected teachings of the historical Buddha (cited in Parry & Jones, 1986, p. 180):

We are what we think
All that we are arises with our thoughts
With our thoughts, we make the world
Speak or act with an impure mind
And trouble will follow you

There is indeed much in the literature of Buddhism to inform the practice of a Western psychotherapist, but there are two unique and quite central aspects of Buddhism that take clinical interventions beyond the well-established path of cognitive-behavioral therapy (CBT). The first of these is an explicit emphasis on intensive practice of mindfulness. The second is a renewed humanistic emphasis on a compassionate relationship between the therapist and the client, which resembles more closely the relationship between a teacher and a student than that between a therapist and a client.

Mindfulness practice is a set of exercises whereby a person comes to develop significant skillfulness as an observer of his or her own mental and emotional processes. Mindfulness involves developing a patient, accepting awareness of a person's own attentional processes on purpose, in the present moment, and nonjudgmentally without succumbing to the flood of likes and dislikes, opinions, prejudices, projections, and fantasies, which usually contaminate our moment-to-moment consciousness. As Levine (2000) described it, mindfulness means learning to pay attention on purpose, in the present moment, for the sake of greater awareness, clarity, and acceptance of present-moment reality.

By practicing mindfulness, clients become aware of just how clouded and distorted their awareness of the world (and themselves) has become. They become intrigued with the process of sorting it all out, nonanalytically and nonjudgmentally. Clients discover how constraining their automatic assumptions have been and how distorting of reality their unawareness has been. They come to glimpse how little of their mind they have been using in day-to-day life. As clients' awareness deepens, mindfulness practice offers unlimited opportunities for them to live their lives in the present moment, to make deliberate and informed decisions, and to take full and complete responsibility for their speech and deeds.

As Aristotle (1960) observed, anger is not just a "hot" emotion; "anger is always attended by a certain pleasure arising from the expectation of revenge" (p. 93). Indeed, *The Iliad*, Homer's epic "song" of the anger of both gods and men, reminds us that much anger is about coercing compliance from those who have made the serious error of disobeying or disagreeing with us. The openness and awareness that unfold through the practice of mindfulness allow one to be more careful, intentional, and precise about one's emotions and behavior.

This intellectual awareness about the motivational nature of one's anger is incomplete, however. It is also crucial to understand that anger does not occur in an interpersonal vacuum. There is great wisdom in the observation, shared by both the Buddha and by CBT, that "we are what we think" and that our angry thoughts are not just responses but actually create a hostile world around us. We do not just have angry feelings and think angry thoughts; we direct these angry impulses and energies toward others. Anger cannot be fully understood, therefore, until its interpersonal nature is taken into account. Thus, it is only logical that the solution to anger must have a profound interpersonal component. That is why the principle of compassionate engagement is so important in a Buddhist/mindfulness understanding of the nature of anger and the path of anger reduction.

Compassion is the wellspring of Buddhist ethics (Bankart, Dockett, & Dudley-Grant, 2003; Khong, 2003; Ragsdale, 2003) and connects every human being with every living thing. It is the true north of one's moral compass, and it is the highest calling of the human heart. In traditional Buddhist teaching (e.g., Gunaratana, 2002) compassion is understood to arise spontaneously as a product of the exercise of morality, mental discipline, and wisdom. But based on my clinical work with Western clients, I am in essential agreement with Alfred Adler that compassion is a human faculty that in a highly agentic and individuated culture virtually always needs to be explicitly addressed and awakened in the course of effective psychotherapy.

The centrality of compassion comes up in two primary contexts in Buddhist therapy. The first is that compassionate concern for the self and others is an essential requirement for mental health and well-being. The second is that compassion must be awakened and nurtured in all human beings. This awakening and nurturing are probably the single most important functions of parents and teachers, and it is the primary mission of psychotherapists of many stripes who concur that psychotherapy must be deeply rooted in an ethic of compassion if it is to have any meaningful probability of achieving its ultimate goals.

Compassion lies at the heart of the "common factors" in all-effective psychotherapies (Hubble, Duncan, & Miller, 1999). The confirmatory data on this point are abundant and persuasive: The therapeutic relationship is without question the single most powerful predictor of therapeutic movement, independent of the relative efficacy of any psychotherapy techniques or protocol. Anthony's psychotherapy, therefore, must be deeply rooted in an ethic of compassion if it is to have any meaningful probability of helping him achieve the goal of changing his life.

Evidence of the Model's Efficacy

Systematic empirical efforts to document the power of a mindfulness model of psychotherapeutic change are likely to be regarded as too recent and too few to convince a committed skeptic. The practice and the principles of "treating" disorders of the heart and the emotions with mindfulness and compassion have been around for thousands of years, but they have not yet enjoyed wide dissemination in the Western scientific community. My hope is that the next generation of clinical research will encourage scholars to look closely at the power of this model on a wide range of human problems and that specifically a mindfulness/Buddhist approach to anger management will receive increased attention from researchers.

Western scientists are beginning to document the effects of mindfulness in a wide variety of psychological domains. Brown and Ryan (2003) documented the impact of mindfulness practice on overall psychological well-being in a recent issue of the *Journal of Personality and Social Psychology*. Carson et al. (2004) elaborated on a recent doctoral dissertation that demonstrated the impact of mindfulness practice on partner relationships following 8 weeks of mindfulness training (including body scan meditation, sitting meditation, partner yoga, walking meditation, loving-kindness meditation, and relationship-focused meditation). Shapiro, Schwartz, and Bonner (1998) tracked a number of changes, including statistically significant reductions in state anxiety and depression and significant increases in both empathy and spirituality in the psychological functioning of medical and premedical students after an 8-week meditation-based stress reduction intervention program, and Kristeller and Johnson (2003) explored the impact of mindfulness training on empathy, compassion, and altruism. In their paper, Kristeller and Johnson (2003, p. 15) conclude:

> Meditative practice is neither necessary nor sufficient to create a sense of compassion toward self or toward others, but it may be that meditation, by systematically providing a tool to suspend engagement in usual thought processes and hence suspension of self-judgment, carries unique value in promoting empathy and compassion. The traditional literature associating meditative practice with spiritual growth suggests that meditation can provide particularly powerful means to actively cultivate universal capacities for love and connectedness.

All of the individual components of a mindfulness/Buddhist approach to anger management have been shown to be therapeutically significant in published reports (Bankart, 2004). However, there have, as yet, been no published accounts of the effectiveness of a comprehensive mindfulness intervention strategy for anger control (Del Vecchio & O'Leary, 2004; DiGiuseppe & Tafrate, 2003). A few studies have been published that, like Dua and Swinden (1992), used a "meditation" component, but a fully randomized trial of a fully integrated mindfulness-based approach to anger management has not yet appeared in the literature. It is important to note that the intervention described in this chapter is much more comprehensive than a meditation-relaxation strategy, which is generally included in therapy outcome research as a minimal-treatment control condition.

Theory and Practice

The problem of anger is located at the center of Buddhist concern for human well-being. Buddhist teachings recognize anger as one of the three great destructive fires, along with greed and delusion, as the essential source of human suffering. These fires generate the intense social and emotional isolation that is the ultimate source of an angry person's distress and plunge the person into a world of shadows and illusion. Their emotional affliction is rooted in an alienating preoccupation with selfish desire that derives from an unenlightened understanding of self and the world. The challenge for the therapist is to help the angry person find the wisdom to awaken from the ignorant delusion that selfish desires can ever be finally satisfied, any obstacle fully eradicated, and suffering permanently eliminated—especially by the application of force. The wisdom of Buddhism is that suffering is universal but that it can be overcome by curbing selfish desire through the cultivation of compassionate concern for and constructive engagement with others.

Thurman summarized the Buddhist perspective on this connection between powerful negative emotions and suffering as follows:

> One of the great sources of our suffering is hatred, and all of its variation: resentment, anger, bitterness, dislike, irritation, aggressiveness, hostility. Hate is very powerful. When we are gripped by hatred we go into a rage and become completely out of control. We smash up our own beloved body and commit suicide. We smash up people whom we love, wives, husbands, children, parents. Rage can turn us into a complete maniac or demon—temporarily. It's one of the most dangerous kinds of energies, very difficult to control. Any force we can marshal within ourselves to prevent and forestall the explosive moment of rage is really beneficial. (Thurman & Wise, 1999, p. 76)

The question that will define the central focus of this approach to the problem of anger is how to uncover and marshal those forces that prevent and forestall the destructive fire of anger. As humanist scientists, we already know where those forces are to be found: They are inherent in one's endowment as a human being. They are in reality not something that has to be learned in therapy so much as they are a vital inherent part of every human being that needs to be reawakened, affirmed, and brought to the center of conscious awareness.

This is a process described by any number of Buddhist teachings; indeed, it is probably the central theme of most of them. In *Meeting the Monkey Halfway* (2000), a Buddhist monk, A. S. Bhikku, asks the reader to direct loving-kindness to one's self, to one's feelings, moods, and perceptions in order to experience love. Here is what Bhikku says about anger:

> Undercut the power of anger by seeing it in the present. Look intently into all its aspects and it will lose its power. Discard every layer of anger; look into your reactions in relation to the offender. Why are you angry? What do you wish to do with this anger? How far and in what direction do you want to go with it? How significant is this in your life? Is this anger worth jeopardizing your well-being? Is it worth all the time you are spending on it? The exercise of questioning your way through your anger will effectively force you into facing the realities of that moment. It will also give you the opportunity to answer those questions honestly. At the end of your investigation, you can be sure that you have lost the momentum of that anger and, therefore, have regained control over your otherwise runaway emotions. This is one of the great escapes from suffering. (p. 73)

THE CASE OF ANTHONY

From the details in the case history, it is safe to assume that there exists an intimate connection between the trauma and pain Anthony experienced as a boy and the suffering he is experiencing today. More than anything else, it is this suffering that engages Anthony into psychological contact with the therapeutic process. Moreover, in a way that he probably cannot imagine, that suffering will ultimately provide him the direction he needs in his life. Anthony's anger, by itself or as a symptom of his depression, is less of a priority than the nature and quality of Anthony's emotional and psychological pain because they will mark the starting point for Anthony's potential for recognizing his capacity for compassion and concern for the well-being of others, and ultimately himself.

This potential is highlighted in the first great lesson that the Buddha taught: *All life is suffering.* As human beings, we live our lives immersed in and surrounded by the apparent unsatisfactoriness of everything, and nothing is ever quite good enough or long enough lasting. Everything that ought to bring us joy and comfort is ephemeral. We have neither the blissful unawareness of the animal world nor the omnipotence and immortality of the gods. We are stuck here, on this earth, for a very limited amount of time, required to work out the conditions of our own survival on a moment-by-moment basis.

The second great lesson was that our suffering is directly tied to our constant and sometimes intense desires. We pursue these desires in ways that often harm and degrade others, as Anthony's uncle did when he sexually abused his adolescent nephew. The effects of our pursuit of desires on others are obvious; the effects on our selves are often more subtle but can certainly be terribly corrosive and self-destructive. Predictably, in the first few weeks of therapeutic work, Anthony will reveal in a fairly typical analytic fashion the emotional contours of his corrupted desires and the power they have assumed over his life. It is not that Anthony's desires are fundamentally any different that anyone else's, but it is doubtful that Anthony has much real awareness of the suffering his desires have caused and continue to inflict upon himself and the people he loves.

The connection between suffering and desire will become self-evident in the first or second therapeutic session. The dilemma is that despite how deeply committed we are to eliminating the suffering from our lives, we tend to quite fiercely resist addressing the necessity of accomplishing this goal by significantly reassessing and moderating our desires. This is where the Buddha's third basic teaching comes to our awareness: Our attachment to our desires holds the key to our release from suffering. As Novaco (1996) suggests, it is easy and common for clients to become attached to their anger and actively resist any efforts to identify anger as a focus of therapeutic treatment. Rather than admonishing angry clients, mindfulness meditation helps them buy some time while their autonomic nervous systems cool off and encourages them to discover available paths to mature happiness—a resolution of the endless suffering that is the price we pay for our unrelenting desire to be right, invulnerable, and in control.

The Problem of Attachments

It is likely that Anthony is going to say that the reason he exploded at the softball game was that the girls were doing something profoundly wrong. Perhaps his players were not acting like they wanted to win the game; in his eyes the team did not give enough evidence of caring about beating their opponents. What was the point of all those hours of practice and all those carefully constructed coaching sessions if the girls were not going to act like they wanted to win?

Playing well, trying hard, and competing to win are legitimate concerns of a coach of a team of people of any age. Anthony's true problem, however, in an existential-Buddhist sense, was that he was mindlessly and selfishly attached to his desire to have the world the way he wanted it to be. Because this problem is so pervasive in the generation of anger, beginning early in therapy we will need to explore in significant depth the nature of Anthony's attachments to his desire to be right, respected, and obeyed.

How does a suffering person address these attachments? This is where the Buddha's fourth lesson comes into play. In this teaching the Buddha said that the way to attack one's desires, and thus to reduce one's suffering, is to follow a course of virtue and moderation—Buddhism's *Eightfold Noble Path*. Anthony needs to reform his life and his way of thinking. This is the heart and soul of mindfulness-based therapy. The Noble Path is the cornerstone of Buddhist ethics, and these ethics are the principles that will directly guide and inform Anthony's therapy. It is a moral code with three primary aspects:

- A concern for the correctness of all of one's behavior. One must consciously and conscientiously strive to live up to the ideals of Right Speech, Right Actions, and Right Livelihood.
- Development of a disciplined, centered, and focused always-on mind: Right Concentration, Right Mindfulness, and Right Effort.
- A passion for equanimity, wisdom, and compassion: Right Thought and Right Understanding.

The term *right* in this connection, according to Khong (2003), "concerns taking responsibility for one's speech, actions, and mental attitudes so that one gains a sense of inner peace and harmony. In this sense, right is synonymous with harmonious" (p. 148). It means taking full and complete *responsibility* for one's thoughts, deeds, and motives—not as matters of some abstract ideal, but as something one does during every waking minute of one's life.

Case Conceptualization

Anthony's anger can therefore be seen as the product of his untrained mind with its undisciplined attention. He is operating in the world as an "isolated skin bag" buffeted from emotion to emotion by the transient events occurring in the world around him. He lacks mature mental and behavioral discipline; his understanding of the nature of the world is deeply flawed. His speech and his actions betray a profound ignorance about his connections to and responsibility for other human beings.

To return to an earlier theme, the key to Anthony's release from his suffering is compassion. His therapist's compassionate connection with him must inspire him to engage in the difficult and serious work (Right Effort) of recovering his humanity through the deliberate cultivation of his mind (Right Concentration) in order to begin to put himself back on the path away from his suffering and toward a path of reconciliation (Right Mindfulness). Apart from carefully monitoring his ways of talking (Right Speech), his public behavior (Right Actions), and his habits of attribution (Right Thought), Anthony needs compassionate responses from his therapist to encourage him in mindful self-reflection and to lead him to develop the deep wisdom that comes from sustained attentional consciousness.

At our initial meetings, Anthony's consciousness will appear to be clouded in pain and confusion. I will therefore be neither surprised nor overly alarmed to learn that Anthony has concluded that suicide is one of his more realistic options at this point in his life; as Nietzsche observed, the idea of suicide has saved a good many lives. His despair is a reflection of the depleted pool of compassion that his family and friends are able to share with him, and he has, more importantly, drained the reservoir of his own compassion. In Buddhism, if your compassion does not include yourself, it is inevitably incomplete (Kornfield, 1993).

That, of course, is the reason he has swallowed his overwhelming pride and brought himself into therapy. The very first thing I hope he recognizes when he walks into my office is that I have been waiting for him to show up. In Zen Buddhism it would be said that Anthony has been through a dry season. Everything vital has withered, and the memory of the last green spring has faded. The course he has been on is no longer viable; the future cannot be sustained. Anthony must be able to recognize the futility of the struggle against the increasingly obvious realities of his situation. At this point in his life, his despair has only one lesson to teach—the old ways of being Anthony have failed. They are finished; they must be fired, dismissed, incinerated. The time has come for him to face *acceptance* of life as it is, right now, here, today, and for all time. The only alternative that is realistic and makes any sense is profound change.

It is possible that Anthony and I could get into a conflict over this, but actually it is unlikely that he will struggle very long or very convincingly against the inevitability of the need for fundamental change. If he does, I would ask him to solve the riddle that the Buddha posed to the village woman who refused to listen to his teachings because she was so deeply angry about the suffering in her own life.

The Buddha told this woman, who had recently lost a child, that she could be released from her suffering if she ate a bowl of rice he would cook for her—but she had first to collect a grain of rice from every household she could find that had not known heartbreak and sorrow. The woman left the Buddha and went from door to door asking for grains of rice from anyone who had not known sorrow; until at last she had knocked on the door of every family in her village. Of course, she returned to the Buddha empty-handed, for no family and no person has lived a life untouched by sorrow. It is written that when the woman realized this, she became suddenly enlightened, but we can at least imagine that she no longer so vehemently denied the ontological realities of human existence.

Framing the Treatment

From the start of treatment, Anthony and I will be in extensive intimate contact over the space of several months. He will be advised that the core assumption of this program of treatment is that anger has stolen his heart and that I will instruct him on a journey of intense self-awareness to help him regain intimate contact with his deepest self. He will discover that buried beneath the corrosive outer layer of his anger, his heart is still engaged in the day-to-day quest for love, meaning, and compassion. His task will not be to *control* or *manage* his anger but to make an earnest and sincere effort to *recover* his true human nature. It really does not matter if Anthony resonates to the idea that, like all human beings, he has a true *Buddha nature* (although that would make it considerably easier to have a conversation with him about the process and his progress through it). What is fundamentally important is a willingness to explore the idea that his anger isolates him from others and alienates his natural consciousness from his human identity, which prevents him from expressing his natural self as a husband, father, coach, and friend.

Through extensive journaling, initially probably including daily e-mail, Anthony and I will collaborate in a very proactive and engaged interpersonal process. In some preconscious way we will seek to install the presence of the Buddha in his bedroom, at his breakfast table, sitting next to him in his car, handing his granddaughter's fresh diaper to him, and, in general, making his Buddha nature available to him with (literally) every breath he takes. The bottom line is that no matter what transpires, neither his Buddha nature nor I are going to go away. As his therapist, I will experience his suffering and I will share in his joy. When he is angry, I will offer him compassion; when he is compassionate, I will offer him my smile. When he messes up, he will be asked to *gaman*,[1] to correct his mistake and to persevere. When he is ultimately on a smooth course, he will be expected to shoulder the responsibility of becoming a Buddha for another troubled suffering soul. The goal of the intervention is nothing short of a radical transformation of his consciousness.

This intensive work will continue for approximately 10 weeks, through a series of graduated exercises (Bankart, 2006) that will show him the way out of his perpetual blind suffering. Over the course of a few months, sessions will help him live his life consistent with his intentions and clearly reflective of his compassionate concern for others. The final phase of our formal relationship will commence when Anthony accepts responsibility for helping another person with the same process, or as we put it in Buddhist speak, when Anthony begins to beat the drum of the Dharma [Truth] in the darkness of the world.

As you read through the following somewhat arbitrary sequence of 10 steps, recognize that the transcendent goal is to help Anthony refill his well of compassion. Some of these steps might fit his situation perfectly; others might need to be modified to meet his background and needs. We might even skip a step or two to focus more clearly on helping Anthony get through a difficult phase. Either way, the constant goal is to flood him with compassion and to help him mindfully recover the essence of what it means to be a loving, connected, aspiring father, husband, and human being.

Ten Steps toward Recovering Natural Mind

Step 1: Preliminary—Mindfulness Meditation

The good news is that Anthony has lots of spare time on his hands. It may at first seem that his chronic unemployment is a violation of the requirement that he be occupied with Right Livelihood, but paradoxically, his unemployment could be a significant blessing in disguise. Anthony needs to take advantage of the considerable freedom he has from "work" at the moment to begin to learn how to practice mindfulness meditation. This process is introduced with a series of graduated mindfulness exercises. To reinforce and supplement these experiences, it would be a good thing for Anthony to participate in a meditation or yoga program in his community for a few hours every week.

In the service of this crucial first step, Anthony will need to explore in some depth his past and current religious practices. The actual practice of mindful meditation is potentially compatible with any religious beliefs that a client brings to the table. Where problems arise, however, is that a client's previous experience with religious organizations and with religious dogma has sometimes left a legacy of mistrust and even cynicism about spiritual experiences and practices of all sorts. Thus, it is important to explore the emotional and intellectual legacy of Anthony's experience as a Roman Catholic and to establish the nontheological grounding of the Buddhist teachings presented in his therapy. For those clients who have at least a neutral and perhaps a positive relationship with religious practices, I will commonly recommend spending an hour or so a day meditating in a church, synagogue, or chapel as a routine part of mindfulness practice. Most clergy are familiar with and supportive of the practice of contemplative prayer, which in many cases can become part of a client's efforts to develop Right Concentration and Right Mindfulness. Mindfulness can also, of course, be practiced by a person with no religious background, inclinations, or beliefs whatsoever.

The initial mindfulness exercises are both brief and carefully focused. For the first week, clients are encouraged to practice no more than 20 minutes at a time, probably two or three times a day as time permits. The focus of these initial efforts is on just that—effort. Is my client willing to invest 20 minutes in developing greater awareness of his or her own physical and mental processes? If 20 minutes is too difficult, can the client do it for 15 or even 10 minutes? The standard practice is to have the client begin by first counting his or her breaths, paying attention to how long it takes to inhale, and then exhale a deep breath of fresh air. The client is then encouraged to gradually lengthen the time it takes to draw in and release breath and to pause for a second or two at the top and the bottom of the breath cycle to observe what is going on in his or her mind.

In general, the next step is to focus on greater awareness of all bodily sensations and functions. A number of low-impact exercises can be used to help Anthony re-establish contact with his basic senses, including taste, sight, and smell. In some cases it can be helpful to include in this phase of the program working on a person's basic sense of balance by joining them in some very basic yoga exercises that involve stretching, walking, and reaching, both with the eyes open and closed. For clients with anger issues, it is important to make them much more aware of their own bodies, especially the muscular tensions that are stored in various muscle groups. Unlike in relaxation therapy, however, this phase of mindfulness training does not focus on *doing* anything with the information gained through careful observation. Rather than instructing clients on how to *change* the tension in their body, they are encouraged simply to take note of it, to become aware of it, and then to pass it gently from their awareness. Clients are thus invited to observe the chronic tension in their jaws, stomachs, or necks. If there is a good reason for them to want to experience this tension, they are free to remain in that state of arousal, but most of the time, angry people discover that they have actually habituated to their chronic arousal and muscle tension and are enlightened to discover that this physical tension serves as a sort of staging ground for their angry thoughts, angry words, and hostile interpersonal communication style.

Particularly in the initial stages of mindfulness practice, much of the focus will be on Anthony's physical well-being. This will benefit him emotionally, but it will also offer the benefit of improving his physical health and increasing his stress hardiness. It is well established that the physiological effects of chronic anger, for example, are reflected in elevated blood pressure and chronic hypertension; Hogan and Linden (2004) have documented finding that anger response styles accounted for 23% of the variance in resting blood pressure readings for men. Similarly, Richards, Alvarenga, and Hof (2000) reported increased levels of total serum cholesterol and low-density lipoproteins in men who were angry and frustrated and who felt unfairly treated. Moreover, these harmful biological correlates of anger are substantially mediated by rumination that serves to prolong angry feelings and provoke the tendency to behave aggressively. Not too surprisingly, angry people who attempt to suppress their ruminations experience substantially higher levels of hypertension and elevated blood pressure (Hogan & Linden, 2004). Thus, even if the initial phases of mindfulness training do little beyond interrupting Anthony's ruminative cycles, it is likely that he will experience health gains from the simple act of attending to his breathing.

To demonstrate just how unhealthy the emotion anger is, clients can be invited to measure their blood pressure and heart rate before and after a session of mindful meditation. You can also invite them to measure their degree of discomfort from headaches, backache, and general fatigue before and after completing a 30-minute body-scan meditation. I have never introduced a client to mindfulness meditation who did not discover on his or her own the causal link between physical and mental stress and the loss of a significant measure of well-being.

Step 2: Preliminary—Journal Keeping and Setting Up Rules for Phone and E-mail Contact

Although not very complicated, the preliminary stages of this approach to treatment are very structured and require a very active, collaborative relationship between the client and the therapist. We need to keep close track on the development of Anthony's expanding conscious awareness to help him process what he is discovering. This will also serve to solidify the therapeutic relationship so that he will feel encouragement to persist in the face of various inevitable resistances and will serve to help him recognize meaningful progress toward his larger goals.

Consistent with the goals of a cognitively based treatment for anger, the ways in which Anthony justifies his anger will be carefully explored. In mindfulness, however, this analysis goes beyond looking at the "irrationality" of self-justification and extends the analysis to looking at the consequences of holding rigidly to the belief that one is morally "right." As Kabat-Zinn (1994) has observed, "anger is the price that we pay for being attached to a narrow view of being right [while] the collective pain we cause others and ourselves bleeds our souls" (p. 242). In practice with men like Anthony, I am consistently struck by how much anger is directly connected with absolutist rules about "right" and "wrong"—views that are justified by an extensive catalog of abstract principles and standards about the acceptable definition of proper human conduct, a great deal of which is defined by rigid sex-specific cultural norms. Thus, the angry man sees himself not only as the last bastion of what is right, proper, and acceptable but also as the pinpointed target of a myriad of moral infractions that he encounters on a daily if not hourly basis. Scratch the surface of any person's anger, in my experience, and you will find the wildly beating heart of an enraged defiant victim. This is the root of what Thomas (2003a) has termed *justified anger*. Indeed, Aquino, Douglas, and Martinko (2004) found that perceptions of victimization are frequently the root of overt anger manifested by employees with a hostile attribution style.

Closely related to the idea of justified anger is the concept of *unrealistic anger*, defined as the negative emotion experienced from going through the process of "trying to assert control over something that does not need correcting or that cannot be corrected" (Sapolsky, 1998, p. 334). Unrealistic anger provokes all of us, but especially young men, into a self-perpetuating series of emotional battles that are biologically dangerous and, over time, even lethal. Thus, the corrosive power of anger is fed by a deep emotional core of craving, aversion, and ignorance that are the central focus of a Buddhist approach to understanding human suffering. The fundamental goal over the course of Anthony's treatment is to help him replace his anger with empathic connection with others (most importantly with his immediate family) that will mature into the wisdom that comes from embracing compassion toward all living creatures. Thus, all of these modes of "crooked thinking" must be observed, recorded, and reflected upon in the therapy session.

With these two preliminaries kept clearly in mind, we can proceed to look at a sample syllabus for a course of 10 therapeutic sessions that will set the agenda for the conversations that will occur before and after mindfulness practice.

A Therapeutic Syllabus

First Session: Taking Stock of His Anger Repertoire

Reflexive expressions of justified and unrealistic anger are deeply socialized into men as masculine virtues by a culture that glorifies strength and violence and is at the same time deeply distrustful of authority and convention. Anyone who works intimately with young men is aware of the pervasive importance of this highly resilient strand in American men's masculinity training (Bankart, 2004).

It is essential in therapeutic work with men that the therapist offer a mindful, psychological buffer zone, a place for introspection, where the client can retreat from the rhetoric of testosterone, demanding respect and maintaining face, as well as defending against any appearance of weakness or uncertainty (Bankart, 2002). I have consistently observed that mindfulness practice can and often does provide a sanctuary for men, especially angry men, in that it allows them to take stock of themselves and their relationship to the world. Most important, perhaps, they can take stock of their relationship with a whole variety of authoritarian teachings and begin the process of sorting out and owning what is true, important, and real. By adopting a mindful orientation toward their personal experience, they will almost certainly experience a wide range of beneficial emotional, psychological, interpersonal, and spiritual effects, as did the highly competitive and agentic medical and premedical students who were introduced to mindfulness meditation by Shapiro, Schwartz, and Bonner (1998).

Indeed, the use of mindfulness practices can release a whole array of demons (Bankart, 2001) that need to be grappled with in a safe and serious place. It involves confronting powerful and often uncharted emotions and grappling with those emotions in a deliberate and constructive way (Greenberg, 2002). It is often the case that clients and students come to resist the difficult, frustrating, and serious work of laying a claim to a sustainable view of the self and the world. It is often necessary to offer a gentle or sometimes not-so-gentle *gaman suru*,[1] an uncompromising request that the student exert what Buddhist teachers call Right Effort (Bankart, 2003b) in his or her quest for enlightenment. It is essential that the angry client not feel preached to or lectured at and that his or her anger be approached in a collaborative effort with empathy, compassion, and loving-kindness. This is not simply some Buddhist sentimentality; it is one of the main findings of researchers who work with angry and violent offenders (Taft et al., 2003). In line with this thinking, the entire gender-package of masculine anger must be uncovered and processed in therapy. This includes each of the following:

- Alcohol/anger inventory
- Gendered anger rules; anger justification
- Anger rhetoric (speech, logic, attribution)

Second Session: Finding the Center, Beginning Self-Awareness

The goal of the second session is to introduce the idea that Anthony has the opportunity to behave heroically when he is confronted with a provocation.

[1]A phrase heard numerous times a day in Japan; it translates roughly as, "Do your best, keep trying, and never be a quitter."

The true hero of Anthony's life operates from within the center of his being. In Buddhist terminology, anger and its co-poisons—greed and delusion (Martin, 2000)—result from the contamination of natural mind. The key idea is that a "pure" mind is both a natural and a compassionate mind. This is a conception that must become the subject of Anthony's meditation in order for him to come to accept the truth imbedded in it. Anthony must dedicate himself to developing and maintaining a clear and compassionate mind.

He needs, through the practice of mindfulness, to become intimately aware of his habitual reflexive patterns of experiencing stress, disagreement, challenge, and disappointment. As Kornfield (1993) wisely put it, he needs to begin the process of confronting the self-protective anger in himself by experiencing a measure of self-directed compassion—he needs to open his mind by first opening his heart. This aspect of Anthony's therapy might involve some measure of bibliotherapy, an opportunity to read and reflect on some of the basic teachings of Buddhist philosophy. Here, for example, is a passage from Gunaratana (2002, p. 192) on the subject of anger.

> But what if someone hurts you? What if someone insults you? You may want to retaliate—which is a very human response. But, where does that lead? "hatred is never appeased by more hatred," it says in the *Dhammapada*. An angry response only leads to more anger. If you respond to anger with loving friendliness, the other person's anger will not increase. Slowly it may fade away. "By love alone anger is appeased," continues the verse in the *Dhammapada*.

Third Session: Exploring "What Is"—Without Trying to Change Anything

To explore the dimension of "acceptance," the therapist provides Anthony with carefully guided exposure to provoking stimuli—not so much in the service of "response prevention" but with careful second-by-second attention to the resulting activity in the body and the mind. Angry thoughts, feelings, and sensations are welcomed as revealing the nature of the untrained, undisciplined, and unenlightened mind. The central parable here is the story of the monk who smiles at the person who is trying to provoke him to anger and simply says: "Thank you; you have been my teacher." The real-life example of this sort of anger control is provided by the Dalai Lama, who when asked if he did not hate the Chinese government for invading his country, killing his people, and destroying his culture replied: "They have stolen my country. Why should I let them steal my heart?"

Fourth Session: Focus on the Physical Body

As previously noted, paying careful attention to the client's diet, physical fitness, and overall physical well-being is an important component of regaining self-control and self-respect. In general, by this point in treatment, it is certainly time to pay attention to Anthony's physical being, including his blood pressure, cholesterol levels, weight, and so forth. At this stage, in addition to chronic patterns of autonomic nervous system arousal, muscle tension, and metabolic disturbance, Anthony would be asked to explore the Type A patterns that pervade his life and to modify those that seem to be getting in the way of his becoming an enlightened being. Because the core of the pathology in Type A responding is in the resentment and hostility chronically experienced, these pervasive feelings become a prime focus for intensive mindful inspection.

Fifth Session: Awareness of Other Human Beings

Perhaps the real "sin" of anger is that it is an emotion rooted in a selfish preoccupation with the self. As we begin the second half of Anthony's treatment program, it will be important for him to complete a very thorough, careful, and honest inventory of the all the important relationships in his life. The Anonymous Random Acts of Kindness Meditation is introduced, and Anthony will be challenged to commit at least one anonymous act of kindness a day for the benefit of someone he loves or cares about a great deal. The focus of the meditation starts with thinking about how to make someone else's day a bit brighter, but the heart of the meditation is in first enjoying that person's unanticipated delight and second in observing how terribly difficult it is to abstain for taking credit for someone else's happiness. I have suggested this meditation to many dozens of men over the past few years and can report that for a significant number of them, this meditation resulted in their first tangible moment of *satori* (a glimpse, at least, of enlightenment). Unwillingness to engage this meditation with creativity, cheerfulness, and sincere interest may be a good indication that the client is not yet ready to progress with the rest of this program.

Sixth Session: Acceptance

Acceptance of the past, the present, and perhaps most important, the futility of struggle is a key psychological process in the therapeutic journey. Probably the most complex idea that Anthony will encounter in his discovery of a Buddhist perspective on his problems is that all causation is circular. Every action both is caused by and is the cause of every other action in the universe. There is no logical possibility of independent action, thought, or consequence. The only alternative to genuine philosophical acceptance is fruitless struggle against the laws of nature. What is paramount, in reality and in truth, however, is the notion of personal agency, personal responsibility, and personal opportunity to improve the conditions of living. No single person can make injustice disappear, for example. However, every human being can take responsibility for the human suffering that injustice creates. Moreover, every person can try to influence those who cause the suffering of others, take some of the suffering away from others by engaging in acts of human kindness, and respond compassionately to the sorrows of fellow creatures. These actions are all grounded in an unflinching acceptance of the world and life as it is, not as it might be in fantasy.

Seventh Session: Obligation—"Sumanai!"

The seventh phase in Anthony's treatment will offer a translation of the principles of Naikan therapy to fit Anthony's life and circumstances. (For a general introduction to Naikan, see Krech, 2002; Reynolds, 1980). Naikan is a very structured introspective therapy that essentially brings a laserlike focus to three questions: What have I received from . . .? What have I given to . . .? and finally, What troubles and difficulties have I caused . . .? (Krech, 2002, pp. 26–27). The goal of Naikan is to help the client recover his or her misplaced and misfocused mind (Reynolds, 1980)—to change focus from narcissistic feelings of entitlement and fantasies of revenge to recognizing a sense of obligation and indebtedness to the people who have loved, nurtured, and provided for him or her. Its focus is not on the guilt that a person will feel after meditation on these questions but on the opportunities the person has to demonstrate recognition of his or her obligations to those people.

This may be the best context in which to process the issue of Anthony's experience of abuse as a youngster. He is, after all, not just a victim of abuse but a survivor and a potential teacher to those who have experienced similar trauma. It is possible that the practice of mindfulness will lead Anthony to realize that he can compassionately create a way for some good come out of his 30 years of suffering. By transforming that suffering into the service of others, especially the protection of his wife, his family, and those who are much younger than he, Anthony has the power to make the world a better, safer, and more humane place. Although it may take quite a bit of time and soul-searching, Anthony may be able to recognize that his anger is a natural but selfish result of his preoccupation with his own suffering, and the best resolution will be to dedicate himself to the protection of others so that they will be less likely to be victimized as he was.

Eighth Session: Forgiveness and Compassion

The Naikan exercises open the Pandora's box of exploring grievances. Anthony is encouraged to begin thinking very deliberately about forgiveness (Coyle & Enright, 1997; DiGiuseppe & Tafrate, 2001), both as a way to better understand and control his angry impulses and, equally important, as a way of beginning to address the underlying issues that are contributing to his depression (Cochran & Rabinowitz, 2000; Troisi & D'Argenio, 2004). He must discover new ways of understanding and meeting his most fundamental needs, essentially a process of creating human meaning, which is a necessary precursor to his ability to manage his emotions and negotiate a successful resolution to interpersonal conflicts (Griffith & Graham, 2004).

The issue of Anthony's ability and willingness to forgive his parents and his uncle is a private decision that only he can decide to make, but there is a distinctive Buddhist perspective on the challenge of forgiveness that might make that process less painful and more interesting. Writing from a Buddhist perspective, Thurman (2005) does not see forgiveness as a gracious act or a transcendent gift between human beings, as many Christian writers have. The Buddhist challenge for an angry person is to cleanse his or her own heart and spirit and make sure that his or her conduct shines a bright light in the world. Thurman hopes that Buddhism will inspire others to live a more responsible and responsive life; holding on to resentments poisons the soul and destroys a person's ability to live compassionately and thus harmoniously in the world.

Like Levine (2000), Thurman urges us to see that forgiveness is a reflection of the constant effort of a human being to follow the path of the Buddha. Forgiveness is an intentional human act that reflects strength of character. Forgiveness occupies the same place in a person's well-ordered life as a list of other virtues, such as tolerance, patience, forbearance, endurance, and transcendent love. For Thurman, in the spirit of the Dalai Lama, "Our enemy is just our opportunity to practice this most rare and important transcendent virtue" (p. 115). Anger evokes enormous energies and vitality, and one must seize this opportunity and convert that energy and vitality into the service of *wisdom* that will deepen our practice of patience, forbearance, tolerance, and love.

This might be the time to explore what Anthony accepts from his religious training as a Catholic about forgiveness of sins and about the power of the human spirit to be forgiving. The Buddhist assumption, and I would put this on the table at the outset, is that Anthony will never be able to develop a real capacity for compassion toward himself until he finds the strength and wisdom to act compassionately toward others. Several other chapters in this book might include this focus; however, I would address this issue explicitly within the context of Anthony's spiritual life.

Ninth Session: Provoking the Dragon

Toward the end of the program, it is important to focus on relapse prevention, which involves knowing what to do in the face of provocation, not being panicked by failure, and knowing how to reconnect with the program to recover the gains that have been temporarily lost. By now, Anthony should be skillful at recognizing the arising of anger in his body and his mind and be able to congratulate himself for handling that arousal in productive ways.

The problem of avoidance must be addressed very explicitly as a critical issue in relapse prevention. Successful therapy cannot be tested if Anthony systematically avoids every "hot-button" situation that might prove challenging to him. It may be time to invite his wife to participate in his treatment in order to get both of them to focus on general issues of avoidance and confrontation in their relationship.

Although basic training in assertiveness has already informed many of the phases of treatment, it may now be necessary to help both Anthony and his wife approach their conflicts and contentions while self-consciously practicing being assertive. Two important ideas at this point are (1) the principle that everyone has the right to disagree respectfully and (2) that there is great power in being able to place your hands over your heart and say to someone who has knowingly or unknowingly provoked you to anger, *Thank you; you have been my teacher.*

Tenth Session: Waking Up the Inner Buddha

The "graduation" session should be a celebration of the wisdom that Anthony has acquired over the past several months. It also serves as the occasion for establishing the ongoing commitment that I will have to Anthony and that he will make to include me in his future journey. The reason that Buddhist psychology does not have a term for "Termination" is that the "cure" can never be considered "finished." Because *all life is suffering*, our human obligation to reduce that suffering does not have an expiration date. To borrow a phrase from Freud, demonstrating concern for and taking personal responsibility for the well-being of others is a process that is truly "interminable."

Follow-Up at 6 Weeks: Identifying Opportunities
to Make a Difference in the World

At the 6-week follow-up appointment, Anthony can be encouraged to take on the project of helping some other person (probably a younger man) find the way out of an angry relationship with the world. The appropriate term here is *mentoring.*

Follow-Up at 3 Months: Responsibility
for Leading Others Out of Suffering

The theme at 3 months would be similar to the agenda at 6 weeks, only now it is termed *leadership.*

Follow-Up at 6 Months: Where Is the Path Taking You?

At 6 months, I hope that I would find myself being educated by Anthony.

CLINICAL ISSUES AND RECOMMENDATIONS

Challenges Specific to this Mode of Treatment

There are challenges for both the therapist and the client that are unique to mindfulness work, above and beyond the challenge of working with angry clients. The most obvious challenge is that from the first day, the entire process must be completely transparent. The principal implication of this is that maintaining a mindfulness practice of your own is necessary to communicate the benefits of regular sustained practice and sensitively evaluate your client's benefits. The heart and soul of the model is personal transformation, the exercising of awareness and choice, and the experiencing of compassionate connection with other beings. The experience of regular meditative practice is subtlety yet pervasively transforming; that is precisely why it is called *transpersonal psychology.* Unless both therapist and client are developing conscious awareness in fundamentally compatible ways, there will be an inevitable disconnect between teaching the procedures and having the experience. This sort of work virtually requires the application of the participant-observer method.

Furthermore, the client must be sincerely committed to both the goals and the methods of this approach for there to be much possibility of deep change. A half-hearted effort is unlikely to result in much of a change in awareness or motivation to change. However, I have often been contacted by former clients 6 months or a year or two after a more or less fruitless mindfulness intervention who indicate that they now have the motivation to actively practice what they only went through the motions of doing while they were in active treatment. Initial experiences with meditation and mindfulness are, indeed, often quite powerful (Walsh, 1978), and seeds for later work are often fruitfully sewn. Whether the client is ready for and receptive to this program should be apparent with the first 2 weeks of treatment.

As mentioned earlier, clients with unpleasant or traumatic prior experiences with religious institutions may be reluctant to embrace a psychotherapeutic approach with manifest spiritual overtones. Other clients may fear that practicing meditation may conflict with the teachings of their religious denomination. Avowed atheists approach this opportunity with principled skepticism and are often delighted to discover that their renunciation of the supernatural does not require them to renounce awareness of a spiritual connection with other living things. Needless to say, however, for a great many people there is a very uneasy relationship between the psychological and spiritual dimensions of life.

It is difficult to predict who will respond favorably to mindfulness practice and, importantly, who would not. I recently led a group of 15 men who, for the most part, responded overwhelmingly positively to the program. One of the men, who was initially skeptical to the point of hostility about the entire program, became thoroughly committed to it. He applied the principles to areas in his life in addition to anger, and his relationships with a wide range of people improved. He became a poster child for the spiritually enhancing power of anonymous random acts of kindness, and he found himself routinely encountering people with a newly open heart. But another man in the group, who initially embraced the program with great enthusiasm, discovered after a few mindfulness sessions a deep undercurrent of anger in his most important relationships and chose not to pursue mindfulness practice. He had learned from his highly successful initial meditative experiences that he was "not ready" to let go of the strong negative emotions that he now perceived to be motivating him to be successful in his chosen career. Clients' early experiences with mindfulness activities such as counting breaths and completing a body scan will reveal whether they are likely to have to confront any major demons in their unconscious (Bankart, 2001).

There is some debate in the field about whether "you have to be somebody before you can be nobody" (Wilber, Engler, & Brown, 1986)—and therefore whether clients with relatively severe self-system deficits (e.g., persons with personality disorders or strong dissociative tendencies) should be discouraged from practicing meditation. There are no clear answers in this debate, but the literature on psychiatric

casualties in meditation demonstrates that most people who have negative experiences are people with significant psychiatric histories who
have gone on very long (several weeks) meditation retreats in the
absence of any psychiatric supervision or support (Shapiro, 1992).
There is no evidence that clients, including people diagnosed with borderline personality disorder, experience negative outcomes from doing
a body scan or counting their breaths.

For others, as my Australian friend Mark Blows has noted in his
long private practice of applying Buddhist principles in outpatient settings, "Not much happens." For them, there are dozens of therapeutic
alternatives, many of which are described in this book and which share
many of the goals and procedures of this program. Often, however,
something does happen—and that something turns out to be powerfully
transforming, not the least bit intimidating or dangerous, and deeply
enriching.

SUMMARY

Application of the ancient principles of mindful meditation has significant value for contemporary therapists involved with the challenge of
treating persons with anger issues. The program described in this chapter
is based on the philosophical premise that all human beings are innately
and even profoundly interconnected with all other living beings and that
anger is in fundamental contradiction to the natural state of human consciousness. Men's anger is deeply rooted within their gender role socialization, and in routine daily life, men often experience difficulty in
separating anger from a wide range of other sex-specific ways of expressing emotional distress. Mindfulness-based therapy may have special
appeal for angry male clients because it privileges the importance of preconscious inner experience over verbal exchange as a therapeutic modality (Bankart, 2006).

The program is unique in that it does not focus on issues of anger
"control" or "management." Rather it emphasizes first recognizing and
then replacing angry feelings and thoughts with acts and gestures reflecting loving kindness—what you can think of as *anger therapy by reciprocal inhibition*. Although the data gathered during various meditative
exercises constitute a cognitive exchange between the client and the therapist, no effort is made to offer logical correction or to provide an alternative construction of reality. The client must discover, with therapeutic
support and guidance, how to respond to frustration, challenge, and
even insult in a way that is reflective of his or her own values and ethical

orientation to the world, in accord with the client's sense of his or her own deepest human nature. The role of the therapist is akin to that of a Socratic dialogue partner, but the source of the wisdom that can transform the anger into effective social discourse is deeply empirical, rooted in the human experience of the client.

This therapeutic approach can be enacted either individually or in small groups, but the emphasis in group settings is not on discussion of the thoughts and feelings of the members. Rather, the group process is focused on discovery, insight into the nature of anger and its consequences, and the sense of shared community that exists when groups of people meditate together. Both the therapist and the group support the application of "right effort" in encouraging clients to make time to practice meditation exercises regularly and encourage one another to engage fully and fearlessly in the process of exploring their consciousness, including their most intimate fears and resentments.

There is a substantial practical benefit to people who practice mindful meditation on a regular basis: It is a highly effective and natural way to combat stress and increase personal effectiveness in daily life. In most of the instances where my clients in this program have realized significantly greater control over anger in their lives, this result has actually been secondary to a much larger impact on the way they encounter and handle stress. When clients work on their anger, they are both surprised and relieved that we actually begin our work together by talking about and working on stress reduction. One of the first discoveries that angry clients make is that anger almost never occurs in the absence of chronic and/or acute stressors.

On the flip side, when clients come to a program on stress management and in the course of that program they are introduced to mindfulness, they very soon become aware of significant reservoirs of anger that are lying just below the level of their conscious awareness. In truth, it was this consistent experience in working with young men that kindled my initial interest in anger as a therapeutic challenge. It took me a while as a therapist to overcome my reluctance to tackle the realities of my stressed clients' anger, but the result of inquiring more deeply into the nature of their anger has brought recognition that anger is a human problem that can be resolved in pretty much the same way that all other human problems can be resolved—through determined effort, focused attention, and the generous application of compassion and wisdom.

One of the most important lessons that one learns from studying and practicing mindfulness is that the realities of the meditative experience are profoundly empirical. It is never necessary to tell a client (or yourself, for that matter) what to expect to discover from a meditative experience. Sharing and comparing those discoveries is both a valuable and fascinating use of therapeutic time, but the process of discovery is as intensely personal as it is profound. The tricky part is, of course, putting what one has learned into daily practice in everyday life. The wisdom of how to accomplish this is what philosophers in the Buddhist tradition call *enlightenment*.

CHAPTER 12

An Adlerian Approach to the Treatment of Anger Disorders

Daniel Eckstein, Al Milliren, Paul R. Rasmussen,
and Robert Willhite[*]

INTRODUCTION TO INDIVIDUAL (ADLERIAN) PSYCHOLOGY

Individual (Adlerian) psychology, as developed by Alfred Adler (1870–1937), "is a cognitive, goal-oriented, social psychology interested in a person's beliefs and perceptions, as well as the effects that person's behavior has on others" (Milliren, Newbauer, & Evans, 2003, p. 91). It not only is a theory of human behavior but also can serve as a comprehensive philosophy of life. As each individual develops a positive sense of worth, he or she becomes more able to make "healthy" choices of behavior and can function with the "courage to be imperfect." Adler was as concerned with social equality, mutual respect, and individual dignity as he was with offering hope to the individual, family, or group that might be experiencing difficulty in meeting the challenges of living. The most universal therapeutic intervention for Adlerians is *encouragement*. These Adlerian concepts can still be evidenced throughout contemporary psychological approaches and personality theory (Watts & Pietrzak, 2000).

[*]The authors would like to acknowledge the invaluable assistance of Sherri Bennett in this chapter.

Although Adler was a contemporary of Freud (and Jung), Adler's theory differed significantly and, in fact, these differences led to his split from the Viennese Psychoanalytic Society. According to Hoffman (1994), it was never clear how they came to be known to one another. In 1902, Freud invited Adler to join the Society, where Adler remained as an active participant until 1911. During this time, Adler was developing his theory based on the extent to which social factors and teleology played a major role in motivation and development. This differed from Freud's view that behavior was biologically or physiologically determined. These differences became so profound that Adler left Freud's group and formed his own society, which ultimately became the Society for Individual Psychology (Milliren, Newbauer, & Evans, 2003). "If a family tree were created for psychology, the Freudian branch would show up as a single branch, while the Adlerian branch would show vigorous growth and branching, bearing fruit that continues to sprout effective therapies up into the postmodern era" (Snow, 2003, p. 5).

One of the major contributors to the growth and development of Adlerian Psychology was Rudolf Dreikurs, M.D. During his early years of practicing psychiatry in Vienna, Dreikurs was involved with Adler and his child guidance clinics. Both Adler and Dreikurs believed that a major focus of individual psychology should be directed to the education of children because this would offer a preventive approach to mental health. In 1937, Dreikurs moved to the United States and during the late-30s and early-40s initiated the opening of child guidance centers in Chicago. While in Chicago, Dreikurs contributed considerably to the understanding of Adler's theory as well as popularizing it throughout the world (Milliren, Newbauer, & Evans, 2003).

Adlerian psychology has a positive and optimistic view of the world—we have choices and need not be victims unless we choose to be. Adlerian psychology is also a phenomenological psychology in that it views one's *perception* of experience as more important than the experience itself.

Adler stressed that all individuals desire to be significant in the world in which they live. In the case of young children, this world is usually the family. Adler believed that if we do not achieve a feeling of significance in childhood, we are likely to develop some form of problematic behavior. Although not always severe, some form of difficulty will arise for the person. Adler said that adult behavior is driven by the "problem." This problem emerges in childhood when the child encounters a problem that, because of his or her situation in life, he or she is not prepared to solve. Solving this problem becomes the child's (often unconscious) "mission in life" and guides many of his or her behaviors and beliefs about the world. This mission is referred to as the *fictional goal*. It is fictional because it is not a realistic objective and therefore can never be achieved to the complete satisfaction of the adult.

Adler believed that as clients become more encouraged and begin to change their view of the world, others, and themselves, they are more able to get past the problem and the *mistaken thinking* that often accompanies it. As clients develop more courage, they are able to stop thinking so individualistically and instead focus on their role within society. Thus focused, the individual can begin to express an increasing capacity for cooperation and contribution or *social interest*. O'Connell (1991) suggested the following "equation" for effective mental health: NH = SE + SI. A *n*atural *h*igh (versus a chemical high) is based on a combination of high *s*elf-*e*steem and high social *i*nterest. This is similar to the "I'm OK/you're OK" position in transactional analysis.

This chapter presents an Adlerian-oriented perspective relative to the emotion of anger with a specific application to the case of Anthony. What follows is a brief overview of the major tenets of Adlerian-Dreikursian psychology and then a discussion of how these tenets can be applied to the topic of anger. An Adlerian approach to conceptualizing the therapeutic process and suggested interventions concludes this chapter.

Theoretical Orientation—A "SUPER" Theory

Fundamental Adlerian principles of human behavior can be illustrated by *SUPER*, an acronym developed by Eckstein (2002). Each letter of the acronym represents a major theoretical Adlerian belief.

SUPER—Social Interest

According to Ansbacher (1991), the most distinctive concept in Adler's individual psychology, but also the one that has the least recognition in general psychological literature, is captured in the German word *Gemeinschaftsgefuehl*. *Gemeinschaftsgefuehl* is generally translated as "social interest" or "social feeling." There is no English word that serves as an accurate translation for the German meaning. Other translations, such as "community feeling," "community sense," or "humanistic identification" (O'Connell, 1991), have also been used. In general, social interest represents the person's capacity to cooperate with others and contribute to the good of the group. This was Adler's measure of the mental health of the individual.

Gemeinschaftsgefuehl, or social interest, was not fully defined in Adler's theory until the later years. From approximately 1916 until his death in 1937, Adler worked to refine his thinking around this simple theme. "What Adler was in search of was a reconciliation between the individual and society, a means of effecting a reintegration of the maladjusted neurotic with his environment through a simple and rational code of conduct that would satisfy the demands of both" (Way, 1962, p. 186). This created a shift in the structure of Adler's theory—from the notion of the individual's striving for superiority or the *will to power*—to a desire to belong, to feel worthwhile, and to be a part of the human community. Social interest, then, became Adler's criterion for normalcy, and an increase in social interest served as the primary goal of therapy.

Existentialist philosophers have used the term *anomie* (rootlessness) to indicate the antipathy of social interest (Ansbacher, 1991). MacIver (1950) observes that *anomie* is a condition in which an individual's sense of social cohesion is broken or fatally weakened. Detachment from a feeling of *embeddedness*, or a lack of "connectedness" to others, results in various antisocial behavior types or severe emotional damage to such individuals.

Slavik (2005) suggests that social interest (SI) is actually more understandable from the perspective of *psychological tolerance* (PT). PT is the amount of threat a person can face without choosing anger and leaving a situation, "caving in" to despair or fear, renouncing one's ability to handle a situation, or in general, withdrawing. PT is plainly related to the habitual coping styles of safeguarding through distancing, exclusion tendencies, antithetical modes of apperception, and limitations in courage (Adler, 1956). A measure of high PT could also serve as a measure of one's willingness to stand out and display *Gemeinschaftsgefuehl*.

Self-defeating strategies for responding to life challenges create discouragement in the individual, leading him or her to withdraw or move away from meaningful contact with others. There is a positive interactive effect involving social interest, self-confidence, and mental health. The more one behaves, feels, and thinks courageously, the more others will respond positively to him or her. This enhances self-confidence, which further expands social interest for both the present reality and for building a better future. A balance of practicality and idealism also highly correlates with a high degree of mental health.

SUPER—Unity

The term *individual psychology* (Adler, 1958) is often misunderstood. In his theory, Adler wanted to stress the idea of the *unity* or *indivisibility* of the person. This was at a time when others were focusing on a personality composed of parts (e.g., Freud's id, ego, and superego and the conscious, subconscious, and preconscious). Adler selected the word *individual*, which in German has the connotation and denotation of unity, an indivisible whole. It refers to the uniqueness of individuals. Like the flower emerging from a single fertilized cell, each person is a unity, rather than an assemblage of parts like a machine. The whole, *unified self* is a focus of Adlerian psychology.

The unified self is what Adler called one's *lifestyle*. The lifestyle, or one's style of life, includes the person's beliefs about self, others, and the world; feelings about one's place in the world and one's world experiences; and the behaviors employed as one moves through life. This is a complex and complete system wherein *each component affects all others*. Obviously, within such a system, any change in any one part will influence changes in other parts of the system. Thus, as we begin to know more about an individual, we can begin to get a glimpse of how that person functions in life. We can make sense of behaviors and the choices the individual makes and help him or her understand the characteristic manner each one uses in "going about going about." This was Adler's idea of the *unity of the personality*—everything connects to everything else about the person.

This concept of the unity of the personality gave rise to one of Dreikurs' innovative contributions to Adlerian theory—the technique of *two points on a line:*

> He used an analogy from geometry applied to the lifestyle concept. "One needs two points to draw a line, and once a line is drawn, one knows an infinite number of points." If a client reveals two apparently independent and contrary facts, a line of logic can be drawn to delineate a picture of a unified, self-consistent life style. The therapist attempts to find the line of logic through intelligent guessing, and if correct, the answer will resolve the puzzle and indicate the basic life style. (Terner & Pew, 1978, p. 247)

The concept of lifestyle, then, includes the characteristic of cutting across ordinary boundaries and uniting what might otherwise be separate entities.

The growing popularity of holistic health and holistic medicine is based on the inter-relationships of mind, body, and spirit *(psychoneuroimmunology)*. For example, many researchers believe that self-hatred is correlated with the breakdown of the immune system in patients with acquired immunodeficiency syndrome (AIDS) and that unresolved anger often accompanies the onset of cancer.

SUPER—*Private Logic*

We don't see things as they are, we see things as we are. (Anais Nin)

Out of the countless events occurring in one's life, each individual decides what conclusions are to be drawn about how life is, in general; how others are and how they should behave toward us; and about one's self—who we are and the nature of our value and worth. *Private logic* is self-created; we give meaning to the events that occur around us.

"We experience reality always through the meaning we give it . . . as something interpreted" (Adler, 1931, p. 3). Such a "private" or "personal" decision-making process relates to the philosophical field known as *phenomenology*. Phenomenology means that one's experiences of reality are subjectively filtered though a personal set of glasses that uniquely focus the world.

A large share of one's private logic surrounds one's movement from a *felt minus* to a *perceived plus*. Our sense of feeling "less than," in one way or another, motivates us to improve upon the situation. We strive for a sense of *significance*, whether it be through belonging, achieving, dominating, or engaging in self-elevation. When we find ourselves in the position of the "underdog," we adopt attitudes and behaviors that we think will change that situation. Anger, for example, is often perceived as the means to an end. We may use it to get what we think we want by overpowering or intimidating others; in reality, it may serve to drive others away.

Private logic is exactly that—the unique, creative, and biased view of the person regarding self, others, and the world. We can only begin to grasp what it is like to be another person by meeting them in their model of the world. Adler (1927) spoke of the need for empathy in clinical situations. In order to understand the private logic of another "we must be able to see with his eyes and listen with his ears" (p. 27). The ability to understand the private inner world of another person is a core condition of therapy. A Native American koan is: "If you want to understand my world, walk a mile in my moccasins."

SUPER—Equality

Equality—to hold no one's head higher (or lower) than your own—is a pivotal principle of individual psychology. Adlerians believe that an authoritarian stance in relationships must be replaced by *a dialogue between equals* in an atmosphere of mutual respect, candor, and acceptance. *Equality* can be defined by contrasting the "vertical" versus the "horizontal" in one's relationships with others. The "horizontal" approach to life views all people as being equally worthy of respect and consideration. Such equality does not mean "sameness" but rather a "no more or less than one" whole human being whose basic birthright is unconditional mutual respect and dignity. By contrast the "vertical" plane measures people in a "one-up" or "one-down" perspective. This vertical dimension is often characterized by elements of power and control in relationships. "Better than/less than" characterizes the vertical plane, whereas "different than" is the horizontal perspective. An orange is different (horizontal plane), not better than (vertical plane), an apple.

Adler coined the term *masculine protest* to describe what was happening in a culture that valued what was defined as being *masculine* over what was *feminine*. In many respects, his views have been seen as a precursor to the sexism upon which the more recent women's movement was founded. In this atmosphere of "better than," both men and women suffer negative consequences. Women protest the inequality. Men are challenged by having an almost impossible standard of being a "real man" from which to be judged. Inferiority and superiority are two sides of the same coin in Adlerian psychology. Both result in a feeling of separateness or disconnection from others.

SUPER—*Reason*

"How is the person seeking to be known?" Most ways of behaving that are eventually accepted by the person reflect the current concept of the self. Adlerians stress that behavior is *purposive* or *goal-directed*. We are all striving for some type of significance or "perfection" in our quest for both belonging and a sense of personal identity. Adler believed it was one's goals, or a *guiding self-ideal*, that motivated behavior. Adlerians call this a type of *master motive*, and this process can be understood from a *teleological* rather than causal perspective—that is, as a *pull by the goal* rather than a push by the drive.

Teleology (from the Greek *teleos*, meaning "goal") means "purposive, moving toward goals." Adler claimed: "Only when we know the effective direction-giving goal of a person may we try to understand his movement" (Ansbacher, 1967, p. 17). Basic life goals, although generally unknown to the person, give direction to all behavior. To the extent that goals are aligned with social interest, the direction of the person's life is useful, positive, and healthy. Conversely, if goals lack social interest and are simply an expression for overcoming perceived inferiorities by achieving personal superiority, the direction of the person's life tends to be useless, negative, and unhealthy.

Dreikurs identified four classic *misguided goals* of behavior, which are formulated in early childhood as being undue *attention, power, revenge*, and *inadequacy*. Dreikurs' four mistaken goals are shorthand explanations/descriptions of consistent patterns of misbehavior in children. Dreikurs (1953) declared that all misbehavior in children could be understood from the perspective of one of these four goals. These goals are largely unconscious in children. Such goals are discouraged methods of striving for significance. Striving for significance is in essence a movement toward fulfillment of the goal to achieve unique identity as well as to belong.

There is a useful distinction between two different kinds of striving. *Striving for perfection* means to move in horizontal fashion with the common sense of communal living, whereas *striving for superiority* means to move in a vertical direction, toward personal superiority over others.

> Movement in striving for perfection and movement in striving for superiority are both efforts to overcome the individual's feelings of inferiority. To the degree that one strives for perfection we can expect positive mental health, a greater sense of well-being, sense of connectedness with others and humanity. To the degree that one is striving for superiority we can expect disease, a sense of separateness." (Manaster & Corsini, 1982)

Anger from an Adlerian Perspective

The word *anger* comes from a Middle English word meaning "grief." It also derives from Latin and Greek words meaning "to strangle." Rather than deal appropriately with our angry feelings, we often choke them off or stuff them (Willhite & Eckstein, 2003). Adler believed that we do not lose our temper; rather, we throw it away in a manner that is consistent with our own private logic. For example, he observed that children of deaf parents, when "having a temper tantrum," do not scream and yell and shout; rather, they stood in sight of their parents and exhibited all the behavioral signs of anger, such as pouting, finger pointing, clinched jaws, and so forth.

Thus, Adlerians treat anger not as something we have or that has us but rather as something we create to achieve a particular goal or end. In effect, we manufacture our emotions to provide us with the energy to accomplish our purposes in life and living. Like the gas in our automobiles, emotions serve to fuel us in the direction of our goals (Dreikurs, 1953). Thus, in the case of the Anthonys in this world, anger is of their own design and execution. It is the counselor's or therapist's responsibility to help them understand "for what purpose" their anger is created. "What is the use?" continually guides us as we share in the therapeutic journey with our clients. In a general sense, Anthony uses his anger to move from a felt minus position, in his view of the world, to one of a plus.

McKay and Maybell (2004, p. 15) distinguish between *anger, rage, aggression,* and *resentment.*

> *Anger* is a feeling natural to the human condition; it is a feeling every human being experiences especially when we are being challenged, threatened, or hurt. There are obviously degrees of anger, and *rage* is

anger at the highest level of intensity. *Aggression* occurs when anger turns from a feeling into a hurtful or harmful action or behavior. When anger turns into rage or aggression, the risk of violence is the greatest. *Resentment* is holding onto and carrying anger as a permanent possession, being weighted down with anger. It usually occurs when you have not fully addressed or resolved being hurt by someone who currently matters, or at one time mattered, in your life.

Resentment also derives from a person's sense of entitlement. According to Eckstein (2006), entitlement is the basic prerequisite for an "advanced course" in anger. When there are long traffic delays, angry people feel entitled to no impediments; teenagers "grounded" by mom or dad are "entitled" to stay out as late as their friends. Anger is a reaction to unfulfilled expectations. Anger says, "I want." According to Adlerian theory, the intensity of the anger depends on what the angry person wants—and how badly they want it. Adler (1927) also noted that "Anger . . . is the veritable epitome of the striving for power and dominance" (p. 210).

Too often, we prefer to blame others for our anger. So often we hear, "See what you made me do?" "You make me so angry" or "You know how mad I get when you. . . ." In these situations, we blame our anger on someone or something else rather than admitting that we created our own anger. As McKay and Maybell (2004) note, guilt often accompanies anger. This is particularly so when one thinks she or he should not have been angry. "Guilt expresses good intentions we really don't have" (p. 22). McKay and Maybell suggest that we "either do wrong or feel guilty, but don't do both; it's too much work!" (p. 22).

As we approach considerations for therapy, it may be useful to keep in mind the following nine essential features of anger (Willhite & Eckstein, 2003):

1. Anger is (almost) universal. Everyone gets angry; at least everyone who's normal.
2. Anger is an appropriate emotion. There is nothing wrong with angry feelings. It is how we display those feelings and deal with them that can become a problem.
3. Anger does not exist in an emotional vacuum. Behind the anger is another emotion, such as hurt, sadness, or disappointment.
4. Anger is expressed in many ways for many purposes. Individuals are creative in their expressions of anger; there is no common pattern. The use of these expressions can also serve many goals or purposes depending on the perception of the individual.
5. Anger feels different to you than it feels to someone else. We each have our own unique style when it comes to our internal anger response.

6. Anger serves many functions, positive as well as negative. Whether the outcome of anger is good or bad depends on whether it is expressed in responsible words and actions.

7. The attempt to hide our anger often affects us more powerfully than the anger itself. And, in the long run, it still plays out with negative consequences.

8. Anger responses are learned. Anger may be a primary emotion, but the way we handle it is usually modeled on someone else's behavior.

9. Anger responses can be altered. This is what provides us with hope. We are only stuck in our patterns of anger if we choose to remain there.

Elements of Adlerian Psychotherapy

"There are probably as many different styles of Adlerian counseling/ therapy as there are individual Adlerians" (Milliren, Newbauer, & Evans, 2003, p. 124). However, certain elements or phases in the practice of counseling and therapy will typically be in evidence. Four elements of the counseling/therapy process have been identified by Dreikurs (1967): relationship and rapport building, information gathering and understanding (by both therapist and client), goal setting and interpretation, and re-education/reorientation. It should be noted that these are not separate stages of the therapeutic process but simply elements that occur within the process as a whole. Although we might begin therapy by focusing on the relationship element, the activity of rapport building is an ongoing function. We also collect information as we go, we continually work toward mutual alignment or agreement on the goal of therapy, and at a minimum, we offer ongoing encouragement and validation to the client.

THE FOUR ELEMENTS OF ADLERIAN COUNSELING AND PSYCHOTHERAPY

The Relationship

Underscoring the entire process of counseling/therapy is the development of a relationship of mutual respect and trust. Consistent with this focus on equality is the agreement between client and counselor on procedure to be followed and the respective roles of each individual. Often, the relationship is defined as collaborative, where the counselor and client work together in a psychological exploration and share joint responsibility for the therapeutic journey. In addition to the standard mental status examination, Adlerians use a lifestyle assessment to further psychological understanding, which may include the following (Walton, 1998):

1. Exploration of the subjective situation: The nature of clients' complaints, problems, or symptoms are explored.
2. Exploration of the objective situation: How clients are functioning in the three life tasks of work, social relationships, and relationships to the other sex is assessed.
3. Family constellation: The exploration of the family constellation provides an indication of how clients found their place within their first social group. This offers a view of the circumstances under which they developed their conclusions about self, others, and the world.
4. Early recollections: Early recollections also represent conclusions clients drew from the circumstances in which they were involved. From the many experiences to which clients have been exposed, they selectively recall only those that coincide with their outlook on life.
5. Disclosure: As part of this shared journey, clients' basic premises about life and the purposes of their behavior, as seen in this psychological investigation, are disclosed. When clients begin to recognize their goals, their conscience often becomes a motivating factor.

Goal Setting and Interpretation

Goal setting and interpretation involve the process of arriving at an agreement as to the goal or goals of the session. Clients often ask, "What would be useful to you now?" or "How might we best spend our time together?" The therapist might suggest a possible goal, but this is always done in a tentative fashion. Although there may be general agreement for the goal of counseling, the therapist offers ongoing opportunities to adjust the goal. The counselor or therapist might ask, "How is this of help to you now?" or "Is this a useful line of pursuit for you?"

Re-Education/Reorientation

Re-education/reorientation involves all those strategies and techniques that might facilitate the client's movement toward the therapeutic goal. Encouragement is a most important factor at this point because the client is attempting to substitute more productive behavior for the less productive.

The use of homework activities is also important because it provides for outside-of-session involvement on the part of the client.

Two new elements have been added to this model: ecology checking and future pacing. It is essential that the therapist regularly check in with the client to make sure that what is occurring in therapy "fits" the client and that it has application to his or her life outside the therapy relationship. Adlerian counseling/psychotherapy is insight-oriented, as are many of the contemporary therapy models. Just as there is a relationship of equals that characterizes all four elements of the counseling model, Adlerians also encourage active participation by the client in all aspects of the therapeutic process. In many respects, the client is the "ultimate judge" of how the process unfolds. These elements are illustrated in Figure 12.1.

Adlerian Applications to the Case of Anthony

Adler (1929) wrote with respect to a female client identified as "Mrs. R." that

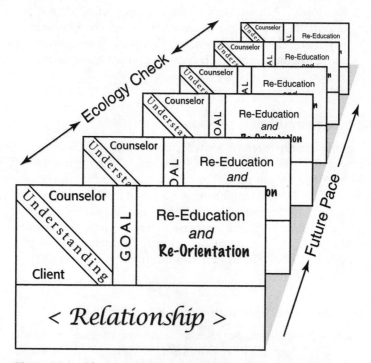

Figure 12.1 The Major Elements of Adlerian Therapy as They Unfold over Time.

With every sentence, with every word of the patient, I consider:

- What is the real meaning of what she is saying?
- What is this person's attitude toward life?
- What do her words mean in the light of her deeds?
- How does she meet the demands life makes of her?
- How does she behave toward her fellow human beings?
- How does she perform her duties (or fail to perform them)?
- Does she tend to reality or illusion? (pp. 4–5)

The first task for an Adlerian, then, would be to gain an understanding of Anthony's basic movement through life in terms of what Adler called his lifestyle.

> A psychologist may commence the study of a life story where he will always find that the particular life he is investigating is directed toward a certain goal. In order to understand a person's life, it is necessary to discover the thread which runs through all his symptoms and which can be traced directly to his goal. We can also call this thread the style of life of a human being. The style of life is the special manner in which a human being faces life and answers the challenge of existence; how he feels, thinks, wants, acts; how he perceives and how he makes use of his perceptions. (Adler, 1929, p. 50)

Although some Adlerians use a formal lifestyle systematic interview (see Eckstein & Kern, 2002, for a suggested interview format), others may choose to use relatively brief components of the formal lifestyle interview. We will use this latter approach in our discussion of the case of Anthony, where the task is to discover his perceptions of life and how he views his place in it. In many respects, we are interested to learn of his hopes, dreams, and desires. Thus, as a place to begin, it is important to form an understanding of Anthony's basic "life is . . .; others are . . .; I am . . .; therefore, I must . . ." core life decisions. This helps to appreciate how Anthony comes to therapy in the present based on what Shulman (1965) called the *preformed working hypothesis* (p. 214).

Consistent with the purposeful goal-directed Adlerian tenets and having discovered the threads of his basic style of life, the next challenge is to work together collaboratively as "joint detectives" to find the "clues" to understanding the payoff for his past antisocial behavior and reduced social interest. In general, there will be a specific focus on the emotion of anger and how he actively "uses" it to achieve things in his life based on his own perception of "how things are supposed to be."

That is the general therapeutic Adlerian "game plan" for Anthony. In reality, what actually evolves in treatment will be in concert with Anthony as he explores his movement through life. The pace and flow of the therapy will be under Anthony's direction, with occasional therapeutic nudges provided by the therapist. As this joint venture unfolds, some of the considerations or specific "clues" to understanding what Eckstein and Kern (2002) describe as Anthony's "psychological fingerprints" would be open for consideration by the Adlerian counselor/therapist. A discussion of these follows.

Anthony's presenting problem must be acknowledged—he is about to lose his family as a result of his anger. The very people who might be accepting of Anthony and his anger are no longer willing to put up with it. Anger is the emotion that many people attempt to use to remove obstacles to gaining that to which they feel entitled. Understanding the nature of his perceived entitlement is a prerequisite to Anthony's comprehending his angry behavior. He uses his anger (albeit maladaptively) to achieve certain ends, most notably, compliance. Both family members and employers resent his use of this powerful and damaging emotion. His "use" of anger has also generated feelings of guilt and embarrassment. He has also struggled with bouts of depression, which might even be construed as silent "temper tantrums."

It is noteworthy that although the reason for treatment is his anger, there are other issues that are likely to be related and will need to be addressed. Most notable is Anthony's problematic work history and his self-defeating behaviors. His history of having been abused sexually is clearly a contributing factor. His initial anger and outrage at the abuse were, in many ways, an understandable way for protecting against the violation of his boundaries. However, holding on to the anger for all this time only hurts Anthony in the present. Forgiveness is ultimately in his own physical and emotional self-interest.

Considering the purpose or use of his anger, the other affective states evidenced in Anthony's behavior make sense. He uses anger to get what he desires in order to meet lifestyle goals when he feels hopeless, given his perceived inadequacy, about actually accomplishing what he wants. His guilt and embarrassment suggest that he has some awareness of his own violation of social and relational rules or expectations. In this regard, guilt is the relationship maintenance emotion signifying a violation of appropriate conduct in a relationship (Rasmussen, 2003). He is aware that anger damages relationships and that he is failing in some way to hold up his end.

Embarrassment is the affective state felt when one has violated a social norm or expectation, and Anthony is apparently aware of the inappropriateness of his public anger displays and is appropriately embarrassed by them. However, embarrassment serves the same purpose for Anthony as would feeling guilty. It is a signal of "good intentions," although a better option would be to do something proactive about it—to change his behavior. Instead, Anthony elects to be embarrassed. Clinically, though, things would be far worse if Anthony did not feel guilt or embarrassment. (For a more in-depth description of an Adlerian "lexicon" of emotions, see Rasmussen, 2003.)

Anthony uses anger in a purposive manner for achieving some interpersonal outcome that he feels entitled to receiving. Given this premise, three critical questions arise:

1. *What is it that he feels entitled to receiving?* There appears to be a series of related outcomes for which he has a sense of entitlement. He seeks compliance from others. He wants others to do and act the ways that he wants them to. This includes doing certain things (e.g., playing softball with intensity, validating his accomplishments) and not doing other things (e.g., making messes, giving him a hard time, asking him to do things he does not want to do).

2. *Is he truly entitled to that outcome, and, if he is, is anger the best way to "get it"?* We are all entitled to respect from others and to outcomes related to safety and security. Beyond these outcomes, we may not be truly entitled to anything. Entitlement is an addiction; anger is a consequence of an unfulfilled expectation.

3. *If he is not necessarily entitled to what he seeks to gain, for what purpose or "payoff" does he think he is entitled to?* Anthony had a basic entitlement related to how his uncle treated him as a child. It seems fair to say that children are entitled to being safe from sexual abuse. It is interesting, however, that in the abusive situation, Anthony did not "use" anger. This underscores the fact that anger is used only when we think it will work. Children being abused by adults often do not see anger as an option. Adults are bigger than they are, and children often feel helpless to actively do anything about it. More typical emotional reactions are repression (simply forgetting it) or dissociation (leave the body during the abuse). Anger often comes out later.

It is possible that therapy with Anthony could successfully end at this point. If Anthony accepted that his anger was inappropriate and he was willing to develop more respectful, patient, and compassionate ways to foster harmonious family feelings, this could be the topic of therapy. Change could be easily facilitated through *instruction and training, role-playing,* and *skill building and implementation.* However, without concomitant changes in his core beliefs, Anthony might easily fall back into the old patterns of behavior.

Anthony's anger and desire for compliance, however, may have deeper roots and probably reflect critical lifestyle assumptions and goals. For Anthony, anger has payoffs, such as avoiding responsibility and not doing things he does not want to do. Such assumptions are common in people who use anger to manage relationships. More involved psychotherapy at this point would include consideration of the origins of his lifestyle assumptions and exploration of his childhood experiences from which he formed his basic ideas about himself, others, and the world. Anthony has created some psychological distance between the core sense of self and the "psychopathology" he says he wants to target in treatment.

Background Lifestyle Personality Clues

As therapy moves forward with Anthony to discover and explore his basic beliefs, the therapist must be cognizant of how Anthony's life decisions affect both his current and his future behaviors. Following are 15 indicators from the case study that Adlerians would use in helping Anthony consider and reconsider his views of self, others, and the world.

1. He is a son in an Italian family. Although this should never be taken at face value and the extent to which this stereotype fits any individual must be considered, Italian sons of immigrant families are often very accommodated. This may leave them with an unrealistic expectation of adulthood; they may lack what Walton (1998) calls the *psychological muscle* necessary for successful problem solving and use of coping strategies.
2. This may be particularly true when the Italian son marries a non-Italian woman who does not cater to his every whim, as is the case with Anthony. That Anthony is the second son and is 6 years younger than his elder brother is also noteworthy. Eckstein (2000) sites empirical studies finding statistical significance of birth order. It is as if Anthony "came in on the third act of the family play." He is already behind and either has to run fast to catch up or give up altogether. A therapist could ask Anthony, "What mistakes did you see being made by your older brother that you learned to avoid in your own life growing up?"

   We do not know much about his brother, so any comments here are pure speculation. That the gap is 6 years might suggest that Anthony was not a planned child. That his mother appeared to favor the first two children and expressed hostilities toward Anthony and his younger sister would be consistent with this speculation. This family dynamic might have contributed to his *wished for* sense of entitlement. He may feel entitled to treatment more in line with that of his older brother and sister. Because we do not know more about his brother, these statements are hypothetical, but the speculation seems very reasonable. Dreikurs (1953) called this process of making guesses "digging gold mines."

3. Anthony focused his attention and resources on athletics rather than on academics. This might suggest that his older siblings were more academically oriented, or at least more obedient to their mother's wishes (his brother was described as nonathletic). Although athletics provided a unique bond with his father and thus led to special attention, this was nonetheless a mixed blessing. No doubt he received considerable validation for these efforts and accomplishments, but his time spent in athletics also took him away from the academic environment, thus contributing to a deficit in necessary adult skills.

4. A significant benefit from attention to schoolwork as a child is the development of a sense of responsibility. Like his father, it appears that Anthony has attempted to regain some athletic validation through the athletic accomplishments of his daughter. He is also using his aggressiveness and tenacity to compel his daughter's team to perform at the highest level. Unfortunately, this is not appreciated and almost serves the opposite purpose.

5. The sexual abuse is another important childhood influence. It is probable that the abuse left Anthony with a legacy of shame (a sense of damage to his core worth via an unalterable event) and self-contempt (a rejection of the self). This might help to accelerate the intensity of his other feelings. Anthony may see himself as ultimately damaged and unacceptable to self and to others.

6. As a result of the abuse, Anthony may elect to compensate for his diminished sense of worth by attempting to become more masculine. This may explain his athletic focus, his interest in guns, his hostility, and his tendency to be a "womanizer." His contempt for and competitiveness with males in positions of authority helps explain his troubled work history. Although Anthony seems to value close relationships with men, he also appears to be untrusting and resentful of men.

7. A core lifestyle conviction may be that men "should" treat him as his grandfather, father (in the early years), and his uncle (initially) treated him. However, this may not be totally satisfactory because, ultimately, they will take advantage of you or hurt you. The "and therefore" conclusion seems to be "therefore, I must be

on the defensive against them." This is indeed a troublesome attitude for someone who, because of his limited career training, will often be occupationally subordinate to other men.

His 21-year stint as a machinist apparently worked as well as it did because his "father figure" employer tolerated his less-than-adequate performance and attitude. When challenged, however, he was defensive and argumentative, which eventually led to his dismissal. This episode may underscore his expectation of accommodation and his conflicted attitude toward men in authority. As long as they are validating, tolerant, and patient, Anthony maintains a positive attitude toward them, even idolizing them to a point. However, when expectations of Anthony that are inconsistent with his own goals or when disappointment in him is expressed, he uses his anger for gaining compliance or revenge.

8. It is likely that Anthony has actually reveled in the joy of victimization, thus allowing him to ignore his own contribution to interpersonal problems. If he is the victim, there is no obligation to change. He enjoys considerable secondary gain via the accommodating behaviors of others.

9. Anthony has spent the greatest part of his life doing what he wants rather than doing what Adlerians call "meeting the needs of the situation." He feels threatened by and resentment toward those who attempt to have power over him. He is self-centered and controlling, with a long history of failing to meet such externalized standards as academic and occupational expectations.

10. Anthony seems to operate by a mistaken belief that "I shouldn't have to do the things I don't want to do." His academic and work history and the history of his marriage all derive from this. In addition, he can use his attention deficit hyperactivity disorder (ADHD) and dyslexia as excuses to further avoid doing things he does not want to do. Although the term *mistaken belief* is more often attributed to Ellis, he credits Adler as being one of the first psychologists to focus on such cognitive distortions.

11. Being lazy is another way of saying that Anthony does not see the benefit of greater activity. Anthony is simply quite happy with minimal accomplishments based on minimal effort. Being the third born and a male in this Italian family may have empowered his sense of entitlement via his ability to get others to do for him because he was smaller and younger.

12. By being tall, athletic, and good looking, Anthony gained significance without effort. Rather than working to foster relationships, he may have simply felt entitled to them. In intimate relationships, Anthony may be rather unskilled, yet sensitive to

the fact that the relationship is not going well. He may not have an appreciation for the fact that he must foster relationships and that when they do not go well—that is, do not go the way that he wants—he forces the issues via hostility and aggression in attempting to get what he wants.

13. If Anthony wants his family to be a healthy one, he needs to better tolerate imperfection in others and accept the responsibility for earning a living. This will require him to be more tolerant of authority figures.

14. One means of connecting effectively with Anthony is to "talk his language." Kopp and Eckstein (2004) suggest that this may be best accomplished through the use of client-generated metaphors. There are at least seven identifiable metaphors that were embedded in the case study: "rage spills over;" "has reached a crescendo," "uses his voice as a weapon," "it just 'takes him' by surprise;" "waiting is torture," "guilt 'triggers' anger;" and "let my guard down." Any one of these can serve as a framework for a focused discussion about Anthony's psychological movement. "How is waiting torturous?" What is it like to feel tortured?" "Are there ways to avoid being tortured?" and so on.

15. It is important to focus on Anthony's strengths rather than his pathology. "One's problems are often the result of the solutions attempted in the past that have failed. Instead of looking for new solutions, the individual continues to behave in a way that adds to the problem . . ." (Milliren, Newbauer, & Evans, 2003, p. 130). By focusing on strengths, Anthony can be encouraged to try new things, building on the assets that are already in his possession. For example, Anthony commented, "I put myself through college." This indicates that he can be proactive on his behalf and does not have to just be reactive in his approach to life challenges. To help Anthony identify additional strengths, he could be invited to visit the website http://www.authentichappiness.com. This website offers a free questionnaire that helps the person identify "signature strengths." Once identified, Anthony's strengths could be used in homework activities to reinforce a more proactive stance in the world on his part.

CLINICAL ISSUES AND RECOMMENDATIONS

It is important here to be reminded of those elements that might serve to interfere with therapeutic progress. For example, Anthony opts to take the stance of the "victim." This sense of blame or powerlessness may have

276 ANGER-RELATED DISORDERS

derived from his prior abuse, but it does not stop him from being more proactive on his behalf. The therapist should be on the lookout for attitudes and behaviors on Anthony's part that serve to support his "victim state." The fact that he seeks "outside refuge" in female relationships is very likely a symptom of his wanting to be taken care of. It is possible that a caring therapist might easily be seduced into becoming the same sort of refuge, thereby reinforcing, rather than minimizing, Anthony's view of self as victim. It would serve Anthony far better to assist him in developing the psychological muscle to be in charge of his life.

Anthony's personal motto seems to be "only work hard if it's fun." This is further complicated by a belief that "others shouldn't make you do what you don't want to do." Not only is this a factor in Anthony's life, but it may also become a major factor in the therapy process. If Anthony perceives that the therapy is too much work or not enjoyable, he may balk or resist making changes. It may be important for confrontations to be served in a relatively gentle manner so that Anthony actually "hears" what is being said to him. The use of a "force field analysis" strategy in which Anthony is asked to weigh the *rewards* against the *costs* of certain behaviors might allow him to self-discover what is more appropriate. The challenge for the therapist will be to maintain a balance of fun and effort as Anthony works to make changes in his life.

Anthony's attitudes (private logic) may not have been an immediate problem when he was a child (others did for him so he only had to do what was fun). Or, his attitudes may be reasonable conclusions given the events in his history (e.g., the abuse). Nonetheless, they do not work well in relation to adult responsibilities. Effective treatment for Anthony would require that he abandon some old and outdated life assumptions and develop career and interpersonal skills that will make it easier for him to effectively function in an adult world. As Anthony becomes armed with self-understanding and is encouraged to develop the "courage to be imperfect," his situation will appear more and more hopeful. Anthony will discover that he no longer needs his anger to manage his world and will be empowered to move through life with a higher level of social interest.

CHAPTER 13

Assimilative Psychodynamic Psychotherapy: An Integrative Approach to Anger Disorders

Jerry Gold

INTRODUCTION TO THE ASSIMILATIVE PSYCHODYNAMIC PSYCHOTHERAPY APPROACH

Overview of the Model

Assimilative psychodynamic psychotherapy (APP) is an integrative approach that relies heavily on contemporary psychodynamic theories of personality structure, psychopathology, and psychological change while freely incorporating ideas, techniques, and strategies from other models of psychotherapy. This therapy has a primary focus on exploration of unconscious processes, resistances, and developmental issues, as do standard psychodynamic models. However, this model incorporates and encourages periods of active, integrative intervention in cognitive, behavioral, emotional, and interpersonal events in a way that is alien to the majority of psychodynamic therapies (Gold & Stricker, 2001; Stricker & Gold, 2005).

APP has been described as "assimilative" (Messer, 1992; Stricker & Gold, 1996) because of the parallel to the descriptions of the processes of assimilation and accommodation in cognitive psychology. In APP a single theoretical structure is maintained, but techniques from other approaches are incorporated within that structure. As these "foreign" interventions are used within the original theoretical framework, the meaning, impact, and utility of those techniques are changed in powerful ways. In proposing the concept of assimilative integration, Messer (1992) argued that all psychological variables must be understood within, and are defined by, their interpersonal, historical, and physical context. Therapeutic interventions are complex interpersonal actions that are defined by the larger context of the therapy. A cognitive method such as cognitive restructuring will mean something entirely different to, and have a different impact on, a client whose current psychotherapy has been conducted within a psychodynamic framework than it will to a client in traditional cognitive therapy.

Active interventions are drawn from other psychotherapies for two simultaneous purposes. The first is the typical use of that technique in its "home" (original) psychotherapy. Cognitive methods are used to change thinking, behavioral methods to modify behavior, and so on. The second purpose is an outgrowth of the immediate psychodynamic status of the therapy. The therapist selects a technique for its hypothesized impact on some important psychodynamic issue that may not be accessible to traditional psychodynamic intervention. The meaning and impact of this active intervention have been changed. It retains its original purpose and effect while being assimilated into the repertoire of psychodynamically effective techniques. As an example, many clients become bogged down in therapy while exploring symptoms such as phobias. It is often the case that the search for the unconscious meaning of a phobia yields repetitive and dryly intellectual material that does not move the therapy along or offer symptomatic relief. The APP therapist may then suggest a behavioral technique such as desensitization for two purposes: (1) to reduce the severity and impact of the phobia (the original, behavioral purpose) and (2), at the psychodynamic level, to resolve the defensive and resistive impact of the symptom on further psychodynamic exploration. It is often the case that successful reduction of anxiety symptoms allows the client to understand the meaning and origin of those symptoms in a fresh and affectively alive way and to be able to better explore the defensive role of the symptom, as well as to gain new insights into the unconscious processes that were defended against by this symptom (a point made by Freud as early as 1914, when he suggested that psychoanalysts must compel phobic clients to face the objects of their fears).

This process of therapeutic and theoretical assimilation is accompanied by accommodation. Intervening actively in a client's cognitive activities, behavior, affect, and interpersonal engagements changes the meaning and felt impact of prior and subsequent psychodynamic exploration and of the theory that guides that work. Psychodynamic ideas, styles, and interventions are redefined and experienced differently in this integrative system as compared with traditional psychoanalytic therapies. Exploration, inquiry, and interpretation, the hallmarks of psychodynamic practice, are expanded in their range of applicability, in the ways that they can be achieved, and in their impact on the client. The therapist can now suggest the use of any active intervention to reach psychodynamic goals. Insight no longer is the exclusive mechanism of change, and action no longer is separated from insight into unconscious processes.

Background of the Approach

Attempts to synthesize the sectarian models or schools of psychotherapy date back to the 1930s, although it was not until the 1980s that these efforts grew into the subdiscipline that we now know as psychotherapy integration (Gold, 1996). The first such study was French's report (1933) that psychoanalysis had to account for, and to make use of, the findings of the behavioral laboratory and of learning theorists. Another highly influential work was the book *Psychoanalytic Therapy*, by Alexander and French (1946). They studied the possibility of psychotherapeutic change arising from a multiplicity of interactive and technical factors and introduced the concept of the "corrective emotional experience." This experience was defined as an interactive event between therapist and client in which the attitudes, emotions, and behavior of the therapist were assumed to change unconscious assumptions and perceptions that were derived from the client's early development and interpersonal history. This idea expanded the psychoanalyst's role from the exclusive provision of insight via interpretation to include also behavioral interaction and the provision of new experience as valid therapeutic endeavors.

Dollard and Miller (1950) attempted to translate psychoanalytic theory into the language and methods of learning theory. Their work was poorly received by their peers but was rediscovered decades later and greatly influenced the thinking of later integrationists. In the 1960s and 1970s a number of creative psychotherapists began to demonstrate that psychodynamic therapy and behavior therapy were not incompatible and could be integrated successful. Examples of this work include that conducted by Beier (1966), who argued that unconscious processes responded to operant conditioning and reinforcement in ways that were true to Skinner's observations, and that done by Feather and Rhodes (1972), whose "Psychodynamic Behavior Therapy" reflected the combination of psychoanalytic understanding with the methods of systematic desensitization.

Most authors credit Wachtel (1977) with establishing the field as a legitimate and popular subdiscipline within psychotherapy with the publication of his book *Psychoanalysis and Behavior Therapy: Toward an Integration.* Wachtel (1977) introduced the sophisticated integrative theory of cyclical psychodynamics, which advanced the viewpoint that unconscious motives, fantasies, and representations of the self and of others were embedded in, and frequently are products of, the person's ongoing interpersonal relationships and behavior. He posited that these psychodynamic variables can be modified therapeutically via traditional insight-oriented interpretation as well as active interventions drawn from the repertoire of behavior therapy, family systems therapy, and gestalt therapy.

The publication of this book heralded a period of time in which psychotherapy integration "came of age" (Arkowitz, 1991) and in which many new models were described. A review of the factors that have promoted an interest in integration within the field of psychotherapy (Norcross & Newman, 1992) revealed the following:

1. The ever-increasing number of schools of psychotherapy
2. The lack of unequivocal scientific support for superior efficacy of any single psychotherapy
3. The failure of any theory to completely explain and predict pathology or personality and behavioral change
4. The rapid growth in the varieties and importance of short-term, focused psychotherapies
5. Greater communication between clinicians and scholars that has resulted in increased willingness to, and opportunity for, experimentation
6. The effects of the grim realities of third-party support for long-term psychotherapies
7. Identification of common factors in all psychotherapies that are related to outcome
8. Growth of professional organizations, conferences, and journals that are dedicated to the exploration of psychotherapy integration

Most discussions of psychotherapy integration (Norcross & Goldfried, 2005) have identified four types or modes of contemporary psychotherapy integration: technical eclecticism, common factors integration, theoretical integration, and assimilative integration.

Technical eclecticism is the most clinical and technically oriented form of psychotherapy integration, and it involves the least attention to the integration of concepts and theories. It is closely related to what generally is called eclectic psychotherapy and can be approached in a very disciplined and coherent manner as well as in a more idiosyncratic form. A broad and comprehensive assessment of the client leads to the selection of clinical strategies and techniques from two or more therapies that may be used sequentially or in combination. Perhaps the most influential version is multimodal therapy (Lazarus, 2005).

Common factors integration starts from the identification of specific effective ingredients of any group of therapies. This approach builds on Rosenzweig's finding (1936) that all therapies share certain change processes, despite their allegiance to particular methods and theories, and also builds on Frank's cross-cultural studies (1961) of various systems of healing. Therapists who work within this perspective therefore aim to identify which of the several known common factors will be most important in the treatment of each individual. Once the most clinically significant common factors are selected, the therapist reviews the spectrum of techniques and psychotherapeutic interactions to locate those that have been found to promote and contain those ingredients. Garfield's common factors–based integrative therapy (2000), which relies on insight, exposure, the provision of new experience, and the provision of hope through the therapeutic relationship, is one well-known form of common factors integration.

Theoretical integration yields a new system of psychotherapy that is the result of the amalgamation of two or more models of personality and psychopathology and the model-specific techniques that produce such psychological change. These integrative theories explain behavior, psychological experience, and interpersonal relationships in multidirectional and interactional terms, investigating the mutual influence of environmental, motivational, cognitive, and affective variables.

Theoretical integration greatly expands the vision and understanding of the therapist when attempting to work with any individual and allows problems at one level or in one sphere of psychological life to be addressed in formerly incompatible ways. That is, the therapist might intervene in a problem in affect tolerance not only to help the client become more comfortable emotionally but to promote change in motivation or to rid the client of a way of thinking about emotion that maintained powerful unconscious feelings. Wachtel's cyclical psychodynamic theory (1977) and its integrative therapy was the first fully developed form of theoretical integration.

Assimilative integration is the fourth and most recently described mode of psychotherapy integration. The premises of this type of integration were described earlier. Another example of assimilative integration, but one that uses a cognitive-behavioral framework as its "home" theory, is cognitive-behavior assimilative integration (Castonguay et al., 2005).

Basic Concepts and Assumptions of the Model

The APP model is based on an expanded version of psychodynamic theory that has been identified as the "three-tier" model of personality structure and change (Stricker & Gold, 1988). These tiers refer respectively to overt behavior (tier 1); conscious cognition, affect, perception, and sensation (tier 2); and unconscious mental processes, motives, conflicts, images, and representations of significant others (tier 3). APP shares with traditional psychoanalytic models a theoretical and clinical emphasis on the exploration of this last sphere of experience. However, the therapist is free to use the complex and multidetermined interconnections between different levels of experience. In this system the therapist recognizes behavior and consciousness as levels of psychological life that are spheres of important work in themselves, unlike traditional psychoanalysis, which treats behavior and conscious experience as superficial phenomena and as clinically relevant only in symbolizing underlying issues.

The three-tier model posits that psychological causation is multidirectional, and it is the interactions of unconscious motivation, conscious experience, action, and the impact of the behavior and attitudes of significant others to which the therapist must attend. The unidimensional theories of change that are typical of most sectarian schools of psychotherapy must be replaced by a multidirectional, circular model (Gold, 1996; Stricker & Gold, 1988). Change begins and can take place within and between any of the three tiers of psychological life. Within the expanded psychodynamic framework of this approach, it is understood that insight can be the cause of change, can be the result of new experiences and ways of adaptation, or may be a moderator variable that promotes the effects of other change processes. Often, it is difficult, if not impossible, to identify the places of insight and active interventions in the causal chain of events that preceded a client's gains.

This model includes a strong emphasis on interpersonal relationships and on the ways in which ongoing interactions with significant others are shaped by variables that can be located in any of the tiers. That is, current interactions with others, and pathogenic patterns of thought and perception, are assumed to be motivated, skewed, and limited by unconscious representations, motives, conflicts, and images. Yet, problematic thinking and troubling interpersonal relationships patterns often express and stabilize unconscious conflicts and representations and prevent interpretive work from being completely effective. These issues, which reflect the immediate impact of others in the client's life, serve to channel the client's actions down well-worn, familiar paths and to maintain the character of the client's unconscious processes.

Mechanisms of Change

The APP model of psychotherapy is positioned firmly within but expands the traditional, insight-oriented framework of psychoanalysis. An expanded and better articulated grasp of the unconscious meanings of one's life experience, an understanding of the impact of intrapsychic conflict, and an enhanced appreciation for the ways in which we unwittingly repeat our histories and find our parents and significant others in current relationships often contributes to psychological freedom, to a more stable and effective sense of identity and self-esteem, and to a lessening of anxiety, depression, and other symptoms. This expansion and exploration of unconscious meaning and representations is accomplished in typical psychodynamic ways: through a detailed inquiry into past and present relationships, fantasies, dreams, behavior, and feelings and through the step-by-step accumulation of hypotheses and inferences about the connections between past and present, intrapsychic and interpersonal, desire and fear, that eventually leads to clarification and interpretation. Historical insight and interactional insight operate in a mutually influential way. Awareness of the role of the past in shaping the present help the client attain greater understanding of her or his current interactions and the ways in which these relationships keep the past alive (Wachtel, 1977).

The differences between this type of therapy and traditional psychoanalytic psychotherapy emerge most significantly when exploration and insight do not achieve their desired ends, in that an exploratory, interpretative approach does not reach or affect certain conflicts, meanings, or other (tier 3) psychodynamic issues. Clients often need to learn new skills or to leave behind maladaptive ways of coping in order to change unconscious meanings and processes. These intrapsychic variables can have enormous staying power in the face of interpretation and insight. Exposure to a feared situation, experience, or emotion can lead to the discovery of new meanings, memories, and conflicts, which neither the client nor the therapist had learned about through standard psychodynamic technique.

A second central change process is the new, ameliorative experience provided by the therapeutic relationship. This is a necessary and sometimes sufficient source of change at all three tiers of experience. A safe, supportive, and mutative interpersonal experience with the therapist allows the client to face the challenges of psychodynamic exploration, as well as to make use of active cognitive, behavioral, interpersonal, and emotional interventions.

The therapeutic relationship is understood to be a unique interpersonal situation in which the client's inner representational world, psychodynamic conflicts, cognitive processes, character traits, interpersonal style, and range of emotional experiences are displayed and are observed and experienced in vivo by the therapist. This experience can present difficulties for the therapist, however. For example, the therapist might find that the client's history, psychodynamics, cognitive limitations, and interpersonal style are exerting pressure on him or her to respond to the client as most others in the client's life have done and will continue to do. It is at this time, though, that the therapist must figure out how to respond benignly and supportively in order to encourage growth, change, and exploration of new intrapsychic and interpersonal possibilities.

As the client feels accepted, secure, and understood in the context of therapy, he or she is more willing and better able to take chances, to question assumptions, and to face painful affects, situations, and internal states. As Bowlby (1980) described, exploration is possible only when one has a secure base of attachment figures to whom to return. Most clients seem to be lacking in this foundation. If the therapist can supply a substitute for this lack, the task of psychotherapy can proceed more confidently and with a much greater chance of success. Many times, success in working with a concrete problem, such as a lack of assertive skills or with dysfunctional cognitions, translates in a deeper way to new perceptions of the therapist and to changes in the therapeutic alliance.

New experience with the therapist often produces change at all three tiers of experience. New ways of thinking or acting with the therapist that are tried and met with acceptance and approval are likely to be experimented with outside of therapy. At a deeper level (tier 3), the therapist's (perhaps) unanticipated positive reaction can go a long way to correct powerful, unconscious images of the self and of others that have been maintained by the client's fears, inhibitions, and/or by interpersonal responses that are ambiguous or as negative as the client had anticipated.

The assimilative nature of this therapy suggests that change processes not usually associated with a psychoanalytically oriented psychotherapy can be relied on to reach the goal of psychodynamic and structural change. So, this therapy might include the change processes of exposure and extinction, the development of new interpersonal skills, cognitive/perceptual change, resolution of unfinished business, increased acceptance and tolerance of emotion, and systemic change, along with and alongside of psychodynamic insight. Often, as has already been suggested, these cognitive, behavioral, experiential, and systemic factors are necessary for their own sake as well as for their role in enhancing psychodynamic exploration and change.

An assimilative shift might be helpful when the client is unable to work within a psychodynamic framework, either at the beginning of therapy or at any point during it. This can occur because the client is relatively unsophisticated, is concrete in his or her thinking, or is threatened by the idea of reconnecting to disavowed experiences and events. A positive therapeutic alliance can be established initially with such persons by beginning the therapy with more immediately accessible tasks and processes, such as those that are typical of cognitive therapy. Similarly, a therapeutic alliance that has been strained or ruptured by distress that is caused by psychodynamic inquiry or by the resistance and transference issues that have emerged through that process can be put back on a positive footing by a shift to a less stressful and more immediately accessible therapeutic procedure. Thus, these techniques are used to help deal with the immediate problems for which they were designed at the levels of behavior and cognition, and at the same time, they can contribute to indirect but powerful work at a more unconscious, psychodynamic level. The therapist can come to be thought of as trustworthy, or this trust can be re-established and interfering anxieties, resistances, and transferences can be managed and resolved without having to be addressed directly.

Most psychoanalytic therapists have experienced, to their chagrin, the limits of interpretation and of insight in correcting powerful psychological representation of other people in the client's life as uncaring, unavailable, hostile, and punitive. In fact, continued interpretation of these issues sometimes becomes repetitive of the original, hurtful experiences. It was for this reason that Alexander and French (1946) added the idea of the corrective emotional experience to psychoanalytic therapy. An assimilative shift can resonate deeply with a client and can powerfully effect and change his or her unconscious representation if its meaning is positive and different from what is expected from others. The therapist who offers a useful and effective way of dealing with life events also is creating an interaction that may correct experience of neglect, rejection, or abuse and one that may become the kernel of new, more benign and deserving self and object representations that cannot be established through interpretative means.

Assimilative shifts can be extremely helpful when the client and therapist are caught in the throes of an enactment (Levenson, 1983). This refers to the type of therapeutic interaction in which the client unwittingly repeats the type of interaction that in part was responsible for his or her pathology. In these situations, the therapist is in some ways transformed into a figure from the client's past and the client responds automatically. There are instances of enactment in which recognition of the enactment and interpretation of it are sufficient for its resolution. At other times, insight and interpretation are unsuccessful. This seems to reflect the client's immersion in the process and his or her inability to recognize the current interaction as a repetition. At such times, the introduction of cognitive, behavioral, or interpersonal techniques can be used to target some component of the problematic interaction (say, perhaps, a lack of assertiveness on the client's part). As the client gains these new skills, he or she often gains a new perspective on the immediate therapeutic interaction and is more able to recognize what has been repeated and *then* to engage in the necessary psychodynamic exploration of that repetition.

Exposure has been identified as a central change process in most forms of psychotherapy, including psychoanalysis (Gold, 1996). As the client makes repeated contact with unconscious wishes and fantasies that are anxiety provoking, an extinction process occurs. However, many sources of anxiety cannot be reached through insight and interpretation alone, because the client's behavioral and cognitive strategies are aimed, consciously and unconsciously, toward the avoidance of situations in which anxiety and other sorts of psychic pain might be experienced. In these instances, the therapist might suggest a behavioral or cognitive exercise that would maximize the possibility of exposure to situations, cognitions, emotions, and unconscious issues that stimulate anxiety and thus offer the opportunity for exposure and extinction at all levels.

Another way to think about the last point is that the integration of cognitive, experiential, systemic, and behavioral interventions expands the range of ways in which the therapist can work with defenses and resistances and with issues that are perceived by the client to be too threatening or too deeply part of his or her reality or for which the client is unprepared. Modes of adaptation that worked in the past but have since ceased to be effective, should objectively be abandoned. However, many clients experience these adaptive mechanisms as the only, or the best, that are available.

A final occasion for an assimilative shift occurs when "neurotic accomplices" (Wachtel, 1977) make their impact felt in the therapy. This term refers to the frequent clinical finding that as the client changes, the important people in his or her life "push back" and try to maintain or reinstate the status quo. Many clients are involved in relationships in which a significant person feels threatened, hurt, or disadvantaged by progress and do their best to get the client to revert to old ways of behaving. At times, exploration of these experiences is sufficient to stabilize and support the client's ongoing efforts at changing. However, some clients fear that they have more to lose in these relationships than they have to gain in therapy, and the treatment therefore bogs down or is abandoned.

These experiences have an impact that goes beyond the immediate interpersonal situation. The unsupportive, disappointed, or disapproving response of a significant other may elicit and reinforce the client's pathological ideas and negative self and object representations, thus reproducing early traumatic developmental experiences. The therapist may, at these times, suggest behavioral and system interventions aimed at helping the client cope with, manage, and master the influence of these "accomplices." In doing so, the client may achieve a new and more satisfying equilibrium in his or her relationships and, at the same time, may have new and positive experiences that become the stuff out of which new patterns of thinking and of unconscious representations are constructed.

Critical Review of Empirical Evidence

APP is exclusively based on clinical experience and has not been examined empirically. This section addresses research about APP and reviews certain existing studies of related forms of integrative psychotherapy that may indirectly address the issue of research support for the current model. The discussion that follows is based on the reviews presented in Stricker and Gold (2002, 2005), wherein the relevance of research findings for this model of psychotherapy were presented in detail.

Any discussion of empirical testing of a particular form of psychotherapy must address its effectiveness and specificity. What is the relative efficacy of this therapy when compared with its component therapies (psychodynamic, cognitive-behavioral, or experiential) or to any other systems of psychotherapy? Should it be found that this integrative approach is more efficacious than its individual components, then we must try to identify those specific psychological characteristics and client populations for which it is most suited. An investigation of the degree (if any) of incremental validity gained by this revision of psychodynamic theory must be part of an effective research agenda. Studies of generalizability must be raised and tested. Can we formalize and offer data-driven guidelines for when and how to move from one intervention to the next, or must clinical intuition dictate exclusively? Is the effectiveness of this approach limited to the clinicians who developed it, or will it be equally powerful when conducted by a broader range of therapists? Can the model be taught?

A portion of the psychotherapy research literature may indirectly reflect on the empirical issues raised by this model and contains a number of studies that support the validity of revised psychodynamic formulations when used as the central focus in treatment. Weiss and Sampson and their colleagues at the Mt. Zion psychotherapy project (Weiss & Sampson, 1986) have developed the Plan Formulation Method, a method of conceptualizing each client's central psychodynamics, which provides a formulation of conscious and unconscious goals, pathogenic beliefs and conflictual emotions, their plans for testing those beliefs, and necessary insights. These authors reported a number of studies that validated the use of these formulations in predicting process changes in psychodynamics over the course of psychotherapy. Studies of the core conflictual relationship theme (CCRT; Luborsky & Crits-Cristoph, 1990) have validated the clinical use of expanded psychodynamic formulations similar to those that are typical of this model. The research of Strupp and his colleagues (Strupp, 1993; Strupp & Binder, 1984) also has demonstrated that is it possible to develop valid and replicable psychodynamically informed formulations of a client's clinical issues that can guide the therapist's clinical strategies and interventions. These psychodynamic formulations are organized as the cyclical maladaptive pattern (CMP), a concept that includes a revised view of psychodynamic processes that resembles the expanded psychodynamic perspective of this therapy: Internal variables are assumed both to influence and to be influenced by interpersonal, cognitive, and emotional states through feedback and feed-forward processes.

This body of research also touches on the issues of generalizability and teachability that were noted previously. Each of the three centers involved in the research cited earlier has created an individualized psychotherapy manual that offers any psychotherapist explicit and data-driven guidelines for formulation of the client's problems and current functioning. Studies of the use of these manuals (Luborsky & Crits-Cristoph, 1990; Strupp, 1993; Weiss & Sampson, 1986) found that compliance to the manual can be demonstrated reliably and that the level of compliance was correlated positively with process variables and with outcome. These findings suggest that modified versions of psychodynamic therapy are teachable and generalizable.

The existing research on integrative psychotherapy may indirectly suggest some answers to the questions of efficacy raised by the description of the approach. Research on a form of technical eclecticism, namely prescriptive psychotherapy (Beutler & Hodgson, 1993), and on the stages of change in psychotherapy (Prochaska & DiClemente, 1992), indicated that integrative psychotherapies are more effective than treatments that address one change factor or a single stage of change and are most effective when interventions are matched to the client's immediate clinical needs and psychological state. This point is a central tenet of the current model. There also are reports of clinical trials of psychodynamically informed integrative psychotherapies, similar to the present model that has yielded preliminary but positive results. Klerman et al. (1984) reported that an integrative, interpersonal psychotherapy for depression outperformed medication and other psychological interventions in a number of studies. Ryle (1997) reported that short- and long-term versions of cognitive analytic therapy (CAT) have been found more effective than purely interpretive or behaviorally oriented approaches. This model is an integrative approach that incorporates cognitive and psychoanalytic ideas and methods.

Perhaps the most significant set of studies of integrative psychotherapy were conducted by Shapiro and his colleagues at the Sheffield Psychotherapy Project (e.g., Shapiro & Firth, 1987; Shapiro & Firth-Cozens, 1990). They investigated the clinical impact of two sequences of combined psychodynamic and cognitive-behavioral therapy: dynamic work followed by active intervention or vice versa. The greatest gains were made and the most comfortable experience of treatment was reported by clients in the dynamic-behavioral sequence. Clients in the behavioral-dynamic sequence demonstrated more frequent deterioration in the second phase of the therapy, and this group did not maintain their gains over time as often as did clients in the dynamic-behavioral group. These results are indirectly supportive of this model, in which psychodynamic work usually precedes and prescribes more active interventions.

An Assimilative Psychodynamic Formulation of Anger Disorder

In the APP model, a formulation of any clinical problem or disorder involves assessing that problem or disorder on each of the tiers of psychological functioning. The ultimate goal is to understand and describe the central psychodynamic issues, including disavowed meanings, fantasies, motivations, conflicts, internal prohibition, and representations of self and of others in relation to the client's conscious cognition, imagery, perceptions, and feelings and in the context of his or her ways of relating to others and of adapting to the world. Among the more crucial issues contained in this formulation are the meeting points of the three tiers and the ways in which processes in one tier affect and maintain processes in another. So, the formulation must contain some description of the way the client's characteristic style of interacting with significant others interferes with or promotes efforts to change conscious thoughts and unconscious meanings and motivations; in addition, it should describe the ways in which dysfunctional thoughts are produced by and in turn reinforce unconscious patterns of representing self and other. This multidirectional formulation resembles the profiles created in more explicitly cognitive-behaviorally oriented psychotherapies, such as the BASIC ID profile favored by Lazarus (2005) in his multimodal therapy. The greatest difference is in this model's explicit addition of the third tier, which is concerned with unconscious meanings and processes.

An anger disorder is a complex psychological and interpersonal construct that refers to the behavior, experience, and inner life of a person who acts in a threatening and/or violent way or who gets "too" angry on a verbal or physical basis more frequently than society deems appropriate. A client with an anger disorder would be understood to be afflicted with a lack of behavioral options (tier 1) other than verbal or physical displays of anger or violence. These behaviors would be seen as being stimulated by a number of dysfunctional thoughts (tier 2) about the self and about others, which would cluster around issues of hurt, humiliation, loss, and vulnerability. Such a person is prone to interpreting the actions of others in a very personalized way, in which small slights, frustration, and disappointment register as major wounds to the person's self-esteem and self-worth. He or she harbors readily activated ideas about being disrespected and disregarded. Emotions such as fear, guilt, shame, and embarrassment dominate the client's affective life. These painful feelings usually are very poorly tolerated, and they are often interpreted as further evidence of the reality of the injury to his or her sense of self that provoked the dysfunctional thinking. At the level of unconscious processes (tier 3), most clients with anger disorders perceive themselves to be vulnerable to psychological injury in close relationships and view other persons as undependable and hostile.

Emotional closeness, interpersonal availability, and openness are construed as highly dangerous, and exposure to the selfish, hateful, exploitative, and abusive wishes and needs of others leads the client to perceive the self as unlovable and as unworthy of love. The arousal of a desire for interpersonal contact and intimacy also activates corresponding self-images that reflect the client's sense of himself or herself as being unworthy of love, as lacking the necessary personal attributes that would garner respect from others, and as being damaged or intrinsically undesirable as a human being. Most, if not all, of these self and object images are derived from hurtful or traumatic developmental experiences with parents and other significant persons. As the client tries to cling to more positive developmental memories, the formative, hurtful interactions are repressed or disavowed or they are recalled but their meaning and impact are rationalized or denied. The client also is plagued by feelings of longing for love and acceptance, which often are so powerful that they come to be felt as cravings. These feelings are much too anxiety provoking for the client to easily recognize and to consciously accept and are disavowed or are experienced in psychologically disguised and indirect ways.

Any psychoanalytically oriented formulation of an anger disorder must recognize that the many hurts in the client's early life have inevitably left their mark in the form of rageful, even murderous, feelings and intentions toward those most implicated in those traumatic experiences. These urges, feelings, and wishes often remain dissociated from the client's awareness. When they are known, they typically exist in an intellectualized and isolated state, wherein the client cannot find a way to acknowledge the importance and ongoing psychological impact of these issues or to alleviate or work through these conflicts and memories.

Finally, what may be lurking "behind" all of these other issues are profound sadness and grief over past events, for all of the loving experiences that were sullied or lost, and for the many missed opportunities in the client's adult life that were caused by fear and anger. These feelings often are accompanied by guilt over the ways in which the client's outbursts of anger or violence have hurt those who he or she has tried to love. These guilty feelings and memories usually are very poorly tolerated and thus remain defended again.

How do all of these issues in the three tiers relate to and impact on one another? Seemingly insignificant slights and hurts in the client's current relationships (tier 1) may connect to and activate the unconscious issues (tier 3) described earlier that are typical of the turbulent unconscious mental life of the client with an anger disorder. That is, a small event may trigger a deeply felt and precariously dissociated constellation of painful memories, self and object images, conflictual feelings, and motivations. The client will rarely be aware of these processes but instead will become preoccupied with familiar thoughts and images of being disregarded, disrespected, shamed, and so on. This two-pronged dysfunctional construal of the interaction magnifies its meaning and impact by some very large factor. The client is left with no subjective choice other than to defend his or her threatened sense of honor or self-worth by going on the offensive, behaviorally and verbally. The interpersonal response of the other person (e.g., fear, withdrawal, escalation) may briefly alleviate the distress felt by the client, but at the same time, it will eventually confirm the client's pathological thinking and basic, unconscious construal of the dangers of interpersonal contact.

Current interactions with others (tier 1) are, at various times, independent and dependent variables in the circular psychological processes that produce and maintain his or her psychopathology. Present-day patterns of angry or violent interaction are motivated, skewed, and limited by unconscious perceptions, motives, conflicts, and images (tier 3), yet these interaction patterns can often reinforce dysfunctional thinking and representational structures. When clients with anger disorder establish and continue relationships, they often unwittingly chose partners who are very much like significant people from their past, or these partners are transformed into replicas of past partners because of the client's aggression and violence. The distance, defensiveness, and hostility exhibited by a friend, spouse, or child may be the result of the client's ongoing hostility. The client may not see this connection and instead will interpret these interpersonal responses as confirmation of the conscious patterns of thought and of the unconscious images of self and other that are implicated in the disorder. Similarly, one's conscious thinking and perception (tier 2) exist in an ongoing, circular, and mutually reinforcing interaction with the client's enduring patterns of relating to others and with his or her more unconscious ways of constructing meaning. Finally, each client's set of character traits, enduring patterns of adapting to the interpersonal world, and patterns of thought and perception limits the chance for new interaction with others and for change at all levels.

THE CASE OF ANTHONY

Case Conceptualization

Anthony is a middle-aged man who has suffered from the effects of abuse, neglect, and loneliness through most of his life. His self-esteem and sense of self-worth are very poor and very vulnerable, and the behavioral strategies that he has used all of his adult life to shore up his self-esteem and to protect himself from feeling the full brunt of his narcissistic injuries have stopped working; in fact, they are adding to his poor opinion of himself. That is, the angry and aggressive outbursts that he has used to get his way, to intimidate others, and to provide a cover for his wounded pride have become an additional source of guilt and shame, acting to confirm and reinforce his deficits in self-esteem.

In applying the three-tier model of personality functioning to this case, it is clear that at tier 1 (overt behavior and interpersonal interactions), Anthony has a very limited repertoire of problem-solving skills and has accompanying deficits in communication and interpersonal cooperation. His chronic problems in managing his emotions and his lack of ability to interact sensitively and maturely with his family have caused Anthony to lose the warmth and comfort that he obtained in the past at home. The emotional distance that now exists between Anthony and his wife and daughters worsens his chronic sense of deprivation, loss, and worthlessness, making him prone to more angry outbursts.

These problems are compounded by a number of cognitive issues (tier 2) that provoke his behavioral problems, are reinforced by those outbursts, and are interwoven with central psychodynamic issues that are discussed later. Anthony thinks of himself as a failure and has many educational, occupational, financial, and relational experiences that can serve as hard evidence for the validity of those thoughts. He apparently has little ability to understand and to empathize with the needs and feelings of others, thus making his relationships one-sided and adding to his difficulties and interpersonal conflicts. He also seems to lose his sense of separateness from others, so he takes on their failures and pain as his own.

Anthony also seems to suffer from what might be described as gaps in his ability to think and from failures to anticipate his reactions to troubling situations. For example, when he became angered at his team, he was unable to think about his emotional reaction and therefore could not slow it down or modulate it. He goes from hurtful event to angry behavioral response without the mediating factors of reality testing, judgment, consideration of alternative interpretations and meanings, and choice of behavioral outcomes. Similarly, Anthony does not seem to know which situations are too "hot" for him and should be understood to be potentially evocative of a loss of control. His history tells us, but apparently does not tell Anthony, that sports are a loaded issue for him, very likely to stimulate images, memories, and feeling connected with his disappointed ambitions, his father's disappointment in him, and other painful interactions. Anthony is not prepared for the stimulation of these issues in the present moment of the game, and as a result, his coping skills are taxed beyond their capacity.

At the level of unconscious psychodynamic processes and representations (tier 3), Anthony remains an abused, exploited, and rejected child who has not come to terms with his mother's inability to love him, his father's disappointment in his inability to live up to his father's expectations, and his parents' failure to protect him from abuse at the hands of his uncle. The abuse itself is, of course, a significant and unresolved source of pain and conflict in Anthony's psychological life, as is his parents' more recent inability to respond appropriately to his disclosure of that abuse. Anthony has much to work on at this level. He has not dealt with the pain, shame, loss, and anger that are associated with his childhood familial experiences, and he denies the impact of the abuse, although his worries about its effects on him suggest that the denial is slipping. Anthony has little, if any, insight into the rapidity with which his internal world of self and object images is activated when he is frustrated, hurt, and disappointed. Despite his lack of awareness of this process, it is easy to hypothesize that Anthony's rageful outbursts are directed at persons and experiences from the past, which are carried in relatively unmodified form in his inner world.

Anthony's problematic functioning at any one tier interacts with his functioning in the other tiers, resulting in circular, mutually provocative, and reinforcing feedback loops. To understand these pathways, Anthony should look at the recent incident on the softball field and consider the event that he identified as most troubling to him. Anthony lashes out at his wife and his daughters when he feels hurt by them, particularly when he construes their attitudes and behavior as shaming, insulting, or humiliating him. This seems to have been the case in the coaching situation that he described, in which his team's "lack of competitive drive" prompted Anthony to become verbally abusive and to throw a baseball bat.

Anthony was unable to separate his sense of self from his perceptions of his daughters and what he assumed to be were negative, critical attitudes on the part of the spectators toward the team, and thus toward him. If his daughters could be seen as not trying hard enough, he, Anthony, was sure to be seen as a foolish failure. Anthony attempted to rid himself of the awful, painful feelings of worthlessness, shame, and embarrassment by attacking the team members and then by throwing the bat. This was an action that had meaning at all three tiers. It exemplifies his lack of control over his emotions, his poor communication skills, and his limited conflict negotiation skills. Cognitively, this event was prompted by his perceptions and thought about being a failure, his difficulties in understanding the motivations and behavior of the girls on his team, and his lack of skill in soothing himself cognitively and emotionally. Finally, this outburst reflected a rapid and deep psychological regression in which Anthony was confronted yet again by the "ghosts" of past hurts and rejections, which lurk in his internal unconscious world. His anger and destructive behavior symbolized his wish to expel and project his pain outwardly and to prove wrong those figures (his grandmother and parents) that had found him unlovable and a failure and also expressed the urge to hurt and punish those persons, past and present, who had made him this vulnerable and fragile.

Initiations and Framing Treatment

The beginning of the therapy is a critical time for most clients and is especially critical for Anthony. He was motivated to start psychotherapy at the age of 48 because his current behavior was frightening him, but the trials and travails of the process of psychotherapy easily could come to outweigh his concerns about his everyday behavior, thus causing a premature end to the treatment.

Establishing an enduring, positive, and trusting therapeutic alliance with Anthony would be very difficult, especially for a male therapist. Anthony has had few male friends, and the close relationships he has had with men have ended in estrangement (his father), abuse (his uncle), and loss (his grandfather). Anthony is an extremely sensitive man whose thoughts and feelings about being a failure and a disappointment to others, especially to men with whom he has been close, are easily activated.

Does this suggest then that Anthony would do better with a female therapist? Perhaps, but his track record is not much better with women.

The relationship with a female therapist is likely to be colored by negative transferences from his relationships with his mother and grandmother. His relationships with his wife and oldest daughter suggest that disappointment and distance replace affection and closeness with women as well. In addition, it is possible that a warm, close relationship with a female therapist could activate memories from the "emotional affair" that he perceived as having damaged his marriage.

He does not trust others lightly. How to establish an effective, positively toned therapeutic alliance is a challenge. Alliance issues must be understood rapidly as the therapist conducts the intake, collects history, and builds up a formulation of Anthony's functioning, diagnosis, strengths, and weaknesses. Once this is accomplished, the therapist will judiciously share his or her findings and formulation and will endeavor to establish a therapeutic contract with Anthony. The therapy must be explained clearly, and Anthony's participation must be described in a way that is comprehensible for him. His cooperation as an equal partner must be obtained during the discussion about how and whether to proceed with this form of psychotherapy. It is crucial that Anthony feel that the relationship is built on mutual respect and collaboration, especially at the beginning of therapy. It is just as critical that the therapy not evoke more issues than Anthony can handle at any given time or cause him to feel like a failure because he cannot understand the therapist's ideas or carry out the therapist's suggestions. This means that psychodynamic exploration and interpretation should be kept to a minimum at the beginning and for a good while, because this client clearly is not yet ready to deal with the pain that such work would evoke. In addition, although work at a cognitive level might be indicated and appropriate at the beginning of therapy, it has its own perils. Anthony describes himself as a poor reader, is unhappy because he did not complete college, and seems to harbor doubts about his intelligence. Much traditional cognitive therapy (cf. Beck, 1995) is based on reading and writing. These techniques certainly might get the therapy off on the wrong foot.

Perhaps the most beneficial way to initially work with such a client is to start with concrete behavioral strategies aimed at problems that he or she identifies as desirable. Does Anthony want to learn to slow down his angry responses? Does he wish to challenge (verbally) his thoughts about being a failure? Perhaps the first goal might be to improve his relationship with Jerome. If he picks the problem to be focused on, feels respected in this choice, and goes on with the help of the therapist, then a number of changes may occur. The problem will improve, his sense of effectiveness will be enhanced, and the foundation of a therapeutic alliance will be solidified. These gains will have an impact on Anthony's functioning at all three tiers, no matter where the work begins. At the level of unconscious functioning, he might begin a corrective emotional experience with the therapist and find a positive, respectful bond with a new person that contradicts and serves as an antidote to his enduring ways of representing himself and others. At the cognitive level, any success is the source of a new and more positive way of thinking about himself; at the behavior level, new skills are significant in their own right.

Many interactions of this type will be necessary before the bond with the therapist is strong enough for the therapy to move into a more exploratory, insight-oriented perspective. The therapist must be mindful of Anthony's enduring readiness to feel slighted, hurt, and rejected and of the ease with which negative transference can be activated. The therapist must anticipate, to the best of his or her ability, the degree to which the process of therapy might too severely tax Anthony's ability to cope and must work to regulate the impact of exploration on Anthony's self-esteem.

Treatment Plan

Therapeutic Goals

A number of short-term, intermediate, and long-term goals can be identified. The first and most important short-term goal is, as described previously, the establishment of a viable therapeutic alliance in which Anthony perceives the therapist as benign, accepting, and supportive and in which Anthony feels respected and safe. This relationship is an absolute requirement for any enduring therapeutic work to occur. It requires the management of Anthony's fragile self-esteem, his readiness to perceive and to react to slights and rejections (real or not), and the rapidity with which his internalized images of past, hurtful relationships are activated in the form of negative transferences. A second set of short-term goals is to enhance Anthony's relationships with his family and with his boss, which will stabilize his self-esteem, lessen his sense of loneliness and isolation, and probably lead to more optimism about the therapy and his chances of succeeding.

Intermediate goals are more cognitive and affective in nature. These include work on Anthony's view of himself as a failure; improvement in Anthony's capacities for empathy with and separation from others, his ability to tolerate emotions and rejection, his ability to anticipate interactions in which he might become angered; and an increase in his ability to substitute thought and delay for immediate gratification and action.

The goals that are most long term involve significant changes in Anthony's psychodynamic issues. The therapy would be aimed at assisting Anthony to work through and resolve the multiple traumas of his childhood and family life, including the grief, sadness, and anger connected with the hostility of his grandmother and mother, the losses of his grandfather and father, and the abuse by his uncle. A related goal is to initiate and complete the mourning processes that must occur for Anthony to detach from this painful history, which he carries around psychologically and which is a constant, although unwitting, shadow. The final goal of therapy is to revise his representational structures: His negative images of himself and of those he loved would be tempered by more benign, lovable, and loving images.

Intervention Techniques and Phases of Treatment

The discussion in the previous sections of this chapter foreshadowed the way this integrative therapy might unfold with Anthony. The goals of the therapy will determine the phases of it. The therapy probably would be conducted in six phases, each of which would blend with the previous and successive phase and each of which would allow for other types of intervention as well. These phases are the assessment and initiation phase, the behavioral phase, the cognitive phase, the psychodynamic phase, the interpersonal/systemic phase, and relapse prevention/termination phase.

In the assessment and initiation phase, the work would focus on collecting enough present-day and historical information to allow the therapist to generate the three-tier formulation, as well as on working toward the establishment of a viable therapeutic alliance. Assessment and reformulation are not limited to this phase but will continue throughout all phases of the therapy. Because this is a psychodynamically oriented therapy and explicit psychodynamic exploration may be reserved for a later phase with Anthony, it is likely that the initial formulation of tier 3 issues will undergo substantial revision or expansion as the therapy progresses.

In the second, behavioral, phase, the work would focus on expanding Anthony's behavioral repertoire to find new and more effective ways of expressing and dealing with his hurt, shame, and injured pride. Techniques might include behavior rehearsal, modeling, social skills training, communication training, and any other behavioral intervention that is supported by research or clinical reports to be effective. This phase probably would be intertwined with the third, cognitive, phase in which standard cognitive techniques such as cognitive restructuring, disputation, imagery, and so on, would be employed. Homework would be used in both of these phases, because it is crucial that Anthony try out and practice any new skills and use his experiences as the source of feedback with which to modify what is done within sessions. Interventions in these phases will, if possible, be selected and used for the dual purposes posited by the assimilative model: for their immediate, traditional impact on behavior and on cognition and for their hypothesized impact on the associated psychodynamic processes.

The fourth phase of therapy would be the psychodynamic phase. If the preceding phases have been successful, a good deal of indirect psychodynamic change will already have been accomplished. For example, if Anthony is able to learn to be more empathic and emotionally tied to his family, then these new skills and warm experiences will help modify his enduring image of himself as ineffective and unlovable and his image of others as hurtful and rejecting.

Further work here will conform, in a flexible way, to standard contemporary psychoanalytic practice: a directed inquiry into Anthony's thoughts, feelings, dreams, memories, and fantasies that would eventuate in interpretive work and increased insight into the impact of his development on his current life. The issues that would be explored would include the internalized, disavowed, remnants of his relationships with his grandparents, parents, and his uncle, especially around the abuse and its aftermath.

This phase will be the most difficult to undertake and to continue. As painful memories and experiences are evoked, the therapeutic alliance may be strained and Anthony is likely to become more resistant and balky. A great deal of preparation will be necessary to make this work possible, as will assimilative shifts into more cognitive and behavioral work to ease Anthony's progress through this part of the therapy. Again, these interventions will have two or more purposes. They will be used to help Anthony cope with the anxieties, emotions, and negative thoughts that are generated by the exploration of his past, and as a result, it is hoped that they will generalize to other stressful interpersonal situations, thereby increasing his interaction competence and sense of mastery. At the same time, the relief offered by these active interventions will remind Anthony of the reality of the therapeutic relationship and may help him clear away defenses, resistances, and negative transferences. If this can be accomplished, the psychodynamic work will continue effectively.

A phase of therapy that focuses on interpersonal and systemic issues often is necessary when the client's "neurotic accomplices" interfere with therapeutic progress or respond to the client's improvement in threatening, abandoning, or otherwise undermining ways. Should this be the case for Anthony, it will be necessary to help him develop the skills to limit the impact of these accomplices or perhaps to include such persons (possibly his wife or daughters, for example) in sessions. Often, this phase occurs after the psychodynamic phase, in which profound characterological changes may be apparent. However, the need for this type of work may occur at any point in the therapy and may recur periodically.

The final phase of the therapy is concerned with relapse prevention and with termination. In this part, Anthony and his therapist would practice identifying particular situations and experiences that in the past would have been likely to trigger Anthony's disordered, angry reactions. This phase will be almost identical to the relapse prevention part of standard cognitive-behavior therapy, but it will also include an additional component. Anthony will be prepared to identify and to process those unconscious meanings and conflicts that might be stirred up by an unpleasant exchange, and he will be ready to work at making the discrimination between the present and the past.

When the client and the therapist have agreed that the therapeutic goals have been reached and an acceptable level of relapse prevention skills has been established, termination proper will begin. Anthony has had his share of serious, painful, and injurious losses. The end of the therapeutic relationship, and the consequent limitations on contact with the therapist, may be acceptable to Anthony and at the same time may elicit thoughts, feelings, and conflicts connected with past separations and disappointments. Anthony may unconsciously construe this separation as yet another example of being a disappointment or failure. Relapses may be the outcome of these reactivated experiences. These events and experiences will be discussed as an inevitable part of the therapy and as an opportunity to apply his new skills in the behavioral, cognitive, psychodynamic, and interpersonal spheres of his experience. Termination also will be an opportunity for a corrective emotional experience that might touch on and modify some of Anthony's long-standing, negative unconscious self and object representation. He and the therapist will have the chance to say goodbye and to process and explore the range of feelings and interactions that have occurred, and Anthony may leave with his head held high and with pride in his accomplishments. If this is the case, he will be able to internalize a new, more competent and lovable image of himself in relation to an accepting, encouraging, and proud parent. These images will go a long way to cushion him when he is hurt and stressed in the future.

Therapeutic Process

A session of APP ordinarily is indistinguishable from traditional psychodynamic therapy unless an integrative shift has occurred in that session. Most sessions are typified by relatively free discussion in which the client takes the lead and talks about whatever is on his or her mind. The therapist listens, asks questions, makes occasional empathic comments, and sometimes offers some new information in the form of clarification or interpretation.

Anthony's therapy probably would deviate from this depiction, especially at the beginning. As noted previously, the unstructured, depth-oriented focus of psychodynamic therapy might be too threatening for him. A structured, focused approach with much therapist input and support would be necessary. The beginning and middle parts of the therapy therefore would resemble the process of cognitive-behavior therapy described by such authors as Beck (1995) or Leahy (2003). The sessions would be organized around a mutually determined agenda that was derived from a problem list, homework would be reviewed, new issues brought up, new homework would be generated, and feedback about the session would be obtained. Later in the treatment, after gains had been made in Anthony's behavior and cognitive functioning and after a relatively stable therapeutic alliance had been established, the therapy might shift to a psychodynamically oriented process of exploration and work toward insight.

There will be one process issue that will be of utmost important at all times in the therapy: The therapist must be alert for enactments of Anthony's past relationships and of his unconscious self and object images. That is, the therapist will continually reflect on the state of the interaction to determine whether the discussion or the issues being addressed are too threatening for Anthony or whether the nature and quality of the interaction have come to resemble some past or present injurious interaction. This search for potential and actual enactments is similar to process work in contemporary interpersonal psychoanalysis (Levenson, 1983), as well as to more interpersonally oriented variants of cognitive therapy (Safran & Segal, 1990).

Timeline and Anticipated Outcome

For this therapy to reach a hypothetical state of complete success, a period of 2 to 3 years of once- or twice-a-week sessions would be a minimum requirement. However, most therapies do not have to be completely successful, and because of the circular nature of change that is assumed, even partial success is likely to produce more success down the road.

Anthony would most likely do well with the earlier phases of the therapy, which are more structured and focused on behavior and cognitive change. This is what he wants and needs, and these aspects of his life are more graspable, concrete, and immediately workable. His fear of his own outbursts and unhappiness with his life are motivating factors. As a result, with about 1 year of therapy, he could make significant progress in changing his conscious ideas about himself and his family and in gaining a large measure of control over his behavior.

Beyond that point, the prognosis becomes murky. It is difficult to make guesses about Anthony's ongoing attachment to therapy and his future interest in more psychodynamic work. Some clients naturally move out of the more structured beginning and middle phases of this type of therapy into a more depth-oriented approach because they have been "turned on" to the process of learning about themselves and they want to complete the job of changing and healing as completely as is possible. Others are happy with their interactional and cognitive gains and recognize, consciously or unwittingly, that further work could be the most painful of all and has the most uncertain outcome. In the instance of this latter outcome, the therapist must be happy with whatever psychodynamic change has accrued through indirect, assimilative intervention and must support the client in his or her decision to end therapy. Then the client can leave with an appreciation of the gains made and with the door open for a possible return. Anthony is likely to fall in the second group of clients. Direct work on his psychodynamic issues could be more than he could bear, and who could blame him for that? He has had enough pain in his life, and his decisions about where and when to stop are deserving of respect and consideration. Otherwise, he and the therapist would be involved in an enactment of his relationship with his father, in which he failed to live up to the other person's expectations.

CLINICAL ISSUES AND RECOMMENDATIONS

The APP model of psychotherapy is based on an expanded and flexible theory of personality. A critical assumption contained within this system is that the probability of success is increased when the client's disorder is assessed and is understood in the broadest context that is possible. Those with the same psychological disorder or with equivalent *Diagnostic and Statistical Manual* (DSM-IV) diagnoses often present unique clinical difficulties and strengths and live in interpersonal networks that may support or hinder progress in therapy in very different ways. The advantage of the three-tier model is its comprehensiveness and its ability to be applied intrapsychically at conscious and subconscious levels, at the level of overt behavior and interpersonal interaction, and at the broader level of the social context. This model allows the therapist to make use of data from the person's history and his or her current life, and it does not privilege any source of data or any type of intervention. However, this model is not useful in the service of prescriptive matching of problem or diagnosis and specific interventions, nor is it useful in the current trend toward manualization of psychotherapies. This version of psychotherapy is highly idiographic and can be usefully applied only when an individualized formulation has been made.

As has been suggested throughout this chapter, this approach places heavy demands on the client and on the therapist, particularly because psychodynamic issues are brought into the process and the therapeutic interaction encourages enactment of past interpersonal difficulties.

This suggests that this therapy is not for everyone. Clients whose presenting complaints lend them to a good prognosis with a more immediately pragmatic and shorter form of therapy should be offered or should be referred to that form. However, when clinical assessment indicates that the client's disorder is reflective of a larger and more entrenched, personality-based complex of motivational, cognitive, behavioral, and systemic factors, then this psychotherapy may ultimately prove to be most advantageous.

CHAPTER 14

Multiple Perspectives on the Conceptualization and Treatment of Anger-Related Disorders

Eva L. Feindler and Alison Byers

INTRODUCTION: A REVIEW OF THE TREATMENT APPROACHES

Chapters written in response to the case of Anthony reveal a wide range of conceptualizations and perspectives on effective interventions. Clearly, it is difficult to fully understand a clinical theoretical orientation from a single case application. This final chapter is an attempt to view the various approaches to treatment simultaneously and to compare them along certain dimensions.

Clinicians across orientations agree that positive therapy outcomes stem from the additive effects of common factors and theory-specific factors. Independent of orientation, therapy is characterized by a process between at least two individuals, therapist and client, who develop a trusting relationship, examine the nature of the presenting problems, and then create more adaptive and successful ways of responding. The importance of the therapeutic alliance is clear in all approaches, as is the need for collaboration between the therapist and the client in delineating treatment goals and evaluating progress. This chapter compares major clinical dimensions of each approach, although some aspects are emphasized in one but not another hypothetical treatment plan.

After reviewing all the treatment chapters and considerable discussion, we decided on several key variables to emphasize in the comparison of different theoretical orientations. Each intervention approach was examined in terms of case conceptualization, treatment formulation, and application to the case of Anthony. This chapter provides a comparison of goals of treatment, hypothesized mechanisms of change, and technical differences in the form and organization of the therapy itself across the eight treatment chapters. Furthermore, the nature of the therapeutic relationship, as well as its role in treatment outcome, is discussed and appears to be a critical variable in every approach. Our choice of dimensions along which to compare theoretical clinical orientations may not be complete; however, it will help readers to examine both similarities and differences. The psychopharmacology chapter, because it does not represent a stand-alone treatment in the case of Anthony, was not included in the comparison of perspectives, nor did we include a comparison of empirical investigations of the various theoretical orientations. Available data are presented in each individual chapter.

Case Conceptualization

Psychoanalytic Therapy

Psychoanalytic therapy combines the intrapsychic conflict and deficit models to conceptualize anger displays as repetitions of past conflicts and defensive efforts to deny vulnerability. Because of the family history of relational deprivation, rejection, and maltreatment, Anthony is characterized by patterns reflecting an insecure and disorganized attachment style with narcissistic vulnerabilities as a result of empathic failures of "self objects." His delayed trauma reaction manifests as shame and deferred aggressive action. His aggressive behavior reflects mechanisms of splitting and projective identification of shameful, weak, and undesirable parts of himself in others. However, the fundamental and distinguishing concept of the psychoanalytic approach is the shift of emphasis from the overt symptom pattern to the underlying personality organization.

Cognitive-Behavioral Therapy

A dual arousal model is used to explain how anger responses are automatic, classically conditioned reactions with little awareness. Particular aversive stimuli serve to increase physiological arousal and trigger angry outbursts. Then, through higher-level cognitive processes (i.e., appraisals, attributions, or biases in social information processing) such outbursts are self-reinforced as justified or effective responses to interpersonal provocation. Angry outbursts and aggressive behaviors are shaped, established, and strengthened through intermittent reinforcement contingencies. Short-term compliance of others, perceptions of power and control, tension reduction, and amelioration of self-righteous indignation serve as positive short-term consequences.

Dialetical Behavior Therapy

Although anger serves a discernible function for a given individual in any given situation, it is seen as a set of maladaptive behaviors evolving from faulty problem solving in response to "intolerable painful affective states." This, combined with problems in affect regulation, is maintained by habitual avoidance of said aversive affective states. Maladaptive behaviors evolve as a result of a combination of biological and environmental factors, specifically, an interaction between a "pervasively invalidating environment" and a biologically wired emotional hypersensitivity that results in an over-reliance on the environment for cues regarding internal states. Dialetical behavior therapy (DBT) embraces "dialectic philosophy," in which the therapist uses a combination of a need for chance and an extensive validation of the client's feelings and efforts. Given the focus of increasing self-awareness, particularly awareness and tolerance of affective states, the Zen practice of "mindfulness" is central to the treatment.

Couples and Family Therapy

Because the primary focus of couples and family therapy is to view individuals in the context of systems, anger outbursts and aggressive behaviors are assumed to serve particular functions in the maintenance of family interaction patterns. Anthony's habitual anger reactions reflect the dysfunctional dynamics in the marital and coparenting subsystems. There seems to be poor articulation of the various roles played by Anthony (husband, father, and grandfather) and of tasks required to negotiate various life cycle transitions for family members. Examination of the clarity and flexibility of boundaries, which reflect the degree of differentiation among members, reveals inconsistent patterns of disengagement and enmeshment. Furthermore, the significant family of origin dysfunction, including trauma, cutoffs, and poor communication, established clear distortions in Anthony's relational schemas.

Emotion-Focused Therapy

Emotion-focused therapy (EFT) characterizes problems in affect regulation as either "over-regulated" or "under-regulated," the two not being mutually exclusive but rather often maladaptively coexisting. The term *over-regulated* is applied to Anthony's expressions of anger as alternately suppressed and explosive, and this pattern is viewed as typical of trauma survivors. However, Anthony also has little insight into or awareness of triggers or means of de-escalating rising anger, hence the concept of "under-regulated." In addition, anger expression is also seen as possibly masking deeper feelings of vulnerability, sadness, fear, and/or pain and may be due to maladaptive core beliefs, which need to be explored and refined to fit more consistently with reality. Finally, Anthony's anger is characterized as "instrumental," suggesting that anger is used to control or manipulate others.

Adapted for trauma survivors, emotion-focused trauma therapy (EFTT) recognizes the role of trauma in disturbance in adult functioning. Thus, Anthony's anger is understood as resulting from his early childhood sexual victimization and the interpersonal failures of significant caregivers; these issues will be a core focus. EFTT maintains that exposure to overwhelming affect causes stress and unique processing of events, which in turn affects adult behavior in part by affecting relationship schemas in adulthood. Avoidance is seen as a faulty coping strategy used to push away unwanted internal experiences and aggression effectively acts as a way to neutralize aversive affective states.

A Buddhist Approach

Buddhist treatment philosophy conceptualizes anger, along with greed and delusion, as one of three essential and unavoidable sources of human suffering. Anger is viewed as a way of coercing compliance from those who disobey or disagree with us, a way of attempting to change what is. Buddhism postulates that suffering is universal and unavoidable and that anger is unproductive and selfish, grounded in a persistent delusion that egoistic desires can ever be satisfied, obstacles removed, or suffering eliminated. In informing psychotherapy, Buddhism postulates that individuals are ruled by factors, which contaminate our moment-to-moment consciousness, such as opinions, automatic assumptions, and prejudices. Only through the disciplined practice of mindfulness can we release ourselves from clouded judgments and distorted realities, which contribute to anger. Buddhism also placed emphasis in the humanistic philosophy that the compassionate relationship with the therapist is essential to learning compassion for the self and understanding the interpersonal nature of anger.

Adlerian Therapy

Anthony has compensated for early childhood feelings of inferiority that resulted from family rejection and trauma by creating a functional life goal of superiority over others. His strivings for significance have taken the negative direction of self-protection, intimidation, and self-centeredness. His anger patterns reflect his striving for dominance and power and are evoked to achieve what he feels entitled to. However, these patterns have led to insecure and volatile relationships, emotional withdrawal, and experiences of shame, which only enhance feelings of inferiority and low self-esteem. Thus, Anthony continues to experience disconnectedness from others and fails to achieve competence in life tasks (occupation, love/sex, and relatedness).

Assimilative Psychodynamic Psychotherapy

According to assimilative psychodynamic psychotherapy, patterns of anger and aggression are motivated, skewed, and limited by unconscious processes, self and object representations and meanings derived from hurtful and traumatic developmental experiences that have been repressed, denied, or rationalized. Anthony's characteristic style of interacting interferes with efforts to change conscious thoughts and reinforces dysfunctional thinking and representational structures. He seems to have few behavioral options other than displays of anger and aggression, which are stimulated by subconscious representations of self and others and deeply felt vulnerability, humiliation, loss, and craving for love and acceptance. Seemingly insignificant hurts or disappointments in his current interactions connect to and activate subconscious issues with little awareness on Anthony's part. The model hypothesizes deficits in the behavioral repertoire (problem-solving, communication, and affect regulations skills) and deficits in cognitive mediation, as Anthony fails to anticipate reactions and evaluates himself as a failure, complicated by intrapsychic conflicts and rageful outbursts.

Goals of Treatment

Psychoanalytic Therapy

Short-Term Goals
- Improve control over angry outbursts
- Improve family relationships, self-esteem, and capacity to work
- Develop capacity for self-reflection, empathy, and regulation of affect
- Develop ability to tolerate range of tender or vulnerable emotions
- Mobilize aggression to empower self
- Increase capacity to maintain interpersonal boundaries

Developmental or Long-Term Goals
- Cultivate awareness of emotions as guides to adaptive behavior, without being compelled toward action forms of discharge
- Develop coherent representation of mental states of self and others
- Repair deficits in personality structure that leave individuals vulnerable to disorganization and rage reactions
- Achieve a change in configuration of compromise formations

Cognitive-Behavioral Therapy

- Understand typical components of own anger sequence
- Conceptualize anger episodes as idiosyncratic aversive triggers, appraised by a set of ideas and beliefs, which yield an internal anger experience that may or may not be expressed
- Disrupt automatic anger patterns by using short-term escape and avoidance strategies
- Restructure cognitive attributions and appraisals of triggering events
- Reduce reactivity of recollections of past abuse
- Understand how interpersonal history has shaped and reinforced ways of responding (cognitively, emotionally, and behaviorally)
- Increase response repertoire to anger triggers
- Explore aspects of forgiveness and empathy
- Enhance problem-solving, negative affect expression, and interpersonal communication skills

Dialetical Behavior Therapy

DBT is a stage-based theory with distinct goals at various stages of treatment. Keep in mind that the treatment protocol was developed to treat chronically suicidal individuals with borderline personality disorder and was adapted to work with other individuals struggling with extreme behavioral dysregulation, such as explosive anger.

Stage 1 Goals
- Establish safety and a connection to treatment
- Confront behavioral dyscontrol and possible life-threatening behavior
- Improve clients' behavioral capacities
- Increase clients' motivation to change
- Help clients generalize new behaviors to all aspects of their lives

- Support therapists
- Structure the therapeutic environment to promote success of both client and therapists

Stage 2 Goals
- Process past traumas and loss through exposure strategies to address post-traumatic symptoms and grief
- Address behaviors characterized as "therapy interfering"

Stage 3 Goals
- Address ordinary problems of living with a focus on problem-solving strategies and skill building
- Decrease "quality-of-life interfering behaviors"

Stage 4 Goals
- Overcome lack of fulfillment or a lack of joy despite generally good objective functioning
- Focus on fulfillment in spiritual or interpersonal realms

Couples and Family Therapy
- Strengthen clients' system by making it more competent or adaptive
- Resolve presenting problem at a level that suggests a high degree of likelihood of maintenance
- Strengthen marital and coparenting alliances
- Enhance sense of spousal dependability, intimacy, and trust
- Enhance family collaboration in managing affect expression in constructive ways
- Encourage sharing of insights, techniques, and accomplishments from individual treatment with family members
- Improve family communication and conflict negotiation skills
- Reconfigure dysfunctional family interaction patterns
- Enhance constructive communication skills and expressions of care or concern
- Understand function of anger within family system

Emotion-Focused Therapy

In EFTT the overall goal is to first evoke the maladaptive emotional structures currently contributing to the maintenance of problems and then to work to change them. In this manner, EFTT hopes to increase both insight (i.e., recognition) and management skills. EFT is an integrative model, and some of the goals reflect the ideas of cognitive-behavioral interventions, such as promoting awareness of the internal states signaling anger, such as growing muscle tension and racing aggressive thoughts. Others are more focused on reflection regarding affective expression. Goals are prioritized idiosyncratically to meet the needs of the client in the moment.

- Gain control over dysfunctional anger experience and expression
- Develop the capacity to experience and adaptively express a full range of primary emotion
- Change cognitions and maladaptive beliefs that give rise to cognitively mediated secondary anger
- Recognize vulnerability, which anger defends against
- Reprocess trauma memories to allow for decrease in anger associated with post-traumatic stress disorder
- Process the sexual victimization and the adaptive and justified feelings associated with failures of caregivers, allowing for their appropriate expression

A Buddhist Approach

The goals are two-pronged in that success is characterized by a combination of increased insight through the disciplined practice of mindfulness, which allows for openness and awareness, and improved skills at recognition and management of anger through typical cognitive-behavioral therapy (CBT) techniques. Goals therefore are as follows:

- Practice mindfulness to become an observer of internal states of consciousness and to accept the present moment nonjudgmentally
- Process representative factors within the anger chain and learn alternative responses to activating events
- Radically transform one's consciousness by taking responsibility for actions and thoughts
- Show compassionate concern for the self and others to allow for effective engagement with others and our own mental health and well-being

Adlerian Therapy

- Achieve symptom relief and strive to achieve unique individual identity and sense of well-being
- Evaluate lifestyle patterns and correct distorted beliefs and ideas about self and others

- Interpret inferiority feelings and fictional final goal of superiority
- Overcome feelings of insecurity and develop greater feelings of connectedness through improved interpersonal relationships
- Redirect strivings for significance into more socially beneficial directions and adopt a contributing way of living
- Replace strategies of self-protection, self-enhancement, and strivings for superiority with courageous social contributions

Assimilative Psychodynamic Psychotherapy

Short-Term Goals Focused on Behavioral Change
- Establish viable therapeutic alliance
- Enhance relationships with others to stabilize self-esteem, reduce emotional isolation, and create optimism about treatment

Intermediate Goals Focused on Cognitive and Affective Change
- Improve capacity for empathy of self and others
- Improve ability to tolerate emotions, rejection, and failures in self and others
- Increase ability to substitute thought and delay for action and immediate gratification

Long-Term Goals Focused on Psychodynamic Issues
- Resolve multiple, developmental traumas
- Initiate and complete mourning process necessary to detach from painful history
- Revise representational structures of self and others toward more benign, lovable, and loving images

Mechanisms of Change

Psychoanalytic Therapy. The emphasis is on increased *awareness* and *insight* of that which has previously not been conscious. The *internalization* of the therapeutic relationship will provide a new pattern and schemas for other relationships. Finally, *reconstruction* will be achieved by connecting current interpersonal patterns to an earlier developmental period.

Cognitive-Behavioral Therapy. The counterconditioning model indicates that repeated *exposure* (imaginal and graduated in vivo) to anger triggers will result in *habituation* and *extinction* of arousal responses. Once these triggers are rendered neutral, new responses (e.g., relaxation or cognitive coping) are paired with triggers as competing, more adaptive responses. Other adaptive responses, such as alternative attributions or assertiveness, are *modeled, rehearsed, shaped* through successive approximations, and *reinforced* through graduated practice in session and as homework.

Dialetical Behavior Therapy. Dialectic thinking is central to DBT and asserts that both *acceptance* of what is and the need for change permanently coexist. This duality allows therapists to support clients in becoming *mindful* of internal states and learning to balance acceptance and the need to learn new behavioral and interpersonal *skills. Validation* allows the client to feel adequately supported and assisted while attempting to engage in more adaptive behaviors, which is essential for clients with extreme emotional dysregulation and a history of invalidating environments.

Couples and Family Therapy. Change in presenting problems is anchored in the in-session *experiential reworking* of interaction patterns among family members. The therapist directs the practice of new patterns with a *balance of focus* on content and process (both verbal and nonverbal) between the alliances and subsystems of family members. Furthermore, a shift in the usual interaction patterns occurs through a *decentering* and *reframing* of anger's function within the family system. *Insight* into transgenerational patterns is also developed.

Emotion-Focused Therapy. Therapeutic change evolves from emotional *exploration* and *interpretation* by the therapist, allowing for a new understanding of the self and others to emerge. Empathy is considered a necessary requirement for change in all EFT, but in trauma treatment in particular, a strong therapeutic relationship is essential for a corrective emotional experience through accurate mirroring of affective states, which enhances the development of appropriate affect regulation. In addition, the *exposure* to and *reprocessing* of traumatic memories allows the activation and processing of associated meanings. Once core affective structures are brought into consciousness, the empathic climate allows a *reframing* of the self, the event, and the perpetrator. By increasing awareness of primary emotions the client experiences changes in self-perception by recognizing and accepting unmet needs as valid and justified. Changes in the perception of abusive or neglectful others reduces the client's perception of the perpetrator as having the power to hurt him or her and assists in the experience of sadness and loss over unmet needs. Anger is similarly processed by *evoking* and *amplifying* how the client experiences the consequences of his or her anger. Using the frequently negative subjective experiences and the *insight* into the unproductiveness of their anger allows the client to change the cognitions at the source of the anger.

A Buddhist Approach. The meditative practice of *mindfulness* is "subtlety yet pervasively transforming." Exercising awareness allows for an increase in choices and improved decision making. In addition, in the process, clients will, with *compassionate support* from the therapist, uncover within themselves compassion and empathy, which permit the healing powers of interpersonal engagement. Mindfulness also brings the knowledge and acceptance that all life is suffering and that our suffering is tied to our desires—suffering ceases when we accept that our desires will go unmet and we will remain wrong, vulnerable, and not in control. *Acknowledgment* that we cannot have the world the way we want it brings acceptance of a course of virtue and moderation.

Adlerian Therapy. The primary mechanism of change in Adlerian therapy is the *insight* clients gain into the ineffectiveness of existing goals. Through increased *recognition* of faulty goal-directed behaviors and reasoning, clients learn to adjust their mistaken thinking, build new skills, and *modify certain cognitive distortions* around finding purpose for their lives.

Part of what creates change is the *modification of the "fictional final goal"* to something more achievable, and hence more satisfying. In so doing, clients develop an increased sense of social cohesion and responsibility, which in turn increases prosocial behaviors and investment in community.

Assimilative Psychodynamic Psychotherapy. Overall, there is an emphasis on *exploration, inquiry,* and *interpretation* of unconscious processes, motives, conflicts, and representations. However, more active change processes are incorporated to facilitate behavioral control of angry outbursts, *cognitive restructuring* of conscious processes, and improvement in interpersonal interaction. Enhanced emotion regulation capacity allows for *gradual exposure* to unconscious material that was previously anxiety provoking. Thus, change processes not usually associated with psychodynamic therapy are incorporated to resolve immediate problems and at the same time to reach goals of psychodynamic and structural change.

Therapeutic Relationship

Psychoanalytic Therapy. The therapist adopts a nonjudgmental, concerned, exploratory, and empathic stance throughout. Functioning as a "participant observer," the therapist will use supportive techniques along with a focus on transference reactions to provide insight into *unconscious* processes. The therapist should maintain a neutral, analytic attitude and avoid direct methods of influence. The initial tasks are to ally with the client's personal goals and understand his or her perspective without endorsing the legitimacy of his or her views. The emerging new and reparative relationship with the therapist is the vehicle for change and is transacted through supportive and expressive interventions.

Cognitive-Behavioral Therapy. Clearly, a good therapeutic alliance is the key to successful treatment; however, that empathic rapport is necessary but not sufficient for positive outcome. The CBT therapist works collaboratively with the client to develop the treatment plan. The potential risks of exposure treatment are explained, and the therapist and the client must reach a joint decision to incorporate this module. Throughout treatment, the CBT therapist is quite directive in planning the sessions' tasks, graduated practice, and homework assignments. The therapist maintains an active role as a teacher, model, coach, and mentor as the client establishes new responses in more in vivo contexts.

Dialetical Behavior Therapy. The dialectic drives the treatment; therefore, flexibility is an important characteristic in successful therapists in DBT. The therapist maintains the position of validation and acceptance on one hand and the need for change on the other, but calls for change must be balanced with infinite patience. In addition, the therapist uses the self and the relationship with the client as a reinforcer for adaptive behavior, meaning a very strong relationship is essential to treatment success. Also, because phone sessions are a component to the treatment, the therapist must have clear boundaries and yet be open to assisting clients in moments of crisis so that in vivo coaching can be implemented. In DBT, the relationship between the client and the therapist is the vehicle through which therapy is made more effective, but in many ways, the relationship *is* the therapy. Because of these many demands, DBT builds in a support system for therapists in the form of team meetings, which are considered ways of ensuring that therapists are on track with their own limits and feelings, with often-difficult clients, and with the protocol.

Couples and Family Therapy. The therapist must establish a therapeutic alliance with each family member and balance the alliances across members to ensure emotional safety for all. Through processes of mimesis and joining, the therapist learns the family "rules" and language and forms a new system with the family. The therapist's role is to encourage family members to interact naturally and to keep them focused (which is the process) on a single problem (the content) long enough to resolve it.

The therapist must manage the family's experience such that each member feels attended to, and he or she must avoid triangulation with members in conflict because this prevents resolution.

Emotion-Focused Therapy. The treatment is collaborative and supportive in that it is guided by the therapist, who must be given permission by the client to be directive. The key therapeutic attributes are considered empathic attunement, knowledge of human emotions, and general theoretical knowledge of personality styles and disorders, as well as the knowledge of a particular client.

A Buddhist Approach. The relationship between the therapist and the client is seen as comparable to that of teacher and student. Compassion guides the interactions, and the therapist is seen as supportive by practicing in a parallel manner. The therapist and the client are in extensive intimate contact over several months. The treatment is flexible in terms of how and when the therapist is available because the therapist joins the client's journey almost as a coach. The process is based on a sense of collaboration and engaged interpersonal interactions, which act as models for the client. Because the therapist shares the process so closely, he or she is said to share the experiences and the feelings of the client. This is the quintessentially participant-observer aspect of a transpersonal model in which the therapist helps the client develop the deep wisdom that comes from the sustained attentional consciousness.

Adlerian Therapy. Adlerians believe that a good therapist-client relationship is founded on a dialogue between equals based on mutual respect, candor, and acceptance and belief in the dignity and importance of each individual. The objective is to ensure that their goals are well aligned and that the therapist is able to model good communication strategies and acting in good faith. Typically, the therapist embraces a "vertical" approach to people, compared with a horizontal approach. Vertical relationships assume that each party is different but equal, as opposed to horizontal thinking, which uses one-up-one-down comparisons. The therapist's main responsibility is to listen for the underlying thinking behind the client's behavior so as to understand the function and rationale for the behavior and to be able to make available alternative choices.

Assimilative Psychodynamic Psychotherapy. The therapist's stance varies with the stages of the integrated model. The therapist is more directive and active in the beginning sessions as behavioral skills and cognitive distortions are treatment emphases. As new ways of thinking and behaving are established, these reactions occur with the therapist in vivo. The therapeutic relationship provides a safe and supportive interpersonal experience, which then begins to shift the powerful unconscious images of self and other. The therapist remains continuously alert for enactments of past relationships and of unconscious self and object images with the dyad. Greater insight into his internal world is facilitated via Anthony's ameliorative relationship experience with the therapist.

Intervention Phases and Strategies

Psychoanalytic Therapy. The authors of this modified psychoanalytic therapy suggest that treatment sessions occur in a face-to-face format for 45 to 50 minutes twice per week. Diagnostic impressions indicate an Axis II personality disorder; the expected duration of treatment will be 2 to 4 years.

Nondirective and supportive techniques dominate the insight-oriented intervention approach. Through clarification, confrontation, interpretation, and reconstruction, the therapist will interpret the meanings of the presenting symptoms to repair characterological deficits, leaving Anthony vulnerable to disorganization and rage reactions. Termination will occur when both the therapist and the client agree that the goals of treatment related to structural personality change have occurred and are likely to endure.

Cognitive-Behavior Therapy. A motivational interviewing framework is used initially to address ambivalence or outright resistance to treatment. Client-centered methods are used to obtain a commitment to treatment and intention to change. Additional assessment would include administration of the Anger Disorder's Scale and the continual use of the Anger Episode's Record, a self-monitoring tool which helps in the functional analysis of a single anger episode. The authors suggest a menu-based approach, which allows the therapist to tailor the intervention plan to a specific anger profile.

Short-term interventions are used early to disrupt automatic anger reactions. The therapist and the client work collaboratively to develop avoidance strategies for predictable triggers and to shape the deliberate use of escape maneuvers. Various counterconditioning and exposure procedures (e.g., progressive muscle relaxation [PMR], marginal desensitization, verbal barbs) are implemented to reduce physiological arousal and interrupt automatic response patterns. Then social skills and cognitive restructuring strategies, which shape alternative ways of thinking and communicating, are established and rehearsed through the use of in-session tasks and homework assignments. In preparation for termination, specific generalization and maintenance strategies are emphasized to review treatment progress, identify and plan for high-risk triggers, and develop skills for managing setbacks.

Dialetical Behavior Therapy. In session, maladaptive behaviors are organized according to a hierarchical focus of treatment. Explosive anger is routinely assessed using behavior analysis and becomes the treatment priority as a "quality-of-life interfering behavior." In cases of interpersonal violence, this category has been expanded to include behaviors that may be interfering with the quality of life of partners or children in the home. If the violence toward others escalates, "life-threatening behavior" directed toward family members becomes the top priority of treatment. In addition, experiences of sexual abuse epitomize the invalidating environment and contribute to deficits in emotion modulation, which are factored into the possibility of an Axis II diagnosis of borderline personality disorder.

Couples and Family Therapy. The initial sessions include all relevant family members, and each is asked to contribute his or her own definition of and relation to the presenting problem. The additional assessment undertaken, the Systemic Therapy Inventory of Change (STIC), is suggested as a way to track change throughout the course of treatment and is given before each session. Following psychoeducation relative to realistic expectations for family functioning, life cycle development, and the physiological aspects of anger arousal, in-session tasks and between-session homework are used to facilitate change in family members' interactions and to enhance generalization to the natural environment. Full family, couples, and individual sessions are scheduled intermittently to help integrate change on multiple system levels. Instruction and behavior rehearsal are used to assist family members in the direct and constructive expression of anger, disappointment, and frustration. Skills in compromise negotiation, conflict de-escalation, and problem solving are practiced. Cognitive strategies are used to reframe anger episodes and to create alternative perspectives to its function. The emotion of anger can be transmitted into caring, compassion, or desire for connection. Emotion-focused strategies are used to promote the sharing of affective experiences and to enhance empathic listening. Finally, more psychodynamic strategies are used to explore and analyze transgenerational influences and to enhance each person's capacity to soothe his or her own anxiety and increase personal capacity for empathy.

Emotion-Focused Therapy. In EFT, the overall goal is to make emotional experiences more accessible and their expression more appropriate.

This is accomplished in a time-limited treatment whereby between 12 and 20 sessions, on average, are found to be effective. There are three phases of treatment. In phase 1 the primary objective is establishing the alliance through empathic understanding and collaboratively formulating goals. This occurs through two processes:

1. Modulation of emotional intensity—both by decreasing arousal through empathic responding and support (i.e., decreasing anger through validation/understanding) and by increasing the experience and expression of previously inhibited/over-regulated emotions
2. Increased emotional awareness and understanding

In phase 2, the goal is to make problematic material as vivid as possible in session through in vivo experiencing of emotion. Multiple techniques are used in this process:

1. Two-chair dialogue for intrapsychic conflict in which the client engages in a dialogue between the two parts of the self that are in conflict in some way (e.g., an experiencing side and an inhibited or blocked/defended part of the self)
2. Imaginal confrontation in which the client makes psychological contact with significant others from his or her past in order to express previously inhibited thoughts or feelings
3. CBT techniques, such as time-outs and assertiveness skills training

The third and last phase focuses on attempting to change self-perception and perceptions of abusive or neglectful others to allow a reformulation of both the self and powerful others. Couples sessions are used as needed, and follow-up, combined with refresher sessions, is indicated after termination to ensure that gains are not lost. At the culmination of treatment, it may be recommended that a client seek collateral support groups and/or refer to readings in particular areas to supplement learning.

A Buddhist Approach. Buddhist treatment places explicit emphasis on the intensive practice of mindfulness, and sessions are set up around a meditation session with both the client and the therapist. Meditation is followed by any necessary didactic process of teaching mindfulness skills focusing on *recognition* of thoughts and feelings. The goal is not *management* but rather replacing negative thoughts and feelings with loving kindness, or "anger therapy by reciprocal inhibition." The bulk of the therapeutic work is composed of 10 sessions, a series of graduated exercises, organized in an idiosyncratic order as deemed necessary for each individual. The duration and frequency of sessions is not rigidly set but rather considered a journey that the client and the therapist embark on together. Two preliminary goals guide the 10 therapeutic sessions, which take place before and after a joint mindfulness practice:

Preliminary 1—learning mindfulness meditation
Preliminary 2—journaling and setting up rules for phone and e-mail contact

In Buddhist work there is a "graduation" as opposed to a "termination" because the relationship between the therapist and the client does not end; it merely shifts. Because "all life is suffering," the journey to accept suffering is lifelong. There is also recommended follow-up at 6 weeks, 3 months, and 6 months, and ultimately, the therapist mentors Anthony as he grows into in his own role as a mentor when he helps others on their journey to mindfulness and acceptance.

Adlerian Therapy. Adlerians are not bound to follow any specific set of techniques. That said, the repertoire of activities is consistent with the basic concepts of individual psychology and is adapted to fit each client. First, the therapist must make a full assessment of the client's functioning, including gaining an understanding of family constellation and conducting a systematic lifestyle interview. Once these are accomplished, cognitive-behavioral interventions are frequently used to modify distorted cognitions, replace maladaptive goals and life objectives, and re-educate the client toward constructive goals. The process of treatment relies on the use of "psychological investigation" and "interpretation" to bring to light faulty thinking and assumptions. Couples therapy and career counseling may be recommended for the current case as well.

Assimilative Psychodynamic Psychotherapy. Assimilative psychodynamic psychotherapy (APP) is an integrative approach that is highly idiographic and *not* driven by diagnosis or by prescriptive matching of intervention technique and symptom pattern. Considered long-term treatment (2–3 years), APP begins with a structured focus, which gradually yields to an unstructured, depth-oriented approach. Cognitive and behavioral techniques are used initially to establish the therapeutic contract, to help solve immediate interpersonal problems, and to restructure distortions and deficits in social information processing. Initially, exploration and interpretation of psychodynamic issues are kept to a minimum to prevent the client from feeling overwhelmed. The relief offered by these CBT strategies increases the safety of the therapeutic relationship and reduces the defensive, resistant, and negative transferences. In addition, successful experiences in improving current relationships create receptivity to psychodynamic strategies of detailed inquiry, exploration of unconscious processes, interpretation, and inferences about connections of past and present experiences. The therapeutic relationship serves a corrective emotional experience and helps shift internal representations of others. A positive, planned termination focuses on relapse prevention as well as the identification and processing of unconscious meanings and conflicts, which may be triggered in the future.

SUMMARY AND INTEGRATION

Clearly, there are many commonalities in the treatments hypothesized for the case of Anthony. Our review of the case discussions underscores the complexity of the case and the interaction of a myriad of individual, familial, and historical components. For each hypothesized treatment approach, there was an articulated theoretical foundation upon which a case conceptualization was developed. This conceptualization served then to formulate treatment goals and to frame the intervention plan. Although the emphasis varied, all of the approaches acknowledged the role of Anthony's early abuse traumas as instrumental to symptom development. Furthermore, all of the approaches clearly indicated that a strong alliance between the client and the therapist would be crucial for successful treatment outcome in this case.

Many chapters in this book included some integration of therapy techniques from other orientations. For the family and couples treatment and the APP approaches, the inclusion of a variety of orientation-based strategies is well integrated in both theory and practice. For most approaches, some psychoeducation, communication skills training, and the teaching of appropriate expression of negative affect were techniques to be incorporated on an "as-needed" basis. Although the designation of treatment as "long term" is a relative judgment, there was flexibility in all approaches and a consensus that various techniques could be interwoven in order to ensure Anthony's psychological growth and improvement in his adaptive functioning. This case was one of a mixed diagnostic picture with a client whose motivation for change was ambivalent at best. Nevertheless, clinicians from a wide variety of theoretical orientations were hopeful that their particular course of treatment would lead to positive outcomes for both Anthony and his family members.

APPENDIX A

Comparative Treatments of Anger-Related Disorders

QUESTIONS FOR AUTHORS TO CONSIDER

1. What would be your therapeutic goals for this client? What are the primary goals and secondary goals?
2. What further information would you want to assist you in developing and implementing treatment for the client? Are there specific assessment tools that you would use, and what would be the rationale for conducting additional assessments?
3. What is your conceptualization of this client's personality, behavior, affective states, and cognitive and current functioning?
4. Are there specific or special techniques that you would implement in therapy with Anthony? What would they be?
5. What are the strengths of this client that can be used in therapy?
6. What pitfalls would you envision in this therapy? What would be the difficulties and their source, and how would you handle these difficulties?
7. How would you address boundaries and limit setting with this client?
8. Are there adjunctive treatments or other forms of treatment (group, couple) that you might recommend? How would they fit within your therapeutic approach?
9. Are there special cautions to be observed in working with this client? Are there any specific resistances you would expect, and how would you deal with them?
10. Are there areas that you would choose to avoid or not address with this client? Why?

11. Would you want to involve significant others in his treatment? Who would you recommend, and how and when would you include them in Anthony's treatment?
12. Is medication a possible treatment option for this client? What effects would you hope that the medication would have?
13. What would be your timeline (duration) for therapy? What would be the ideal frequency and duration of the sessions? (How would termination best be decided?)
14 What is your prognosis for this case? What results would you expect from your treatment of Anthony?
15. What would be the issues to be addressed in termination? How would termination be structured?
16. What do you see as the hoped-for changes for this client in order of importance?

References

Abelson, R. P. (1981). Psychological status of the script concept. *American Psychologist, 36,* 715–729.

Abernethy, A. D. (1995). Managing racial anger: A critical skill in cultural competence. *Journal of Multicultural Counseling and Development, 23,* 96–102.

Achmon, J., Granek, M., Golomb, M., & Hart, J. (1989). Behavior treatment of essential hypertension: A comparison between cognitive therapy and biofeedback of heartrate. *Psychosomatic Medicine, 51,* 152–164.

Adams, D. (1988). Treatment models of men who batter: A profeminist analysis. In K. Yllo & M. Bograd (Eds.), *Feminist perspectives on wife abuse* (pp. 176–199). Newbury Park, CA: Sage.

Adler, A. (1929). *The science of living.* New York: Greenberg.

Adler, A. (1958). *What life should mean to you.* (A. Porter, Ed). New York: Prestige. (Original work published 1931).

Alberti, R. E., & Emmons, M. L. (2001). *Your perfect right.* Atascadero, CA: Impact Publishers.

Alexander, F., & French, T. (1946). *Psychoanalytic therapy.* New York: Ronald Press.

Allen, D. (2000). Recent research on physical aggression in persons with intellectual disability: An overview. *Journal of Intellectual and Developmental Disability, 25*(1), 41–43.

Altaribba, J. (2003). Does carono equal "liking"? A theoretical approach to conceptual non-equivalence between languages. *International Journal of Bilingualism, 7,* 305–322.

American Psychiatric Association. (1994). *Diagnostic and statistical manual of mental disorders* (4th ed.). Washington, DC: Author.

American Psychiatric Association. (2000). *Diagnostic and statistical manual of mental disorders* (4th ed., text revision). Washington, DC: Author.

Amrhein, P. C., Miller, W. R., Yahne, C. E., Palmer, M., & Fulcher, L. (2003). Client commitment language during motivational interviewing predicts drug use outcomes. *Journal of Consulting and Clinical Psychology, 71,* 862–878.

Anastasi, A., Cohen, N., & Spatz, D. (1948). A study of fear and anger in college students through the controlled diary method. *Journal of Genetic Psychology, 73,* 243–249.

Ansbacher, H. (1967). A restatement of Adler's position. In R. R. Ansbacher, *The individual psychology of Alfred Adler* (2nd ed.). New York: Harper & Row.

Ansbacher, H. (1991). The concept of social interest. *Individual Psychologist, 47*(1), 30–44.

Aquino, K., Douglas, S., & Martinko, M. J. (2004). Overt anger in response to victimization: Attributional style and organizational norms as moderators. *Journal of Occupational Health Psychology, 9,* 152–164.

Arasteh, A. R., & Sheikh, A. A. (1989). Sufism: The way to universal self. In A. A. Sheikh & K. S. Sheikh (Eds.), *Eastern and western approaches to healing* (pp. 146–179). New York: Wiley.

Ardrey, R. (1970). *The social contract.* New York: Atheneum.

Aristotle. (1960). Rhetoric. In L. Cooper (Ed. & trans.), *The rhetoric of Aristotle.* Englewood Cliffs, NJ: Prentice Hall.

Arkowitz, H. (1991). Introductory statement: Psychotherapy integration comes of age. *Journal of Psychotherapy Integration, 1,* 1–4.

Atkinson, D. R., Kim, B. S. K., & Caldwell, R. (1998). Ratings of helper roles by multicultural psychologists and Asian American students: Initial support for the three-dimensional model of multicultural counseling. *Journal of Counseling Psychology, 45,* 414–423.

Averill, J. R. (1982). *Anger and aggression: An essay on emotion.* New York: Springer/Verlag.

Averill, J. R. (1983). Studies on anger and aggression: Implications for theories of emotion. *American Psychologist, 38,* 1145–1160.

Avis, J. (1991). Power politics in therapy with women. In T. J. Goodrich (Ed.), *Women and power: Perspectives for family therapy* (pp. 183–200). New York: W.W. Norton.

Ayme, S. (2004). *Determinants et analyse de l'etat de colere chez les ensignants d'eps exercant en reseau d'education prioritaire.* Unpublished doctoral dissertation, University of Lyon, France.

Babcock, J. C., Costa, D. M., Green, C. E., & Eckhardt, C. I. (2004). What situations induce intimate partner violence? A reliability and validity study of the Proximal Antecedents to Violent Episodes (PAVE) Scale. *Journal of Family Psychology, 18,* 322–442.

Bach, G., & Goldberg, H. (1974). *Creative aggression.* Garden City, NY: Anchor Books.

Bacon, M. K., & Ashmore, R. D. (1985). How mothers and fathers categorize descriptions of social behavior attributed to daughters and sons. *Social Cognition, 3,* 193–217.

Ball, T. (2001, September). *Termination: The holocaust of the Klamath.* Paper presented at the meeting of the Takini Network, Santa Ana, NM.

Bankart, C. P. (1997). *Talking cures: A history of Western and Eastern psychotherapies.* Pacific Grove, CA: Brooks Cole.

Bankart, C. P. (2000, August). *Building bridges: Applying Eastern wisdom in Western contexts.* Paper presented at the 108th Annual Convention of the American Psychological Association, Washington, DC.

Bankart, C. P. (2001, August). *Releasing the demons: Teaching men to meditate.* Paper presented at the 109th Annual Convention of the American Psychological Association, San Francisco.

Bankart, C. P. (2002). Mindfulness as a useful adjunct in therapeutic work with men. *SPSMM Bulletin, 7,* 5–7.

Bankart, C. P. (2003a). Five manifestations of the Buddha in the West. In K. H. Dockett, G. R. Dudley-Grant, & C. P. Bankart (Eds.), *Psychology and Buddhism: From individual to global community* (pp. 45–69). New York: Kluwer Academic Publishers.

Bankart, C. P. (2003b). A Western psychologist's inquiry into the nature of Right Effort. *Constructivism in the Human Sciences, 8,* 63–72.

Bankart, C. P. (2004, July). *Mindfulness, compassion, and reason: Anger management strategies for men.* Presented at the 112th Annual Convention of the American Psychological Association, Honolulu, Hawaii.

Bankart, C. P. (2006). *Freeing the angry mind: How men can use mindfulness and reason to save their lives and their relationships.* Oakland, CA: New Harbinger Publications.

Bankart, C. P., Dockett, K. H., & Dudley-Grant, G. R. (2003). On the path of the Buddha: A psychologist's guide to the history of Buddhism. In K. H. Dockett, G. R. Dudley-Grant, & C. P. Bankart (Eds.), *Psychology and Buddhism: From individual to global community* (pp. 13–44). New York: Kluwer Academic Publishers.

Bankart, C. P., Koshikawa, F., Nedate, K., & Haruki, Y. (1992). When East meets West: Contributions of Eastern traditions to the future of psychotherapy. *Psychotherapy, 29,* 141–149.

Baron, R. (1983). Social influence theory and aggression. In R. G. Geen & E. L. Donnerstein (Eds.), *Aggression: Theoretical and empirical reviews: Issues in research* (Vol. 2, pp. 173–190). New York: Academic Press.

Bateman, A., & Fonagy, P. (2001). Treatment of borderline personality disorder with psychoanalytically-oriented partial hospitalization: An 18-month follow-up. *American Journal of Psychiatry, 158*(1), 36–42.

Bates, J. E. (1989). Concepts and measures of temperament. In G. A. Kohnstamm, J. E. Bates, & M. K. Rothbart (Eds.), *Temperament in childhood.* Chichester, England: Wiley.

Baumeister, R. F., Smart, L., & Boden, J. M. (1996). Relation of threatened egotism to violence and aggression: The dark side of high self esteem. *Psychological Review, 103,* 5–33.

Beck, A. T. (1963). Thinking and depression. *Archives of General Psychiatry, 9,* 324–333.

Beck, A. T. (1964). Thinking and depression: Theory and therapy. *Archives of General Psychiatry, 10,* 561–571.

Beck, A. T. (1971). Cognition, affect, and psychopathology. *Archives of General Psychiatry, 24,* 495–500.

Beck, A. T. (1976). *Cognitive therapy and the emotional disorders.* New York: International Universities Press.

Beck, A. T. (1999). *Prisoners of hate: The cognitive basis of anger, hostility, and violence.* New York: HarperCollins.

Beck, A. T. (2002). Prisoners of hate. *Behaviour Research and Therapy, 40,* 209–216.

Beck, A. T., Freeman, A., Davis, D. D, et al. (2004). *Cognitive therapy of personality disorders* (2nd ed.). New York: Guilford Press.

Beck, J. S. (1995). *Cognitive therapy: Basics and beyond.* New York: Guilford Press.

Beck, R., & Fernandez, E. (1998). Cognitive-behavioral therapy in the treatment of anger: A meta-analysis. *Cognitive Therapy & Research, 22,* 63–74.

Behzadi, K. G. (1994). Interpersonal conflict and emotions in an Iranian cultural practice: Qahr and ashti. *Culture, Medicine and Psychiatry, 18,* 321–359.

Beier, E. G. (1966). *The silent language of psychotherapy.* Chicago: Aldine.

Benson, H. (1975/2000). *The relaxation response.* New York: William Morrow.

Ben-Zur, H., & Zeidner, M. (1988). Sex differences in anxiety, curiosity, and anger: A cross-cultural study. *Sex Roles, 19,* 335–347.

Berg-Cross, L., & Takushi-Chinen, R. (1995). Multicultural training models and the person-in-culture interview. In J. Ponterotto, J. M. Casas, L. A. Suzuki, & C. M. Alexander (Eds.), *Handbook of multicultural counseling* (pp. 333–356). Thousand Oaks, CA: Sage.

Bernard, J. (1981). *The female world.* New York: Free Press.

Bernardez, T. (1987). Women and anger: Cultural prohibitions and the feminine ideal. In *Work in progress: Stone Center for Developmental Services and Studies.* Wellesley, MA: Wellesley College, Stone Center.

Berkowitz, L. (1990). On the formation and regulation of anger and aggression: A cognitive-neoassociationistic analysis. *American Psychologist, 45,* 494–503.

Bertalanffy, L. (1968). *General systems theory: Foundations, development, applications.* New York: Braziller.

Beutler, L. E., & Hodgson, A. B. (1993). Prescriptive psychotherapy. In G. Stricker & J. R. Gold (Eds.), *Comprehensive handbook of psychotherapy integration* (pp. 151–163). New York: Plenum.

Bhat, K. N. (1999). The role of biofeedback-assisted anger control in reversing heart disease. *Dissertation Abstracts International, 60* (5-B), 2326.

Bhikkhu, A. S. (2000). *Meeting the monkey halfway.* York Beach, ME: Samuel Weiser.

Birditt, K. S., & Fingerman, K. L. (2003). Age and gender differences in adults' descriptions of emotional reactions to interpersonal problems. *Journal of Gerontology: Psychological Sciences, 58,* 237–245.

Birnbaum, D. W., & Croll, W. L. (1984). The etiology of children's stereotypes about sex differences in emotionality. *Sex Roles, 10,* 677–691.

Bion, W. R. (1957). Attacks on linking. In *Second thoughts.* New York: Jason Aronson, 1984.[SK8]

Bishop, S. R., Lau, M., Shapiro, S., Carlson, L., Anderson, N. D., Carmody, J., Segal, V., Abbey, S., Speca, M., Velting, D., & Devins, G. (2004). Mindfulness: A proposed operational definition. *Clinical Psychology, Science and Practice, 11,* 230–241.

Bohus, M., Haaf, B., Stiglmayer, C., Pohl, U., Bohme, R., & Linehan, M. M. (2000). Evaluation of inpatient dialectical behavior therapy for borderline personality disorder—A prospective study. *Behavior Research and Therapy, 38,* 875–887.

Boszormenyi-Nagy, I., Grunebaum, J., & Ulrich, D. (1991). Contextual therapy. In A. S. Gurman & D. P. Kniskern (Eds.), *Handbook of family therapy* (Vol. 2, pp. 200–238). Philadelphia: Brunner/Mazel.

Boszormenyi-Nagy, I., & Spark, G. M. (1973). *Invisible loyalties: Reciprocity in intergenerational family therapy.* Oxford, England: Harper & Row.

Boszormenyi-Nagy, I., & Ulrich, D. N. (1981). Contextual family therapy. In A. Gurman & D. Kniskern (Eds.), *Handbook of family therapy* (pp. 159–186). New York: Brunner/Mazel.

Bowen, M. (1978). *Family therapy in clinical practice.* Northvale, NJ: Jason Aronson.

Bowlby, J. (1980). *Attachment and loss* (Vol. III: Loss, sadness, and depression). New York: Basic Books.

Bowlby, J. (1988). *A secure base.* New York: Basic Books.

Bracken, B. A., & McCallum, R. S. (2001). Assessing intelligence in a population that speaks more than two hundred languages: A nonverbal solution. In L. A. Suzuki, J. G. Ponterotto, & P. J. Meller (Eds.), *Handbook of multicultural assessment* (2nd ed., pp. 405–431). San Francisco: Jossey-Bass.

Brenner, C. (1982). *The mind in conflict.* New York: International Universities Press.

Brenner, C. (1992). The structural theory and clinical practice. *Journal of Clinical Psychoanalysis, 1*(3), 369–380.

Brenner, C. (2000). Observations of some aspects of current psychoanalytic theories. *Psychoanalytic Quarterly, 69*(4), 597–632.

Breunlin, D., Schwartz, R., & Mac Kune-Karrer, B. (1992). *Metaframeworks: Transcending the models of family therapy.* San Francisco: Jossey-Bass.

Brewin, C. R. (2001). A cognitive neuroscience account of posttraumatic stress disorder and its treatment. *Behaviour Research & Therapy, 39*(4), 373–393.

Briere, J. (1995). *Trauma symptom inventory professional manual.* Odessa, FL: Psychological Assessment Resources, Inc.

Briere, J. (1996). A self-trauma model for treating adult survivors of severe child abuse. In J. Briere & L. Berliner (Eds.), *The APSAC handbook on child maltreatment* (pp. 140–157). Thousand Oaks, CA: Sage.

Briggs, J. (1970). *Never in anger.* Cambridge, MA: Harvard University Press.

Briscoe, Y. B. (2002). A cognitive behavioral anger management intervention for women with histories of substance abuse. *Dissertation Abstracts International, 62* (11-B), 5358.

Brislin, R. W., Bochner, S., & Lonner, W. J. (1975). *Cross-cultural perspectives on learning.* New York: Wiley.

Britton, R. (1995). Psychic reality and unconscious belief. *International Journal of Psychoanalysis, 76,* 19–23.

Brody, L. R. (1996). Gender, emotional expression, and parent child boundaries. In R. Kavanaugh (Ed.), *Emotion: Interdisciplinary perspectives* (pp. 139–170). Mawwah, NJ: Erlbaum.

Brondolo, E. (2000). *Anger management training.* Unpublished manuscript, St. John's University, New York.

Brown, K. W., & Ryan, R. M. (2003). The benefits of being present: Mindfulness and its role in psychological well-being. *Journal of Personality and Social Psychology, 84,* 822–848.

Brown, K. (2001). A theory of forgiveness in marriage and family therapy: A critical review of the literature. *Dissertation Abstracts International, 62* (1-B), 538.

Buss, A. H., & Plomin, R. (1975). *A temperament theory of personality development.* New York: Wiley.

Buss, A. H., & Plomin, R. (1984). *Temperament: Early developing personality traits.* Hillsdale, NJ: Erlbaum.

Cairns, R. B., Cairns, B. D., Neckerman, H. J., Ferguson, L. L., & Gariepy, J. L. (1989). Growth and aggression: I. Childhood to early adolescence. *Developmental Psychology, 25,* 320–330.

Campbell, D. T. (1975). On the conflicts between psychology and moral traditions. *American Psychologist, 30,* 1103–1126.

Campbell, E. A., & Guiao, I. Z. (2004). Muslim culture and female self-immolation: Implications for women's health research and practice. *Health Care for Women International, 25,* 782–793.

Campbell, M., Small, A. M., Green, W. H., Jennings, S. J., Perry, R., Bennett, W. G., Anderson, L. (1984). Behavioral efficiency of haloperidol and lithium carbonate: A comparison in hospitalized aggressive children with conduct disorder. *Archives of General Psychiatry, 41,* 650–656.

Caner, E. M., & Caner, E. F. (2002). *Unveiling Islam: An insider's look at Muslim life and beliefs.* Grand Rapids, MI: Dregel.

Carriere, M. F. (2003). *Anger expression as a predictor of outcome in emotion focused therapy for adult survivors of childhood abuse.* Unpublished Master's thesis, University of Windsor, Windsor, Ontario, Canada.

Carson, J. W., Carson, K. M., Gil, K. M., & Baucom, D. H. (2004). Mindfulness-based relationship enhancement. *Behavior Therapy, 35,* 471–494.

Carver, C. S., & Scheier, M. F. (1990). Principles of self-regulation: Action and emotion. In E. T. Higgins & R. M. Sorrentino (Eds.), *Handbook of motivation and cognition: Foundations of social behavior* (Vol. 2, pp. 3–52). New York: Guilford Press.

Castonguay, L., Newman, M., Borkovec, T., Holtforth, M., & Maramba, G. (2005). Cognitive-behavioral assimilative integration. In J. Norcross & J. Goldfried (Eds.), *Handbook of psychotherapy integration* (2nd ed., pp. 241–262). New York: Oxford University Press.

Cattell, R. B., & Scheier, I. H. (1961). *The meaning and measurement of neuroticism and anxiety.* New York: Ronald Press.

Chang, E. C., D'Zurilla, T. J., & Sanna, L. J. (2004). *Social problem solving: Theory, research and training.* Washington DC: American Psychological Association.

Chemtob, C. M., Novaco, R. W., Hamada, R. S., & Gross, D. M. (1997). Cognitive behavioral treatment for severe anger in posttraumatic stress disorder. *Journal of Consulting and Clinical Psychology, 65,* 184–189.

Chemtob, C. M., Novaco, R. W., Hamada, R. S., Gross, D. M., & Smith, G. (1997). Anger regulation deficits in combat-related posttraumatic stress disorder. *Journal of Traumatic Stress, 10,* 17–36.

Christensen, C. P. (1995). Cross-cultural awareness development: An aid to the creation of anti-racist feminist therapy. In J. Adleman & G. M. Enguidanos (Eds.), *Racism in the lives of women: Testimony, theory, and guides to antiracist practice* (pp. 209–227). New York: Harrington Park Press.

Clare, A. (2000). *On men: Masculinity in crisis.* London: Chatto & Windus.

Coccaro, E. F. (2003). Intermittent explosive disorder. In E. F. Coccaro (Ed.), *Aggression psychiatric assessment and treatment* (pp. 149–166). New York: Marcel Dekker.

Coccaro, E. F., & Kavoussi, R. I. (1997). Fluoxetine and impulsive aggressive behavior on personality-disordered subjects. *Archives of General Psychiatry, 54,* 116–120.

Cochran, S. V., & Rabinowitz, F. E. (2000). *Men and depression: Clinical and empirical perspectives.* New York: Academic Press.

Cohen, J. (1988). *Statistical power analysis for the behavioral sciences* (2nd ed.). Hillsdale, NJ: Lawrence Erlbaum.

Coon, D. W., Thompson, L., Steffen, A., Sorocco, K., & Gallagher-Thompson, D. (2003). Anger and depression management: Psychoeducational skill training interventions for women caregivers of a relative with dementia. *Gerontologist, 43,* 678–689.

Cox, D. L., Stabb, S. D., & Bruckner, K. H. (1999). *Women's anger: Clinical and developmental perspectives.* Philadelphia: Brunner/Mazel.

Cox, D. L., Stabb, S. D., & Hulgus, J. F. (2000). Anger and depression in girls and boys: A study of gender differences. *Psychology of Women Quarterly, 24,* 110–112.

Cox, D. L., Van Velsor, P., & Hulgus, J. F. (2004). Who me, angry? Patterns of anger diversion in women. *Health Care for Women International, 25,* 872–893.

Coyle, C., & Enright, R. (1997). Forgiveness intervention with post-abortion men. *Journal of Consulting and Clinical Psychology, 65,* 1042–1046.

Crick, N. R., & Grotpeter, J. K. (1995). Relational aggression, gender, and social-psychological adjustment. *Child Development, 66,* 710–722.

Cross, S. E., & Madson, L. (1997). Models of the self: Self-construals and gender. *Psychological Bulletin, 122,* 5–37.

Dahlen, E. R., & Deffenbacher, J. L. (2000). A partial component analysis of Beck's cognitive therapy for the treatment of general anger. *Journal of Cognitive Psychotherapy, 14,* 77–95.

Damasio, A. (1994). *Descartes' error: Emotion, reason, and the human brain.* New York: Grosset/Putnam.

Damasio, A. (1999). *The feeling of what happens: Body and emotion in the making of consciousness.* Fort Worth, TX: Harcourt College.

Davison, G. C., Williams, M. E., Nezami, E., Bice, T. L., & DeQuattro, V. L. (1991). Relaxation, reduction in angry articulated thoughts, and improvements in borderline hypertension and heart rate. *Journal of Behavioral Medicine, 14,* 453–468.

Deffenbacher, J. L. (1988). Cognitive-relaxation and social skills treatments of anger: A year later. *Journal of Counseling Psychology, 35,* 234–236.

Deffenbacher, J. L. (1999). Cognitive-behavioral conceptualization and treatment of anger. *Journal of Clinical Psychology. Special Treating anger in psychotherapy, 55*(3), 295–309.

Deffenbacher, J. L. (2003). Anger disorders. In E. F. Coccaro (Ed.), *Aggression psychiatric assessment and treatment* (pp. 89–111). New York: Marcel Dekker.

Deffenbacher, J. (1992). Trait anger: Theory, findings, and implications. In J. N. Butcher & C. D. Spielberger (Eds.), *Advances in personality assessment* (Vol. 9, pp. 177–201). Hillsdale, NJ: Lawrence Erlbaum.

Deffenbacher, J. L., & Deffenbacher, D. M. (2003). Where is the anger in introductory and abnormal psychology texts? *Teaching of Psychology, 30,* 65–67.

Deffenbacher, J. L., & Lynch, R. S. (1998). Cognitive/behavioral intervention for anger reduction. In V. E. Caballo (Ed.), *Manual para el tratamiento cognitivo-conductual de los trastornos psicologicos* (Vol. 2, pp. 639–674). Madrid, Spain: Siglo XXI.

Deffenbacher, J. L., & McKay, M. (2000). *Overcoming situational and general anger: A protocol for the treatment of anger based on relaxation, cognitive restructuring and coping skills training.* Oakland, CA: New Harbinger.

Deffenbacher, J. L., & Stark, R. S. (1992). Relaxation and cognitive-relaxation treatments of general anger. *Journal of Counseling Psychology, 39,* 158–167.

Deffenbacher, J. L., Dahlen, E. R., Lynch, R. S., Morris, C. D., & Gowensmith, W. N. (2000). An application of Beck's cognitive therapy to general anger reduction. *Cognitive Therapy and Research, 24,* 689–697.

Deffenbacher, J. L., Demm, P. M., & Brandon, A. D. (1986). High general anger: Correlates and treatment. *Behaviour Research and Therapy, 24,* 481–489.

Deffenbacher, J. L., Filetti, L. B., Lynch, R. S., Dahlen, E. R., & Oetting, E. R. (2002). Cognitive-behavioral treatment of high anger drivers. *Behaviour Research and Therapy, 40,* 895–910.

Deffenbacher, J. L., Huff, M. E., Lynch, R. S., Oetting, E. R., & Salvatore, N. F. (2000). Characteristics and treatment of high anger drivers. *Journal of Counseling Psychology, 47,* 5–17.

Deffenbacher, J. L., McNamara, K., Stark, R. S., & Sabadell, P. M. (1990a). A comparison of cognitive-behavioral and process oriented group counseling for general anger reduction. *Journal of Counseling and Development, 69,* 167–172.

Deffenbacher, J. L., McNamara, K., Stark, R. S., & Sabadell, P. M. (1990b). A combination of cognitive, relaxation, and behavioral coping skills in the reduction of general anger. *Journal of College Student Development, 31,* 351–358.

Deffenbacher, J. L., Oetting, E. R., Lynch, R. S., & Morris, C. D. (1966). The expression of anger and its consequences. *Behaviour Research & Therapy, 34,* 575–590.

Deffenbacher, J. L., Oetting, E. R., Huff, M. F., Cornell, G. R., & Dallager, C. J. (1996). Evaluation of two cognitive-behavioral approaches to general anger reduction. *Cognitive Therapy & Research, 20,* 551–573.

Deffenbacher, J. L., Oetting, E. R., Huff, M. E., & Thwaites, G. A. (1995). Fifteen-month follow-up of social skills and cognitive-relaxation approaches to general anger reduction. *Journal of Counseling Psychology, 42,* 400–405.

Deffenbacher, J. L., Richards, T. L., & Kogan, L. R. (2002, August). *Long-term effects of relaxation and cognitive therapies for driving anger.* Paper presented at the 110th Annual Convention of the American Psychological Association, Chicago.

Deffenbacher, J. L., Story, D. A., Brandon, A. D., Hogg, J. A., & Hazaleus, S. L. (1988). Cognitive and cognitive-relaxation treatments of anger. *Cognitive Therapy and Research, 12,* 167–184.

Deffenbacher, J. L., Story, D. A., Stark, R. S., Hogg, J. A., & Brandon, A. D. (1987). Cognitive-relaxation and social skills interventions in the treatment of general anger. *Journal of Counseling Psychology, 34,* 171–176.

Deffenbacher, J. L., Thwaites, G. A., Wallace, T. L., & Oetting, E. R. (1994). Social skills and cognitive-relaxation approaches to general anger reduction. *Journal of Counseling Psychology, 41,* 386–396.

Del Vecchio, T., & O'Leary, K. D. (2004). Effectiveness of anger treatments for specific anger problems: A meta-analytic review. *Clinical Psychology Review, 24,* 15–34.

Derogatis, L. R. (1993). *BSI: Brief Symptom Inventory.* Minneapolis: National Computer Systems.

Diaz, L. A. (2000, August). A comparison of cognitive restructuring and systematic desensitization techniques for anger reduction with an inmate population. *Dissertation Abstracts International, 61* (2-B), 1078.

DiGiuseppe, R. (2005). *Treatment of anger-related disorders.* Presentation at New York City Family Court Mental Health Service Grand Rounds.

DiGiuseppe, R., & Tafrate, R. C. (2001). A comprehensive treatment model for anger disorders. *Psychotherapy, 38,* 262–271.

DiGuiseppe, R., & Tafrate, R. C. (2003). Anger treatment for adults: A meta-analytic review. *Clinical Psychology: Science and Practice, 10,* 70–84.

DiGuiseppe, R., & Tafrate, R. C. (2004). *The anger disorders scale.* Toronto, Canada: Multi-Health Systems (MHS).

DiGuiseppe, R., Tafrate, R. C., & Eckhardt, C. (1994). Critical issues in the treatment of anger. *Cognitive and Behavioral Practice, 1,* 111–132.

Dimeff, L., Risvi, S. L., Brown, M., & Linehan, M. M. (2000). Dialectical behavior therapy for substance abuse: A pilot application to methamphetamine-dependent women with borderline personality disorder. *Cognitive and Behavioral Practice, 7,* 467–468.

Dingfelder, S. F. (2005). Closing the gap for Latino patients. *Monitor on Psychology, 36*(1), 58–61.

Dollard, J., & Miller, N. E. (1950). *Personality and psychotherapy.* New York: McGraw-Hill.

Driekurs, R. (1953). *Fundamentals of Adlerian psychology.* New York: Greenberg. (Original work published in 1933).

Driekers, R. (1967). *Psychodynamics, psychotherapy & counseling.* Chicago: Alfred Adler Institute.

Dua, J. K., & Swinden, M. L. (1992). Effectiveness of negative thought reduction, meditation, and placebo training treatment in reducing anger. *Scandinavian Journal of Psychology, 33,* 135–146.

duMont, P. M., Droppleman, E., Droppleman, P. G., & Thomas, S. P. (1999). The lived experience of anger among a sample of French women. *Journal of Multicultural Nursing and Health, 5*(1), 19–26.

Dutton, D. G. (1995). Propensity for Abusiveness Scale (PAS). *Journal of Family Violence, 10,* 203–221.

Dutton, D. G. (1998). *The abusive personality: Violence and control in intimate relationships.* New York: Guilford Press.

Dutton, D. G. (1999). Traumatic origins of intimate rage. *Aggression and Violent Behavior, 4*(4), 431–447.

Eagly, A., & Steffen, V. J. (1986). Gender and aggressive behavior: A meta-analytic review of social psychological literature. *Psychological Bulletin, 100,* 309–330.

Eamon, K. C., Munchua, M. M., & Reddon, J. R. (2001). Effectiveness of an anger management program for women inmates. *Journal of Offender Rehabilitation, 34,* 45–60.

Eckhardt, C. I., & Deffenbacher, J. L. (1995). Diagnosis of anger disorders. In H. Kassinove (Ed.), *Anger disorders: Definition, diagnosis, and treatment.* Washington, DC: Taylor and Francis.

Eckstein, D. (2000). Empirical studies indicating significant birth-order related personality differences. *Journal of Individual Psychology, 56*(4), 481–494.

Eckstein, D. (2006). An Adlerian approach to anger. In *Contemporary approaches of treatment.* Milton Friedman Series. Victoria, BC: Trafford.

Eckstein, D., & Kern, R. (2002). *Psychological fingerprints* (5th ed.). Dubuque, IA: Kendall/Hunt Publishing Company.

Edmondson, C. B., & Conger, J. C. (1996). A review of treatment efficacy for individuals with anger problems: Conceptual, assessment, and methodological issues. *Clinical Psychology Review, 16,* 251–275.

Eells, T. D., & Lombart, K. G. (2003). Case formulation and treatment concepts among novice, experienced and expert cognitive-behavioral and psychodynamic therapists. *Psychotherapy Research, 13*(2), 187–204.

Eells, T. D. (1997). Psychotherapy case formulation: History and current status. In T. D. Eells (Ed.), *Handbook of psychotherapy case formulation* (pp. 1–25). New York: Guilford Press.

Ekman, P. (1993). Facial expression and emotion. *American Psychologist, 48,* 384–392.

Elliott, R., Greenberg, L. S., & Lietaer, G. (2003). Research on experiential psychotherapies. In M. J. Lambert, A. E. Bergin, & S. L. Garfield (Eds.), *Handbook of psychotherapy and behavior change* (5th ed., pp. 499–539). New York: Wiley.

Ellis, A. E. (1962). *Reason and emotion in psychotherapy.* New York: Lyle Stuart.

Ellis, A. E. (1973). *Humanistic psychotherapy.* New York: McGraw-Hill.

Ellis, A. E. (1991). The revised ABC's of rational-emotive therapy (RET). *Journal of Rational-Emotive and Cognitive Behavior Therapy, 9*(3), 139–172.

Ellis, A. E. (1994). *Reason and emotion in psychotherapy: Revised and updated.* New York: Carol Publishing.

Ellis, A. (1976). Techniques of handling anger in marriage. *Journal of Marriage and Family Counseling, 2,* 305–315.

Ellis, A. E., & Tafrate, R. (1997). *How to control your anger before it controls you.* Secaucus, NJ: Carol Publishing.

Enright, R. D. (2001). *Forgiveness is a choice.* Washington, DC: APA Books.

Eron, L. D., Gentry, J. H., & Schlegel, P. (Eds.). (1994). *Reason to hope: A psychosocial perspective on violence and youth.* Washington, DC: American Psychological Association.

Fagot, B. I., Leinbach, M. D., & Hagan, R. (1986). Gender labeling and the development of sex-typed behaviors. *Developmental Psychology, 22,* 440–443.

Feather, B. W., & Rhodes, J. W. (1972). Psychodynamic behavior therapy. I: Theory and rationale. *Archives of General Psychiatry, 26,* 496–502.

Fehrenbach, P. A., & Thelen, M. H. (1982). Behavioral approaches to the treatment of aggressive disorders. *Behavior Modification, 6,* 465–497.

Fields, B., Reesman, K., Robinson, C., Sims, A., Edwards, K., McCall, B., Short, B., & Thomas, S. P. (1998). Anger of African American women in the South. *Issues in Mental Health Nursing, 19,* 353–373.

Fine, G. A. (1987). *With the boys: Little League baseball and preadolescent culture.* Chicago: University of Chicago Press.

Fischer, A. H., Rodriguez Mosquera, P. M., van Vianen, A. E., & Manstead, A. S. (2004). Gender and culture differences in emotion. *Emotion, 4,* 87–94.

Fiske, S. T. (1993). Controlling other people: The impact of power on stereotyping. *American Psychologist, 48,* 621–628.

Fivush, R. (1991). Gender and emotion in mother–child conversations about the past. *Journal of Narrative and Life History, 1,* 325–341.

Foa, E. B. (2000). Psychosocial treatment of posttraumatic stress disorder. *Journal of Clinical Psychiatry. Special focus on posttraumatic stress disorder, 61*(Suppl. 5), 43–51.

Foa, E. B., & Rothbaum, B. O. (1998). *Treating the trauma of rape: Cognitive-behavioral therapy for PTSD.* New York: Guilford Press.

Folger, R., & Baron, R. A. (1996). Violence and hostility at work: A model of reactions to perceived injustice. In G. R. Vanden Bos & E. Q. Bulatao (Eds.), *Violence on the job: Identifying risks and developing solutions* (pp. 51–85). Washington, DC: American Psychological Association.

Fonagy, P. (2001). *Attachment theory and psychoanalysis.* New York: Other Press.

Fonagy, P., Gergely, G., Jurist, E., & Target, M. (2002). *Affect regulation, mentalization, and the development of the self.* New York: Other Press.

Foote, S. L., & Morrison, J. H. (1987). Extrathalamic modulation of cortical function. *Annual Review of Neuroscience, 10,* 67–95.

Frank, J. (1961). *Persuasion and healing.* Baltimore: Johns Hopkins.

French, T. M. (1933). Interrelations between psychoanalysis and the experimental work of Pavlov. *American Journal of Psychiatry, 89,* 1165–1203.

Freud, S. (1905). Three essays on sexuality. *Standard Edition, 7,* 135–243.

Freud, S. (1914). Remembering, repeating, and working through. *Standard Edition, 12,* 147–156.

Freud, S. (1915a). Instincts and their vicissitudes. *Standard Edition, 14,* 111–140.

Freud, S. (1915b). The unconscious. *Standard Edition, 14,* 166–215.

Freud, S. (1920). Beyond the pleasure principle. *Standard Edition, 18,* 7–64.

Freud, S. (1926). Inhibitions, symptoms, and anxiety. *Standard Edition, 20,* 87–172.

Freud, S. (1946). Instincts and their vicissitudes. In *Collected papers* (Vol. 4, pp. 60–83). London: Hogarth. (Original work published 1921).

Freud, S. (1949). *An outline of psychoanalysis* (J. Strachey, Trans.). New York: W. W. Norton.

Fried, R. (1999). *Breathe well, be well.* New York: Wiley & Sons.

Frijda, N. H. (1986). *The emotions.* Cambridge, MA: Cambridge University Press.

Fruzzetti, A. E., & Iverson, K. M. (2004). Mindfulness, acceptance, validation, and "individual" psychopathology in couples. In S. C. Hayes, V. M. Follette, & M. M. Linehan (Eds.), *Mindfulness and acceptance: Expanding the cognitive-behavioral tradition.* New York: Guilford Press.

Fruzzetti, A. E., & Levensky, E. R. (2000). Dialectical behavior therapy for domestic violence: Rationale and procedures. *Cognitive and Behavioral Practice, 7,* 435–447.

Garfield, S. (2000). Eclecticism and Integration: A personal retrospective view. *Journal of Psychotherapy Integration, 10,* 341–356.

Gates, G. S. (1926). An observational study of anger. *Journal of Experimental Psychology, 9,* 325–331.

Geffner, R., & Mantooth, C. (1999). *Ending spouse/partner abuse: A psychoeducational approach for individuals and couples.* New York: Springer.

Geiger, T. C., Zimmer-Gembeck, M. J., & Crick, N. R. (2004). The science of relational aggression: Can we guide intervention? In M. M. Moretti, C. L. Odgers, & M. A. Jackson (Eds.), *Girls and aggression: Contributing factors and intervention principles* (pp. 27–40). New York: Kluwer Academic/Plenum.

Gelles, R. J., & Straus, M. A. (1988). *Intimate violence.* New York: Simon & Schuster.

Gerzina, M. A., & Drummond, P. (2000). A multimodal cognitive-behavioural approach to anger reduction in an occupational sample. *Journal of Occupational and Organizational Psychology, 73,* 181–194.

Ghazzal, Z. (1998). From anger on behalf of God to "forbearance" in Islamic medieval literature. In B. Rosenwein (Ed.), *Anger's past: The social uses of an emotion in the middle ages* (pp. 203–230). Ithaca, NY: Cornell University Press.

Gilligan, J. (1997). *Violence: Reflections on a national epidemic* (p. 222). New York: Vintage Books.

Gold, J. (1996). *Key concepts in psychotherapy integration.* New York: Plenum.

Gold, J., & Stricker, G. (2001). Relational psychoanalysis as a foundation for assimilative integration. *Journal of Psychotherapy Integration, 11,* 47–63.

Goldfried, M. R. (1995). Toward a common language for case formulation. *Journal of Psychotherapy Integration, 5,* 221–244.

Goldner, V., Penn, P., Sheinberg, M., & Walker, G. (1990). Love and violence: Gender paradoxes in volatile attachments. *Family Process, 29,* 343–364.

Gondolf, E. W., Heckert, D. A., & Kimmel, C. M. (2002). Nonphysical abuse among batterer program participants. *Journal of Family Violence, 17*(4), 293–314.

Gottman, J. M., Jacobson, N. S., Rushe, R. H., & Shortt, J. W. (1995). The relationship between heart rate reactivity, emotionally aggressive behavior, and general violence in batterers. *Journal of Family Psychology, 9*(3), 227–248.

Gottman, J. M., Katz, L. F., & Hooven, C. (1997). *Meta-emotion: How families communicate emotionally.* Hillsdale, NJ: Lawrence Erlbaum.

Gottesfeld, M. L. (1981). Countertransference and ethnic similarity. In G. Henderson & M. Primeaux (Eds.), *Transcultural health care* (pp. 32–37). Menlo Park, CA: Addison-Wesley.

Greene, B. (1990). Sturdy bridges: The role of African American mothers in the socialization of African American children. *Women and Therapy, 10,* 205–225.

Greenberg, L. S. (2002a). Integrating an emotion-focused approach to treatment in psychotherapy integration. *Journal of Psychotherapy Integration, 12,* 154–189.

Greenberg, L. S. (2002b). *Emotion-focused therapy: Coaching clients to work through their feelings.* Washington, DC: American Psychological Association.

Greenberg, L. S., & Foerster, F. (1996). Task analysis exemplified: The process of resolving unfinished business. *Journal of Consulting and Clinical Psychology, 64*(3), 439–446.

Greenberg, L. S., & Malcolm, W. (2002). Resolving unfinished business: Relating process to outcome. *Journal of Consulting and Clinical Psychology, 70*(2), 406–416.

Greenberg, L. S., & Paivio, S. C. (1997). *Working with emotions in psychotherapy.* New York: Guilford Press.

Greenberg, L. S., & Rice, L. N. (1997). Humanistic approaches to psychotherapy. In P. L. Wachtel (Ed.), *Theories of psychotherapy: Origins and evolution* (pp. 97–129). Washington, DC: American Psychological Association.

Greenberg, L. S., Korman, L. M., & Paivio, S. C. (2002). Emotion in humanistic psychotherapy. In D. J. Cain (Ed.), *Humanistic psychotherapies: Handbook of research and practice* (pp. 499–530). Washington, DC: American Psychological Association.

Greenberg, L. S., Rice, L. N., & Elliott, R. (1993). *Facilitating emotional change: The moment-by-moment process.* New York: Guilford Press.

Griffith, B. A., & Graham, C. C. (2004). Meeting needs and making meaning: The pursuit of goals. *Journal of Individual Psychology, 60,* 25–41.

Grodnitzky, G. R., & Tafrate, R. C. (2000). Imaginal exposure for anger reduction in adult outpatients: A pilot study. *Journal of Behavior Therapy and Experimental Psychiatry, 31,* 259–279.

Gross, J. J. (1998). The emerging field of emotion regulation: An integrative review. *Review of General Psychology. Special New Directions in Research on Emotion, 2*(3), 271–299.

Grover, S. M., & Thomas, S. P. (1993). Substance use and anger in mid-life women. *Issues in Mental Health Nursing, 14,* 19–29.

Guessoum, A. (1986). Tolerance and psychiatry: An Islamic view. *Psychiatrie Francaise, 17,* 55–60.

Gunaratana, B. H. (2002). *Mindfulness in plain English.* Boston: Wisdom Publications.

Gurman, A. S., & Kniskern, D. P. (Eds.). (1981). *Handbook of family therapy* (Vol. 1, pp. 96–133). New York: Brunner/Mazel.

Haaga, D. A. F., Davison, G. C., Williams, M. E., Dolezal, S. L., Haleblian, J., Rosenbaum, J., Dwyer, J. H., Baker, S., Nezami, E., & DeQuattro, V. (1994). Mode-specific impact of relaxation training for hypertensive men with Type A behavior pattern. *Behavior Therapy, 25,* 209–223.

Hagerman, R. J., Bregman, J. D., & Tirosh, E. (1998). Clonidine. In S. Reiss & M. G. Aman (Eds.), *Psychotropic medications and developmental disabilities. The international consensus handbook.* Columbus, OH: Ohio State, Nisonger Centre.

Hall, J., Stevens, P., & Meleis, A. (1994). Marginalization: A guiding concept for valuing diversity in nursing knowledge development. *Advances in Nursing Science, 16*(4), 23–41.

Hamner, M. B., & Robert, S. (2004). Posttraumatic stress disorder: differential diagnosis and management. *Current Psychosis and Therapeutics Reports, 2,* 109–115.

Hanna, F. J. (2002). *Therapy with difficult clients: Using the precursors model to awaken change.* New York: Guilford Press.

Harre, R. (Ed.). (1986). *The social construction of emotions.* Oxford: Blackwell.

Harris, M. B. (1996). Aggression, gender, and ethnicity. *Aggression and Violent Behavior, 1,* 123–146.

Hatch, H., & Forgays, D. (2001). A comparison of older adolescent and adult females' responses to anger-provoking situations. *Adolescence, 36,* 557–570.

Hayes, S. C. (2004). Acceptance and commitment therapy and the new behavior therapies: Mindfulness, acceptance, and relationship. In S. C. Hayes, V. M. Follette, & M. M. Linehan (Eds.), *Mindfulness and acceptance: Expanding the cognitive-behavioral tradition.* New York: Guilford Press.

Hayes, S. C., Wilson, K. G., Gifford, E. V., Follette, V. M., & Strosahl, K. (1996). Experiential avoidance and behavioral disorders: A functional dimensional approach to diagnosis and treatment. *Journal of Consulting and Clinical Psychology, 64*(6), 1152–1168.

Hazaleus, S. L., & Deffenbacher, J. L. (1986). Relaxation and cognitive treatments of anger. *Journal of Consulting and Clinical Psychology, 54,* 22–226.

Henderson, G., & Primeaux, M. (1981). *Transcultural health care.* Menlo Park, CA: Addison-Wesley.

Herman, J. L. (1992). *Trauma and recovery.* New York: Basic Books.

Hermans, H. J. M., & Kempen, H. J. G. (1998). Moving cultures: The perilous problems of cultural dichotomies in a globalizing society. *American Psychologist, 53,* 1111–1120.

Hightower, N. (2002). *Anger Busting 101.* Houston: Bayou Publishing.

Hines-Martin, V., Malone, M., Kim, S., & Brown-Piper, A. (2003). Barriers to mental health care access in an African American population. *Issues in Mental Health Nursing, 24,* 237–256.

Hoffman, E. (1994). *The drive for self: Alfred Adler and the founding of individual psychology.* Reading, MA: Addison-Wesley.

Hogan, B. E., & Linden, W. (2004). Anger response styles and blood pressure: At least don't ruminate about it. *Annals of Behavioral Medicine, 27,* 38–49.

Holowaty, K. A. M. (2004). *Characteristics of client-identified helpful aspects of emotion focused trauma therapy for reprocessing memories of childhood abuse.* Paper presented at the 35th Annual Meeting of the Society for Psychotherapy Research, Rome, Italy.

Holtzworth-Munroe, A. (2000). A typology of men who are violent toward their female partners: Making sense of the heterogeneity in husband violence. *Current Directions in Psychological Science, 9*(4), 140–143.

Holtzworth-Munroe, A., & Hutchinson, G. (1993). Attributing negative intent to wife behavior: The attributions of martially violent versus nonviolent men. *Journal of Abnormal Psychology, 2,* 206–211.

Holtzworth-Munroe, A., & Meehan, J. C. (2004). Typologies of men who are maritally violent: *Scientific and clinical implications. Journal of Interpersonal Violence, 19*(12), 1369–1389.

Howells, K., & Day, A. (2003). Readiness for anger management: Clinical and theoretical issues. *Clinical Psychology Review, 23,* 319–337.

Hubble, M. A., Duncan, B. L., & Miller, S. D. (Eds.). (1999). *The heart and soul of change: What works in therapy.* Washington, DC: American Psychological Association.

Hyman, S. E. (1998). Brain neurocircuitry of anxiety and fear: implications for clinical research and practice. *Biological Psychiatry, 44,* 1201–1203.

Illovsky, M. E. (2003). *Mental health professionals, minorities, and the poor.* New York: Brunner-Routledge.

Ivey, A. E. (1995). Psychotherapy as liberation: Toward specific skills and strategies in multi-cultural counseling and therapy. In J. G. Ponterotto, J. M. Casas, L. A. Suzuki, & C. M. Alexander (Eds.), *Handbook of multicultural counseling* (pp. 53–72). Thousand Oaks, CA: Sage.

Izard, C. E. (1977). *Human emotions.* New York: Plenum Press.

Izard, C. E. (1990a). Facial expressions and the regulation of emotions. *Journal of Personality and Social Psychology, 58*(3), 487–498.

Izard, C. E. (1990b). The substrates and functions of emotion feelings: William James and current emotion theory. *Personality & Social Psychology Bulletin. Special Centennial Celebration of The Principles of Psychology, 16*(4), 626–635.

Jack, D. C. (1999). *Behind the mask: Destruction and creativity in women's aggression.* Cambridge, MA: Harvard University Press.

Jack, D. C. (2001). Anger. In J. Worell (Ed.), *Encyclopedia of women and gender* (Vol. 1). San Diego: Academic Press.

Jacobson, N. S., & Christenson, A. (1996). *Integrative couples therapy.* New York: Norton.

Jacobson, N. S., & Gottman, J. M. (1998). *When men batter women: New insights into ending abusive relationships.* New York: Simon & Schuster.

Jacobson, N. S., & Truax, P. A. (1991). Clinical significance: A statistical approach to defining meaningful change in psychotherapy research. *Journal of Consulting and Clinical Psychology, 59,* 12–19.

Jarry, J. L., & Paivio, S. C. (2004). *Comparative outcome of two versions of emotion focused trauma therapy for reprocessing memories of childhood abuse: A dismantling study.* Paper presented at the 35th Annual Meeting of the Society for Psychotherapy Research, Rome, Italy.

Javier, R. A., Barroso, F., & Muqoz, M. A. (1993). Autobiographical memories in bilinguals. *Journal of Psycholinguistic Research, 22,* 319–338.

Jensen, J. B. (2004). Conduct disorder and other disruptive behaviors: Pediatric Psychopharmacology. *Current Psychosis and Therapeutics Report, 2,* 104–108.

Johnson, A., Johnson, O., & Baksh, M. (1986). The colors of emotions in Machiguenga. *American Anthropologist, 88,* 674–681.

Johnson, S. M. (2002). *Emotionally focused couple therapy with trauma survivors: Strengthening attachment bonds.* New York: Guilford Press.

Johnson, S. M., & Greenberg, L. S. (1985). Emotionally focused couples therapy: An outcome study. *Journal of Marital and Family Therapy, 11*(3), 313–317.

Johnson, S. M., & Greenberg, L. S. (1988). Relating process to outcome in marital therapy. *Journal of Marital and Family Therapy, 14*(2), 175–183.

Jones, J., & Trower, P. (2004). Irrational and evaluative beliefs in individuals with anger disorders. *Journal of Rational Emotive and Cognitive-Behavior Therapy, 22,* 153–170.

Jouriles, E. N., & O'Leary, K. (1985). Interspousal reliability of reports of marital violence. *Journal of Consulting & Clinical Psychology, 53*(3), 419–421.

Kaariainen, I. T. (2002): Psychopharmacology of major depression. In M. A. Reinecke & Davison M. R. (Eds.), *Comparative treatments of depression* (pp. 427–451). New York: Springer Publishing.

Kabat-Zinn, J. (1994). *Wherever you go there you are: Mindfulness meditation in everyday life.* New York: Hyperion.

Kassinove, H. (Ed.). (1995). *Anger disorders: Definition, diagnosis and treatment.* Washington, DC: Taylor and Francis.

Kassinove, H., & Tafrate, R. C. (2002). *Anger management: The complete practitioner's guidebook for the treatment of anger.* Atascadero, CA: Impact Publishers.

Kassinove, H., & Sukhodolsky, D. G. (1995). Anger disorders: Basic science and practical issues. In H. Kassinove (Ed.), *Anger disorders: Definition, diagnosis, and treatment.* Washington, DC: Taylor and Francis.

Kassinove, H., McDermott, S., & Terricciano, S. (2005). Effects of the barb treatment for anger responses to insults: Cognitive restructuring or extinction? Manuscript submitted for publication.

Kassinove, H., Sukhodolsky, D. G., Tsytsarev, S. V., & Solovyova, S. (1997). Self-reported constructions of anger episodes in Russia and America. *Journal of Social Behavior and Personality, 12,* 301–324.

Kaufman, L. M., & Wagner, B. R. (1972). Barb: A systematic treatment technology for temper control disorders. *Behavior Therapy, 3,* 84–90.

Kavanagh, K. H., & Kennedy, P. H. (1992). Promoting cultural diversity: Strategies for health care professionals. Newbury Park, CA: Sage.

Kay, D. C. (2002). Angry men and medication: *Anger Busting 101* (pp. 187–192). Houston: Bayou Publishing.

Kendler, K. S., Kessler, R. C., Walters, E. E., MacLean, C., Neale, M. C., Heath, A. C., & Eaves, L. J. (1995). Stressful life events, genetic liability, and onset of an episode of major depression in women. *American Journal of Psychiatry, 152*(6), 833–842.

Kennedy, H. G. (1992). Anger and irritability. *British Journal of Psychiatry, 161,* 145–153.

Kernberg, O. F. (1970). Factors in the psychoanalytic treatment of narcissistic personalities. *Journal of the American Psychoanalytic Association, 18,* 51–85.

Khong, B. S. L. (2003). Role of responsibility in Daseinanalysis and Buddhism. In K. H. Dockett, G. R. Dudley-Grant, & C. P. Bankart (Eds.), *Psychology and Buddhism: From individual to global community* (pp. 139–159). New York: Kluwer Academic Publishers.

Kim, B. S. K., Ng, G. F., & Ahn, A. J. (2005). Effects of client expectation for counseling success, client–counselor worldview match, and client adherence to Asian and European American cultural values on counseling process with Asian Americans. *Journal of Counseling Psychology, 52,* 67–76.

Kimmel, J. (1976). The rational barb in the treatment of social rejection. *Rational Living, 11,* 23–25.

Klein, M. (1946). Notes on some schizoid mechanisms. *International Journal of Psychoanalysis, 27,* 99–110.

Klein, M. (1975). Love, guilt and reparation & other works (pp. 1921–1945). New York: Delta.

Klerman, G. L., Weissman, M. M., Rounsaville, B. J., & Chevron, E. S. (1984). *Interpersonal psychotherapy of depression.* New York: Basic Books.

Knafo, D. (2004). Introduction. In D. Knafo (Ed.), *Living with terror, working with trauma: A clinician's handbook* (pp. 1–15). Lanham, MD: Jason Aronson.

Knafo, D., & Feiner, K. (2005). Unconscious fantasies and the relational world. Hillsdale, NJ: Analytic Press.

Kogan, L. R., Richards, T. L., & Deffenbacher, J. L. (2001, August). *Effects of relaxation and cognitive therapy for driving anger reduction.* Paper presented at the 109th Annual Convention of the American Psychological Association, San Francisco.

Kohut, H. (1971). *The analysis of the self.* New York: International Universities Press.

Kohut, H. (1972). Thoughts on narcissism and narcissistic rage. *Psychoanalytic Study of the Child, 27,* 360–400.

Kohut, H. (1977). *The restoration of the self.* New York: International Universities Press.

Koons, C. R., Robins, C. J., Tweed, J. L., Lynch, T. R., Gonzalez, A. M., Morse, J. Q., Bishop, G. K., Butterfield, M. I., & Bastian, L. A. (2001). Efficacy in using dialectical behavior therapy in women veterans with borderline personality disorder. *Behavior Therapy, 32*(2), 371–390.

Kopp, R., & Eckstein, D. (2004). Using early memory metaphors and client-generated metaphors in Adlerian therapy. *Journal of Individual Psychology, 60*(2), 163–174.

Kopta, S. M., Howard, K. I., Lowry, J. L., & Beutler, L. E. (1994). Patterns of symptomatic recovery in therapy. *Journal of Consulting and Clinical Psychology, 62*(5), 1009–1016.

Kornfield, J. (1993). *A path with heart.* New York: Bantam Books.

Krech, G. (2002). *Naikan: Gratitude, grace, and the Japanese art of self-reflection.* Berkeley: Stone Bridge Press.

Kristeller, J. L., & Johnson, T. (2003, June). *Cultivating loving-kindness: A two-stage model of the effects of meditation on empathy, compassion, and altruism.* Paper presented at the conference, Works of Love: Scientific and Religious Perspectives on Altruism, Villanova, PA.

Krystal, H. (2004). Optimizing affect function in the psychoanalytic treatment of trauma. In D. Knafo (Ed.), *Living with terror, working with trauma: A clinician's handbook* (pp. 283–296). Lanham, MD: Jason Aronson.

Lachmund, E., & DiGiuseppe, R. (1997, August). *How clinicians assess anger: Do we need an anger diagnosis?* Advances in the diagnosis, assessment, and treatment of angry clients. Symposium held at the annual meeting of the American Psychological Association, Chicago.

Lachmund, E., DiGiuseppe, R., & Fuller, J. R. (2005). Clinicians' diagnosis of a case with anger problems. *Journal of Psychiatric Research, 39*(4), 439–448.Lakoff, G., & Johnson, M. (1999). *Philosophy in the flesh: The embodied mind and its challenge to Western thought.* New York: Basic Books.

Larkin, K. T., & Zayfert, C. (1996). Anger management training with mild essential hypertensives. *Journal of Behavioral Medicine, 19,* 415–433.

Lazarus, A. A. (2005). Multi-modal therapy. In J. Norcross & M. Goldfried, (Eds.), (2005). *Handbook of psychotherapy integration* (2nd ed., pp. 105–120). New York: Oxford University Press.

Lazarus, R. (1991). Progress on a cognitive-motivational-relational theory of emotion. *American Psychologist, 46,* 819–834.

Leahy, R. (2003). *Cognitive therapy techniques.* New York: Guilford Press.

Lebow, J. L. (Ed.). (1995). Open-ended therapy: Termination in marital and family therapy. In R. H. Mikesell, D. Lusterman, & S. H. McDaniel (Eds.), *Integrating family therapy: Handbook of family psychology and systems theory.* Washington DC: APA Books.

Lebow, J. L. (2003a). Integrative approaches to couple and family therapy. In T. L. Sexton, G. R. Weeks, & M. S. Robbins (Eds.), *Handbook of family therapy: The science and practice of working with families and couples*. New York: Routledge.

Lebow, J. (2003b). Integrative family therapy for disputes involving child custody and visitation. *Journal of Family Psychology, 17,* 181–192.

LeDoux, J. E. (1995). Emotion: Clues from the brain. *Annual Review of Psychology, 46,* 209–235.

Leff, J. (1973). Culture and the differentiation of emotional states. *British Journal of Psychiatry, 123,* 299–306.

Leichsenring, F., & Leibing, E. (2003). The effectiveness of psychodynamic therapy and cognitive behavior therapy in the treatment of personality disorders: A meta-analysis. *American Journal of Psychiatry, 160*(7), 1223–1232.

Leifer, R. (1999). Buddhist conceptualization and treatment of anger. *Journal of Clinical Psychology, 55,* 339–351.

Lerner, H. (1977, Winter). The taboos against female anger. *Menninger Perspective,* pp. 5–11.

Levant, R. F. (1995). Toward the reconstruction of masculinity. In R. F. Levant & W. S. Pollack (Eds.), *A new psychology of men* (pp. 229–251). New York: Basic Books.

Levenson, E. (1983). *The ambiguity of change.* New York: Basic Books.

Levine, M. (2000). *The positive psychology of Buddhism and yoga.* Mahwah, NJ: Lawrence Erlbaum.

Levy, R. I. (1983). Introduction: Self and emotion. *Ethos, 11,* 128–134.

Linden, W., Hogan, B. E., Rutledge, T., Chawla, A., Lenz, J. W., & Leung, D. (2003). There is more to anger coping than "in" or "out." *Emotion, 3*(1), 12–29.

Linehan, M. M., & Schmidt, H., III. (1995). The dialectics of effective treatment of borderline personality disorder. In W. T. O'Donohue & L. Krasner (Eds.), *Theories of behavior therapy: Exploring behavior change* (pp. 553–584). Washington, DC: American Psychological Association.

Linehan, M. M. (1993a). *Cognitive behavioral therapy of borderline personality disorder.* New York: Guilford Press.

Linehan, M. M. (1993b). *Skills training manual for treating borderline personality disorder.* New York: Guilford Press.

Linehan, M. M., Armstrong, H. E., Suarez, A., Allmon, D., & Heard, H. L. (1991). Cognitive behavioral treatment of chronically parasuicidal borderline patients. *Archives of General Psychiatry, 48,* 1060–1064.

Linehan, M. M., Dimeff, L. A., Reynolds, S. K., Comtois, K. A., Shaw Welch, S., Heagerty, P., & Kivlanhan, D. R. (2002). Dialectical behavior therapy versus comprehensive validation plus 12-step for the treatment of opioid dependent women meeting criteria for borderline personality disorder. *Drug and Alcohol Dependence, 67,* 13–26.

Linehan, M. M., Heard, H. L., & Armstrong, H. E. (1993). Naturalistic follow-up of a behavioral treatment for chronically parasuicidal borderline patients. *Archives of General Psychiatry, 50,* 971–974.

Linehan, M. M., Schmidt, H., Dimeff, L. A., Craft, J. C., Kanter, J., & Comtois, K. A. (1999). Dialectical behavior therapy for patients with borderline personality disorder and drug-dependence. *American Journal of Addiction, 8,* 279–292.

Linehan, M. M., Tutek, D. A., Heard, H. L., & Armstrong, H. E. (1994). Interpersonal outcome of cognitive behavioral treatment for chronically suicidal borderline patients. *American Journal of Psychiatry, 151,* 1771–1776.

Linkh, D. J., & Sonnek, S. M. (2003). An application of cognitive-behavioral anger management training in a military occupational setting: Efficacy and demographic factors. *Military Medicine, 168,* 475–478.

Little, L. K. (1998). Anger in monastic curses. In B. H. Rosenwein (Ed.), *Anger's past: The social uses of an emotion in the Middle Ages* (pp. 9–35). Ithaca, NY: Cornell University Press.

Livesley, W. J. (2003). *Practical management of personality disorder.* New York: Guilford Press.

Lorenz, K. (1966). *On aggression.* New York: Harcourt, Brace, & World.

Luborsky, L., & Crits-Cristoph, P. (1990). *Understanding transference: The CCRT method.* New York: Basic.

Lunt, I., & Poortinga, Y. H. (1996). Internationalizing psychology. *American Psychologist, 51,* 504–508.

Lusk, J. T. (1992). *30 scripts for relaxation imagery and inner healing* (Vol. 1). Duluth, MN: Whole Person Associates.

Lynch, T. R. (2000). Treatment of elderly depression with personality disorder comorbidity using dialectical behavior therapy. *Cognitive and Behavioral Practice, 7,* 468–477.

Lytton, H., & Romney, D. M. (1991). Parents' differential socialization of boys and girls: A meta-analysis. *Psychological Bulletin, 109,* 267–296.

MacIver, R. (1950). The ramparts we guard. In E. A. Schuler, *Outside readings in sociology* (4th ed., pp. 782–788). New York: Crowell.

Malone, R. P., Delaney, M. A., Luebbert, J. F., Cater, J., & Campbell, M. (2000). A double-blind placebo-controlled study of lithium in hospitalized aggressive children and adolescents with conduct disorder. *Archives of General Psychiatry, 57,* 649–654.

Manaster, G., & Corsini, R. J. (1982). *Individual psychology.* New York: F. E. Peacock.

Marlatt, G. A., & Gordon, J. R. (Eds.). (1985). *Relapse prevention: Maintenance strategies in the treatment of addictive behaviors.* New York: Guilford Press.

Martin, P. (2000). *The Zen path through depression.* New York: Harper Collins.

Martin, C. L., & Fabes, R. A. (2001). The stability and consequences of young children's same-sex peer interactions. *Developmental Psychology, 37,* 431–446.

Maybury, K. K. (1997). *The influence of status and sex on observer judgments of anger displays.* Unpublished doctoral dissertation, University of California, Davis.

Mayne, T. J., & Ambrose, T. K. (1999). Research review on anger in psychotherapy. *Journal of Clinical Psychology, 55,* 353–363.

Maxmen, J. S., & Ward, N. G. (1995). *Essential psychopathology and its treatment* (2nd ed. rev. for DSM-IV). New York: W. W. Norton.

McCann, R. A., Ball, E. M., & Ivanoff, A. (2000). DBT with an inpatient forensic population: The CMHIP forensic model. *Cognitive and Behavioral Practice, 7,* 447–456.

McGoldrick, M., Gerson, R., & Shellenberger, S. (1999). *Genograms: Assessment and intervention.* New York: Norton.

McKay, G. D., & Maybell, S. A. (2004). *Calming the family storm* (p. 15). Atascadero, CA: Impact Publishers.

Mcvey, M. E. (2000, January). Exposure and response prevention versus rational self-statements in the treatment of angry men. *Dissertation Abstracts International, 61* (6-A), 2197.

Meichenbaum, D. H. (1985). *Stress inoculation training.* New York: Pergamon.

Meloy, J. R. (1992). *Violent attachments.* Northvale, NJ: Aronson.

Messer, S. B. (1992). A critical examination of belief structures in integrative and eclectic psychotherapy. In J. C. Norcross & M. R. Goldfried (Eds.), *Handbook of psychotherapy integration* (pp. 130–168). New York: Basic.

Messer, S. B. (2004). Evidence-based practice: Beyond empirically supported treatments. *Professional Psychology: Research and Practice, 35*(6), 580–588.

Meyer, R. G., & Deitsch, S. E. (1996). *The clinician's handbook* (4th ed., pp. 386–411). Boston: Allyn and Bacon.

"Midlife in Bhubaneswar." (1995). *MIDMAC Bulletin Number Four.* Vero Beach, FL: MIDMAC, The Research Network on Successful Midlife Development.

Miller, J. B. (1983). The construction of anger in women and men. In *Work in progress: Stone Center for Developmental Services and Studies.* Wellesley, MA: Wellesley College, Stone Center.

Miller, W. R., & Rollnick, S. (1991). *Motivational interviewing: Preparing people to change addictive behavior.* New York: Guilford Press.

Miller, W. R., & Rollnick, S. (2002). *Motivational interviewing: Preparing people for change* (2nd ed.). New York: Guilford Press.

Milliren, A., Evans, T., & Newbauer, J. (2003). Adlerian counseling and psychotherapy. In D. Capuzzi & D. Gross, *Theories of counseling & psychotherapy.* Upper Saddle River, NJ: Merrill.

Millon, T., Davis, R., & Millon, C. (1997). *Millon clinical multiaxial inventory—III Manual* (3rd ed.). Minneapolis: National Computer Systems.

Minuchin, S. (1974). *Families and family therapy.* Cambridge, MA: Harvard University Press.

Monroe, S. M., Rohde, P., Seeley, J. R., & Lewinsohn, P. M. (1999). Life events and depression in adolescence: Relationship loss as a prospective risk factor for first onset of major depressive disorder. *Journal of Abnormal Psychology, 108*(4), 606–614.

Moon, J. R., & Eisler, R. M. (1983). Anger control: An experimental comparison of three behavioral treatments. *Behavior Therapy, 14,* 493–505.

Morey, L. C. (1991). *Personality Assessment Inventory.* Odessa, FL: Psychological Assessment Resources, Inc.

Morawski, J. G. (1987). The troubled quest for masculinity, femininity, and androgyny. In P. Shaver & C. Hendrick (Eds.), *Review of personality and social psychology* (Vol. 7, pp. 44–69). Beverly Hills: Sage.

Muir, E. (1993). *Mad blood stirring: Vendetta and factions in Friuli during the Renaissance.* Baltimore: Johns Hopkins.

Muller, R. T., Sicoli, L. A., & Lemieux, K. E. (2000). Relationship between attachment style and posttraumatic stress symptomatology among adults who report the experience of childhood abuse. *Journal of Traumatic Stress, 13*(2), 321–332.

Mumford, G. (2004). Explosive growth of suicide terrorism brings psychological scientists to the table. *Psychological Science Agenda, 18*(11), 1–2.

Murphy, C. M., & Baxter, V. A. (1997). Motivating batterers to change in the treatment context. *Journal of Interpersonal Violence, 12,* 607–619.

Murray, R., & Zentner, J. P. (1979). *Nursing concepts for health promotion.* Englewood Cliffs, NJ: Prentice Hall.

Myers, J. E. B., Berliner, L., Briere, J., Hendrix, C. T., Jenny, C., & Reid, T. A. (2002). *The APSAC handbook on child maltreatment* (2nd ed.). Thousand Oaks, CA: Sage.

New Freedom Commission on Mental Health. (2003). *Achieving the promise: Transforming mental health care in America: Final report* (DHHS Publication No. SMA-03-3832). Rockville, MD: Author.

Norcross, J., & Goldfried, M. R. (Eds.). (2005). *Handbook of psychotherapy integration* (2nd ed.). New York: Oxford University Press.

Norcross, J., & Newman, C. (1992). Psychotherapy integration: Setting the context. In J. C. Norcross & M. R. Goldfried (Eds.), *Handbook of psychotherapy integration* (pp. 47–83). New York: Basic.

Novaco, R. W. (1975). *Anger control: The development and evaluation of an experimental treatment.* Lexington, MA: D.C. Heath.

Novaco, R. W. (1996). Anger treatment and its special challenges. *NCP Clinical Quarterly, 6*(3). Retrieved April 12, 2004, from http://www.ncptsd.org/publications/cq/v6/ns/novaco.html.

Novaco, R. W. (1997). Remediating anger and aggression with violent offenders. *Legal and Criminological Psychology, 2,* 77–88.

Novaco, R. W. (1998). Aggression. In H. Friedman (Ed.), *Encyclopedia of mental health* (pp. 13–26). San Diego: Academic Press.

Novaco, R. W. (2003). *The Novaco Anger Scale and Provocation Inventory.* Los Angeles: Western Psychological Services.

O'Connall, W. (1991). Humanistic identification. *Individual Psychologist, 47*(1), 26–27.

O'Leary, K. D. (2001). Psychological abuse: A variable deserving critical attention in domestic violence. In K. D. O'Leary & Maiuro (Eds.), *Psychological abuse in violent domestic relations* (pp. 3–28). New York: Springer.

Owens, L. D., Shute, R., & Slee, P. (2000). "Guess what I just heard!": Indirect aggression among teenage girls in Australia. *Aggressive Behavior, 26,* 67–83.

Paivio, S. C. (1999). Experiential conceptualization and treatment of anger. *Journal of Clinical Psychology. Special Treating Anger in Psychotherapy, 55*(3), 311–324.

Paivio, S. C. (2004). *Comparative processes of two versions of emotion focused trauma therapy for reprocessing memories of childhood abuse.* Paper presented at the 35th Annual Meeting of the Society for Psychotherapy Research, Rome, Italy.

Paivio, S. C., & Carriere, M. F. (in press). Contributions of EFT to the understanding and treatment of anger and aggression. In T. Cavell (Ed.), *Understanding anger and aggression.* Hilldale, NJ: Erlbaum.

Paivio, S. C., & Greenberg, L. S. (1995). Resolving "unfinished business": Efficacy of experiential therapy using empty-chair dialogue. *Journal of Consulting and Clinical Psychology, 63*(3), 419–425.

Paivio, S. C., & Greenberg, L. S. (2000). Emotion focused therapy for interpersonal trauma. *NC-PTSD Clinical Quarterly, 9*(2), 22–29.

Paivio, S. C., & Jarry, J. L. (2002). *Comparative efficacy and active ingredients of two emotionally focused therapies for resolving child abuse trauma.* Ontario Mental Health Foundation.

Paivio, S. C., & Laurent, C. (2001). Empathy and emotion regulation: Reprocessing memories of childhood abuse. *Journal of Clinical Psychology. Special Treating Emotion Regulation Problems in Psychotherapy, 57*(2), 213–226.

Paivio, S. C., & Nieuwenhuis, J. A. (2001). Efficacy of emotion focused therapy for adult survivors of child abuse: A preliminary study. *Journal of Traumatic Stress, 14*(1), 115–133.

Paivio, S. C., & Patterson, L. A. (1999). Alliance development in therapy for resolving child abuse issues. *Psychotherapy: Theory, Research, Practice, Training, 36*(4), 343–354.

Paivio, S. C., & Shimp, L. N. (1998). Affective change processes in therapy for PTSD stemming from child physical abuse. *Journal of Psychotherapy Integration, 8,* 211–229.

Paivio, S. C., Hall, I. E., Holowaty, K. A. M., Jellis, J. B., & Tran, N. (2001). Imaginal confrontation for resolving child abuse issues. *Psychotherapy Research, 11*(4), 433–453.

Pan, H., Neidig, P., & O'Leary, K. D. (1994). Male-female and aggressor-victim differences in the factor structure of the Modified Conflict Tactics Scale. *Journal of Interpersonal Violence, 9,* 366–382.

Parker-Sloat, E. (2003). Client-therapist ethnicity and gender matching as predictors of length of treatment and goal completion at a practicum training clinic. *Dissertation Abstracts International, 64* (6-B), 2934.

Parks, G. A., & Marlatt, G. A. (2000). Relapse prevention therapy: A cognitive-behavioral approach. *The National Psychologist, 9.*

Parry, S. J., & Jones, G. A. (1986). Beyond illusion in the psychotherapeutic enterprise. In G. Claxton (Ed.), *Beyond therapy: The impact of Eastern traditions on psychological theory and practice* (pp. 173–192). London: Wisdom Press.

Pence, E., & Paymar, M. (1993). *Education groups for men who batter: The Duluth model.* New York: Springer.

Perelberg, R. J. (Ed.). (1999). *Psychoanalytic understanding of violence and suicide.* New York: Routledge.

Perry, J., Banon, E., & Ianni, F. (1999). Effectiveness of psychotherapy for personality disorders. *American Journal of Psychiatry, 156*(9), 1312–1321.

Peyroux, C. (1998). Gertrude's furor: Reading anger in an early medieval saint's life. In B. H. Rosenwein (Ed.), *Anger's past: The social uses of an emotion in the Middle Ages* (pp. 36–55). Ithaca, NY: Cornell University Press.

Phinney, J. S. (1996). When we talk about American ethnic groups, what do we mean? *American Psychologist, 51,* 918–927.

Piaget, J. (1954). *The construction of reality in the child.* Oxford, England: Basic Books.

Pinsof, W. M. (1995). *Integrative problem-centered therapy: A synthesis of family, individual, and biological therapies.* New York: Basic Books.

Pinsof, W., Zinbarg, R., Mann, B., Lebow, J., Knobloch-Fedders, L., Friedman, G., & Karam, E. (2005). *The systemic therapy inventory of change.* The Family Institute at Northwestern University.

Plant, E. A., Hyde, J. S., Keltner, D., & Devine, P. G. (2000). The gender stereotyping of emotions. *Psychology of Women Quarterly, 24,* 81–92.

Poll: Minorities find Whites insensitive, bossy. (1994, March 4). *USA Today,* p. 3A.

Pollack, W. S. (2000). The Columbine syndrome: Boys and the fear of violence. *National Forum: The Phi Kappa Phi Journal, 80*(4), 39–42.

Ponterotto, J. (1988). Racial/ethnic minority research in the *Journal of Counseling Psychology:* A content analysis and methodological critique. *Journal of Counseling Psychology, 35,* 410–418.

Ponterotto, J. G., Casas, J. M., Suzuki, L. A., & Alexander, C. M. (1995). *Handbook of multicultural counseling.* Thousand Oaks, CA: Sage.

Ponterotto, J. G., Gretchen, D., & Chauhan, R. V. (2001). Cultural identity and multicultural assessment: Quantitative and qualitative tools for the clinician. In L. A. Suzuki, J. G. Ponterotto, & P. J. Meller (Eds.), *Handbook of multicultural assessment* (2nd ed., pp. 67–99). San Francisco: Jossey-Bass.

Power, M. J., & Dalgleish, T. (1997). *Cognition and emotion: From order to disorder.* Hove, East Sussex, UK: Psychology Press.

Prochaska, J. O., & DiClemente, C. C. (1992). The transtheoretical approach. In J. C. Norcross & M. R. Goldfried (Eds.), *Handbook of psychotherapy integration* (pp. 300–334). New York: Basic.

Prochaska, J. O., Norcross, J. C., & DiClemente, C. C. (1995). *Changing for good.* New York: Avon.

Ragsdale, E. S. (2003). Value and meaning in gestalt psychology and Mahayana Buddhism. In K. H. Dockett, G. R. Dudley-Grant, & C. P. Bankart (Eds.), *Psychology and Buddhism: from individual to global community* (pp. 105–124). New York: Kluwer Academic.

Ramirez, J. M., Fujihara, T., & van Goozen, S. (2001). Cultural and gender differences in anger and aggression: A comparison between Japanese, Dutch, and Spanish students. *Journal of Social Psychology, 141,* 119–121.

Random House Webster's College Dictionary. (2001). New York: Random House.

Rasmussen, P. R. (2003). The adaptive purpose of emotional expression: A lifestyle elaboration. *The Journal of Individual Psychology, 59*(4), 388–409.

Rathus, J. H., Cavuoto, N., & Passarelli, V. (2006). Dialectical behavior therapy for intimate partner violence. In R. A. Baer (Ed.), *Mindfulness-based treatment approaches* (pp. 333–354). Boston: Academic Press.

Rathus, J. H., & Miller, A. M. (2002). Dialectical behavior therapy adapted for suicidal adolescents. *Suicidal and Life-Threatening Behavior, 32,* 146–157.

Rathus, J. H., & Feindler, E. (2004). *Assessment of partner violence.* Washington, DC: American Psychological Association.

Ravello, G. (2000, July). Prevention of child abuse and neglect: Anger management for expectant mothers involved in home-visitation programs. *Dissertation Abstracts International, 61* (1-B), 547.

Remer, P., & Oakley, D. (2005). Counselor self-disclosure. *The Feminist Psychologist, 32*(1), 8–10.

Reay, A. M., & Browne, K. D. (2002). The effectiveness of psychological interventions with individuals who physically abuse or neglect their elderly dependents. *Journal of Interpersonal Violence, 17,* 416–431.

Reilly, P. M., & Shopshire, M. S. (2002). *Anger management for substance abuse and mental health clients.* Washington, DC: U.S. Department of Health and Human Services, Substance Abuse and Mental Health Services Administration (SAMHSA).

Reynolds, D. K. (1980). *The quiet therapies: Japanese pathways to personal growth.* Honolulu: University of Hawaii Press.

Rhodewalt, F., & Morf, C. C. (1998). On self-aggrandizement and anger: A temporal analysis of narcissism and affective reactions to success and failure. *Journal of Personality and Social Psychology, 74*(3), 672–685.

Richards, J. C., Alvarenga, M., & Hof, A. (2000). Serum lipids and their relationships with hostility and angry affect and behaviors in men. *Health Psychology, 19,* 393–398.

Richards, T. L., Deffenbacher, J. L., Filetti, L. B., Lynch, R. S., & Kogan, L. (2001, August). *Short- and long-term effects of interventions for driving anger reduction.* Paper presented at the 109th Annual Convention of the American Psychological Association, San Francisco.

Riley, W., Treiber, F., & Woods, M. (1989). Anger and hostility in depression. *The Journal of Nervous and Mental Disease, 177,* 668–674.

Rimm, D. C. Hill, G. A., Brown, N. N., & Stuart, J. E. (1974). Group assertive training in treatment of expression of inappropriate anger. *Psychological Reports, 34,* 791–798.

Rizzuto, A.-M., Meissner, W. W., & Buie, D. H. (2004). *The dynamics of human aggression.* New York: Brunner-Routledge.

Robins, S., & Novaco, R. W. (1999). A systems conceptualization and treatment of anger. *Journal of Clinical Psychology, 55,* 325–337.

Rogler, L. H. (1999). Methodological sources of cultural insensitivity in mental health research. *American Psychologist, 54,* 424–433.

Rosaldo, R. I. (1984). Grief and a headhunter's rage: On the cultural force of emotions. In S. Plattner & E. M. Bruner (Eds.), *Text, play, and story: The construction and reconstruction of self and society* (pp. 178–195). Washington, DC: American Ethnological Society.

Rosenwein, B. H. (Ed.). (1998). *Anger's past: The social uses of an emotion in the Middle Ages.* Ithaca, NY: Cornell University Press.

Rosenzweig, S. (1936). Some implicit common factors in diverse methods of psychotherapy. *American Journal of Orthopsychiatry, 6,* 412–415.

Rothbart, M. K., & Bates, J. E. (1998). Temperament. In N. Eisenberg (Ed.), *Handbook of child psychology* (5th ed.). *Social, emotional and personality development* (Vol. 3, pp. 105–176). New York: Wiley.

Rottenberg, J., & Gross, J. (2003). When emotion goes wrong: Realizing the promise of affective science. *Clinical Psychology: Science & Practice, 10*(2), 227–232.

Rubin, T. (1970). *The angry book.* New York: Collier.

Russell, J. A. (1991). Culture and the categorization of emotions. *Psychological Bulletin, 110,* 426–450.

Ryle, A. (1997). *Cognitive analytic therapy and borderline personality disorder: The model and the method.* New York: John Wiley.

Safran, J. D., & Segal, Z. (1990). *Interpersonal process in cognitive therapy.* New York: Basic Books.

Sandhu, D. S. (1997). Psychosocial profiles of Asian and Pacific Islander Americans: Implications for counseling and psychotherapy. *Journal of Multicultural Counseling and Development, 25*(1), 7–22.

Sapolsky, R. M. (1998). Why *zebras don't get ulcers: An updated guide to stress, stress-related disease, and coping.* New York: W. H. Freeman.

Sartre, J.-P. (1948). *The emotions: Outline of a theory* (Bernard Frechtman, Trans.). New York: Philosophical Library.

Saussy, C. (1995). *The gift of anger: A call to faithful action.* Louisville, KY: Westminster John Knox Press.

Sayar, K., Guzelhan, Y., Solmaz, M., Ozer, O. A., Ozturk, M., Acar, B., & Arikan, M. (2000). Anger attacks in depressed Turkish outpatients. *Annals of Clinical Psychiatry, 12,* 213–218.

Scheffler, R. M., & Miller, A. B. (1991). Differences in mental health service utilization among ethnic subpopulations. *International Journal of Law and Psychiatry, 14,* 363–376.

Scherer, K. R. (1997). The role of culture in emotion-antecedent appraisal. *Journal of Personality and Social Psychology, 73,* 902–922.

Schiraldi, G. R., & Kerr, M. H. (2002). *The anger management sourcebook* (p. 14). New York: Contemporary Books.

Schlichter, K. J., & Horan, J. J. (1981). Effects of stress inoculation on the anger and aggression management skills of institutionalized juvenile delinquents. *Cognitive Therapy and Research, 5,* 359–365.

References   349

Schumacher, J. A. (2001). Risk factors for male-to-female partner physical abuse. *Aggression and Violent Behavior, 6,* 281–352.

Segall, M. H., Lonner, W. J., & Berry, J. W. (1998). Cross-cultural psychology as a scholarly discipline: On the flowering of culture in behavioral research. *American Psychologist, 53,* 1101–1110.

Seldes, G. (1985). *The great thoughts.* New York: Ballantine Books.

Seneca. (1963). *On anger.* In J. W. Basore (Trans.), *Moral essays.* Cambridge, MA: Harvard University Press.

Shapiro, D. H. (1992). Adverse effects of meditation: A preliminary investigation of long-term meditators. *International Journal of Psychosomatics, 39*(special issue nos. 1–4), 62–67.

Shapiro, D., & Firth, J. (1987). Prescriptive vs. exploratory psychotherapy: Outcomes of the Sheffield Psychotherapy Project. *British Journal of Psychiatry, 151,* 790–799.

Shapiro, D., & Firth-Cozens, J. (1990). Two year follow-up of the Sheffield Psychotherapy Project. *British Journal of Psychiatry, 157,* 389–391.

Shapiro, S. L., Schwartz, G. E., & Bonner, G. (1998). Effects of mindfulness-based stress reduction on medical and premedical students. *Journal of Behavioral Medicine, 21,* 581–599.

Shields, S. A. (2002). *Speaking from the heart: Gender and the social meaning of emotion.* Cambridge, UK: Cambridge University Press.

Shin, S.-M., Chow, C., Camacho-Gonsalves, T., Levy, R. J., Allen, I. E., & Leff, H. S. (2005). A meta-analytic review of racial-ethnic matching for African American and Caucasian American clients and clinicians. *Journal of Counseling Psychology, 52,* 45–56.

Shulman, B. (1965). A comparison of Allport's and the Adlerian concept of life styles: Contributions to a psychology of the self. *Individual Psychologist, 3,* 14–21.

Siegman, A. W., & Smith, T. W. (1994). *Anger, hostility, and the heart.* Hillsdale, NJ: Erlbaum.

Simeon, J., Milin, R., & Walker, S. (2002). A retrospective chart review of risperidone use in treatment-resistant children and adolescents with psychiatric disorders. *Prog.Neuropsychopharmacol Biological Psychiatry, 26,* 267–275.

Simmons, R. (2002). *Odd girl out: The hidden culture of aggression in girls.* New York: Harcourt.

Skinner, B. F. (1945). The operational analysis of psychological terms. *Psychological Review, 52,* 270–277.

Slavik, S. (2005). Professed skills of experienced counselors implicit in early recollections. *The Canadian Journal of Adlerian Psychology, 35,* 62–76.

Smedley, A., & Smedley, B. D. (2005). Race as biology is fiction, racism as a social problem is real. *American Psychologist, 60,* 16–26.

Snow, S. (2003). *Extended family tree: Adler lives on in modern therapies.* Retrieved November 30, 2003 from www.commcure.com/adler.html.

Solomon, R. C. (1993). *The passions.* Indianapolis: Hackett.

Spector, R. E. (1996). *Cultural diversity in health and illness* (4th ed.). Stamford, CT: Appleton & Lange.

Spence, J. T., & Buckner, C. E. (2000). Instrumental and expressive traits, trait stereotypes, and sexist attitudes. *Psychology of Women Quarterly, 24,* 44–62.

Spielberger, C. D. (1988). *Professional manual for the State-Trait Anger Expression Inventory.* Odessa, FL: Psychological Assessment Resources.

Spielberger, C. D. (1991). *State-Trait Anger Expression Inventory: Revised research edition, professional manual.* Odessa, FL: Psychological Assessment Resources.

Spielberger, C. D. (1999). *Manual for the State Trait Anger Expression Inventory—2.* Odessa, FL: Psychological Assessment Resources.

Spielberger, C. D., Johnson, E. H., Russell, S. F., Crane, R. J., Jacobs, G. A., & Worden, T. J. (1985). The experience and expression of anger: Construction and validation of an anger expression scale. In M. Chesney & R. Rosenman (Eds.), *Anger and hostility in cardiovascular and behavioral disorders* (pp. 5–30). New York: Hemisphere.

Spielberger, C. D., Krasner, S. S., & Soloman, E. P. (Eds.). (1988). The experience, expression, and control of anger. In M. A. Chesney & R. H. Rosenman (Eds.), *Anger and hostility in cardiovascular and behavioral disorders.* New York: Hemisphere/McGraw-Hill.

Sroufe, L. A. (1995). *Emotional development: The organization of emotional life in the early years.* Cambridge, MA: Cambridge University Press.

Stanley, B., Ivanoff, A., Brodsky, B., Oppenheim, S., & Mann, J. (1998, November). *Comparison of DBT and "treatment as usual" in suicidal and self-mutilating behavior.* Paper presented at the 32nd annual meeting of the Association for the Advancement of Behavior Therapy, Washington, DC.

Steffen, A. M. (2000). Anger management for dementia caregivers: A preliminary study using video and telephone interventions. *Behavior Therapy, 31,* 281–299.

Stern, S. B. (1999). Anger management in parent-adolescent conflict. *American Journal of Family Therapy, 27,* 181–193.

Sterns, C. Z., & Stearns, P. N. (1986). *Anger: The struggle for emotional control in American history.* Chicago: University of Chicago Press.

Stevenson, J., & Meares, R. (1992). An outcome study of psychotherapy for patients with borderline personality disorder. *American Journal of Psychiatry, 149*(3), 358–362.

Straus, M. A., Hamby, S. L., Boney-McCoy, S., & Sugarman, D. (1996). The revised Conflict Tactics Scales (CTS2): Development and preliminary psychometric data. *Journal of Family Issues, 17,* 283–316.

Stricker, G., & Gold, J. (1988). A psychodynamic approach to the personality disorders. *Journal of Personality Disorders, 2,* 350–359.

Stricker, G., & Gold, J. (1996). An assimilative model for psychodynamically oriented integrative psychotherapy. *Clinical Psychology: Science and Practice, 3,* 47–58.

Stricker, G., & Gold, J. (2002). Psychotherapy integration: An assimilative, psychodynamic model. In J. Lebow (Ed.), *Handbook of psychotherapy.* New York: John Wiley & Sons.

Stricker, G., & Gold, J. (2005). Assimilative psychodynamic psychotherapy. In J. Norcross & M. Goldfried (Eds.), *Handbook of psychotherapy integration* (2nd ed., pp. 221–240). New York: Oxford University Press.

Struthers, R., & Lowe, J. (2003). Nursing in the Native American culture and historical trauma. *Issues in Mental Health Nursing, 24,* 257–272.

Strupp, H. H. (1993). Psychotherapy research: Evolution and current trends. In T. K. Fagan & G. R. VandenBos (Eds.), *Exploring applied psychology: Origins and critical analyses* (pp. 121–133). Washington, DC: American Psychological Association.

Strupp, H. H., & Binder, J. L. (1984). *Psychotherapy in a new key: A guide to time limited dynamic psychotherapy.* New York: Basic Books.

Sue, D. W., & Sue, D. (1999). *Counseling the culturally different: Theory and practice* (3rd ed.). New York: Wiley.

Suinn, R. M. (1990). *Anxiety management training.* New York: Plenum.

Sukhodolsky, D. G., Demertzis, K. H., & Kostogiannis, C. (2001, August). *Cognitive appraisals and anger in interpersonal contexts: U.S. versus Greece comparison.* Paper presented at the American Psychological Association, San Francisco.

Sullivan, H. S. (1970). *The Psychiatric Interview.* New York: Norton.

Tafrate, R. C. (1995). Evaluation of treatment strategies for adult anger disorders. In H. Kassinove (Ed.), *Anger disorders: Definition, diagnosis, and treatment* (pp. 109–130). Washington, DC: Taylor and Francis.

Tafrate, R. C., & Kassinove, H. (1998). Anger control in men: Barb exposure with rational, irrational, and irrelevant self-statements. *The Journal of Cognitive Psychotherapy, 12,* 187–211.

Tafrate, R. C., & Kassinove, H. (2003). Cognitive behavior therapy with anger disordered patients: Strategies for the beginning phase of treatment. In R. Leahy (Ed.), *Overcoming roadblocks in cognitive behavior therapy.* New York: Guilford Press.

Tafrate, R., Kassinove, H., & Dundin, L. (2002). Anger episodes in high and low trait anger community adults. *Journal of Clinical Psychology, 58,* 1573–1590.

Taft, C. T., Murphy, C. M., King, D. W., Musser, P. H., & DeDeyn, J. M. (2003). Process and treatment adherence factors in group cognitive-behavioral therapy for partner violent men. *Journal of Consulting and Clinical Psychology, 71,* 812–820.

Tanaka-Matsumi, J. (1995). Cross-cultural perspectives on anger. In H. Kassinove (Ed.), *Anger disorders: Definition, diagnosis, and treatment* (pp. 81–90). Washington, DC: Taylor and Francis.

Tavris, C. (1989). *Anger: The misunderstood emotion* (Rev. ed.). New York: Simon and Schuster.

Telch, C., Agras, W., & Linehan, M. M. (2001). Dialectical behavior therapy for binge eating disorder. *Journal of Consulting and Clinical Psychology, 69*(6), 1061–1065.

Terner, J., & Pew, W. L. (1978). *The courage to be imperfect: The life and work of Rudolf Dreikurs.* New York: Hawthorn.

Terracciano, S. (2000, January). Effects of barb exposure and rational statement rehearsal on anger and articulated thoughts in angry married men: Extinction or cognitive restructuring. *Dissertation Abstracts International, 61* (6-B), 3294.

Thomas, S. P. (1989). Gender differences in anger expression: Health implications. *Research in Nursing and Health, 12,* 389–398.

Thomas, S. P. (1991). Toward a new conceptualization of women's anger. *Issues in Mental Health Nursing, 12,* 31–49.

Thomas, S. P. (Ed.). (1993). *Women and anger.* New York: Springer.

Thomas, S. P. (1995). Women's anger: Causes, manifestations, and correlates. In C. D. Spielberger & I. G. Sarason (Eds.), *Stress and emotion: Anxiety, anger, and curiosity* (Vol. 15, pp. 53–74). Washington, DC: Taylor and Francis.

Thomas, S. P. (2001). Teaching healthy anger management. *Perspectives in Psychiatric Care, 37,* 41–48.

Thomas, S. P. (2003a). Men's anger: A phenomenological exploration of its meaning in a middle-class sample of American men. *Psychology of Men and Masculinity, 4,* 163–175.

Thomas, S. P. (2003b). "None of us will ever be the same again": Reactions of American mid-life women to 9/11. *Health Care for Women International, 24,* 853–867.

Thomas, S. P. (2004, November). *Women's anger in the United States, France, and Turkey.* Paper presented at the International Congress on Women's Health Issues, Sao Pedro, Brazil.

Thomas, S. P., & Atakan, S. (1993). Trait anger, anger expression, stress, and health status of American and Turkish mid-life women. *Health Care for Women International, 14,* 129–143.

Thomas, S. P., & Pollio, H. R. (2002). *Listening to patients.* New York: Springer.

Thomas, S. P., Smucker, C., & Droppleman, P. (1998). "It hurts most around the heart": A phenomenological exploration of women's anger. *Journal of Advanced Nursing, 28,* 311–322.

Thomas, S. P., & Williams, R. (1991). Perceived stress, trait anger, modes of anger expression, and health status of college men and women. *Nursing Research, 40,* 303–307.

Thomas, S. P. (2003). Men's anger: A phenomenological exploration of its meaning in a middle class sample of American men. *Psychology of Men & Masculinity, 4,* 163–175.

Thompson, C. L. (1996). *Reaching across boundaries of culture and class: Widening the scope of psychotherapy.* New York: Jason Aronson.

Thurman, C. W. (1985). Effectiveness of cognitive-behavioral treatments in reducing Type A behavior among university faculty. *Journal of Counseling Psychology, 32,* 74–83.

Thurman, R. (2005). *Anger.* New York: Oxford University Press. The quote from the Buddha at the end of Chapter 1 is based on the Sangharashgita translation of *Dhammapada, The Way of Truth,* p. 423. This material appears in the frontispiece of Thurman's book.

Thurman, R., & Wise, T. (1999). *Circling the sacred mountain: A spiritual adventure through the Himalayas*. New York: Bantam Books.

Tolman, R. M. (1989). The development of a measure of psychological maltreatment of women by their male partners. *Violence and Victims, 4*, 159–177.

Troisi, A., & D'Argenio, A. (2004). The relationship between anger and depression in a clinical sample of young men: The role of insecure attachment. *Journal of Affective Disorders, 79*, 269–272.

Tweed, R. G., & Dutton, D. G. (1998). A comparison of impulsive and instrumental subgroups of batterers. *Violence and Victims, 13*(3), 217–230.

Twenge, J. M. (2001). Changes in women's assertiveness in response to status and roles: A cross-temporal meta-analysis, 1931–1993. *Journal of Personality and Social Psychology, 81*, 133–145.

Underwood, M. K. (2003). *Social aggression among girls*. New York: Guilford Press.

U.S. Census Bureau. (2001). *United States Census 2000, summary files 1 and 2*. Retrieved December 5, 2003, from http://www.census.gov/Press-Release/www/2001/sumfile1.html and sumfile2.html.

U.S. Department of Health and Human Services. (2001). *Mental health: Culture, race, and ethnicity—A supplement to mental health: A report of the Surgeon General*. Rockville, MD: U.S. Department of Health and Human Services, SAMHSA, Center for Mental Health Services.

U.S. Surgeon General's Report on Mental Health. (1999). *Mental health: A report of the Surgeon General—Overview of cultural diversity and mental health services*. Rockville, MD: U.S. Department of Health and Human Services, SAMHSA, Center for Mental Health Services.

van der Kolk, B. A. (1996). The body keeps the score: Approaches to the psychobiology of posttraumatic stress disorder. In B. A. van der Kolk, A. C. McFarlane, & L. Weisaeth (Eds.), *Traumatic stress: The effects of overwhelming experience on mind, body, and society* (pp. 214–241). New York: Guilford Press.

van der Kolk, B. A., McFarlane, A. C., & Weisaeth, L. (1996). *Traumatic stress: The effects of overwhelming experience on mind, body, and society*. New York: Guilford Press.

Verheul, R., van den Bosch, L. M., Koeter, M. W. J., de Ridder, M. A. J., Steijnen, T., & van den Brink, W. A. (2003). A 12-month randomized clinical trial of dialectical behavior therapy for women with borderline personality disorder in the Netherlands. *The British Journal of Psychiatry, 182*, 135–140.

Wachtel. P. L. (1977). *Psychoanalysis and behavior therapy: Toward an integration*. New York: Basic.

Walen, S., DiGiuseppe, R., & Dryden, W. (1992). *A practitioner's guide to rational emotive therapy* (2nd ed.). New York: Guilford Press.

Walsh, R. N. (1978). Initial meditative experiences: Part II. *Journal of Transpersonal Psychology, 10*, 1–28.

Walton, F. X. (1998). Use of the most memorable observation as a technique for understanding choice of parenting style. *The Journal of Individual Psychology, 54*(4), 487–494.

Wampold, B. E. (2001). *The great psychotherapy debate*. Hillsdale, NJ: Erlbaum.

The war against women. (1994, March 28). *U.S. News and World Report*, p. 44.

Watson, J., & Bedard, D. (2005). *Clients' emotional process in psychotherapy: A comparison between cognitive-behavioral and process-experiential psychotherapy*. Paper presented at the Ohio Society for Psychotherapy Research, Toledo, OH.

Watts, R. E., & Pietrzak, D. (2000). Adlerian "encouragement" and the therapeutic process of solution-focused brief therapy. *Journal of Counseling & Development, 78*(4), 442–447.

Way, L. (1962). *Adler's place in psychology*. New York: Collier Books.

Webster's New World College Dictionary (4th ed.). (2000). New York: MacMillan.

Weidner, G., Istvan, J., & McKnight, J. D. (1989). Clusters of behavioral coronary risk factors in employed women and men. *Journal of Applied Social Psychology, 19*, 468–480.

Weiss, J., & Sampson, H. (1986). The research: A broad view. In *The psychoanalytic process* (pp. 337–348). New York: Guilford Press.

Whelton, W. J. (2004). Emotional processes in psychotherapy: Evidence across therapeutic modalities. *Clinical Psychology and Psychotherapy, 11*(1), 58–71.

Whiteman, M., Fanshel, D., & Grundy, J. F. (1987). Cognitive-behavioral interventions aimed at anger of parents at risk for child abuse. *Social Work, 32*, 469–474.

Wilber, K., Engler, J., & Brown, D. P. (1986). *Transformation of consciousness: Conventional and contemplative perspectives on development*. Boston: New Science Library/Shambala.

Willhite, R., & Eckstein, D. (2003). The angry, the angrier, and the angriest relationships. *The Family Journal, 11*(2), 76–83.

Williams, D. R., Yu, Y., Jackson, J. S., & Anderson, N. B. (1997). Racial differences in physical and mental health: Socio-economic status, stress and discrimination. *Journal of Health Psychology, 2*, 335–351.

Williams, J. E., Paton, C. C, Siegler, I. C., Eigenbrodt, M. L., Nieto, F. J., & Tryoler, H. A. (2000). Anger proneness predicts coronary heart disease risk. *Circulation, 101*, 2034–2039.

Williamson, P., Day, A., Howells, K., Bubner, S., & Jauncey, S. (2003). Assessing offender readiness for change problems with anger. *Psychology, Crime, and Law, 9*, 295–307.

Wilson, D. L., Davidson, K., & Reneau, S. (2000, April). *Implementing a cognitive-behavioral anger intervention with African Americans*. Paper presented at the Society of Behavioral Medicine, Nashville, TN.

Worell, J., & Remer, P. (2003). *Feminist perspectives in therapy: Empowering diverse women*. Hoboken, NJ: Wiley.

Zeldin, T. (1977). *France, 1848–1945, Vol. 2, Intellect, Taste and Anxiety*. Oxford: Clarendon.

Zlotnick, C., Elkin, I., & Shea, M. (1998). Does the gender of a patient or the gender of a therapist affect the treatment of patients with major depression? *Journal of Consulting and Clinical Psychology, 66,* 655–659.

Zubieta, J. K., & Alessi, N. E. (1992). Acute and chronic administration of trazodone in the treatment of disruptive behavior disorders in children. *Journal of Clinical Psychopharmacology, 12,* 346–351.

Zuckerman, M. (1990). Some dubious premises in research and theory on racial differences. *American Psychologist, 45,* 1297–1303.

Index

—JOURNAL—

Violence and Victims

Roland D. Maiuro, PhD, Editor-in-Chief

"...an indispensable resource...for the latest and most sophisticated work in the field."
— **L. Kevin Hamberger**, PhD
Medical College of Wisconsin, Racine, WI

"Violence and Victims has steadily provided interested readers with the best and latest of sound qualitative and quantitative investigations of criminal violence against children, young people, and adults in the United States and internationally."
— **Russ Immarigeon,** Contributing Editor
Crime Victims Report

This journal reliably serves as an exceptional forum for the latest developments in theory, research, policy, clinical practice, and social services in the area of interpersonal violence and victimization, including legal and media reports as well as book reviews.

Sample Articles Include:

- Factors That Influence Battered Women to Leave Their Abusive Relationships
- Child Abduction, Parents' Distress and Social Support
- Help-Seeking and Coping Strategies for Intimate Partner Violence in Rural and Urban Women
- Domestic Violence Cases Involving Children
- A Comparative Study Examining Associations Between Women's Drug-Related Lifestyle Factors and Victimization Within the Family
- Intimate Partner Violence

ISSN 0886-6708 • Volume 21 (2006)
Published Six Times Annually: February, April, June, August, October, December

11 West 42nd Street, New York, NY 10036-8002 • Fax: 212-941-7842
Order Toll-Free: 877-687-7476 • Order On-line: www.springerpub.com

Conduct Disorders

A Practitioner's Guide to Comparative Treatments

W. M. Nelson III, PhD, ABPP
A. J. Finch, Jr., PhD, ABPP
K. J. Hart, PhD, ABPP, Editors

"*In a word,* Conduct Disorders *delivers. That is, it sets out to permit practicing clinicians from different theoretical orientations to describe what works best for conduct-disordered youth...organized and informative...an impressive collection of clinically informed and research knowledge that educates the graduate student and satisfies the experienced clinician.*"

—**Philip C. Kendall,** PhD, ABPP
Professor, Director of Child and Adolescent Anxiety Disorders Clinic
Temple University

With a focus on the main population for which conduct disorder is a problem—children and adolescents—this book not only looks at the history of diagnosis in this population, but uses one case study to investigate several up-to-date treatments used by practicing clinicians from different theoretical orientations. A discussion of what these clinicians believe are the best treatments for this population is included.

Partial Contents:

The Case of "Michael" • The Psychoanalytic Approach to the Treatment of Conduct Disorder • Family Therapy • Cognitive-Developmental Treatment of Conduct Disorder • Behavioral Treatment for Youth with Conduct Disorder • Cognitive-Behavioral Psychotherapy for Conduct Disorder • Multisystemic Therapy in the Treatment of Adolescent Conduct Disorder • The Continuum of Residential Treatment Care for Conduct Disordered Youth • Pharmacologic Considerations in the Treatment of Conduct Disorder

2006 • 400pp • 0-8261-5615-0 • hard

11 West 42nd Street, New York, NY 10036-8002 • Fax: 212-941-7842
Order Toll-Free: 877-687-7476 • Order On-line: www.springerpub.com

From the Family Violence Series

Gender-Inclusive Treatment of Intimate Partner Abuse

A Comprehensive Approach

John Hamel, LCSW

Foreword by Donald Dutton

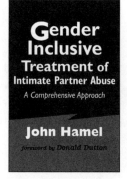

"...Hamel's work is well-written, comprehensive, very practical, and easily surpasses the current books on the subject...This book will be useful and essential reading for all social workers, psychologists, family therapists, and victimologists interested in domestic violence."

—Dr. Albert Roberts
Professor of Social Work and Criminal Justice
Director of Faculty and Curriculum
Rutgers, The State University of New Jersey

This breakthrough handbook for mental health professionals and educators concerned with domestic violence offers practical, hands-on materials for conducting assessments and providing treatments that take the entire family system into account. Rich with research that shows women are abusive within relationships at rates comparable to men, the book eschews the field's reliance on traditional domestic violence theory and treatment, which favors violence intervention for men and victim services for women and ignores the dynamics of the majority of violent relationships.

Partial Contents

Part I Assessment: Summary of Domestic Violence Research • Issues and Problems in Domestic Violence Assessment • Conducting Domestic Violence Assessments • Assessment Forms • Special Considerations in Domestic Violence Assessment • **Part II Treatment**: General Features • Working with Victims • The Treatment Plan • Group Work • Family Interventions

2005 • 328pp • soft • 0-8261-1873-9